HANDS-ON SQ

The Language, Querying, Reporting, and the Marketplace

Robert Groth

with contributions from David Gerber

Prentice Hall PTR
Upper Saddle River, New Jersey 07458
http://www.prenhall.com

Library of Congress Cataloging-in-Publication Data

Groth, Robert.
    Hands-on SQL : the language, querying, reporting, and the
    marketplace / Robert Groth, with contributions from David Gerber.
        p.   cm.
    Includes index.
    ISBN 0-13-486143-4
    1. SQL (Computer program language) I. Gerber, David.
    II. Title.
    QA76.73.S67G77   1997   96-17526
    005.75'6--dc20   CIP

Editorial/production supervision: *Jane Bonnell*
Cover design director: *Jerry Votta*
Cover design: *Design Source*
Manufacturing manager: *Alexis R. Heydt*
Acquisitions editor: *Paul W. Becker*
Editorial assistant: *Maureen Diana*

© 1997 by Prentice Hall PTR
Prentice-Hall, Inc.
A Simon & Schuster Company
Upper Saddle River, New Jersey 07458

The publisher offers discounts on this book when ordered in bulk quantities. For more information, contact Corporate Sales Department, Prentice Hall PTR, One Lake Street, Upper Saddle River, NJ 07458. Phone: 800-382-3419; FAX: 201- 236-7141; E-mail: corpsales@prenhall.com

Omnis 7 is a registered trademark of Blythe Software, Inc. Delphi is a registered trademark of Borland International, Inc. DB2, DB2/2, and DB2/6000 are registered trademarks of International Business Machines Corporation. Oracle is a registered trademark of Oracle Corporation. NonStop SQL is a registered trademark of Tandem. Forest & Trees is a registered trademark of Trinzic Corporation. All other products are trademarks of their respective owners.

Printed in the United States of America
10   9   8   7   6   5   4   3   2   1

ISBN 0-13-486143-4

Prentice-Hall International (UK) Limited, *London*
Prentice-Hall of Australia Pty. Limited, *Sydney*
Prentice-Hall Canada Inc., *Toronto*
Prentice-Hall Hispanoamericana, S.A., *Mexico*
Prentice-Hall of India Private Limited, *New Delhi*
Prentice-Hall of Japan, Inc., *Tokyo*
Simon & Schuster Asia Pte. Ltd., *Singapore*
Editora Prentice-Hall do Brasil, Ltda., *Rio de Janeiro*

Contents

2 Database Design 2-1

PART 2 RAPID TUTORIAL

9 Views

10 Privileges and Use of GRANT and REVOKE

15 Fourth Generation Languages   15-1

16 Database Middleware   16-1

PART 4   EXPANDING HORIZONS

Preface

SQL has enjoyed over 20 years of innovation since R. F. Boyce and D. D. Chamberlin wrote the first article on the language in 1973. Every database vendor in the market today has some tie to the SQL language. With the number of years and wealth of development surrounding the SQL language, why is it that so few of the software innovations based on the SQL language are used to help us learn the language?

This book, *Hands-On SQL: The Language, Querying, Reporting, and the Marketplace,* resulted from a frustration with the academic approach to teaching the use of the SQL language. Of the many books published to introduce the SQL language to the general public, this is the first to use software query tools, graphical interfaces, and a relational database engine to simplify the introduction to SQL.

Hands-On SQL: The Language, Querying, Reporting, and the Marketplace includes a CD-ROM containing Centura Software Corporation's SQLBase™, a leading relational database for personal computers, and the award-winning, end-user query tool Quest. The combination of these tools makes learning SQL easier than ever.

Purpose of This Book

This book provides an innovative, easy approach to learning SQL and discusses how SQL is used in the industry.

This book takes a distinctly different approach to introducing SQL than other books currently on the market. The emphasis of this book is on market focus and rapid-fire, hands-on teaching style.

Market Focus

SQL can be viewed as the assembly language of information storage and retrieval. To gain a reasonable understanding of what SQL is all about, you must have a broad perspective on how it is being used within the market today.

Much has been done within the industry to extend the power of this query language. Development tools currently on the market allow you to create SQL-based applications capable of connecting to Oracle®, DB2™, Sybase®, Informix®, Centura Software's SQLBase, and a wealth of other databases without writing a single line of code.

The SQL market has matured to where you would not realistically want to use SQL without using several of the many tools available to assist you in such things as the creation of reports, queries, and front-end database applications. A clear demonstration of the market's maturity was Sybase's 1994 purchase of Powersoft, a prominent player in application development tools for the SQL market, for an excess of nine hundred million dollars.

This book broadens the scope of what is relevant to learning SQL. Not only should you learn the syntax needed to use SQL, but you should also learn about the query tools, report writers, development environments, class libraries, and the many extensions to SQL that have made the language so valuable in the industry today.

Rapid-Fire, Hands-on Teaching Style

This book also provides a rapid-fire, hands-on approach to learning SQL syntax. By devoting three hours of your time, you can use the enclosed CD-ROM to familiarize yourself with all the major components of the SQL language.

The CD-ROM includes Centura Software Corporation's SQLWindows Solo™ and exercises relating to this book. Included with SQLWindows Solo is the award-winning 4GL, SQLWindows, the relational engine, SQLBase, and the end-user query tool, Quest™. Quest offers a rapid learning environment for demonstrating the basics of the SQL language quickly and easily, allowing you to build a query statement graphically, via the point and click method, or interactively. You can then see the SQL statements you have created and view their results when you apply them to the relational database. In this book, you will interactively enter SQL commands via Quest.

Once we cover SQL syntax itself, we expand the exercise to show how easy it is to turn those queries into reports and graphs.

By the end of this book you should:

- Have a basic understanding of the SQL language.

- Increase your own marketability by understanding how SQL is used in the database industry today.

- Be able to differentiate between the different SQL-based product offerings on the market. The differences in SQL offerings among Oracle, Informix, Sybase, and DB2, Microsoft®, and Centura Software are specifically addressed.

Audience

This book gives a general overview of the SQL market today and was written for a broad-based audience. The book will be useful to:

- *Application Developers*

  Application developers build client applications that access databases, using front-end products like SQLTalk™, SQLWindows, and the SQL/API™.

- *Database Administrators (DBAs)*

  Database administrators perform day-to-day operation and maintenance of the database. They design the database, create database objects, load data, control access, perform backup and recovery, and monitor performance.

- *PC Owners/End Users*

  End users use SQL to query and change data. Casual users who want to access data from relational databases should know the basics of SQL and the tools available to them.

- *Students*

  Students desiring a practical introduction to the basics of SQL and what is being done in the SQL market can start with this book.

- ***Systems Analysts and Consultants***

  Consultants can benefit from the discussions of the vendors involved in this market and specifically from Chapter 13, which discusses the differences in SQL.

Scope of the Book

Hands-On SQL: The Language, Querying, Reporting, and the Marketplace does not attempt to explain the ANSI SQL-86, SQL-89, or SQL-92 standards. The American National Standards Institute has come out with these standards as conformance guidelines that all SQL vendors should adhere to. In reality, these standards have been a least common denominator approach to the SQL language, and, depending on the database you are working with, SQL will greatly vary. If you want to learn more about the ANSI standard, see *Understanding the New SQL: A Complete Guide* by Jim Melton and Alan R. Simon. Jim Melton, from Digital Equipment Corporation, was the editor of the SQL-92 standard. In typical management by committee fashion, the standard itself is over 500 pages.

CD-ROM Installation Requirements

The minimum system requirements for installing the SQL Solo CD-ROM included by arrangements with Centura Software Corporation are:

- CPU: 386-based PC or higher
- RAM: 4 Mbytes (8 MBytes recommended)
- Hard disk space: 35 MBytes minimum required
- CD-ROM drive

The installed software enables you to run the CD-ROM-based tutorial included in this book. Additional files have been added specifically for this book beyond those provided by Centura Software.

Organization of This Book

Hands-On SQL: The Language, Querying, Reporting, and the Marketplace is divided into four parts:

Starting Out: Chapter 1 introduces basic concepts of the SQL language and provides a brief history. Chapter 2 introduces database design and discusses the database example to be used in this book.

Rapid Tutorial: Chapters 3 through 13 provide a hands-on approach to learning the SQL language. The tutorial uses a database of Fortune 500 companies and factual information about their revenue and other fundamental statistics. A database is created, data is inserted and updated, and then this data is queried by means of the SQL SELECT command. Performance issues, indexes, views, permissions, and system catalogs are all discussed in a quick, hands-on style. Chapter 13 specifically addresses the differences in SQL between implementations from Sybase, Microsoft, Informix, Oracle, IBM, and Centura Software.

Embedded SQL: Chapters 14, 15, and 16 look at embedding the SQL code in application languages and 4GL tools. We look at a range of vendors that provide simplified methods for rapid application prototyping. Chapter 16 explores the recent popularity of ODBC and other database connectivity options.

Expanding Horizons: Chapters 17, 18, and 19 look at tools and technologies that make SQL easier to use and discuss future directions of SQL and relational technology. Chapters 17 and 18 are devoted to end-user query and report tools available today. Chapter 19 examines future directions for the industry.

The chapters are listed below.

Chapter	Description
Preface	This preface discusses the purpose, audience, and outline of this book.
Chapter 1 *Introduction to SQL*	Chapter 1 introduces the concepts of SQL and relational database technology, as well as the database players in this industry.
Chapter 2 *Database Design*	Chapter 2 introduces the database example used in this book and talks about design issues.
Chapter 3 *Creation of a Database*	Chapter 3 teaches how to create a database and how to drop a database and its elements.
Chapter 4 *INSERT, UPDATE, and DELETE*	Chapter 4 teaches how to insert, update, and delete records within the database and introduces basic operators used with SQL as search conditions.
Chapter 5 *Retrieving Data/ The SELECT Statement*	Chapter 5 introduces the SELECT statement, which is the basis for retrieving data.
Chapter 6 *Functions and the Clauses ORDER BY, GROUP BY, and HAVING*	Chapter 6 expands on the use of the SELECT statement. This chapter introduces GROUP BY, ORDER BY, and HAVING clauses as well as functions, and, in particular, aggregate functions.
Chapter 7 *Joins and Unions*	Chapter 7 discusses unions and joins with SELECT statements.
Chapter 8 *Complex Queries and Performance*	Chapter 8 expands on how to use subqueries and looks at performance issues.
Chapter 9 *Views*	Chapter 9 covers database views.

Chapter	Description
Chapter 10 *Privileges and Use of GRANT and REVOKE*	Chapter 10 discusses privileges and using the GRANT and REVOKE commands.
Chapter 11 *System Tables and Stored Procedures*	Chapter 11 discusses system tables and stored procedures.
Chapter 12 *Data Integrity and Constraints*	Chapter 12 discusses referential integrity concepts and transaction analysis.
Chapter 13 *SQL Variations*	Chapter 13 discusses the database specifics for the major vendors, including Sybase, Oracle, Informix, and IBM.
Chapter 14 *Writing Applications Using SQL*	Chapter 14 looks at embedded SQL, including ODBC.
Chapter 15 *Fourth Generation Languages*	Chapter 15 looks at 4GLs and the market trends in rapid application development with SQL.
Chapter 16 *Database Middleware*	Chapter 16 looks at middleware and connecting SQL applications to multiple servers. Industry trends in middleware are examined.
Chapter 17 *A Look at Query Tools*	Chapter 17 looks at query tools in the industry and what they have to offer.
Chapter 18 *Report Writers*	Chapter 18 looks at component report writer products and discusses functionality of these products and the report writing capability of the query tools discussed in Chapter 17.
Chapter 19 *Database Directions*	Chapter 19 looks at future directions of SQL and relational technology.
Appendix A *SQL Vendors*	Appendix A provides a list of the companies and products mentioned in this book as players in the relational market.

Chapter	Description
Appendix B *Installing SQL Solo*	Appendix B outlines the steps to install SQL Solo and the book exercises for the hands-on use of SQL.
Appendix C *The LEAD Toolkit:* *A Demonstration*	Appendix C demonstrates a tool that generates a database and an application based on a database logical model.

Acknowledgments

This book would not have been completed without the help of many individuals. Several people who have been instrumental to this project are Lani Barton, Craig Donato, Tom George, Kevin Johnson, and Darci Wright. Many thanks to my wife, Michele Groth, for her painstaking review of the book.

I would like to acknowledge Dave Gerber for writing Chapter 13 on variations in the SQL language. Several sections of this book are also based on his contributions to work done for Centura Software Corporation, which they have graciously allowed me to include.

Special thanks to Centura Software Corporation for providing the use of the SQLWindows Solo product with this book as well as providing access to documentation used in this book. Thanks also to Client Server Designs, in particular Ric Gagliardi and Alex Sorobitz, for the generation of a demonstration of their LEAD toolkit based on this book's sample database.

1   Introduction to SQL

This chapter introduces the basics of the SQL language, defines specific terms used with the SQL language, discusses the relational database model, and covers vendors currently considered leaders in the SQL / relational database market.

The chapter is organized as follows:

1.1   What Is SQL?

The Structured Query Language, or SQL, is a standard method used for accessing databases. SQL (pronounced "es-que-ell" or "sequel") defines a complete set of commands that lets you access a relational database. It has a simple command structure for data definition, access, and manipulation.

SQL was intended to be used with programming languages, so standard SQL does not have commands for interactive screen dialogue or for more than very crude report formatting.

SQL is nonprocedural. When you use SQL, you specify *what* you want done, not *how* to do it. To access data, you need only name a table and the columns; you do not have to describe an access method. For example, a single command can update multiple rows in a database without specifying the row's location, storage format, and access format.

SQL has several layers of increasing complexity and capability. End users with little computer experience can use SQL's basic features; programmers can use the advanced features they need.

1.1.1   Why Use SQL?

SQL's features make it the most widely used language for relational databases. There are many reasons why SQL has obtained such a market following:

- **Market acceptance**

  While other languages could easily offer the functionality of SQL, SQL is used by the lion's share of the relational database market. The very fact that so many use SQL motivates others to follow.

- **Power**

  SQL is powerful. SQL is a complete database language, so you can use it for data definition, data control, and transaction management. SQL commands are simple to use in their basic form, but they have the flexibility to do complex operations.

- **Ease of use**

  People can easily access and manipulate data without becoming involved with the physical organization and storage complexities of that data.

1.1.2   SQL History

SQL began with a paper published in 1970 by E. F. Codd, a mathematician working at the IBM Research Laboratory in San Jose, California. In this paper, "A Relational Model of Data for Large Shared Data Banks" (*Communications of the ACM*, Vol. 13, No. 6, June 1970), Codd formulated the principles of a relational system for managing a database and described a relational algebra for organizing the data into tables.

Four years later, another important paper followed: "SEQUEL: A Structured English Query Language" (*Proceedings of the 1974 ACM SIGMOD Workshop on Data Description, Access and Control*, May 1974) by D. D. Chamberlin and R. F. Boyce. Both its authors were (like Codd) researchers at IBM's San Jose Research Laboratory. Their paper defined a language (the ancestor of SQL) designed to meet the requirements of Codd's relational algebra.

Two years after that, Chamberlin and others developed a version of the language, SEQUEL/2, and shortly after that IBM built a prototype system called System R that implemented most of its features. Around 1980 the name changed to SQL, often pronounced "sequel."

Both the American National Standards Institute (ANSI) and the International Organization for Standardization (ISO) are developing SQL as a standard interface to a relational database management system.

1.1.3 ANSI Standard

The American National Standards Institute has attempted to bring conformity to the SQL language. While the SQL language varies immensely from vendor to vendor, and commercial vendors always try to extend and improve the language, a series of specifications have progressed steadily toward standardizing elements of the language.

ANSI released documents with the proposed standard in 1986, 1989, and 1992 (SQL-86, SQL-89, and SQL-92). SQL-92 is by far the most complete. It has come a long way toward making a broad set of guidelines as well as minimizing potential areas of incompatibilities between vendors. For example, SQL-89 said nothing about system tables, which are an integral part of any relational database. Most vendors do not fully adhere to the ANSI standards and frequently add functionality not yet addressed in standard specifications.

The variants of the SQL language are numerous. Chapter 13 discusses the differences of some of the leading SQL variants, including vendor products such as the Sybase® SQL Server™ and Microsoft® SQL Server, Informix® Online™, Oracle® 7, and the IBM® DB2™ product.

1.2   SQL Parts

SQL allows you to perform a wide variety of actions, such as:

- Creating tables in the database
- Storing data
- Retrieving data
- Changing data and table structures
- Combining data and performing calculations on it
- Providing data security

Although SQL commands and syntax vary from vendor to vendor, they can be grouped into categories that remain fairly constant. Actual commands listed here are based on SQLBase, which is used in the hands-on exercises in this book. Chapter 12 discusses SQL variations among vendors.

1.2.1 Commands for Data Definition Language (DDL)

These commands create database objects such as tables or views.

ALTER TABLE	CREATE EVENT
CREATE INDEX	CREATE TABLE
CREATE TRIGGER	CREATE VIEW
DROP	ERASE

1.2.2 Commands for Data Manipulation Language (DML)

These commands delete data from and insert or update data into tables within a database.

DELETE	INSERT
UPDATE	

1.2.3 Commands for Data Query Language (DQL)

The SELECT command retrieves data.

SQL lets you build complex queries by means of the SELECT statement and relational operators (such as >, <, =, >=, <=, or <>) that enable you to express a search condition. A query can use a join to pull data from different tables and correlate it by matching on a common row that is in all the tables.

The input to one query can be the output of another query. A nested query is called a *subselect*.

Queries can be nested within INSERT, UPDATE, and DELETE commands to specify the scope of the operation.

1.2.4   Transaction Control Commands

These commands ensure data integrity when changing data. They ensure that a logically related sequence of actions that accomplish a particular result in an application (a logical unit of work) are either performed or cancelled in their entirety.

COMMIT   ROLLBACK
SAVEPOINT

1.2.5   Data Administration Commands

These commands help you analyze system performance and operations.

AUDIT MESSAGE   START AUDIT
STOP AUDIT

1.2.6   Data Control Commands

The following commands perform these functions:

- Create and maintain databases
- Create and maintain partitions
- Assign users to databases and tables

ALTER DATABASE	ALTER DBAREA
ALTER PASSWORD	ALTER STOGROUP
CHECK DATABASE	CHECK INDEX
CHECK TABLE	CREATE DATABASE
CREATE DBAREA	CREATE EVENT
CREATE INDEX	CREATE STOGROUP
CREATE SYNONYM	CREATE TABLE
CREATE TRIGGER	CREATE VIEW
DEINSTALL DATABASE	DROP DATABASE
DROP DBAREA	DROP EVENT
DROP INDEX	DROP STOGROUP
DROP SYNONYM	DROP TABLE
DROP TRIGGER	DROP VIEW
GRANT	INSTALL DATABASE
LOCK DATABASE	REVOKE
UNLOCK DATABASE	UPDATE STATISTICS
SET DEFAULT STOGROUP	

1.3   Example of an SQL Command

The following example shows an SQL query both in conversational English and actual SQL syntax.

What we want to do in English

Give me a list of everyone who lives in Palm Tree who has a salary greater than $15,000.

How we do it with SQL

Figure 1-1 shows an example of an SQL statement in the top window. The result table below returned one row, with the entry Mick Michaelson. Mick Michaelson is the only person living in Palm Tree with the specified salary. To retrieve the information we wanted, information was extracted from two tables, EMP_PRIVATEINFO and EMP_JOBINFO.

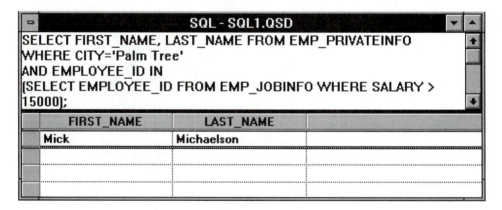

Figure 1-1   *How We Do It with SQL*

1.4   SQL and the Relational Model

SQL was designed as a language specifically for relational databases. In reality, SQL is now used to connect to almost every database management system, from stand-alone engines on the personal computer to legacy systems on a mainframe. Products like Trinsic's InfoHub™ or Information Builder's EDA/SQL™ work as an SQL-engine front end to mainframe data. Also SQL front ends to personal databases from dBASE IV™ to Access™ to

BTrieve™ to Paradox™ are readily available today even though these databases have specific limitations in the relational, client/server market.

While to understand SQL it is necessary to look at the relational database model, one should understand all database models in the market today. The hierarchical and network database models still enjoy popularity in the corporate world. Moreover, the object-oriented database model is rapidly gaining attention and popularity. (SQL is being used, appropriately or inappropriately, even with the object-oriented model.)

First, we look at five basic database models used today: file system, hierarchical, network, relational, and object-oriented model. Then, we examine the specifics of the relational model.

1.4.1 File System Model

A file system is the simplest model used for a database. In this management system, data is stored in a file, or series of files, sequentially on a disk. The "flat-file" approach, as it is called, offers no real benefits other than simplicity and low cost.

1.4.2 Hierarchical Model

One approach widely used in the 70s was the hierarchical model. This database model is still used today on mainframes such as IBM's IMS™ system and on PCs with Microsoft DOS. The hierarchical model organizes data in a tree structure from a "root node," as shown in Figure 1-2.

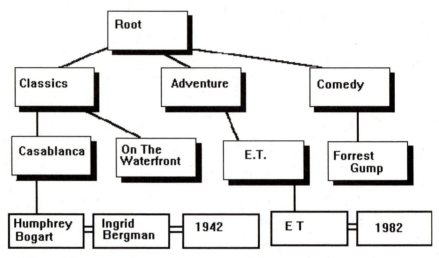

Figure 1-2   *Example of a Hierarchical Model*

As the example above demonstrates, a tree structure simplifies the search for data because you no longer search sequentially: You traverse down the nodes of the tree. Still, this design has significant issues.

For one thing, the initial structure of the database determines how data is related. You would have to completely redesign the database to change this. For example, in the diagram above, we have created a linked list of actors based on a particular movie. We could have made a linked list of movies based on a particular actor. Although you may have several ways you want to relate your information, the hierarchy limits you to one representation.

Second, the design of a hierarchical database can easily lead to confusions in relationships. For example, while I might consider Forrest Gump to be a comedy, someone else may consider it a classic several years from now.

1.4.3   Network Design Model

The approach to DBMS used as the network system was defined by the Conference on Data Systems Language (CODASYL). An example of this type of model is shown in Figure 1-3.

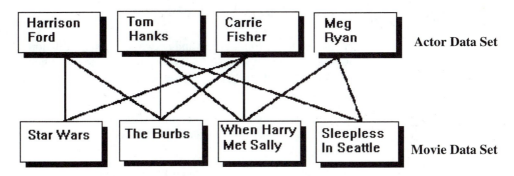

Figure 1-3   *Example of the Network Design Model*

In this model, we base our design on *data sets*. This model has two data sets:

- Actor data set
- Movie data set

The lines between the sets represent the relationships between movies and actors. The biggest advantage to this model is its flexibility. We could easily create another data set, such as the director data set, and connect that set to both the movie data set and the actor data set without too much pain. The drawback is the complexity of creating a model like this. As you add data sets, the connections become difficult to understand.

Like the hierarchical model, the network database model is procedural and record-at-a-time. To find a record, you have to navigate or find a path to the record you want and give multiple procedural commands that tell the system to walk down that path, step by step. You need a detailed understanding of how the data is stored. Once you have created a database and loaded data into it, it can be difficult to change.

The network database model (again, like the hierarchical model) stores some data as values and other data as pointers. For example, in a network system, the data that *When Harry Met Sally* was made in 1989 would be stored as a value in a field. The data that Meg Ryan starred in *When Harry Met Sally* would be stored as a pointer from the movie data set to the corresponding actor data set.

With network models, pointers are used to associate records to one another in a network. You must decide whether to store data as a pointer or as a value when you define the database.

1.4.4 Relational Model

In contrast to the hierarchical and network models, a relational system provides automatic navigation. You do not have to know how the database stores data in order to retrieve, change, or destroy that data. This makes it easy to access data.

The relational model is a collection of tables based on a set of rules that describe their relation to each other. The model is compelling for its power and simplicity.

Relational database systems can use any value to link one table to another, and you define relationships between values when you query the data, not when you create the tables. This gives you maximum flexibility to create spontaneous queries.

It was only in 1981 that IBM released their first relational database, called SQL/DS, based on SQL. By 1983 the first release of DB2 was introduced. Many vendors were on IBM's heels and actively joined in on developing relational databases early in the process. Oracle actually beat IBM to the market. Gupta (now Centura Software Corporation) introduced the first relational database on a personal computer in 1986.

1.4.5 Object-Oriented Model

The object-oriented model describes a data element as an object with attributes and its own identification. You do not use a unique value in a table as the means to retrieve information; rather, you base queries on object identifiers.

This model is discussed in Chapter 18, where we discuss future directions of database technology. Chapter 18 also discusses several of the vendors that integrate the SQL language and the object-oriented model.

1.5   Relational Model

A relational database is a collection of information stored in tables. The tables themselves resemble how information stored in nonrelational tables might look. When you define a database, you give a name to an eventual collection of tables and associated indexes.

A single database can contain all the data associated with one application or with a group of related applications. Collecting data into one database lets you start or stop access to all the data in one operation and grant authorization for access to all the data as a unit.

A database contains one or more *tables*. Each table has a name and contains a specific number of *columns* (vertical) and unordered *rows* (horizontal). Each column in a row is related in some way to the other columns in the same row. Figure 1-4 illustrates the model.

Column

PROD_NUM	PROD_NAME	PRICE	PRICE_DATE
113	Wall Mount Fluorescent Type 602	150	3/11/93
114	Overhead Track Type 401	125	3/11/93
115	Exterior Flood Type D01	100	3/11/93
116	Overhead Fluorescent Type 202	150	3/11/93
117	Wall Mount Spot Type A1	100	3/11/93
118	Overhead Track Type 400	100	3/11/93
119	Exterior Flood Type D02	125	3/11/93

Row

Figure 1-4   *PRODUCTS Relational Table*

Each column has a name and a data type. Each column contains a data value at the intersection of a row and a column.

In theory, no row in a table should be a duplicate of any other row. For instance, in the table PRODUCTS in Figure 1-4, the columns defined are *prod_num*, *prod_name*, *price*, and *price_date*. If I had entered two rows in this table with the same product name, there would be two duplicate rows in the table. The column, *product_num,* could be used to differentiate the two entries. (The two rows could have the same product name, but the products could have different colors and therefore have a different product number.) In such cases, there will be a column or combination of columns that are different for each order, and so the columns uniquely identify the row.

In a relational system, multiple tables are defined. These tables can be connected to create virtual tables so that interrelated data can be matched up and extracted in ways that may not have been intended by the creator of the database.

1.6   Definition of Terms

Several concepts and objects are fundamental to the SQL language. Objects (such as databases, tables, indexes, and views) and concepts (such as primary keys, foreign keys, referential constraints, joins, and system catalogs) are fundamental to SQL and relational technology. Several of the most significant objects and concepts are defined below.

1.6.1 Database

A *database* is a set of SQL objects. When you define a database, you give a name to an eventual collection of tables and associated indices.

Note: Several database vendors use *schema* interchangeably with database.

1.6.2 Table

A database contains one or more *tables*. Each table has a name and contains a specific number of columns (vertical) and unordered rows (horizontal). Each column in a row is related in some way to the other columns in the same row.

In Figure 1-1, we showed an SQL statement accessing and linking two relational tables, EMP_PRIVATEINFO and EMP_JOBINFO. Figure 1-5 shows the EMP_JOBINFO relational table.

Table - GUPTA:EMP_JOBINFO					
EMPLOYEE_ID	**DEPARTMENT_ID**	**TITLE**	**SALARY**	**BONUS**	**START_DATE**
1	2220	Senior Engineer	20000	50	6/12/86
2	2210	Manager	15000	25	7/12/87
3	2220	Staff Engineer	25000	25	10/15/89

Figure 1-5   *The EMP_JOBINFO Relational Table*

1.6.3   Index

An *index* is an ordered set of pointers to the data in a table, stored separately from the table. Each index is based on the values of data in one or more columns of a table. For example, a phone book can use last name, sorted alphabetically, as an index.

An index provides two benefits:

- **Improves performance.** Access to data is faster.

- **Ensures uniqueness.** A table with unique fields in the index cannot have two rows with the same values in the column or columns that form the index key.

1.6.4   View

A *view* is an alternate way of representing data that exists in one or more tables. A view can include all or some of the columns from one or more *base tables*. You can also base a view on other views or on a combination of views and tables.

A view looks like a table, and you can use it as though it were a table. You can use a view name in an SQL command as though it were a table name. You cannot do some operations through a view, but you do not need to know that an apparent table is actually a view.

A table has a storage representation, but a view does not. When you store a view, SQLBase stores the definition of the view in the system catalog, but SQLBase does not store any data for the view itself because the data already exists in the base table or tables.

A view lets different users view the same data in different ways. This allows programmers, database administrators, and end users to see the data as it suits their needs.

An example view may show only first name and phone number from a table with other columns such as last name and address.

1.6.5 Join

A *join* retrieves rows from more than one table. This operation is called a join because the rows retrieved from the different tables are joined on one or more columns that appear in two or more of the tables.

1.6.6 Primary Key

A table can have a *primary key,* which is a column or a group of columns whose value uniquely identifies each row. In Figure 1-6, the table EMP_PRIVATEINFO has a column, *employee_id,* that uniquely identifies that row; therefore, it can be used as a primary key.

Table - GUPTA:EMP_PRIVATEINFO				
EMPLOYEE_ID	FIRST_NAME	LAST_NAME	ADDRESS	CITY
1	Bill	Williams	1 First Street	Grand Canyon
2	Patty	Patterson	22 Lonesome Drive	Oily City
3	Mick	Michaelson	300 Ocean Boulevard	Palm Tree

Figure 1-6   *The EMP_PRIVATEINFO Relational Table*

1.6.7 Foreign Key

Columns of other tables may be *foreign key,* whose values must be equal to values of the primary key of the first table. Figure 1-6 shows an example of a foreign key, where the column, *employee_id*, in the table EMP_PRIVATEINFO is a foreign key to the EMP_JOBINFO table (which has this same column). The column, *employee_id*, can be both a primary key to itself and a foreign key to the table EMP_JOBINFO.

1.6.8   Referential Integrity

If a column is a primary key, then it must be a unique value. If a column is a foreign key, then that column must appear as a column in another table. Such rules as these are referred to as *referential integrity*.

1.6.9   System Catalog

Each database has a *system catalog* that contains tables created and maintained by SQLBase. These tables contain information about the tables, views, columns, indexes, and security privileges for the database. The system catalog is sometimes called a *data dictionary*.

When you create, change, or drop a database object, SQLBase changes rows in the system catalog tables.

A system catalog contains fields, such as the name, size, type, and valid values of each column stored in a table. A system catalog also holds information about the tables and views that exist in the database and how they are accessed. A user can query the data dictionary tables just like any other table.

1.7   Relational Database Vendors

Following is a list of major relational database vendors in the market today. This list is by no means complete, but is meant to represent the more dominant players. All products are trademarks or registered trademarks of their respective companies.

Borland International, Inc. (Interbase)
100 Borland Way
Scotts Valley, CA 95066
(408)431-1000

PRODUCT: Interbase

PLATFORMS: Windows, Netware, HP-UX, Sun Solaris, IBM AIX, SGI, SCO UNIX, other UNIX variants, DEC VMS

POSITION: Interbase has been targeted for a long time to the UNIX market. Just recently it has been ported to the Microsoft Windows marketplace, in conjunction with the release of Borland's Delphi applications development environment.

Cincom Systems, Inc. (Supra)
2300 Montana Ave
Cincinnati, OH 45211
(800) 543-3010

PRODUCT: Supra Server

PLATFORMS: UNIX, Windows NT, VMS, IBM's MVS and OS/2

POSITION: Cincom does not have the market share of competitors like Informix, Sybase, Oracle, or IBM, but they do have some unique differentiators.

Cincom's government division announced in 1994 that they would accept 99 cents for Federal users if these users trade in competing products. Cincom capitalizes on its compatibility with the Federal Information Processing Standard 127-1 for SQL to go after the government market. Cincom also stated its intention to work with Unisql to integrate Unisql's object-oriented DBMS technology with their own.

Computer Associates International Inc (CA-Ingres)
One Computer Associates Plaza
Islandia, NY 11788
(516) 543-3010

PRODUCT: CA-Ingres

PLATFORMS: Microsoft Windows, most major UNIX versions, including Sun Solaris, AIX, HP-UX, VAX/ VMS, and OS/2

POSITION: Computer Associates has been a major player in mainframe database packages, with CA-IDMS and CA-Datacom. With the 1994 acquisition of The Ask Group, owner of Ingres, they plan to make a more prominent play in the relational database market.

The Ask Group acquisition was CA's forty-eighth. CA has a reputation for making problematic software companies pay off (The Ask Group lost $70 million in the quarter preceding the takeover). Ingres has solid products, including connectivity software, that tie into CA's mainframe strengths. Computer Associates also acquired rights to remarket Centura Software's SQLBase under its own label as an Ingres relational engine for Microsoft Windows.

Centura Software Corporation (SQLBase, SQLBase Ranger)
1060 Marsh Rd
Menlo Park, CA 94025
(415) 321-9500

PRODUCT: SQLBase, SQLBase Ranger

PLATFORMS: Windows, Windows 95, Windows NT, Novell Netware, Sun Solaris

POSITION: Centura Software positions itself as a database for branch automation and mobile computing. Bruce Scott, co-founder of Gupta (now Centura Software), and his team wrote the first relational database for the PC in 1986. Since then, Centura Software has been a market leader in relational databases for branch computing. They have earned a reputation for offering the fastest relational implementation on a Novell server. The company focuses more on a data replication strategy to other vendors' RDBMS. SQLBase Ranger on a laptop can replicate that data to other high-end database servers.

Centura has never fought for the high relational databases market but has focused on a small memory footprint for department servers and desktop applications.

IBM (DB2, DB2/2, DB2/6000)
Old Orchard Road
Armonk, NY 10504
(914) 765-1900

PRODUCT: DB2 5.0, DB2/6000 for AIX, DB2/2 for OS/2

PLATFORMS: Microsoft Windows, MVS, AIX, AX/400, OS/2, Sun Solaris, HP-UX

POSITION: You will hear IBM market DB2 as an "end-to-end" product. They run DB2 on everything from the mainframe down to the PC. IBM is putting a lot of resources into porting DB2 onto more platforms, and IBM has many success stories at the high and low ends. The main criticisms from analysts have been that there is more than one code base for DB2 ports and that IBM does not push client/server technologies. Criticism aside, IBM is aggressively marketing DB2 and pushing to merge their code base.

Informix (INFORMIX-Online, INFORMIX-SE)
4100 Bohannon Dr
Menlo Park, CA 94025
(415) 926-6300

PRODUCTS: Informix-Online 7.1 Informix-SE 7.1

PLATFORMS: Windows NT, Sun Solaris, HP-UX, IBM AIX, most of the major UNIX platforms

POSITION: Informix is the third largest relational database software company, behind Sybase and Oracle. The INFORMIX-Online 5.0 distinguishes itself by 1) being written for UNIX operating systems and 2) being able to scale with symmetric multiprocessing machines and also parallel processing. Because of Informix's concentration on the UNIX platforms, they have consistently delivered an extremely fast and reliable database on UNIX platforms.

Informix also differentiates itself by offering an easier-to-use entry level database offering called INFORMIX-SE. INFORMIX-SE targets small- to mid-range application environments.

Microsoft (SQL Server)
One Microsoft Way
Redmond, WA 98052
(206) 882-8080

PRODUCT: SQL Server 95

PLATFORMS: Windows NT

POSITION: While Microsoft and Sybase's cooperation in relational technology is cooling, Microsoft's technology is named like and based on Sybase's RDMS. Microsoft can capitalize on their position by pushing a low- end relational server on the Windows NT platform that offers hard-to-beat functionality as well as a great price / performance ratio. Microsoft's pricing strategy will likely inflict pain on database players such as Sybase, Oracle, and Informix, but Microsoft has a lot to learn in direct sales and service.

SQL Server supports most major features today, including data replication, central management, parallel backup, SMP support, and declarative referential integrity. Their major play is in their bundling of SQL Server with NT, including graphical administration tools and ease of use.

Oracle Corporation (Oracle)
500 Oracle Parkway
Redwood Shores, CA 94065
(415) 506-7000

PRODUCTS: Oracle 7, Oracle 8

PLATFORMS: Oracle boasts over 80 distinct platforms, including Windows, Windows NT, Macintosh, 40+ UNIX versions, VMS, MVS, VM, HP MPE/XL, Siemens, ICL, OS/2, and Novell Netware

POSITION: A leader in enterprise-level relational databases, Oracle offers a broad suite of tools and services. Oracle is the number one player in the enterprise-level relational database market. Their clear strength is the scalability across platforms. They run on all major hardware and operating system platforms available worldwide. Also, Oracle's product is mature and offers all of the check-off items required by corporate America for enterprise-level database management. Oracle has, however, been shy when benchmarking against competition, which may point to the fact that if you are the most scalable across hardware platforms, you might not always have the best performance. Oracle 8 has been touted as a major boost to Oracle's performance, especially in the symmetric multiprocessing arena.

Oracle has also distinguished itself with the Oracle Parallel Server, which runs on loosely coupled machines. These highly specialized machines are mainly used in Fortune 500 companies and research institutions. When there is a need, Oracle reaches into the very high end.

Oracle has recently forayed into the desktop market by scaling down their database to sit on Windows and Macintosh. They are at a disadvantage in the low-end arena because of the size of the database and the amount of memory they require, but their desktop solutions position them to have the broadest offering in the market.

Oracle Corporation (Rdb/VMS)
500 Oracle Parkway
Redwood Shores, CA 94065
(415) 506-7000

PRODUCT: Rdb

PLATFORMS: VMS

POSITION: Oracle purchased Rdb from DEC. Oracle has maintained a strong presence in the VMS marketplace and clearly hopes to eventually move the existing Rdb installed base over to Oracle's own technology.

Oracle will maintain the Rdb product for some time but will continue to push a migration strategy to Oracle.

Progess Software (Progress)
14 Oak Park
Bedford, MA 01730
(617) 280-4000

PRODUCT: Progress 7.0

PLATFORMS: SunOS, HP-UX, DG/UX, and Microsoft Windows

POSITION: Progess is known for its integration of its database and 4GL product, which it markets under the Progress 7.0 label. While Progress is not competing head to head with the likes of Informix, Sybase, or Oracle, Progress has undertaken a strategy of licensing its relational technology to other software vendors for reuse. Progress has been able to ship large numbers of its RDBMS through different names and labels.

Quadbase Systems, Inc. (Quadbase-SQL)
2855 Kifer Rd., Ste. 203
Santa Clara, CA 95051
(408) 982-0835

PRODUCT: Quadbase-SQL and Quadbase-SQL SB Server

PLATFORMS: Windows, Windows NT, Novell Netware

POSITION: Quadbase positions itself by packaging its engine in a client development kit targeted at Visual Basic, C, C++, FoxPro, and other application developers. Quadbase has made an ODBC driver to serve as the native API to their database.

Sybase, Inc. (SQL Server)
6475 Christie Avenue
Emeryville, CA 94608
(510) 596-3500

PRODUCT: SQL Server Release 10, SQL Server Release 11

PLATFORMS: Windows NT, Bull, DEC VMS, DEC OSF, DG AViiON, HP-UX, IBM AIX, ICL, Motorola 88k, NCR System 3000, NEC, Novell Netware, OS/2, Pyramid S, Sequent, Silicon Graphics, Stratus, SunOS, Sun Solaris, Unisys

POSITION: A leader in enterprise-level relational databases, Sybase offers a broad suite of tools and services.

Sybase has distinguished itself as a company focused on client/server computing. To bolster this image, Sybase has made strategic relations with Microsoft, which has its own version of SQL Server and also has made strategic acquisitions of network interoperability products as well as Powersoft, a leader in the client/server application development arena. Sybase, like Informix, has centered on UNIX platforms, but it has branched out to other platforms as well, most notably Netware, OS/2, and DEC VMS.

Sybase has several formidable tasks ahead of it. First, they must successfully integrate Powersoft's technology. They must also face strained relations with Microsoft. Their dealings with Microsoft have been problematic, with Microsoft now charting a divergent course from Sybase.

On the low end, Sybase inherited Watcom's relational engine as part of the Powersoft aquisition, which has been a strong low-end, desktop relational engine. Sybase plans to integrate the Watcom engine to make it appear more like their own RDBMS. The effort will take many man years to complete and, if successful, could give Sybase a great positioning in the low-end market.

Sybase (SQL Anywhere)
Watcom, a subsidiary of Sybase.
Waterloo, Ontario
(519) 886-3700

PRODUCT: Watcom 4.0

PLATFORMS: Windows, Windows 95, Windows NT, OS/2, DOS, Novell

POSITION: SQL Anywhere (previously known as Watcom) is a direct competitor to SQLBase in competing at the branch automation and mobile computing segment of the relational market. With Sybase's purchase of Powersoft, SQL Anywhere has headed in the direction of being "SQL Server Lite." The database is a relative newcomer on the market, having been written by university students in Waterloo in the early 90s, it now has asynchronous replication to Sybase System 11.

SQL Anywhere gained a large market share extremely fast by being the first to offer limited free runtimes, where, as long as a user did not create new databases, tables, or columns, developers could deploy the database as they are accustomed to do with products like dBASE, BTrieve, Paradox, and FoxPro.

Tandem (NonStop SQL)
19333 Valco Parkway
Cupertino, CA 95014
(408) 285-6000

PRODUCT: NonStop SQL/ MP

PLATFORMS: Tandem machines

POSITION: Tandem boasts an extremely reliable, high-end relational database for mission-critical applications. Tandem boasts over 5000 large-scale database licenses deployed. Tandem is now targeting data warehousing solutions by adding such unique SQL features as its Multidimensional Access Method (MDAM) for decision-support applications.

XDB Systems Inc (XDB)
14700 Sweitzer Lane
Laurel, MD 20707
(301) 317-6800

PRODUCT: XDB 4.0

PLATFORMS: Windows, Windows NT, OS/2, Sun Solaris, AIX, HP-UX, Novell Netware

POSITION: XDB Systems has a strategy of supplying DB2-compatible databases. They tout more than 60,000 licenses for XDB DBMS, making them a player in the low-to mid-range relational market.

4th Dimension Software, Inc. (4D First and 4D Server)
One Park Plaza, 11th Fl.
Irvine, CA 92714
(714) 757-4300

PRODUCT: 4D First, 4D Server

PLATFORMS: Macintosh

POSITION: 4th Dimension provides a relational client/server database and a development tool, Object Master, for the Macintosh platform. With over 6000 developers worldwide, they offer a unique alternative to client/server technology for the Apple community. Their multiuser server supports AppleTalk and TCP/IP protocols.

A Note on XBase Products:

Many personal PC databases offer SQL front ends today, including dBASE, Paradox, Access, FoxPro, and Clipper. While these databases are useful and prevalent in the PC world, there are significant issues this class of databases faces when dealing with multiuser, networked environments. For many databases in this class, referential integrity issues may not be addressed at all.

1.8 Summary

In this chapter, we looked at the origins of SQL and covered the basic commands used with this language. We also described the relational database model. The SQL language and the relational model do not always go hand in hand. For example, Microsoft Access can use an SQL interface even though the underlying database model is a flat-file system. SQL was specifically designed to be used with a relational database model, but because of its market acceptance, it is widely used in a manner not originally intended by the researchers who developed the language at IBM.

This chapter also defined important terms used with the SQL language and a relational database. Specifically we introduced the concepts of *tables*, *columns*, *indexes*, and *views*, as well as *joins*, *primary* and *foreign keys*, and *referential integrity*. These concepts will be used many times in the following chapters.

Finally, we introduced major database vendors in the SQL market today. The list was by no means exhaustive, but it is representative of the market and points to the broad acceptance of SQL in corporate America. The last part of this book, Expanding Horizons, elaborates on the SQL market and introduces other players in this market beyond the traditional database vendors. For now, we have a good basis for looking at the first step in creating a database: designing the logical model.

2 Database Design

This chapter steps through the process of database design. Simple design techniques are introduced to build a sample database that is also used in the Rapid Tutorial in Chapters 3 through 11. The design process is not only central to proper data management, but is also one of the most complex issues an application's developer will face. Understanding a database design greatly simplifies the process of learning SQL. While not all database design processes are covered here, this chapter provides a broad overview helpful in learning SQL.

The chapter is organized as follows:

- Section 2.1 Approaching Database Design
- Section 2.2 Steps of Database Design
- Section 2.3 Creation of a Logical Model
- Section 2.4 Normalization
- Section 2.5 Database Diagram
- Section 2.6 Logical Data Modeling Tools
- Section 2.7 Summary

2.1 Approaching Database Design

To properly begin learning SQL, it is useful to begin at the first step in the database design: the process of designing a logical data model. The *conceptual* schema, sometimes referred to as the *logical data model*, is based on the natural characteristics of the data without regard to how the data may be used or physically stored. The assumption is that the logical perspective of an organization's data resource is the least likely to change over time and is therefore the most stable. It is also the easiest way to learn why a relational database is designed as it is. Many PC users are used to databases that contain over a thousand columns in one table. (Note that Oracle, which is used at the enterprise level in large corporations, supports a maximum of only 256 columns.)

The next step, which we approach in Chapter 3, is designing a physical model, or *internal schema* of a database. The *internal schema* is a mapping of the conceptual model to the physical constructs of the target database management system (DBMS). For example, in performing this translation, the database designer may introduce new physical objects or alter the conceptual objects to achieve better performance or capacity and a more usable database. These design changes can be made to exploit the hardware or software environment of an implementation platform. Since these changes should not be visible at the conceptual level, the actual meaning of the data does not change.

We could spend a great deal of time on database design. Many books have been written on this topic; however, since learning the SQL language is our main objective, we will leave this area once we have an initial structure for our database. Inevitably, we will return to database design in order to discuss performance issues surrounding the SQL language.

2.1.1 Advantages to a Structured Approach

Many readers frequently question the need to step through a rigorous design process, even for complex data structures. Unfortunately, database design is central to system performance and data integrity. Taking a systematic approach to database design will end up saving everyone a great deal of time. The main advantages of a structured database design are database integrity, increased performance, elimination of redundancy, and database independence.

Database Integrity

There are numerous situations that place integrity, or data consistency, in jeopardy. For example: hardware sometimes fails; software will have bugs; users will not always enter data in the same format; and application developers may not agree on how they want to store their information. For integrity problems like these, there are no easy solutions, but for others, we can avoid data inconsistency altogether by properly designing our database.

To properly design a database, we must first understand the integrity rules we intend to follow.

There are several forms of integrity. For example, we might dictate an integrity rule for a table of Fortune 500 companies where the primary key will never be null (every company has to have a company ID number). There could be an application depending on the *company ID* field that would not work otherwise. This is known as an *entity integrity rule.* An example of another integrity rule could be that when a company name is used in more than one table, the name must be spelled the same way in both places. This is an example of a *referential integrity rule.*

Proper database design must create a list of the known integrity rules before we can create a database that enforces them.

Increased Performance

When users complain of the relative performance problems when using SQL to query a database, more often than not the design of their database has more to do with performance than how they structure their queries. From personal experience, one biotech firm local to the Bay Area was able to increase the performance of their Oracle-based application by a factor of 100 simply by creating a few indexes on key tables.

Careful attention to database design insulates user needs from database performance and capacity concerns.

Elimination of Redundancy

With the number of tables one usually creates with a relational model, it is easy for data redundancy to creep into a design. A structured approach eliminates this; however, having the same information stored in multiple tables can be critical for performance reasons. There are trade-offs to the data redundancy issue: Data could also take up needed disk space, especially when you get tens of thousands of rows of data in a single table.

Database Independence

The major advantage of using a structured approach is that as the physical characteristics of the data and/or the target DBMS change over the life of the database, database designers can adjust the physical constructs of the internal schema *without affecting existing program modules.* Similarly, the users' views of the data can be changed as their requirements change without affecting the manner in which the data is physically stored. Without the three schema (or similar) architecture, changes to the physical database can require costly effort wasted on maintenance of existing program modules.

2.1.2 A Note on Standards

There are several different approaches to database design, but most agree on the basic concepts discussed in this chapter. The ANSI/X3/SPARC Study Group on Database Management Systems has defined a generalized architecture or framework for a database system. The group's architecture is still not generally used commercially, but it does provide a push toward merging the common threads of most techniques. Several of the guidelines are discussed in this chapter.

2.2 Steps of Database Design

The easiest way to understand the design process is to visualize it. Figure 2-1 illustrates a step-by-step path through the database design process.

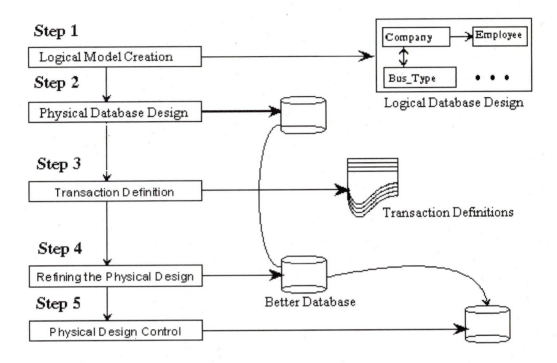

Figure 2-1 *Database Design Steps and Deliverables*

2.2.1 Explaining the Steps

Now that we have outlined a flow process for database design in Figure 2-1, we can explain each of the steps in enough detail to get a broad picture of the whole process.

Step 1) Logical Model Creation

This chapter specifically addresses the issues of logical data modeling, as it is the first step in the creation of a database. Logical data modeling, or the creation of the conceptual schema, is a (relatively) well-known process within the database industry. Many books and training courses are available on the subject. Consequently, this chapter does *not* attempt to present an exhaustive treatment of this material. Rather, this chapter introduces you to the logical database design process. Readers who are interested in a more detailed presentation of the material are encouraged to read one of the many excellent books available on the subject or to attend a local training course.

In addition, the database industry has standardized on the *entity-relationship diagram*, or ERD, to represent the conceptual schema. Consequently, many computer-aided software engineering (CASE) vendors market tools for entity relationship diagramming. You may find one of these tools beneficial in the creation of your conceptual schema. Many software development tools provide integration of this schema, including vendors such as LBMS, Intersolv, Bachman, Popkin, Visual Systems, and LogicWorks.

Step 2) Physical Database Design

In Chapter 3 we cover the tasks necessary to create the first-cut internal schema or physical database design. The database constructed in Chapter 3 is an initial prototype only, representing the logical data requirements in their simplest form, without any processing requirements. The first-cut physical schema is constructed by applying some simple conversion rules to the entity relationship diagram.

Also, many of the CASE tools discussed above automatically generate the first-cut internal schema. Such CASE tools can convert an entity relationship diagram to one of many relational database vendors compatible SQL DDL (data definition language). You have a level of database independence when this level of functionality exists and is automated for you.

Step 3) Transaction Definition

The primary goal of *physical* database design is to ensure that the database provides the required level of performance. Typically, database performance is measured in terms of transaction performance. So, the objective of physical database design is to ensure every database *transaction* meets or exceeds its performance requirements. The transaction definition is a yardstick by which the rest of the database design process is judged.

Chapter 12 discusses this more advanced level of data definition. We will create transaction definitions because they represent detailed and critical processing requirements. A final database design must meet these requirements in order to be completed successfully.

Step 4) Refining the Physical Design

Chapter 8 revisits the physical database created in Chapter 3, with the goal of introducing design optimization methods that improve its performance and capacity. At this point in the database design process, general guidelines are applied to the first-cut physical database design to produce a better physical database design.

Step 5) Physical Design Control

Physical design control is the iterative process of adjusting the internal schema to meet the objectives set in the transaction definitions. Transactions that fail to meet processing requirements are examined for possible improvements that target their particular database accesses. Our goal is to find an acceptable trade-off between conflicting requirements of all of the transactions that make up the complete system. This process is iterative; it repeats until all critical transactions are performing effectively.

2.3 Creation of a Logical Model

In this section, we go through a series of examples, as well as introduce the important concepts of logical modeling in order to build a sample logical model diagram, which is shown in Section 2.5. Specifically, we do the following:

- Explain and design an *entity relationship diagram* (ERD).

- Show a diagram of a simple ERD diagram.

- Introduce specific terms and concepts of this logical diagram, including entities, relationships, cardinality, dependency rules, attributes, domains, and primary and foreign keys.

This is a lot to cover, but once you have it, you are well on the way to creating your first logical model.

2.3.1 Entity Relationship Diagrams (ERD)

Logical data modeling uses diagram symbols, a model (or picture) of the data required to meet the objectives of the system being developed. The resulting model is called an *entity-relationship diagram* (ERD).

Techniques are applied to this model to verify its accuracy, completeness, and stability. The model can then be translated into a physical database design, possibly for multiple implementation platforms, by performing a transformation process that meets specific performance requirements as well as any special characteristics of the chosen physical architecture.

The most basic objects of logical data modeling are the *entity* and the *relationship*. *Keys, attributes*, and *domains* are not assigned diagram symbols, but are important background objects for logical data modeling. Each of these concepts is discussed below.

Entities and Relationships

Entities are the basic information units of an ERD and are equivalent to tables in the finished physical database design. Entities represent a person, place, concept, or event in the real world about which information is needed. Examples of entities are customers, orders, invoices, employees, and warehouses. Entities are represented by boxes in our diagram.

Relationships are connections between one or more entities. These are represented graphically by lines containing various symbols that convey characteristics of the relationship. The majority of relationships involve only two entities and are called binary relationships. These are often broadly classified according to how many occurrences of an entity type can appear on each side of the relationship, as shown in Figure 2-2.

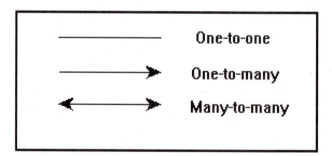

Figure 2-2   *Defining Types of Relationships Among Entities*

2.3.2 Our Sample Database ERD

Figure 2-3 depicts the sample database used in this book, which is included on the accompanying CD-ROM. This database describes over 250 of the Fortune 500 companies in the United States.

The entities described by our sample database are:

- COMPANY
- EMPLOYEES
- BUS_TYPES
- BUS_CODES
- STOCK
- STOCK_PRICE
- LOCATIONS
- REVENUE
- DEPARTMENTS

Each entity, or grouping of data, will become a table in our relational database. The lines between the entities indicate the type of relationship between them. We will use the arrows described in Figure 2-2 as notation to establish relationships between entities.

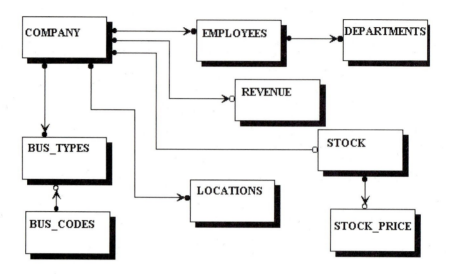

Figure 2-3   *Example ERD for Corporate Database for Fortune 500 Companies*

2.3.3   *Entities, Relationships, and Cardinality*

An important characteristic of the relationship is its *cardinality*, which describes the allowable number of occurrences of each entity type involved in the relationship. In Figure 2-3, *minimum cardinality* (which can be either zero or one) is described through the use of circles at the ends of the lines. The circle can be either hollow, indicating zero, or filled in, indicating one.

Maximum cardinality (which can be either one or many) is described through the use of arrows. The absence of the arrow means a maximum of one entry is allowed, whereas the presence of an arrow means a maximum of many (more than one).

Examples of Minimum Cardinality

In Figure 2-3, there are hollow circles by the entities REVENUE, STOCK, STOCK_PRICE, and BUS_TYPES. The hollow circle indicates that entries are optional, but at most one entry is allowed. The entities COMPANY, LOCATIONS, BUS_TYPES, BUS_CODES, and EMPLOYEES all designate a mandatory requirement that at least one row be present in each of the tables noted by the darkened circles next to each entity.

Examples of Maximum Cardinality

The use of one-way arrows from the COMPANY entity to other entities, like EMPLOYEES, indicates a *one-to-many* relationship. This relationship can be stated as a rule: For each company there can be many employees. The lack of any arrows between the entities COMPANY and STOCK implies a *one-to-one* relationship between them. Here the rule would be: A company will have no more than one stock record.

There are also cases of *many-to-many* relationships, which are denoted by arrows at both ends of the lines. Figure 2-3 does not have an example of this. We could have denoted the COMPANY / EMPLOYEE relationship to be many-to-many. A employee could work for more than one company, which is true for contractors as well as board members.

2.3.4 *Dependency Rules*

The type of relationship, where an entity has both minimum and maximum cardinality of one with another entity, is often called a *dependency*. For example, from the EMPLOYEES entity perspective, the minimum cardinality of COMPANY is one. The maximum cardinality of the relationship is also one, since there is no arrow on the COMPANY side of the relationship. The EMPLOYEE entity is said to be dependent on COMPANY, since it could not exist without a relationship to a single occurrence of COMPANY. All of the dependencies in a database should be written up as a set of rules.

We can summarize the relationships we have created with the following set of rules.

- An employee works for one, and only one, company.
- There can be one or many employees working for each company.
- There are zero, one, or many revenue entries for each company.
- There can be one or many location entries for each company.
- There is either zero or one stock entry for each company.
- There can be one or many business types for each company.
- Each location, employee, stock, business type, and revenue entry is related to one, and only one, company.
- There are zero, one, or many business types related to each business code.
- There is a one-to-one relationship between an employee and his department.

- There are zero, one, or many stock price entries for each stock record.

2.3.5 Attributes and Domains

Attributes are simply characteristics of entities. They either describe or identify an entity. Examples of descriptive attributes for the COMPANY, EMPLOYEES, and STOCK_PRICE entities are listed below:

COMPANY Entity:

- *comp_name*
- *comp_id*
- *corp_addr*
- *city*
- *state*
- *zip*

EMPLOYEES Entity:

- *emp_name*
- *emp_id*
- *title*
- *dep_code*

STOCK_PRICE Entity:

- *symbol*
- *stock_date*
- *stock_value*

Following the transformation of the logical design into a physical database, entities will become tables and attributes will become columns in tables.

Domains are the logical value sets that attributes possess. The definition of domain given here is the usage specified by E. F. Codd when he published the relational data model. Attributes such as *stock_value* could have domain called CURRENCY, for example, because the possible values of these attributes are a discrete set of those real numbers that are represented by the picture 999,999...,999.99. Likewise, the attribute *stock_date* could have the DATE domain, in which 02/29/1992 is a set member, but 02/29/1993 is not.

Domains provide a means to perform semantic validation of query statements, particularly for join operations. When tables are joined on columns that are not defined on the same domain, the results will not be meaningful. An example of this is SELECT * FROM EMPLOYEES WHERE EMPLOYEES.emp_id = COMPANY.emp_id. Although domains do not have to be specified for a data model since they are not at this point transformed into any physical design object, their inclusion can provide a means of manually validating the join criteria used in SQL statements. They are also useful in the physical design process for determining physical data types of table columns.

2.3.6 Primary and Foreign Keys

Identifying attributes are also called keys. The two most important keys for database design are *primary* and *foreign keys*. An example of a primary key in the entity COMPANY is *comp_id*, which is a unique attribute used to locate a specific entry within the entity. These keys provide the means by which relational databases support referential integrity. The *comp_id* key ensures that every entry is unique. The *comp_name* could also be used as the primary key, but long character strings do not make a good choice as an identifier for performance reasons.

For a logical data model to be complete, every entity must have a primary key identified. This primary key can consist of either a single attribute or may be composed of two or more attributes, in which case it is called a concatenated or composite key. The entity EMPLOYEES has a *composite primary key* of *comp_id* and *emp_id*. Both attributes are needed to uniquely identify an entry in EMPLOYEES.

The two critical characteristics of a primary key are uniqueness and nonredundancy. Uniqueness refers to the fact that the value of a primary key for a given occurrence of an entity must not be duplicated in any other occurrence of the same entity type. The physical design implication is that a unique index must be able to be placed on a primary key successfully. The nonredundancy characteristic of a primary key, which applies to concatenated keys only, means that each of the attributes that constitute the primary key must be essential to its uniqueness, so that if any attribute was removed, then the key would no longer be unique. This last rule prevents extraneous information from being placed into keys. These rules for forming primary keys are important in the normalization process.

Figure 2-4 illustrates primary and foreign keys.

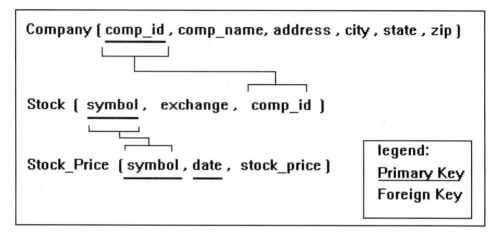

Figure 2-4   *Example of Mapping Between Primary and Foreign Keys*

Foreign keys must be created in an entity type to indicate the specific occurrence of another entity with which this entity has a relationship. The attributes of the foreign key must match the primary key of the related entity exactly. The foreign key appears in the entity that is on the many side of a one-to-many relationship or may appear on either side of a one-to-one relationship. When the relationship is many-to-many, an intermediate table will contain the foreign keys of both entities involved in the relation.

2.4   Normalization

To design a relational database correctly, you use a process called *data normalization*. There are actually five steps to this process, but for performance reasons, the fourth and fifth steps are not commonly used. We will examine the first three steps.

The normalization process is a logical design technique that is especially well suited for use with relational systems because of its capability to directly implement the results without any translation. Performing normalization:

- Reduces data redundancy

- Protects against update and deletion anomalies

- Provides a more flexible, longer lasting database design

The resulting database will be easier to maintain and will not require major, high-cost, structural changes as often as do unnormalized designs. This is due to the inherent stability of basing the data structures on the natural organization of the basic business information flowing through the corporation rather than structuring it with only a limited user or application perspective.

While the processes that a business performs on its data may change often, the data items that are operated on by those processes can be structured to reflect the nature of the company's business. This means that the application processes, embodied in program logic, can be more quickly changed to keep pace with company needs. The underlying database remains the same, reflecting the basic information inherent in the environment. Attaining this level of stability is the goal of data normalization.

2.4.1   Normal Form

The normal form is a specific level of normalization achieved by a set of tables making up a database design. Each successive normal form represents a more stable and controlled stage of design. Higher levels of normal forms always require the design to be in each lower level of normalization. As an example, second normal form requires the design to be in first normal form, third normal form requires both first and second forms, and so on.

A number of normal forms are defined, and work is continuing so that more forms may appear in the future. Most current texts on database design address normal forms one through five, although only the first three are needed for most tables. For this reason, only the first three forms are summarized in Table 2-1. Consult more detailed database design texts for a more in-depth discussion of additional normal forms.

Table 2-1 *Summary of Normal Forms, Rules, and Steps Needed to Achieve the Next Form*

Form	Description	Transform
Unnormalized Data		**Decompose all data structures into flat, two-dimensional tables.**
First Normal Form	**Records with no repeating groups**	
Second Normal Form	**All nonkey data items fully functionally dependent on primary key**	**For tables with composite primary keys, ensure that all other attributes are dependent on the whole key. Split tables apart as required to achieve this.**
Third Normal Form	**All nonkey data items independent of each other**	**Remove all transitive dependencies, splitting the table apart as required. No nonkey attribute should represent a fact about another nonkey attribute.**

2.4.2 First Normal Form

Converting an unnormalized relation called COMPANY into first normal form is shown in Figure 2-5. This conversion involves breaking the table apart, with each table having its own primary key identified. Any repeating elements are also removed from the relations at this point, so that each resulting table is *flat*, meaning that each column has a unique name and no columns consist of multiple elements (such as an array). This simple step places these data items into first normal form.

Primary keys are indicated by the attributes that are underlined.

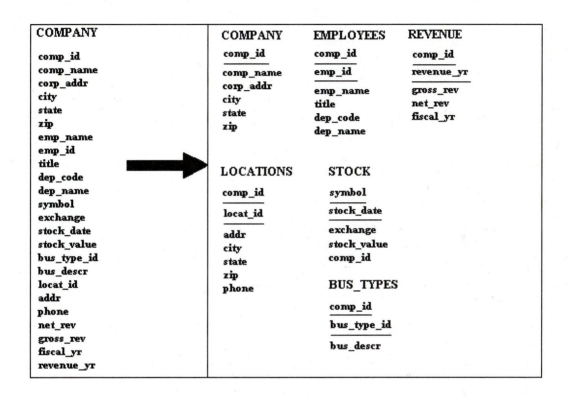

Figure 2-5 *First Normal Form: Conversion of an unnormalized relation, COMPANY, into six separate relations in first normal form.*

2.4.3 Second Normal Form

Figure 2-6 illustrates further normalization of the previous example, where the *stock_value* relation violates second normal form. The small arrows indicate the key attributes that each nonkey attribute depends on. The other relations in the previous example are already in second normal form.

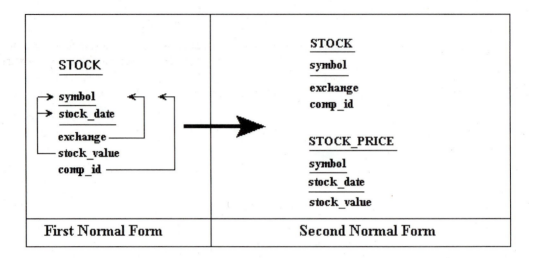

Figure 2-6   *Second Normal Form*

Further transformations are required to bring the data structure from Figure 2-6 into second normal form. As Figure 2-6 shows, the STOCK relation violates second normal form and must be broken apart. The nonkey attributes of *exchange* and *comp_id* are dependent only on part of the primary key, *symbol*. The table is therefore transformed so that *symbol* is the entire primary key, with the two attributes that depend on it remaining in the table. The *stock_date* and *stock_value* attributes, which depended on the entire key of the original STOCK relation, are placed into a new relation, STOCK_PRICE, along with the original composite key. Figure 2-7 illustrates one other table, BUS_TYPE, that needs to be put in second normal form. The relation, BUS_TYPES, needs conversion so that the *bus_descr* attribute only depends on one of the primary keys, *bus_type_id.*

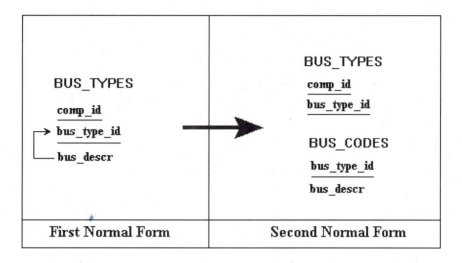

BUS_TYPES

comp_id

bus_type_id

bus_descr

First Normal Form

BUS_TYPES

comp_id

bus_type_id

BUS_CODES

bus_type_id

bus_descr

Second Normal Form

Figure 2-7   *Second Normal Form, Continued*

As Figure 2-7 shows, the BUS_TYPES relation violates second normal form and must be broken apart. The nonkey attribute *bus_descr* is dependent only on part of the primary key, *bus_type_id*. The table, BUS_CODES, is therefore created so that *bus_type_id* is the entire primary key, with the attribute, *bus_descr* in the table. The original table, BUS_TYPE, loses its dependent attribute.

The main reasons to normalize a small table such as this are to reduce data redundancy and to reduce the number of changes necessary should you change the domain of *bus_descr*.

The entire set of relations is now in second normal form.

2.4.4 Third Normal Form

Figure 2-8 illustrates further normalizing our example to third normal form: The EMPLOYEES relation violated third normal form because of nonkey attributes that are dependent on other nonkey attributes, as shown by the arrows. These attributes are broken out into new relations, the original relation as a foreign key to the new relation. This foreign key attribute is *dep_code* in the EMPLOYEES relation.

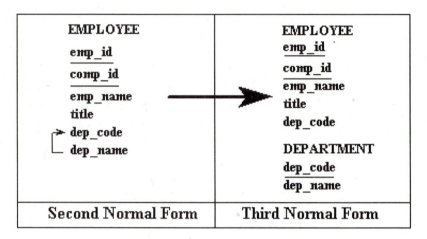

Figure 2-8   *Third Normal Form*

One remaining transformation must be done on our data from Figure 2-5 in order to get all the relations into third normal form. As shown in Figure 2-8, the EMPLOYEES relation violates third normal form and must be transformed into two tables. The nonkey attribute *dep_name* depends on another nonkey attribute, *dep_code*. Even though *dep_name* is currently in the EMPLOYEES table, it does not depend on the primary keys directly, but is dependent through the *dep_code*, which is dependent on the primary key.

This is called a *transitive dependency* and is removed by creating a new table with a primary key of the transitive attribute in the original relation. This transitive attribute then becomes a foreign key to the new table. The attributes in the original relation that were transitively dependent are now placed in the new table, where they are fully dependent on the primary key only. The DEPARTMENT relation in Figure 2-8 is formed through this process. The data originally described in Figure 2-5 is now entirely in third normal form.

2.4.5 Denormalization

Now that we have looked at the benefits associated with data normalization, a few words about denormalization are in order. Denormalization is the process of taking a database design out of third normal form (or some higher form) for performance reasons. One may denormalize by either redundantly storing prime attributes or by adding aggregate attributes to the database.

Some database designers routinely denormalize during logical database design. However, the only reason to denormalize is to achieve greater performance. In addition, because of the added complexities of a denormalized database, denormalization should occur only as a last resort after all other means of increasing performance have failed. The logical design should still be maintained in (at least) third normal form in order to facilitate clear thinking about its structure and meaning.

2.5 Database Diagram

Figure 2-9 illustrates the first cut at our logical database schema. Primary keys are underlined. Now that we have this diagram, we can create a physical database from it!

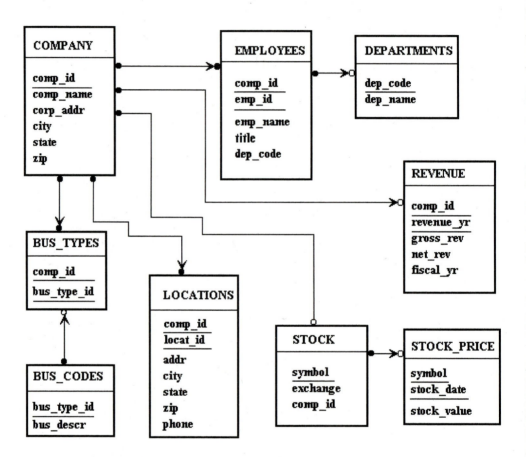

Figure 2-9 *Logical Schema for our Fortune 500 Database*

2.6 Logical Data Modeling Tools

Several logical data modeling tools exist to simplify the process we have just stepped through. These tools include, ERwin/ERX™, from Logic Works, Inc., InfoModeler™, from Asymetrix, and S-Designer™ from SDP Technologies, Inc., a subsidiary of Sybase.

2.6.1 Logical Modeling Tools: Checklist

These tools help you automate the process of logical data modeling. Obviously, ease of use and good performance are factors that any software tool will have, but logical modeling tools also offer a range of functionality to look at. Typical checklist items in evaluating these products include the following:

Development of the logical model

A good logical modeling tool should be easy to use when generating a logical model, especially when establishing relationships of tables with primary and foreign keys. Upon completion of an entity relationship diagram, a logic modeler should be able, among other things, to generate a normalized diagram and use a rules-based tool to check for any inconsistencies or redundant names.

Logical modeling reports

The ability to print out a logical diagram for viewing is an important piece of logic modelers. A diagram would be able to be broken into smaller views and printed. Some reporting tools will print out business rules for a diagram in an English-oriented fashion.

Creation of physical database designs

Once a logical model has been created, a logic modeling tool should be able to create a physical database model, including column lengths, data types, primary and foreign keys, referential integrity rules, and indexes. An ability to create triggers and to denormalize a database is also of value.

Physical design reports

Reporting information about a physical database model is very similar to printing a logical model, although more RDBMS-specific information is required. Reporting about specifics like database types, column names, and referential integrity rules should be available.

Generation of a database schema

Once a physical model has been created, a logical modeling tool will generate the SQL statements appropriate to the specific back-end RDBMS. Some modeling tools will allow you to write generic stored procedures that will also generate specific stored procedure statements for a specific database.

Maintenance of logical and physical models

Changes in a logical model should cause changes to a physical schema; changes to a physical schema should cause changes to the logical model. Maintenance activities ensure that the logical and physical models are congruous.

Reverse engineering of databases

Given that you have an Oracle, Informix, or specific DDL script from a RDBMS vendor, a logical modeling tool should be able to create a logical diagram. You should also be able to port an existing database from one RDBMS to another, using reverse engineering.

Documentation and technical support

Documentation and technical support are critical factors in looking at any software tool. Because logical modeling is a complex process, proper documentation and support are paramount.

2.6.2 Logical Modeling Vendors

Logic Works (ERwin/ERX)
1060 Route 206
Princeton, NJ 08540
(609) 252-1177

PRODUCT: ERwin/ERX for Windows, ERwin/ERX for NT (specialized version for 4GL vendors)

PLATFORMS: Windows , Windows 95, and Windows NT

POSITION: Logic Works has added several features to make this product attractive, including the ability to create compatible stored procedures and trigger generation. They have an easy-to-use modeling tool that is aided by their creation of versions of their product for specific 4GLs, including PowerBuilder, SQLWindows, and Oracle*CASE.

Sybase (S-Designer)
6475 Christie Avenue
Emeryville, CA 94608
(510) 596-3500

PRODUCT: S-Designer

PLATFORMS: Windows, Windows 95, and Windows NT

POSITION: SDP, a French company that created S-Designer, was acquired by Sybase. S-Designer offers many advanced features, including 32-bit support, support for customizable stored procedures and triggers, reverse engineering of databases through ODBC connectivity. They have an easy-to-use interface and good integration to 4GL development tools, such as Centura Software's SQLWindows and PowerBuilder. Since acquisition, S-Designer is being packaged with the PowerBuilder product.

Asymetrix (InfoModeler)
110-110th Ave N.E., Suite 700
Bellevue, WA 98004
(206) 462-0501

PRODUCT: InfoModeler

PLATFORMS: Windows, Windows 95

POSITION: InfoModeler builds a repository of facts, in English, that can be used to develop a logical model diagram. They use a methodology referred to as ORM (Object Role Modeling) and require familiarity of this style of design. Paul Allen, a founder of Microsoft, is behind this company, seeing the need for PC-based database modeling tools.

2.6.3 Data Transformation Tool

The following vendor tool, Data Junction, while not a data modeling tool, is very helpful in transferring data formats across a large number of file formats.

Tools and Techniques, Inc. (Data Junction)
2201 Northland Dr
Austin, Texas 78756
(512) 459-1308

PRODUCT: Data Junction

PLATFORMS: Windows, Windows 95

POSITION: Data Junction provides an easy-to-use graphical interface to define input and output files for data conversion. Almost every file format can be converted. They use a "hub and spoke" paradigm. Any data file can be defined as a spoke. You can drag and drop data fields from a data source to a target data source once you set up these files as "spokes." Then, filters are set, and the data "spokes" go through the "hub" for automatic data conversion.

2.7   Summary

The most important concepts from this chapter can be summarized by the following points.

- Databases can be logically described as logical models to help the developer understand the relationships of entities or tables in a database. This diagram is referred to as an *entity relationship diagram (ERD)*.

- An ERD defines the limits on how many entries in one table can relate to entries in another table. This is referred to as defining *cardinality* and is useful in setting dependency rules.

- We used examples to demonstrate *primary* and *foreign keys* for our database example. Primary and foreign keys are used specifically as identifiers to uniquely point to entries within our database. These keys become significant when we look at performance and data integrity in the next chapter and beyond.

- *Normalization* is a powerful tool used with relational databases to ensure database integrity as well as the appropriateness of your design.

In this chapter, we covered the basic steps of logical data modeling. It is not uncommon for large software companies to spend a year or more and a team of engineers to work on and perfect database designs used in complex business applications. Almost always, these engineers, or data modelers, will use a design tool like LogicWorks ERwin to lay out the design. These tools are becoming sophisticated enough to physically generate a database for you from your logical model.

3   Creation of a Database

In this chapter, we cover the tasks necessary to create the first-cut physical database design. The entity-relationship diagram (ERD) created in Chapter 2 will be converted to SQL data definition language (DDL) in order to create the desired physical database.

The chapter is organized as follows:

3.1   Physical Database Creation

In Chapter 2, a logical model for the database, COMPANY, was created. This section illustrates how this sample database is created by use of the SQL command, CREATE.

3.1.1   CREATE DATABASE Command

Here is the SQL command to create the database COMPANY:

```
CREATE DATABASE COMPANY
```

This statement is simple and complete. We can add other options to this command. For example, we could say:

CREATE DATABASE *COMPANY* LOG TO ACCTFILES

This particular command uses the option, LOG TO, which is particular to SQLBase. The LOG TO addition specifies that you can place the log file on a disk separate from the database for better performance and integrity.

Vendors often vary the syntax of commands. For example, the ANSI standard uses the word SCHEMA in place of DATABASE, as shown below:

CREATE SCHEMA *COMPANY*

Each vendor will have different options that accompany the CREATE command (as will all SQL commands), but the basics are the same. In Chapter 13, database-specific SQL variations are discussed.

There is one thing to be especially aware of when creating a database. A database will have the concept of being owned by a specified user. With SQLBase, the database is owned by a user named SYSADM. This user has privileges that other users of the database will not have. In the case of a multiuser database, you will have many users who may not have the privilege of creating databases or tables.

Creating a database is really the simplest of commands. If there are options to be specified with the database, most SQL variations have an ALTER command to allow for changes in a database and its tables at a later time.

Removing a database is also simple to do. To remove the database, you can also use the DROP command.

DROP DATABASE *COMPANY*

This command removes an existing database. We can then recreate the database or send it on its way to the eternal resting place of the relationally dead.

3.1.2 Creating Tables

Once a database is created, the next step is to create tables within the database. The simple CREATE command for this is structured:

CREATE TABLE *table-name*
(column-name datatype [NULL | NOT NULL],
column-name datatype [NULL | NOT NULL],.....)

One table created in Chapter 2 was the COMPANY table, which had the columns *comp_id*, *comp_name*, *corp_addr*, *city*, *state*, and *zip*. Following the syntax for the CREATE TABLE command, the statement to create the table COMPANY looks something like the statement below. The lines beginning with "/*" and ending with "*/" are comments.

```
CREATE TABLE COMPANY
(COMP_ID INTEGER NOT NULL,
COMP_NAME VARCHAR (40) NOT NULL,
CORP_ADDR VARCHAR (50) NOT NULL,
CITY VARCHAR (40) NOT NULL,
STATE VARCHAR (2) NOT NULL,
ZIP VARCHAR (20), NOT NULL)

/* The NOT NULL statement indicates that a */
/* specific column must always contain a value */
/* for every row that exists. */
```

Several things about this statement can be observed:

- The table is named COMPANY.

- For each column in the base table, we provided names. In this case *comp_id, comp_name, corp_addr, city, state,* and *zip* are the column names.

- We had to choose the appropriate data types for the columns within the table. INTEGER and VARCHAR are the two data types used in this example.

- NOT NULL was specified after each column, meaning that these columns must always contain a value. Conversely, we could have specified NULL to signify that no value at all is initially specified for the column. The use of these are optional, as denoted by the square brackets. Note that NULL is the default.

Beyond the observations that were just made, there are some simple guidelines to keep in mind when creating a table. First of all, always verify that the table name, in this case, COMPANY, is both unique and descriptive about the information contained within the table. Second, the column names should also be unique and descriptive of the values they contain.

We also need to be concerned about requiring values for specific columns in a table. For example, in the previous chapter, we declared the *comp_id* column to be a primary key to the table COMPANY. A primary key is a unique identifier and therefore needs to contain a value. In this case, we enforced that *comp_id* is NOT NULL.

There are also guidelines on using data types. We will look at data types in much more detail later; however, before an involved discussion on data types, we show another example.

Statements needed to create our sample database are shown below. We then create the database. Once we reach this point, we go back and discuss the syntax and data types in more detail.

3.1.3 Using the Data Definition Language (DDL)

We have absorbed enough knowledge of the CREATE TABLE command at this point to transform our logical data diagram from the previous chapter into basic statements, which we will use to begin building our sample database. Again, note that the lines beginning with "/*" and ending with "*/" are comment lines.

```
/* TABLE: COMPANY */

CREATE TABLE COMPANY (COMP_ID INTEGER NOT NULL,
COMP_NAME VARCHAR (40) NOT NULL,
CORP_ADDR VARCHAR (50) NOT NULL,
CITY VARCHAR (40) NOT NULL,
STATE VARCHAR (2) NOT NULL,
ZIP VARCHAR (20) NOT NULL,
PRIMARY KEY (COMP_ID))


/* TABLE: BUS_TYPES */
CREATE TABLE BUS_TYPES (COMP_ID INTEGER NOT NULL,
BUS_TYPE_ID INTEGER NOT NULL,
PRIMARY KEY (COMP_ID, BUS_TYPE_ID))


/* TABLE: BUS_CODES */

CREATE TABLE BUS_CODES (BUS_TYPE_ID INTEGER  NOT NULL,
BUS_DESCR VARCHAR (40) NOT NULL,
PRIMARY KEY (BUS_TYPE_ID))
```

```
/* TABLE: EMPLOYEES */

CREATE TABLE EMPLOYEES (COMP_ID INTEGER NOT NULL,
EMP_ID INTEGER NOT NULL,
TITLE VARCHAR (50),
EMP_NAME VARCHAR (40) NOT NULL,
DEP_CODE INTEGER NOT NULL,
PRIMARY KEY (COMP_ID,EMP_ID))

/* TABLE: LOCATIONS */

CREATE TABLE LOCATIONS (COMP_ID INTEGER NOT NULL,
LOCAT_ID SMALLINT NOT NULL,
ADDR VARCHAR (50),
CITY VARCHAR (40),
STATE VARCHAR (2),
ZIP VARCHAR (20),
PHONE VARCHAR (25),
PRIMARY KEY (COMP_ID,LOCAT_ID))

/* TABLE: REVENUE */

CREATE TABLE REVENUE (COMP_ID INTEGER NOT NULL,
REVENUE_YR INTEGER NOT NULL,
GROSS_REV FLOAT,
NET_REV FLOAT,
FISCAL_YR VARCHAR (10),
PRIMARY KEY (COMP_ID,REVENUE_YR))

/* TABLE: STOCK */

CREATE TABLE STOCK (COMP_ID INTEGER NOT NULL,
SYMBOL VARCHAR (8) NOT NULL,
EXCHANGE VARCHAR (8),
PRIMARY KEY (SYMBOL))

/* TABLE: STOCK_PRICE */

CREATE TABLE STOCK_PRICE (
SYMBOL VARCHAR (8) NOT NULL,
STOCK_DATE TIMESTAMP NOT NULL,
STOCK_VALUE DECIMAL (6,3),
PRIMARY KEY (SYMBOL,STOCK_DATE))
```

```
/* TABLE: DEPARTMENTS */

CREATE TABLE DEPARTMENTS (
DEP_CODE INTEGER NOT NULL,
DEP_NAME VARCHAR (40) NOT NULL,
PRIMARY KEY (DEP_CODE))
```

The example code above demonstrate the basics of the CREATE TABLE statement. The example also introduces new data types and the use of the PRIMARY KEY statement. Both data types and primary keys are covered in much more detail later in this chapter.

The next section steps through the creation of this database, using the software contained in the CD-ROM at the back of this book. While there are many topics yet to be covered, some hands-on experience will reinforce what has been learned so far.

3.2   Exercises: Creation of a Database

Appendix B outlines the steps to install the SQL Solo software and the exercises on your personal computer. Once you have loaded this software, you can step through each of the exercises yourself.

Exercise 3.2.1:   Creating the Database

After completion of the steps in Appendix B, SQLBase and Quest will be available from your Windows program manager. You can get started right away. We will provide you enough information to start building your first database.

1.   Double-click on the Quest icon in your Gupta program group, as shown in Figure 3-1.

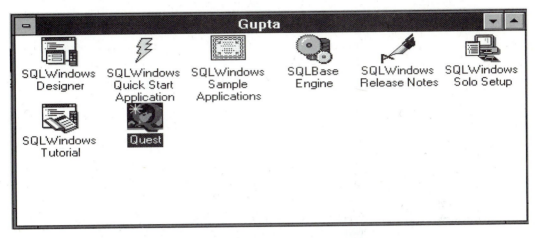

Figure 3-1 *Starting Quest from the Main Window*

2. Once Quest is running, select **Database** from the Utilities menu (Figure 3-2). Select **Create** from the cascaded menu.

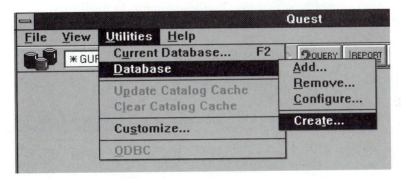

Figure 3-2 *Creating the Database*

3. Type *COMPANY* in the database name field. You should no longer see Gupta, but rather COMPANY in the field, as shown in Figure 3-3.

Figure 3-3 *Naming the Database*

Exercise 3.2.2:   Creating the Tables

4.   If the SQL button is not visible, click on the arrows shown in Figure 3-4 to get to the SQL button. Click on the **Open** button and then on the **SQL** button (Figure 3-3).

5.   Quest prompts for a file to open. Choose the file c:\sqlbase\exercises\chapter3\ex3-1.qsd, as shown in Figure 3-4. The file contains the SQL statements to create our sample database tables. Click **OK**.

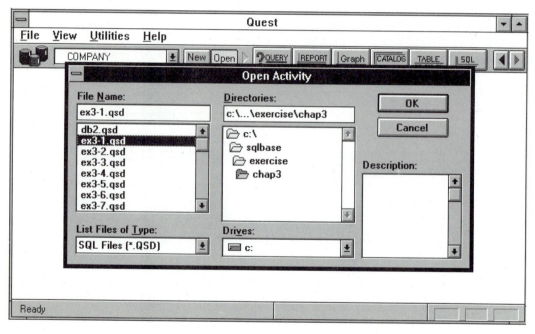

Figure 3-4   *Selecting a File*

6. As shown in Figure 3-5, under the SQL menu, choose **Execute All SQL**. The CREATE TABLE commands will be executed one by one.

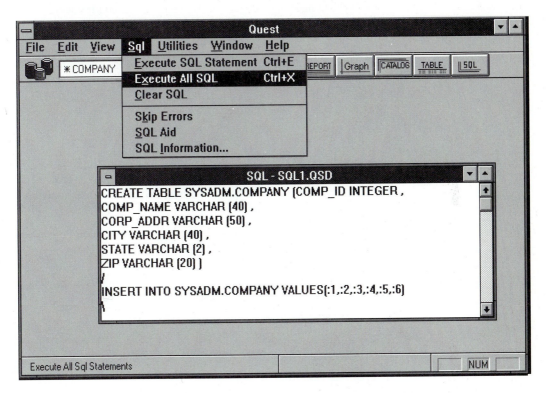

Figure 3-5 *Executing CREATE TABLE Commands*

7. To verify that the tables and columns for this database have been created, pull down the SQL menu. Choose **SQL Aid** (shown, but not chosen, in Figure 3-5). A pop-up window shows you the tables now in the COMPANY database and the columns in each table.

8. Take your time to look at the SQL language brought up in the SQL Activity window. Notice in the first CREATE TABLE statement that instead of using the table name, COMPANY, by itself, this SQL script uses SYSADM.COMPANY. SYSADM is a user name, which has not yet been discussed. This user name assigns ownership of the table COMPANY to the user SYSADM.

A relational database has the concept of users. By default, the administrator of SQLBase is SYSADM. Other users can be defined, and, as we will learn, privileges can also be granted and revoked.

9.   You should also notice a COMMIT command at the end of the SQL script that was executed. The COMMIT command is a way to tell a relational database to end the current transaction, which is discussed in more detail later. A transaction has one or more SQL commands that must either all be executed or none at all.

3.3   Data Types

In the previous exercise, data types for columns specified in the CREATE TABLE command had names like VARCHAR (40) and VARCHAR (2). These data type names are usually vendor specific; we address them in more detail.

All relational tables have the same basic types of data, including character data types, whole numbers, decimal numbers, monetary data types, timestamps, and binary data. This section primarily discusses the data types used by SQLBase, as these are used in the exercises in this book. Chapter 13 discusses the variations of data types among vendors.

The general data types that SQLBase uses to store data are:

- Character
- Numeric
- Date and time

The data type determines:

- The value and length of the data as stored in the database
- The display format when the data is displayed

All SQL vendors vary in how they choose to represent data types, especially in the number of bytes used in storing a particular data type. The logic modeling tools mentioned earlier, like LogicWorks, actually take the different data types into account and create the SQL statements for you for the particular database vendor. Other tools, such as Tools and Technique's Data Junction convert data into the correct format for you, independently of the database and the system you choose to use. As this particular part of database design can be tedious and time consuming, these products are widely used.

Let us look at the data types more closely.

3.3.1 Null Values

A *null value* indicates the absence of data. Any data type can contain a null value. A null value has no storage.

Null is *not* equivalent to zero or to blank; it is the same as *unknown*. A value of null is *not* greater than, less than, or equivalent to any other value, including another value of null. To retrieve a field value on a null match, the NULL predicate must be used.

Empty strings have a null value.

3.3.2 Character Data Types

A character string is a sequence of letters, digits, or special characters. For SQLBase, all character data is stored as variable-length strings.

For DB2 SQL compatibility, SQLBase allows several alternative keywords to declare the same data type. Every vendor has variations of the keywords used for data types.

An empty string has a null value.

All character data types can store binary data.

Character data is stored as case sensitive. To search for case-insensitive data, you can issue a SELECT statement with the @UPPER or @LOWER functions. For example, the following query returns only uppercase SMITHs:

```
SELECT LNAME FROM EMP
WHERE @UPPER(LNAME) = 'SMITH';
```

CHAR (or VARCHAR)

A length *must* be specified for this data type. The length determines the maximum length of the string. The length cannot exceed 254 bytes. To specify the length of a CHAR or VARCHAR string, follow the variable with a numeric value in parenthesis. For example,

```
CHAR (11)
VARCHAR(25)
CHAR(10)
```

You can use CHAR columns in comparison operations with other characters or numbers and in most functions and expressions.

LONG VARCHAR (or LONG)

This data type stores strings of any length. The difference between a CHAR (VARCHAR) and a LONG (LONG VARCHAR) data type is that a LONG type can store strings longer than 254 bytes and is not specified with a length attribute.

Both text and binary data can be stored in LONG VARCHARs. However, only character data can be retrieved through SQLTalk.

SQLBase uses the LONG VARCHAR as a BLOB equivalent. A "BLOB" is a term used in the industry to refer to large images or large amounts of binary data (Binary Large OBject).

You can store a bitmap file as a LONG field. SQLBase stores the entire file in the field with no compression, which means that all of the file's data is present in the database file. If the bitmap file is large, you can store it outside the database file to save space. To do this, store only the file name in the database and use a program to access the bitmap file through its stored file name.

A LONG data type is stored as a linked list of pages. Since it is variable length, no space is preallocated. This means that if no data is entered, no pages are allocated, and if data is entered, only enough pages to hold the LONG are allocated.

3.3.3 Numeric Data Types

SQLBase allows these numeric data types:

Exact Data Types	Approximate Data Types
DECIMAL (or DEC) INTEGER (or INT) NUMBER SMALLINT	DOUBLE PRECISION FLOAT REAL

Unique to other versions of RDBMS, SQLBase uses its own internal representation of numbers. Data is cast on input and output to conform to the restrictions of the data type.

Precision and scale are maintained internally by SQLBase. *Precision* refers to the total number of allowable digits. *Scale* refers to the number of digits to the right of the decimal point.

Numbers with up to 15 decimal digits of precision can be stored in the exact data types. Numbers in the range of 1.0e-99 to 1.0e+99 can be stored in the approximate data types.

SQLBase supports integer arithmetic. For example,

INTEGER / INTEGER = INTEGER

Number columns can be used in any comparison operations with other numbers and can occur in all functions and expressions.

NUMBER

A superset of all the other numeric data types, NUMBER is not associated with a particular scale or precision. Any number up to 15 digits of precision can be stored and retrieved regardless of the fraction value; a NUMBER data type, on the other hand, supports up to 23 precision digits.

Use NUMBER in either of the following situations:

- You do not need to control precision or whole numbers.

- You need SQLBase to automatically give you the largest precision available.

DECIMAL (or DEC)

This data type is associated with a particular scale and precision. Scale is the number of fractional digits, and precision is the total number of digits. For example, $10,000.25 uses a precision of 7 and a scale of 2. If precision and scale are not specified, SQLBase uses a default precision and scale of 5,0.

Use the DECIMAL data type when you need to control precision and scale, such as in currency.

The position of the decimal point is determined by the precision and the scale of the number. The scale cannot be negative or greater than the precision. The maximum precision is 15 digits.

This data type can store a maximum of 15 digits. The valid range is:

-999999999999999 to +999999999999999

Another way to express the range is to say that the value can be *-n* to *+n*, where the absolute value of *n* is the largest number that can be represented with the applicable precision and scale.

The DEC notation is compatible with DB2. Following are some DECIMAL examples:

DECIMAL (8,2)
DECIMAL (5,0)   (same as INTEGER precision)
DECIMAL
DEC

Currency

Although SQLBase does not have a specific CURRENCY data type, this data type is common to other vendors. With SQLBase, you can use DECIMAL instead. A suggested setting is DECIMAL (15,2).

INTEGER (or INT)

This data type has no fractional digits. Digits to the right of the decimal point are truncated. An INTEGER can have up to 10 digits of precision:

-2147483648 to +2147483647

The INT notation is compatible with DB2.

SMALLINT

This data type has no fractional digits. Digits to the right of the decimal point are truncated. Use this number type when you need whole numbers. A SMALLINT can have up to 5 digits of precision:

-32768 to +32767

SQLBase does not store a SMALLINT value relative to the size of a 16-bit or 32-bit integer but approximates it with the same number of digits. C programmers should check for overflow.

DOUBLE PRECISION

This data type specifies a column containing double-precision floating-point numbers.

FLOAT

This data type stores numbers of any precision and scale. A FLOAT column can also specify a precision:

FLOAT (*precision*)

If the specified precision is between 1 to 21 inclusive, the format is single-precision floating point. If the precision is between 22 and 53 inclusive, the format is double-precision floating point.

If the precision is omitted, double-precision is assumed. Some examples are:

```
FLOAT
FLOAT (20)
FLOAT (53)
```

REAL

This data type specifies a column containing single-precision floating-point numbers.

3.3.4 Date/Time Data Types

SQLBase supports these data types for date and time data:

- DATETIME (or TIMESTAMP)
- DATE
- TIME

You can use date columns in comparison operations with other dates. You can also use dates in some functions and expressions.

Internally, SQLBase stores all date and time data in its own floating-point format. The internal floating-point value is available through an application program API call.

This format interprets a date or time as a number with the form:

DAY.TIME

DAY is a whole number that represents the number of days since December 30, 1899. December 30, 1899 is 0, December 31, 1899 is 1, and so forth.

TIME is the fractional part of the number. Zero represents 12:00 AM.

March 1, 1900 12:00:00 PM is represented by the floating-point value 61.5 and March 1, 1900 12:00:00 AM is 61.0.

Wherever a date/time string can be used in an SQL command, a corresponding floating-point number can also be used.

DATETIME (or TIMESTAMP)

This data type is used for columns that contain data that represents both the date and time portions of the internal number.

You can input DATETIME data by using any of the allowable date and time formats listed for the DATE and TIME data types.

When a part of an input date/time string is omitted, SQLBase supplies the default of 0, which converts to December 30, 1899 (date part) 12:00:00 AM (time part).

TIMESTAMP can be used instead of DATETIME for DB2 compatibility.

The time portion of DATETIME has resolution to the second and microsecond. The time portion of TIMESTAMP has resolution to the microsecond.

DATE

This data type stores a date value. The time portion of the internal number is zero. On output, only the date portion of the internal number is retrieved.

TIME

This data type stores a time value. The date portion of the internal number is zero. On output, only the time portion of the internal number is retrieved.

TIME has resolution to the second.

3.4   Data Type Guidelines

Every database vendor has certain guidelines for using data types.

3.4.1 Guidelines for Columns

After the columns are identified, data types need to be added. Here are some guidelines for data types:

- Choosing among some data types becomes a matter of documentation, which may be useful for range validation. As an example, defining a classification code column in SQLBase, such as LEDGER_SUBCODE in a general ledger application, as CHAR(3) documents the fact that values must always consist of three characters (perhaps falling into the range "10A" to "99Z") instead of defining the data type as VARCHAR(3).

- If the usage of a numeric data item requires it to be of a fixed width, use the DECIMAL data type with the required precision and an appropriate scale. If an integer is desired, use DECIMAL with a scale of zero. This helps to communicate external formatting requirements more clearly.

- Avoid the use of INTEGER and SMALLINT data types in general. Use these only for internal control fields such as cycle counters. Formatting these fields for external display use can be difficult because of the indeterminate display width.

- Avoid using CHAR or VARCHAR for data that will always be numeric. Using a numeric data type will ensure that the field will always be populated with valid numeric data.

- Avoid the use of the REAL (or FLOAT or DOUBLE PRECISION) data type except for situations calling for scientific measurement information containing a wide range of values. The exponent-mantissa format of these data types lacks the exact precision associated with other numeric data types and also causes floating-point operations to be performed for their manipulation. Floating-point operations take longer than other mathematical operations.

- Use the DATE and TIME formats when expressing chronological data.

- Use DATETIME (or TIMESTAMP) for control. Many designers include a TIMESTAMP field for tracking row creation and updates.

3.4.2   Null Usage

When defining data types for columns, you will also need to specify the column's ability to assume the null value. Note that null is a special value that indicates either "unknown" or "not applicable." Users and programmers not accustomed to the use of nulls may have problems remembering to include host variable declarations and tests for nulls in columns that allow them. Nulls can also cause problems when they are in columns that are used for joining tables. For example, "missing data" may be disconcerting to a user of a query that joins tables where one table has null values. Consider the following factors when deciding whether to allow a null value in a column:

- Columns participating in primary keys should always be defined with NOT NULL, since they are required to be populated with unique values for each row.

- Foreign keys should generally be defined with NOT NULL. Whenever a child table is dependent on a parent, the foreign key to the parent table cannot be null, since the existence of a child occurrence without a parent would violate the dependency rule of the relationship.

- Use NOT NULL WITH DEFAULT for columns with DATE, TIME, or DATETIME data types to allow current date and time data to be stored in the field automatically. This is particularly useful for row creation timestamps.

- Allow nulls for those columns that will have need for the unknown or inapplicable meaning of the null value. The null value works especially well in numeric fields where aggregate functions like SUM and AVERAGE are used.

- Use NOT NULL WITH DEFAULT for all columns not meeting one of the above criteria.

3.5 Indexes and Primary and Foreign Keys

So far we have introduced the CREATE TABLE command and discussed data types. The table we have created, however, is not really complete. There is no indication of which columns are primary or foreign keys.

In this section we discuss adding primary and foreign keys to our tables. We also introduce the ALTER and CREATE INDEX commands.

3.5.1 Primary and Foreign Keys and Referential Integrity

Referential integrity is the verification that links between table rows are valid at all times. The links are implemented through common values contained in primary and foreign keys in the related rows. These rows may exist in the same table or in separate tables.

The table containing the primary key is said to be the *parent* table in the relationship, and the table containing the foreign key is called the *child* table. (Although these terms "parent" and "child" are widely accepted in relational terminology, they connote a hierarchical, dependent relationship between the tables. Of course, a relationship implemented through primary and foreign keys could be of several types other than hierarchical.) It is important to remember that these terms are meaningful only in the context of a single relationship, since a child table in one relationship could be a parent table in another relationship and vice versa.

By defining a table's primary and foreign keys when you create the table, you enforce the validity of relationships within the DBMS itself without requiring any special coding conventions by the user. For instance, without system-enforced referential integrity, an order entry program would have to retrieve a row from the customer table (corresponding to the customer number entered by the operator) in order to verify that the customer actually existed. With referential integrity, the child order table contains the customer number as a foreign key to the parent customer table, and the program no longer needs to check for the existence of the customer. When the order row is inserted, the DBMS will realize that the referential integrity definition requires it to read the customer table to verify the existence of a row with a primary key that matches the contents of the foreign key in the order record. If this row is found in the customer table, then the order row can be inserted successfully. Otherwise, the insert will fail and an appropriate SQL error code will be returned to the program to indicate that a referential integrity error occurred.

Sometimes concerns are raised about the possible performance penalties that can be incurred through the use of system-defined and system-enforced referential integrity. In the vast majority of cases, the DBMS itself is able to maintain a higher level of consistency with a lower cost. The two most important factors contributing to this are its ability to perform integrity checks for *all* database accesses and its ability to *always* use the most efficient access technique available to perform the referential checks.

3.5.2   Example of Primary Keys

Adding primary keys to our database implements the relationships specified by us in Chapter 2 in the logical diagram (Figure 2-9). For example, with the table COMPANY, the column used as the primary key is *comp_id*. To make the *comp_id* column the primary key requires the following code:

```
CREATE TABLE COMPANY (COMP_ID INTEGER NOT NULL,
COMP_NAME VARCHAR (40) NOT NULL,
CORP_ADDR VARCHAR (50) NOT NULL,
CITY VARCHAR (40) NOT NULL,
STATE VARCHAR (2) NOT NULL,
ZIP VARCHAR (20), NOT NULL
PRIMARY KEY (COMP_ID))

CREATE UNIQUE INDEX XPKCOMPANY
ON COMPANY
(COMP_ID)
```

Two new statements have been used. One, a PRIMARY KEY statement was added to the CREATE TABLE statement. Two, the CREATE UNIQUE INDEX command was used to identify this column as unique.

This process required the following steps:

1. Identify the primary key of each table within the CREATE TABLE statement.

2. Build unique indexes for each primary key of each table.

3.5.3 CREATE INDEX Command

An index is primarily used as a mechanism to increase performance on a table. It is also used for placing referential constraints on a table. Indexes are critical to tuning system performance.

To give an analogy of how an index is useful: When looking for a number in the Yellow Pages, you don't want to go through every number in that particularly fat book to find the number you want. Typically, you use an index to speed the search.

In the previous section, we used the CREATE INDEX command to create a primary key. Later in the book, we discuss indexes in more detail. For now, it is important to know how to create an index.

To create an index, XCOMPID, on the column *comp_id* from the table COMPANY, the simplest form of the command is:

CREATE INDEX XCOMPID ON COMPANY (comp_id)

Types of Indexes

In the previous example, an index was created that did not place any constraint on the column, *comp_id*. To make *comp_id* a primary key, however, it is necessary to specify that this column is unique. In this case, you will actually use a CREATE UNIQUE INDEX command.

There are three general types of indexes: composite indexes, unique indexes, and clustered indexes.

Composite indexes use two or more columns as a unit. For example, you couple columns to create such an index:

> CREATE INDEX XPlayer_name on TEAM(first_name, last_name)

To search on a name, the creation of an index on both the first name and last name of an individual simplifies any subsequent search on that name.

Unique indexes prevent duplication of data. No two rows are permitted the same index value. Primary key columns make use of this to enforce referential integrity. By definition, a primary key always contains a unique value. For example:

> CREATE UNIQUE INDEX XPLayer_name on TEAM(first-name,last-name)

This command ensures that a player's name is always unique. In the previous example, two players could have the same name.

A *Clustered index* is an index that sorts both logically and physically. Clustered indexes are used to increase performance on rows where values can be easily sorted. Clustered indexes continually sort rows of a table.

The CREATE INDEX Command and the Primary Key

For the creation of the primary key, use a UNIQUE index, which is an index that allows only one occurrence of any value within a column. So, for example, our COMPANY table has a primary key column named *comp_id*. A UNIQUE INDEX on *comp_id* would ensure that no two rows within the COMPANY table will have the same *comp_id*.

When we created our sample database in the first set of exercises, we named the columns constituting the primary key of each table. This was done by using the PRIMARY KEY clause of the CREATE TABLE statement. Since the primary key is also required to be unique, another step is required before the primary key definition is complete.

Following each table's CREATE TABLE statement, code a CREATE UNIQUE INDEX statement that builds a unique index on the primary key columns of the table. Include only those columns that are in the primary key, and index them in the same order as they are specified in the PRIMARY KEY definition clause of the CREATE TABLE statement. As shown previously for our example, this would be:

```
CREATE UNIQUE INDEX XPKCOMPANY
ON COMPANY (COMP_ID)
```

The indicator, "XPK," in the index name was used to signify that this is a primary key index. This was chosen for clarity as a standard convention for primary key indexes in the book's exercises. Inadvertently dropping such an index would have detrimental effects on the desired referential integrity for the database.

3.5.4 Adding Foreign Keys

Specifying the FOREIGN KEY requirements of our database requires the use of the ALTER TABLE command. At the end of our example statement, following all CREATE TABLE/INDEX statements, we can code an ALTER TABLE statement that adds the foreign key definitions needed for each child table in the database.

For example:

```
ALTER TABLE EMPLOYEES
FOREIGN KEY FKDEP_CODE (DEP_CODE)
REFERENCES DEPARTMENTS
ON DELETE RESTRICT
```

The ALTER TABLE command has just been introduced; because it has a lot of options, we discuss this command in more detail.

3.5.5 ALTER TABLE Command

The ALTER TABLE command can do several things, including:

- Adding, dropping, or modifying a column
- Renaming a column or table
- Adding or dropping a primary key
- Adding or dropping a foreign key

Adding, Dropping, or Modifying a Column

A simple example of an ALTER TABLE command to add a column is:

ALTER TABLE EMPLOYEE ADD Home_Phone VARCHAR (20)

In this example, a column, *Home_Phone*, was added to the table EMPLOYEE.

To modify this command in order to change the column from 20 to 40 characters and to ensure that the column always has a value in it (with the NOT NULL argument), use the following command:

ALTER TABLE EMPLOYEE MODIFY Home_Phone
VARCHAR (40) NOT NULL

To drop this column, the following command can be used:

ALTER TABLE EMPLOYEE DROP Home_Phone

There are restrictions on such commands. For example, you cannot drop a column that is indexed, a column belonging to a primary or foreign key, or a system-defined column in the system catalog.

Renaming a Column or Table

For renaming a column, the ALTER TABLE command looks something like this:

ALTER TABLE EMPLOYEE RENAME Title Position

The sample database is called COMPANY; so is a table within the database. For renaming a table to avoid confusion, the command looks like this:

ALTER TABLE COMPANY RENAME TABLE COMP

Adding or Dropping a Primary Key

The example in Section 3.5.2 showed that a primary key clause can be added to a CREATE TABLE statement. A primary key can also be added by using the ALTER TABLE statement. For example,

ALTER TABLE EMPLOYEE PRIMARY KEY (EMP_NO)

Adding or Dropping a Foreign Key

A foreign key is specifically added with an ALTER TABLE statement. An example of this is:

ALTER TABLE EMPLOYEES FOREIGN KEY (DEP_CODE)
REFERENCES DEPARTMENTS ON DELETE RESTRICT

Selection of appropriate referential integrity constraints requires an understanding of the business rules governing the way applications can delete and update data. Use of this knowledge allows the database designer to select the appropriate delete rules from among the three options available in SQLBase. These options are:

- *Restrict*, which disallows deletion of parent rows if any child rows exist. This is the default and is generally the safest option.

- *Set Null*, which sets the foreign key values of child rows to null when parent rows are deleted.

- *Cascade*, which deletes child rows when parent rows are deleted.

There are also implications of delete rules resulting from the transitive relationships among three or more tables that can cause restrictions to be placed on the designer's selection. Many coding options can be constrained through the use of referential integrity. The designer must consider all these factors when selecting appropriate referential integrity constraints for the database.

3.5.6 ALTER TABLE Diagram

The ALTER TABLE statement has many clauses and options that can be used with it. In general, to simplify reading such SQL statements, a command diagram is used. A simplified command diagram for the ALTER Table diagram is shown in Figure 3-6.

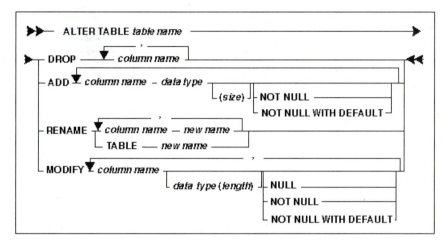

Figure 3-6   *ALTER TABLE Statement Diagram*

Table 3-1 shows the conventions for the SQL command diagram.

Table 3-1   *SQL Command Conventions*

Symbol	Description
▶▶	A double arrow pointing right means the start of a command.
⟶	A single arrow pointing right means a continuation line of a command.
◀◀	A double arrow pointing left means the end of a command.
UNIQUE	Optional clauses and keywords (such as UNIQUE) hang off the main or continuation lines.

Table 3-1   *SQL Command Conventions (Continued)*

Symbol	Description
ASC DESC	If there is an optional item with alternate choices, the choices are in a vertical list. In this example, ASC and DESC are alternate nonmandatory options. ASC is underlined, which means it is the default and can be omitted. If an item is mandatory, the first alternative is on the main line (this example is from the UPDATE command).
table name view name	
– (⬇ column name) –	When arguments of the same type (such as a list of column names) can be repeated, an arrow pointing downward is suspended above the argument. A delimiter or operator on this line shows what separates each argument (such as commas separating column names).

Clauses with the ALTER TABLE Command

ADD Adds a column to a table. ADD is the default clause if no clause is specified.

DROP Removes a column from a table. If the column has data, the data is lost.

You cannot drop any of the following:

- Indexed column
- Column belonging to a primary or foreign key
- System-defined columns in the system catalog

MODIFY Changes the attributes for a column.

You can increase the length of a character column, but you cannot decrease the length. You specify the data type when you increase the length of a character column.

You *cannot* change the data type of a column.

You *cannot* change the length of a numeric column.

NULL   Removes a NOT NULL attribute for a column.

NOT NULL   Adds a NOT NULL attribute to a column that currently accepts nulls.

If the column contains NULL values, you cannot redefine the column as NOT NULL.

You cannot modify system-defined columns in the system catalog.

NOT NULL WITH DEFAULT

Prevents a column from containing null values and allows a default value other than the null value.

The NOT NULL WITH DEFAULT clause is compatible with DB2.

RENAME   Renames a table or column. System catalog tables and system-defined columns in the system catalog cannot be renamed.

3.5.7 Completed Example of Adding Primary Keys and Foreign Keys

The following example reprints the SQL statements for Section 3.1.3 used to create our sample database, COMPANY, highlighting the additional SQL statements to add primary and foreign keys. Notice that foreign keys were added to the COMPANY and EMPLOYEES tables.

```
/* TABLE: COMPANY */

CREATE TABLE COMPANY (COMP_ID INTEGER NOT NULL,
COMP_NAME VARCHAR (40) NOT NULL,
CORP_ADDR VARCHAR (50) NOT NULL,
CITY VARCHAR (40) NOT NULL,
STATE VARCHAR (2) NOT NULL,
ZIP VARCHAR (20), NOT NULL
PRIMARY KEY (COMP_ID))

CREATE UNIQUE INDEX XPKCOMPANY
ON COMPANY(COMP_ID)

/* TABLE: BUS_TYPES */

CREATE TABLE BUS_TYPES (COMP_ID INTEGER NOT NULL,
BUS_TYPE_ID INTEGER NOT NULL,
PRIMARY KEY (COMP_ID, BUS_TYPE_ID)

CREATE UNIQUE INDEX XPKBUS_TYPE
ON BUS_TYPES (COMP_ID,BUS_TYPE_ID)

/* TABLE: BUS_CODES */

CREATE TABLE BUS_CODES (BUS_TYPE_ID INTEGER NOT NULL,
BUS_DESCR VARCHAR (40) NOT NULL,
PRIMARY KEY (BUS_TYPE_ID))

CREATE UNIQUE INDEX XPKBUS_CODES
ON BUS_CODES (BUS_TYPE_ID)

/* TABLE: EMPLOYEES */

CREATE TABLE EMPLOYEES (COMP_ID INTEGER NOT NULL,
EMP_ID INTEGER NOT NULL,
TITLE VARCHAR (50),
EMP_NAME VARCHAR (40) NOT NULL,
DEP_CODE INTEGER NOT NULL,
PRIMARY KEY (COMP_ID,EMP_ID))

CREATE UNIQUE INDEX XPKEMPLOYEES
ON EMPLOYEES (COMP_ID,EMP_ID)

ALTER TABLE EMPLOYEES
```

```
FOREIGN KEY FKDEP_CODE (DEP_CODE)
REFERENCES DEPARTMENTS
ON DELETE RESTRICT;

/* TABLE: LOCATIONS */

CREATE TABLE LOCATIONS (COMP_ID INTEGER NOT NULL,
LOCAT_ID SMALLINT NOT NULL,
ADDR VARCHAR (50),
CITY VARCHAR (40),
STATE VARCHAR (2),
ZIP VARCHAR (20),
PHONE VARCHAR (25),
PRIMARY KEY (COMP_ID,LOCAT_ID))

CREATE UNIQUE INDEX XPKLOCAT
ON LOCATIONS (COMP_ID,LOCAT_ID)

/* TABLE: REVENUE */

CREATE TABLE REVENUE (COMP_ID INTEGER NOT NULL,
REVENUE_YR INTEGER NOT NULL,
GROSS_REV FLOAT,
NET_REV FLOAT,
FISCAL_YR VARCHAR (10),
PRIMARY KEY (COMP_ID,REVENUE_YR))


CREATE UNIQUE INDEX XPKREVENUE
ON REVENUE (COMP_ID,REVENUE_YR)

/* TABLE: STOCK */

CREATE TABLE STOCK (COMP_ID INTEGER NOT NULL,
SYMBOL VARCHAR (8) NOT NULL,
EXCHANGE VARCHAR (8),
PRIMARY KEY (SYMBOL))

CREATE UNIQUE INDEX XPKSYMBOL
ON STOCK (SYMBOL)

ALTER TABLE STOCK
FOREIGN KEY FKCOMP_ID (COMP_ID)
REFERENCES COMPANY ON DELETE RESTRICT
```

```
/* TABLE: STOCK_PRICE */

CREATE TABLE STOCK_PRICE (
SYMBOL VARCHAR (8) NOT NULL,
STOCK_DATE TIMESTAMP NOT NULL,
STOCK_VALUE DECIMAL (6,3),
PRIMARY KEY (SYMBOL,STOCK_DATE))

CREATE UNIQUE INDEX XPKSTOCK_VAL
ON STOCK_PRICE (SYMBOL,STOCK_DATE)

/* TABLE: DEPARTMENTS */

CREATE TABLE DEPARTMENTS (
DEP_CODE INTEGER NOT NULL,
DEP_NAME VARCHAR (40) NOT NULL,
PRIMARY KEY (DEP_CODE))

CREATE UNIQUE INDEX XPKDEP_CODE
ON DEPARTMENTS(DEP_CODE)
```

It is important to remember that *both* the PRIMARY KEY clause of the CREATE statement *and* the CREATE UNIQUE INDEX are required before SQLBase considers the primary key definition for the table to be complete.

Adding foreign keys through this ALTER technique guarantees that each table's primary key definition is completed (with its associated index) prior to being referenced in a foreign key clause by some other table.

3.6   Exercises

These exercises cover many of the SQL commands that have been introduced in this chapter, including CREATE TABLE, CREATE INDEX, DROP TABLE, DROP INDEX, and ALTER TABLE.

The exercises consist of many files of the format, <filename>.qsd. The process for opening these SQL scripts is shown below. It will be used repeatedly throughout this book. Note that all of the scripts shown here can also be built topically with this query tool, although you do not learn the SQL syntax explicitly as you do in these exercises.

In the first exercise, you will drop the table you created in Section 3.2. The process described in this exercise is repeated for the rest of the exercises.

Exercise 3.6.1: Using the DROP TABLE Command

1. Double-click on the Quest icon in your Gupta program group, as shown in Figure 3-7.

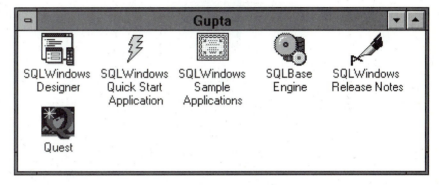

Figure 3-7   *Opening Quest*

Quest is opened. By default (unless the workspace is saved), Quest connects to the sample database, GUPTA.

2. For this exercise, connect to the COMPANY database. If the COMPANY database is not already available as a database, connect to the COMPANY database by pulling down the **Utilities** menu and using the **Add** function. Click on the COMPANY database you have created.

Type *COMPANY* in the database name field, as shown below.

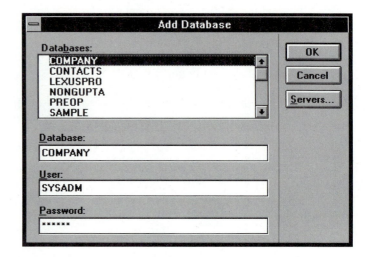

Figure 3-8   *Selecting COMPANY Database*

Open the SQL script

3. Click on the **Open** button and then on the **SQL** button.

Figure 3-9   *Opening the SQL Script*

4. Quest prompts for a file, as shown below. All exercise files for this book reside in c:\sqlbase\exercise. For this exercise, the first script to open is c:\sqlbase\exercise\chap3\ex3-2.qsd. The file contains the SQL statements for the first exercise.

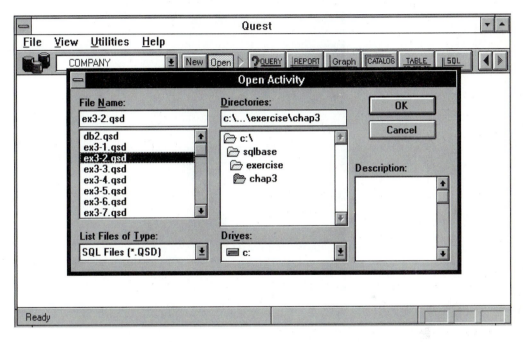

Figure 3-10   *Selecting a File*

5. From the SQL menu, choose **Execute All SQL**.

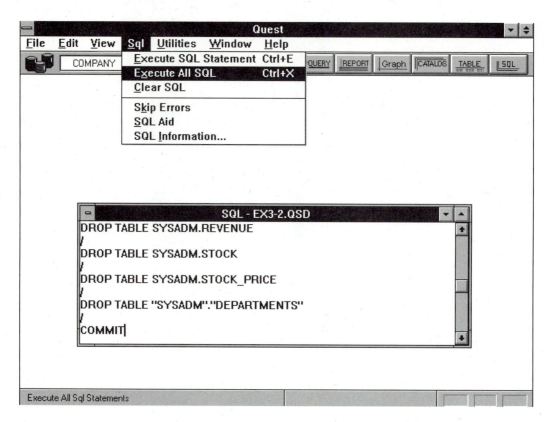

Figure 3-11 *Executing SQL Script*

This exercise will drop all tables created in the exercises in Section 3.2.

6. If you choose the **SQL Aid** menu item, as shown above but not selected, you summon a window that shows all the tables and columns that are available in this database.

7. To close the exercise, select the **Close** option from the File menu of Quest.

Exercise 3.6.2: Using the CREATE TABLE Statement and Primary Keys

In this exercise, the tables just dropped will be recreated with the primary key and the CREATE UNIQUE INDEX statements needed for referential integrity.

1. Make sure you are connected to the COMPANY database.

2. We will repeat the steps from our first exercise. That is, click on the **Open** button and then on the **SQL** button. Choose the file c:\sqlbase\exercise\chap3\ex3-3.qsd. Click **OK**.

3. Under SQL menu, choose **Execute All SQL**.

   The database tables will be recreated. This time, the PRIMARY KEY statement was added to the CREATE TABLE statement. (In the next chapter, we demonstrate the use of the primary key when performing an INSERT statement.)

   The primary key and unique index for the table, STOCK, was specifically not added in this script; in the next exercise, we show you how to go back and do it.

4. To close the exercise, choose the **Close** option from the File menu of Quest.

Exercise 3.6.3: Using the CREATE INDEX Command

This exercise creates indexes of different types. The primary key for the table, LOCATIONS, in the last exercise was not created. The primary key for locations is actually a composite index on the columns, *comp_id* and *locat_id*.

1. Make sure you are connected to the COMPANY database.

2. Repeat the steps from our first exercise. That is, click on the **Open** button and then on the **SQL** button. Choose the file c:\sqlbase\exercise\chap3\ex3-4.qsd. Click **OK**.

3. The command to be executed is:

   CREATE INDEX XPKLOCAT ON
   LOCATIONS (COMP_ID, LOCAT_ID)

From the SQL menu, choose **Execute All SQL**.

The index is created. If you don't specify that this index is unique, two rows can currently share the same value. To make this index specifically enforce unique values, the index is dropped and recreated with the UNIQUE clause.

Drop the Index and Recreate with a Unique Index

4. Click on the **Open** button and then on the **SQL** button. Quest prompts for a file. Choose the file c:\sqlbase\exercise\chap3\ex3-5.qsd. The file contains the SQL statements to drop all the tables from the previous lab. Click **OK**.

5. The commands to be executed are:

    DROP INDEX XPKLOCAT

    CREATE UNIQUE INDEX XPKLOCAT ON
    LOCATIONS (COMP_ID,LOCAT_ID)

    From the SQL menu, choose **Execute All SQL.**

Create an Index on First Three Digits of a Number

The following example makes use of *functions*. Functions are predefined operations that many relational databases provide. In this case, a function, '@LEFT', is used to create an index on the first three characters of the column, *phone*, from the table LOCATIONS.

1. Click on the **Open** button and then on the **SQL** button. Quest prompts for a file. Choose the file c:\sqlbase\exercise\chap3\ex3-6.qsd. Click **OK**.

2. The command to be executed is:

    CREATE INDEX PHONE_IDX ON
    LOCATIONS (@LEFT(PHONE,3))

    This index is not a primary key and, by this book's convention, '_IDX' was added to the name to indicate that PHONE_IDX was an index.

3. From the SQL menu, choose **Execute All SQL.**

    An example of such an index dramatically increasing performance of a query is the case where an end user may want to do a search on a company by area code. For example:

Code:

> SELECT COMP_ID FROM LOCATIONS WHERE
> @LEFT(PHONE,3)= '415'

English Translation:

> GET ALL COMPANY ID NUMBERS FROM THE TABLE,
> LOCATIONS WHERE THE AREA CODE EQUALS '415'

4. To close the exercise, select the **Close** option from the File menu of Quest.

Exercise 3.6.4:   Using the ALTER TABLE Command

1. Make sure you are connected to the Company database. If you have changed, pull down the Utilities menu and use the Add function. Click on the Company database you have created.

2. Repeat the steps from our first exercise. That is, click on the **Open** button and then on the **SQL** button. Choose the file c:\sqlbase\exercise\chap3\ex3-7.qsd.

Adding, Dropping, or Modifying a Column

3. SQL statements will be executed one at a time, instead of all at once.

   The first example of an ALTER command, adding a column to our sample database, is:

   > ALTER TABLE EMPLOYEE ADD Home_Phone VARCHAR (20)

   In this first example, a column, *Home_Phone*, was added to the table EMPLOYEE.

Choose the first statement in the SQL Activity Window by clicking on it. From the **SQL** menu, choose **Execute SQL Statement**.

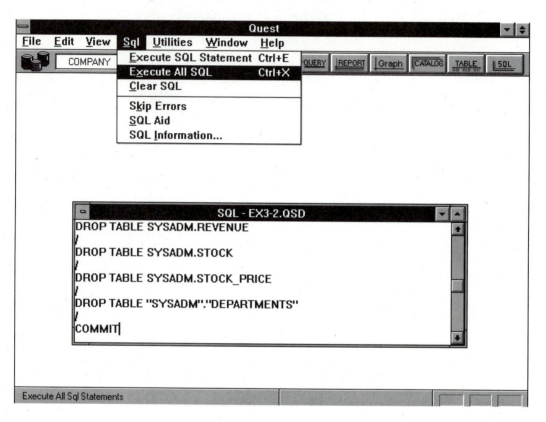

Figure 3-12   *Using the ALTER TABLE Command*

4. Now move to the next command line by clicking on the line in the SQL Activity window. To modify the previous command in order to change the column from 20 to 40 characters and to ensure that the column always has a value in it (with the NOT NULL argument), execute the following command:

    ALTER TABLE EMPLOYEES MODIFY Home_Phone
    VARCHAR (40) NOT NULL

Once this line is selected, from the SQL menu, choose **Execute SQL Statement**.

5. Choose the next line by clicking on it. From the SQL menu, choose **Execute SQL Statement**. The next command executed, shown below, drops the *home_phone* column:

    ALTER TABLE EMPLOYEES DROP Home_Phone

Renaming a Column or Table

6. Choose the next line by clicking on it. From the SQL menu, choose **Execute SQL Statement**. The next command executed, shown below, renames a column *title* to *position*:

    ALTER TABLE EMPLOYEES RENAME COLUMN Title Position

7. Again, choose the next line by clicking on it. The sample database is called COMPANY, as is a table within the database. This can be confusing, so the next command renames the COMPANY table to COMP.

    ALTER TABLE COMPANY RENAME TABLE COMP

    From the SQL menu, choose **Execute SQL Statement**.

Adding a Primary Key

8. This step shows how to add the primary key for the table, STOCK, which was omitted in the file ex3-3.qsd.

    Move to the next line by clicking on it. You can also add a primary key by using the ALTER TABLE statement with the CREATE UNIQUE INDEX statement shown below:

    CREATE UNIQUE INDEX SYMBOL_IDX ON STOCK(SYMBOL)

    ALTER TABLE STOCK PRIMARY KEY (SYMBOL)

9. From the SQL menu, choose **Execute SQL Statement** to execute the CREATE INDEX statement. Click on the next statement. Choose **Execute SQL Statement** again to execute the ALTER TABLE statement. The primary key is created!

10. To close the exercise, select **Close** from the File menu of Quest.

Exercise 3.6.5: Adding Foreign Key Statements with the ALTER TABLE Command

1. A foreign key is specifically added with a ALTER TABLE statement like the one below:

   ```
   ALTER TABLE EMPLOYEES FOREIGN KEY (dep_code)
   REFERENCES DEPARTMENTS ON DELETE RESTRICT
   ```

   Click on the **Open** button and then on the **SQL** button. Choose the file c:\sqlbase\exercise\chap3\ex3-8.qsd.

2. From the SQL menu, choose **Execute All SQL**.

   The database tables will be recreated. This time, we add the FOREIGN KEY statement to our sample database.

3. To close the exercise, select **Close** from the File menu of Quest.

3.7   Summary

Congratulations! This chapter has covered a lot of ground. You should now have a good understanding of the process of creating a database. This chapter has built upon the concepts introduced in Chapters 1 and 2. The subsequent chapters discuss how to use our database.

We have specifically looked at the statements for creating a physical database. The statements, often called the data definition language (DDL), include:

- CREATE DATABASE / DROP DATABASE
- CREATE TABLE / DROP TABLE
- CREATE INDEX / DROP INDEX
- ALTER TABLE

The hands-on exercises demonstrate the basics of these commands. Take the time to run the examples if you still have questions on these commands.

You should have also gained a better understanding of *data types* used to define how data in columns is stored. Data types is one area in which all database vendors vary, so you should be especially aware of how the data types are used.

Finally, this chapter provided a more complete understanding of how *indexes, primary* and *foreign keys*, and *referential integrity* are used. This book revisits these concepts, but the fundamentals of how they are used are stated most clearly in this chapter.

4   INSERT, UPDATE, and DELETE

In the last chapter, we created a physical database. This chapter discusses inserting, updating, and deleting data records within that database. The three SQL statements that map to inserting, updating, and deleting data are: INSERT, UPDATE, and DELETE. Not too difficult to remember! Collectively these commands are known as data manipulation language (DML).

The chapter is organized as follows:

Section 4.1 INSERT Command
Section 4.2 Exercises: Using the INSERT Command
Section 4.3 UPDATE Command
Section 4.4 Search Conditions with the UPDATE Command
Section 4.5 Predicates with the UPDATE Command
Section 4.6 Exercises: The UPDATE Command
Section 4.7 DELETE Command
Section 4.8 Exercises: The DELETE Command
Section 4.9 Summary

4.1   INSERT Command

The INSERT command inserts rows of data into a table. A basic INSERT might look like this:

```
INSERT INTO COMPANY
VALUES (1,'Albertson Inc.','250 Parkcenter
Blvd','Boise','ID','83726')
```

In the example above, values are inserted into the table COMPANY. There is, however, no mention of the columns of the table that data is inserted into. The columns are implicit. Another way to achieve the same result is:

```
INSERT INTO COMPANY
(COMP_ID,COMP_NAME,CORP_ADDR,CITY,STATE,ZIP)
VALUES (1,'Albertson Inc.','250 Parkcenter
Blvd','Boise','ID','83726')
```

This statement explicitly references the columns. It has the same effect as the first statement; only all the columns are listed out.

4.1.1   Inserting Values into Selected Columns

When an INSERT command is used to insert only a few columns into a table, then the columns must be implicitly declared. For example:

```
INSERT INTO COMPANY
(COMP_ID,COMP_NAME,STATE)
VALUES (1,'Albertson','ID')
```

In this example, only three columns are being filled: the columns *comp_id*, *comp_name*, and *state*.

Inserting Many Rows of Data

Rather than issuing many INSERT commands one after the other to insert multiple rows of data, you can use a *bind variable*. An example of using bind variables is:

```
INSERT INTO COMPANY
VALUES (:1,:2,:3,:4,:5,:6)
\
1,'Albertson S Inc','250 Parkcenter Blvd','Boise','ID','83726'
2,"Airborne Freight Corp","3101 Western
Ave","Seattle","WA","98111"
/
```

In the example above, the bind variable, :1, signifies the value of the first column to be inserted and is replaced for every row (the number 1 for the first row and 2 for the second row).

The bind variable, :2, signifies the value of the second column, replaced by the string 'Albertson' for the first row, 'Airborne Freight Corp' for the second row, and so forth. The left slash, \, and the right slash, /, begin and end the list of rows to be inserted.

4.1.2 Restrictions on the INSERT Command

Today, enterprise-level relational databases can handle the insertion of extremely large amounts of data. The number of records to be inserted is limited only by the amount of available disk space.

More commonly, restrictions on insertions to a database are based on referential constraints. For example, the second of two INSERT commands below would not be allowed when used against the sample database we created in Chapter 3.

```
INSERT INTO COMPANY
VALUES (1,'Albertson Inc','250 Parkcenter
Blvd','Boise','ID','83726')
INSERT INTO COMPANY
VALUES (1,'Ford','1 Ford Lane','Detroit','MI','50034')
```

In these statements, two identical values are inserted into the *comp_id* column. The second command would have failed because *comp_id* is a primary key and therefore must be unique. Remember that we created a unique index on the primary key, *comp_id*, in the last chapter. In this case, *comp_id* has the value 1 more than once; therefore, it is not allowed.

Another restriction on the INSERT command is that a primary key must not be null. For example, the following statement will not work:

```
INSERT INTO COMPANY
VALUES (,'Anheuser Busch Inc',
'One Busch Place','St Louis','MO','63118')
```

In the example above, the primary key, *comp_id*, is null, which is not allowed.

The previous two restrictions can be summarized by the following guidelines for inserting data into a parent table with a primary key:

- Do not enter nonunique values for the primary keys, as in the example above.

- Insert only non-null values for any column of the primary key.

Another restriction on the INSERT command is a restriction based on the permissions a user has to execute a command. Earlier it was mentioned that a database has specific users. Users can be restricted from using certain commands, as is covered in later chapters. (Two commands, GRANT and REVOKE, control whether you can execute an INSERT.)

4.1.3 Foreign Key Restriction Rules

Use the following guidelines when inserting data into a dependent table with foreign keys:

- Each non-null value inserted into a foreign key column must be equal to a value in the primary key.

- The entire foreign key is regarded as null if any column in the foreign key is null. The INSERT statement does not perform any referential checks for a null foreign key and will therefore successfully complete (as long as there are no unique index violations).

- An INSERT into either the parent table or dependent table will not work if the index enforcing the primary key of the parent table has been dropped (resulting in an incomplete table).

4.1.4 The INSERT Command Diagram

We covered the basics of the INSERT command. Now, look at a simplified diagram of the INSERT command for SQLBase (Figure 4-1). We will be adding to our knowledge of this command as we progress through the book.

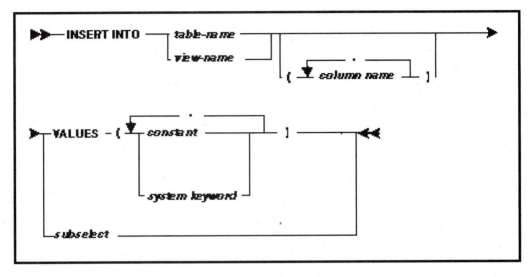

Figure 4-1   *INSERT Command Diagram*

The different pieces of the command are referred to as **clauses**. Below are brief descriptions of the clauses we have covered:

Clauses

INTO	Always used after the INSERT.
table name	(including any qualifier) Must reference a table that exists in the database.
column name	One or more column names in the specified table or view for which you provide insert values. You can name the columns in any order.
	If you omit the column list, you are implicitly using a list of all the columns, in the order they were created in the table or view, and must therefore provide a value for each column.
	You cannot omit a column name or insert null data into a column defined as NOT NULL.
VALUES	Contains one row of column values to be inserted. The values can be constants, bind variables, or system keywords.
	Separate the column values with commas. Do *not* put a space before or after the comma.

To embed characters such as commas, surround the string with double quotes. To embed double quotes, enclose the string with additional single quotes.

System keywords such as NULL, USER, SYSTIME, SYSDATE, SYSDATETIME cannot be used with inserts that use bind variables. However, you can enter them directly, as shown in the following example:

INSERT INTO TABLE1 values (SYSDATETIME)

subselect We have not discussed the SELECT command yet (covered in the next chapter). The subselect clause inserts the rows of a result table produced by a SELECT command, which retrieves data. The number of columns retrieved must match the number of columns being inserted. Similarly, the rows of the select must match the create definition with respect to data types and length of data. SQLBase attempts data type conversions where possible. You can use a self-referencing INSERT here; in other words, you can insert from the same table in this subselect clause.

4.2   Exercises: Using the INSERT Command

Exercise 4.2.1:   Inserting Data into a Table

In this example, you will insert data into the tables you created in the first exercise.

1.   Once again, make sure you are connected to the COMPANY database by pulling down the Utilities menu and using the **Add** function. Click on the COMPANY database.

2.   Click on the **Open** button and then on the **SQL** button as shown below.

Figure 4-2   *Starting Up*

3. Quest prompts for a file, as shown below. Choose the file c:\sqlbase\exercise\chap4\ex4-1.qsd. Click **OK**.

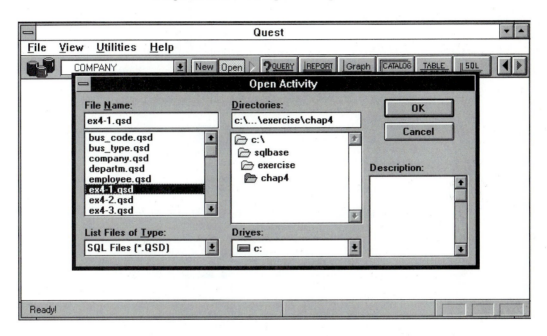

Figure 4-3 *Opening a SQL File*

4. The first INSERT command to be executed is shown below:

```
INSERT INTO COMP
VALUES (3,'Albertson S Inc','250 Parkcenter
Boulevard','Boise','ID','83726-0020')
```

Select the first INSERT command with your mouse. Do not choose Execute ALL SQL as in the previous chapter. Choose the **Execute SQL Statement** menu option as shown below. The objective is to step through a series of INSERT commands, one by one.

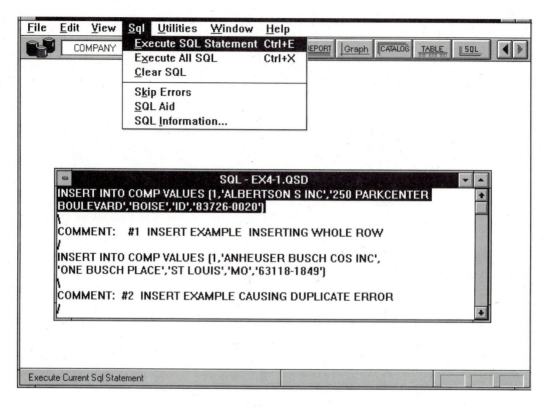

Figure 4-4   *Executing One SQL Statement at a Time*

5.   The second INSERT command should cause an error.

> INSERT INTO COMP
> VALUES (1,'Anheuser Busch Cos Inc',
> 'One Busch Place','St Louis','MO','63118-1849')

Select this INSERT statement with your mouse. Choose the **Execute SQL Statement** menu option, as shown in Figure 4-4, to execute the second INSERT command.

In this case, a row was inserted with a duplicate *comp_id* column value of 1. Since *comp_id* is a primary key, it must have a unique value.

This call will generate an error, as shown below.

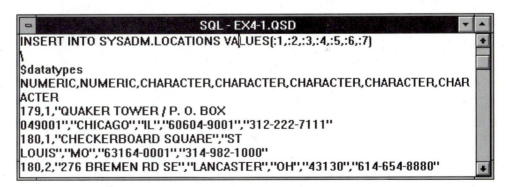

Figure 4-5   *Duplicate Column Values on a Primary Key Column*

6.   The third INSERT command demonstrates insertion into only a few columns:

> INSERT INTO COMP (COMP_ID,COMP_NAME) VALUES (252,'Zenith')

Click on this INSERT statement and choose **Execute SQL Statement** option from the SQL menu.

With this INSERT command, only the columns *comp_id*, *comp_name* are used.

7.   The fourth INSERT command shows insertion, using bind variables as shown below:

```
SQL - EX4-1.QSD
INSERT INTO SYSADM.LOCATIONS VALUES(:1,:2,:3,:4,:5,:6,:7)
\
$datatypes
NUMERIC,NUMERIC,CHARACTER,CHARACTER,CHARACTER,CHARACTER,CHAR
ACTER
179,1,"QUAKER TOWER / P. O. BOX
049001","CHICAGO","IL","60604-9001","312-222-7111"
180,1,"CHECKERBOARD SQUARE","ST
LOUIS","MO","63164-0001","314-982-1000"
180,2,"276 BREMEN RD SE","LANCASTER","OH","43130","614-654-8880"
```

Figure 4-6   *An INSERT Command with Bind Variables*

Click on this INSERT statement and choose **Execute SQL Statement** from the SQL menu.

8. Click on the COMMIT statement and choose **Execute SQL Statement** from the SQL menu to commit the insertions you have done.

9. To close, choose the **Close** option from the File menu.

Exercise 4.2.2:   Loading the Sample Database

The sample database to be loaded has values for approximately 150 of the Fortune 500 companies in America. Databases will have automated load facilities to speed this process, but to give you more experience, this exercise demonstrates inserting into this database table by table.

1. Once again, make sure you are connected to the COMPANY database by pulling down the Utilities menu and using the **Add** function. Click on the COMPANY database.

2. Click on the **Open** button and then on the **SQL** button.

3. Choose the file: c:\sqlbase\exercises\chap4\company.qsd. Click **OK**.

4. Choose the **Execute All SQL** menu option. You have inserted the values for the first table into the sample database.

5. Choose **Close** from the File menu to close the file.

Repeating the Process

6. There are nine load files, one for each table in our database. Repeat process from steps 2 through 4 for each of these tables. Here are the load files for the sample database:

   - c:\sqlbase\exercises\chap4\company.qsd (already inserted)
   - c:\sqlbase\exercises\chap4\bus_type.qsd
   - c:\sqlbase\exercises\chap4\bus_code.qsd
   - c:\sqlbase\exercises\chap4\departm.qsd
   - c:\sqlbase\exercises\chap4\employee.qsd
   - c:\sqlbase\exercises\chap4\location.qsd
   - c:\sqlbase\exercises\chap4\revenue.qsd
   - c:\sqlbase\exercises\chap4\stock.qsd
   - c:\sqlbase\exercises\chap4\stock_pr.qsd

For each file listed, open the file, as in steps 2 and 3. Then, execute the files, as in step 4. Be sure to close each file after executing the commands. The SQL activity within Quest has limited buffer size; it was not originally intended for use in loading the amount of data that we are loading here.

Seeing the Results

7. A quick way to see the results on the table is to open a table through Quest. First, choose **Open** and **Table** as shown below.

Figure 4-7   *Opening a Table*

8. Now, choose the table, COMPANY, shown below.

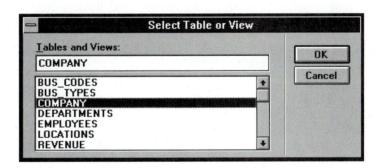

Figure 4-8   *Selecting a Table*

9.   You will see the following:

Figure 4-9   *A Look at the Company Table*

4.3   UPDATE Command

The UPDATE command updates the value of one or more columns of a table or view, based on the specified search conditions.

The UPDATE command in basic form looks like this:

```
UPDATE table-name
SET column-name = expression
[WHERE search_conditions]
```

SET Clause

The SET clause of this statement specifies columns that we desire to change. After the SET statement, you need to specify a column name and a value (or expression). For example,

```
UPDATE REVENUE
SET net_rev = 4500000
```

This statement updates every single *net_rev* column in our database. In essence, the statement is saying, "Change the value of the column, *net_rev,* in every row of the table REVENUE to be 4,500,000."

Usually, you want to narrow down the number of rows that are updated. To do this, use the WHERE clause.

WHERE Clause

The WHERE clause can limit the number of rows that are to be updated. The WHERE clause is quite a powerful clause with many search conditions. This clause is also used heavily with other SQL statements. An example of a statement using a WHERE clause is:

```
UPDATE EMPSAL
SET SALARY = 45000
WHERE EMPNO= 1004
```

In this example, only the row in the table, EMPSAL, which has a column, EMPNO, equal to the value 1004, is updated.

More Examples

This example uses the "||" symbol, which concatenates two strings, to prefix with the letter T all titles in the EMPLOYEE table. This example updates every row in the table.

```
UPDATE EMPLOYEES SET TITLE= 'T'||TITLE
```

Assuming the table EMPLOYEES had a column, *salary*, we could give all employees in department 2500 a 10% raise by issuing the following command (the "*" symbol is used to multiply two numbers):

```
UPDATE EMPLOYEES SET SALARY = SALARY*1.10
WHERE DEP_CODE = 32
```

4.3.1 Referential Issues and the UPDATE Statement

Referential integrity can cause several issues when an UPDATE command is used. To demonstrate this point, Figure 4-10 below shows a primary key/foreign key dependency of the table EMPLOYEES and COMPANY.

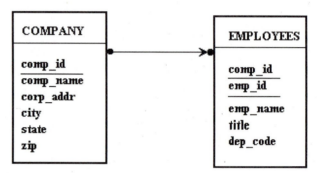

Figure 4-10   *Referential Integrity Example*

The following UPDATE statement shows a potential problem:

```
UPDATE COMPANY SET COMP_ID = 3000
WHERE COMP_ID = 4
```

In this example, the column, *comp_id*, is changed in the table, COMPANY, but not in the table, EMPLOYEES. This is an obvious problem, given the dependency of the one table on the other.

If you are updating a parent table, you cannot modify a primary key for which dependent rows exist. Doing so would violate referential constraints for dependent tables and would leave a row without a parent. In addition, you cannot give a primary key a null value.

Any non-null foreign key values that you enter must match the primary key for each relationship in which the table is a dependent.

If an UPDATE against a table with a referential constraint fails, an error message is returned.

RESTRICT Clause

In a database with referential integrity, the only UPDATE rule that can be applied to a parent table is RESTRICT. This means that any attempt to update the primary key of the parent table is restricted to cases where there are no matching values in the dependent table.

4.3.2 UPDATE Command Diagram

We covered the basics of the UPDATE command. Now, let's look at the UPDATE command diagram for SQLBase (Figure 4-11).

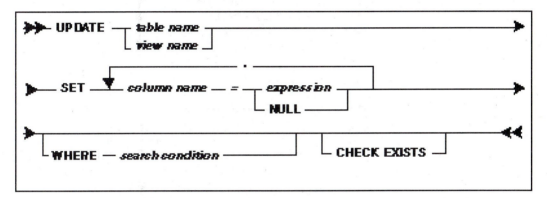

Figure 4-11 *Update Command Diagram*

Below are brief decriptions of the clauses we have covered with UPDATE.

Clauses

table name	(including any qualifier) Must reference a table that exists. The UPDATE command can also update what is known as a view. (Views can also be used with the INSERT command; they are covered later.)
column name	Identifies the columns to be updated in the table or view. Columns derived from an arithmetic expression or a function cannot be updated.
expression	Item or combination of items yielding a single value.
SET	If the update value is specified as null, the column must have been defined to accept null values.
	If a unique index is specified on a column, the update column value must be unique or an error results. Note that for a multicolumn index, it is the *aggregate* value of the index that must be unique.

WHERE search condition

> Specifies the rows to be updated based on a search condition.
>
> When this clause is used, it is called a searched UPDATE.

CHECK EXISTS

> Specifies to return an error if at least one row is not updated. This clause can be used in any context, including in chained commands.

4.4   Search Conditions with the UPDATE Command

A search condition in a WHERE clause qualifies the scope of a query by specifying the particular conditions that must be met. The WHERE clause can be used in the UPDATE command as well as in the DELETE and SELECT commands discussed further on:

A search condition contains one or more *predicates* connected by the logical (Boolean) operators OR, AND, and NOT.

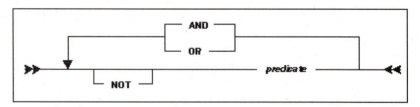

Figure 4-12   *Search Condition Boolean Operators*

The types of predicates that can be used in a search condition are discussed in section 4.5, *Predicates*.

The specified logical operators are applied to each predicate and the results are combined according to the following rules:

- Boolean expressions within parentheses are evaluated first.
- When the order of evaluation is not specified by parentheses, then NOT is applied before AND.
- AND is applied before OR.
- Operators at the same precedence level are applied from left to right.

A search condition specifies a condition that is *true*, *false*, or *unknown* about a given row or group. NOT (true) means false, NOT (false) means true, and NOT (unknown) is unknown (false). AND and OR are shown in the truth table (Table 4-1).

Assume P and Q are predicates. The first two columns show the conditions of the individual predicates, P and Q. The next two columns show the condition when P and Q are evaluated together with the AND operator and the OR operator. If an item in an expression in a search condition is null, then the search condition is evaluated as unknown (false).

Table 4-1   *Search Condition Boolean Operators Truth Table*

P	Q	P and Q	P or Q
True	True	True	True
True	False	False	True
True	Unknown	Unknown	True
False	True	False	True
False	False	False	False
False	Unknown	False	Unknown
Unknown	True	Unknown	True
Unknown	False	False	Unknown
Unknown	Unknown	Unknown	Unknown

An example of using the OR operator is shown below.

```
UPDATE REVENUE SET net_rev = 1200000
WHERE COMP_ID = 4 OR COMP_ID = 7
```

The OR operator returns true if either condition is met. In the last example, if the COMP_ID is 4 or if it is 7, the NET_REV column is updated.

The AND operator returns true only if both conditions could be met. The previous example would not meet this condition because the COMP_ID can not be equal to 4 and equal to 7 at the same time.

The NOT operator negates a condition. For example:

```
UPDATE REVENUE SET net_rev = 1200000
WHERE NOT COMP_ID = 9 OR COMP_ID > 12
```

This conditions updates the REVENUE table when *comp_id* is not 9 or when *comp_id* is greater than 12.

Nulls and Search Conditions

If a search condition specifies a column that might contain a null value for one or more rows, be aware that such a row is *not* retrieved, because a null value is not less than, equal to, or greater than the value specified in the condition. The value of a null is *unknown* (false).

To select values from rows that contain null values, use the NULL predicate (explained later in this chapter):

```
WHERE column name IS NULL
```

SQLBase does not distinguish between a null and zero length string on input. Consider the following command that inserts a zero-length string into the column, *city*:

```
INSERT INTO COMPANY (COMP_ID,CITY) VALUES (400,")
```

The following command updates not only the null rows, but also the row with the zero-length string.

```
UPDATE COMPANY SET STATE = "AND ZIP "
WHERE CITY = NULL
```

This last UPDATE set the columns *state* and *zip* to zero-length strings any time the column, *city*, is NULL.

Examples of Search Conditions

The example below updates rows for the table, STOCK_PRICE, to January 1, 1996, where column, *symbol*, begins with P or R and *stock_value* is NULL.

```
UPDATE STOCK_PRICE SET STOCK_DATE = '01-JAN-1996'
WHERE (SYMBOL LIKE 'P%' OR SYMBOL LIKE 'R%') AND
STOCK_VALUE = NULL
```

The underscore (_) and the percent (%) are the pattern-matching characters:

_   Matches *any single character.*

%   Matches *zero or more characters.*

The backslash (\) is the escape character for percent (%), underscore (_), and itself—if you actually wanted to match those symbols rather than use them as wildcards.

4.5   *Predicates with the UPDATE Command*

A predicate in a WHERE clause specifies a search condition that is true, false, or unknown with respect to a given row or group of rows in a table.

Predicates use operators, expressions, and constants to specify the condition to be evaluated.

These types of predicates are described in this section:

- Relational
- BETWEEN
- NULL
- EXISTS
- LIKE
- IN

4.5.1 *Predicates with Relational Operators*

Relational operators, are used to perform comparisons between values. These operators are shown in Figure 4-13.

=	[Equal To]	<>	[Not Equal]
<	[Less Than]	<=	[Less Than or Equal]
>	[Greater Than]	>=	[Greater Than or Equal]

Figure 4-13   *Relational Operators*

The following example uses the "greater than or equal" operator:

```
UPDATE REVENUE SET net_rev >= 5000000
WHERE net_rev = 5200000
```

English Translation of Update

The example above, translates in English to: Update the table, REVENUE, setting the column, *new_rev*, to 5,000,000 when *net_rev* is greater than or equal to 5,200,000.

In this example, we could easily change the where clause. For example, we could change the >= operator to a <> operator and completely reverse the meaning of the update so that any row in table, REVENUE, that does not have column, *net_rev,* containing 5200000 is updated.

```
UPDATE SET REVENUE = 5000000
WHERE net_rev <> 5200000
```

In each of these scenarios, we are making comparisons between numeric values. We can also make comparisons with character strings.

```
UPDATE SET STATE = 'CA'
WHERE CITY = 'SANTA CLARA'
```

We can also make character comparisons, however, the results often surprise those not familiar with how ASCII characters are ordered. For example, the character 'A' is less than (<) the character 'a.' Also, the character '2' is less than (<) the character 'A.'

4.5.2 BETWEEN Predicate

The BETWEEN predicate compares a value with a range of values. The BETWEEN predicate is inclusive.

Figure 4-14 diagrams the BETWEEN predicate.

Figure 4-14   *BETWEEN Predicate Diagram*

The following is a BETWEEN example:

UPDATE COMPANY SET STATE = 'CA'
WHERE (ZIP BETWEEN '90205' AND '60000')

4.5.3   NULL Predicate

The NULL predicate tests for null values. Figure 4-15 shows its structure.

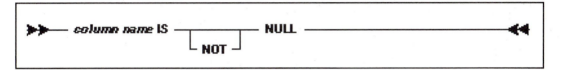

Figure 4-15   *NULL Predicate Diagram*

The following line shows a NULL example:

UPDATE COMPANY SET STATE = '' WHERE ZIP IS NULL

4.5.4   EXISTS Predicate

The EXISTS predicate tests for the existence of certain rows in a table. Figure 4-16 shows its structure.

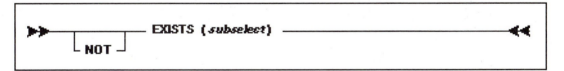

Figure 4-16   *EXISTS Predicate Diagram*

The following example updates the column, *locat_id*, to 5 in the table, LOCATIONS if the column, *city*, has a value of 'Menlo Park' and the column, *comp_name*, has the value 'INFORMIX'.

UPDATE LOCATIONS SET LOCAT_ID = 5 WHERE EXISTS
(SELECT * FROM COMPANY WHERE CITY = 'Menlo Park' and
COMP_NAME = 'INFORMIX')

The EXISTS predicate uses the SELECT statement (covered in more detail in the next chapter).

4.5.5 LIKE Predicate

The LIKE predicate searches for strings that match a specified pattern. The LIKE predicate can only be used with CHAR or VARCHAR data types. Figure 4-17 shows its structure.

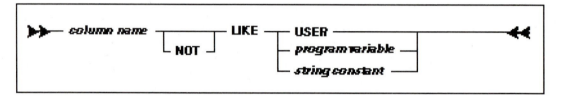

Figure 4-17   *LIKE Predicate Diagram*

The following examples show how LIKE predicates are used.

The example is true for any name with the string 'Pepsi' anywhere in it. You may be searching for 'Pespsi, INC' or 'Pepsi Corp', but are not sure exactly how the name looks.

    UPDATE COMPANY ZIP = 50532 WHERE COMP_NAME LIKE
    '%PEPSI%'

The example below shows a condition that is true for any two-character state code beginning with 'M'.

    UPDATE LOCATIONS ADDR = NULL WHERE JOB LIKE 'M_'

4.5.6 IN Predicate

The IN predicate compares a value to a collection of values. The collection of values can be either listed in the command or the result of a subselect. If there is only one item in the list of values, parentheses are not required.

Figure 4-18 shows the IN predicate's structure.

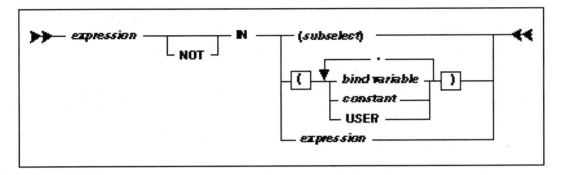

Figure 4-18 *IN Predicate Diagram*

The following examples show IN predicates.

UPDATE EMPLOYEES DEP_CODE= 42 WHERE TITLE in
('MTS', 'Technical Staff', 'Engineer', 'Senior Engineer')

4.6   Exercises: The UPDATE Command

Exercise 4.6.1:   Using the UPDATE Command

In this example, you will perform simple update commands.

1. Once again, make sure you are connected to the COMPANY database. If not, pull down the Utilities menu and using the **Add** function, click on the COMPANY database.

2. Click on the **Open** button and then on the **SQL** button as shown below.

Figure 4-19 *Opening the SQL Activity*

3. Quest prompts for a file. Choose the file c:\sqlbase\exercise\chap4\ex4-2.qsd. Click **OK.**

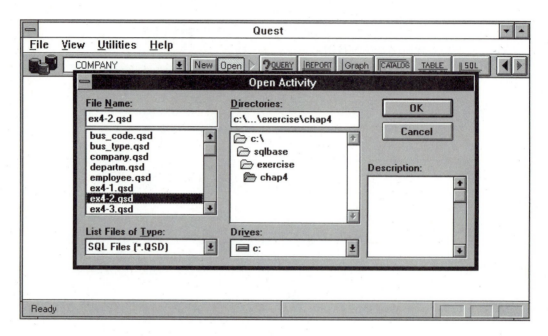

Figure 4-20   *Opening the SQL File*

4. The First UPDATE Command to be executed, as shown in Figure 4-21 is:

UPDATE EMPLOYEES
SET SALARY = 100000
WHERE EMPNO= 1

To update the column *salary*, we must first create this column with an ALTER TABLE command:

ALTER TABLE EMPLOYEES ADD SALARY INTEGER

Choose the ALTER TABLE command with your mouse. Choose the **Execute SQL Statement** menu option as shown below.

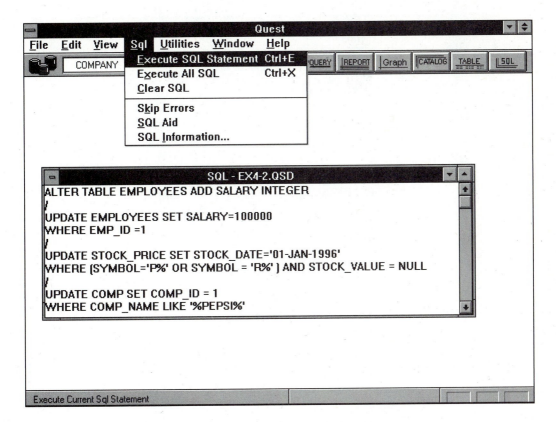

Figure 4-21 *Executing ALTER TABLE Statements*

5. To show the effect of the UPDATE we are about to do, open the table EMPLOYEES by selecting **Open** and **Table** and then choosing the EMPLOYEE table to view. The table will appear as shown in Figure 4-22.

Table - COMPANY:EMPLOYEES					
COMP_ID	EMP_ID	POSITION	EMP_NAME	DEP_CODE	SALARY
1	1	Controller	BROATCH, ROBERT E.	1	
1	2	Chairman of the Board	COMPTON, RONALD E.	1	
1	3	VP	BENANAV, GARY	1	
2	1	Chairman of the Board	CLINE, ROBERT S.	1	
3	1	Chief Executive Officer	MICHAEL, GARY	1	
3	2	Chief Operations Office	CARLEY, JOHN	1	
3	3	Chief Financial Officer	OLSON, A. CRAIG	1	
4	1	Chairman of the Board	BOSSIDY, LAWRENCE	1	
4	2	President	BURNHAM, DANIEL P	1	
4	3	Chief Financial Officer	BARTER, JOHN W.	1	
5	1	Chairman of the Board	ALLEY, WILLIAM J	1	
5	2	Chief Financial Officer	HENSON, ARNOLD	1	
5	3	Chief Operations Office	HAYS, THOMAS C.	1	
6	1	Chairman of the Board	STAFFORD, JOHN R.	1	
6	2	Chief Financial Officer	CONSIDINE, JOHN	1	

Figure 4-22   *A Look at the EMPLOYEES Table*

Notice no values are in the *salary* column just created.

6.   Select the first UPDATE command with your mouse. Again choose the
Execute SQL Statement menu option to execute the INSERT
command.

7. Now, pull down the Table menu from menu bar of Quest and choose the **Refresh** option. You should now see the following table shown below:

COMP_ID	EMP_ID	POSITION	EMP_NAME	DEP_CODE	SALARY
1	1	Controller	BROATCH, ROBERT E.	1	100000
1	2	Chairman of the Board	COMPTON, RONALD E	1	
1	3	VP	BENANAV, GARY	1	
2	1	Chairman of the Board	CLINE, ROBERT S.	1	100000
3	1	Chief Executive Officer	MICHAEL, GARY	1	100000
3	2	Chief Operations Office	CARLEY, JOHN	1	
3	3	Chief Financial Officer	OLSON, A. CRAIG	1	
4	1	Chairman of the Board	BOSSIDY, LAWRENCE	1	100000
4	2	President	BURNHAM, DANIEL P	1	
4	3	Chief Financial Officer	BARTER, JOHN W.	1	
5	1	Chairman of the Board	ALLEY, WILLIAM J	1	100000
5	2	Chief Financial Officer	HENSON, ARNOLD	1	
5	3	Chief Operations Office	HAYS, THOMAS C.	1	
6	1	Chairman of the Board	STAFFORD, JOHN R.	1	100000
6	2	Chief Financial Officer	CONSIDINE, JOHN	1	

Table - COMPANY:EMPLOYEES

Figure 4-23 *A Modified EMPLOYEES Table*

8. The Second UPDATE command should update the column, *stock_date*, from the STOCK_PRICE table. This example is shown below.

```
UPDATE STOCK_PRICE SET STOCK_DATE = '01-JAN-1996'
WHERE (SYMBOL LIKE 'P%' OR SYMBOL LIKE 'R%') AND
STOCKVALUE = NULL
```

Select this UPDATE command with your mouse. Again choose the **Execute SQL Statement** menu option to execute the second INSERT command.

9. The third UPDATE command shows insertion into only a few columns:

```
UPDATE COMP SET COMP_ID = 1
WHERE COMP_NAME LIKE '%PEPSI%'
```

Select this UPDATE command with your mouse. Again, choose the **Execute SQL Statement** menu option to execute the second update command.

10. This UPDATE command should cause an error.

In this case, there is already a row with a *comp_id* of value 1. So, this call generates the error shown below.

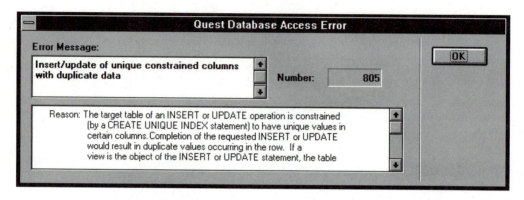

Figure 4-24   *UPDATE Command Error Message*

11. The next UPDATE command to be executed is:

UPDATE EMPLOYEES SET POSITION= 'T'||POSITION

The || symbol is used with SQLBase to concatenate strings. Select this statement with your mouse. Choose the **Execute SQL Statement** menu option to execute the UPDATE command.

This UPDATE appends a T to all values in the column, *position,* as shown in Figure 4-25.

12. The next UPDATE command shows the use of a multiplication operator, *, on the column, *salary.* We could give all employees in department 1 a 10% raise by issuing the following command:

UPDATE EMPLOYEES SET SALARY = SALARY*1.10
WHERE DEP_CODE = 1

Select this UPDATE command with your mouse. Choose the **Execute SQL Statement** menu option to execute the UPDATE command.

13. To see the results of the last two UPDATE statements, pull down the **Table** menu from the menu bar and choose **Refresh.** You will see the T

appended to the entries in the *position* column as well as the change in the *salary* column as a result of the last statement.

COMP_ID	EMP_ID	POSITION	EMP_NAME	DEP_CODE	SALARY
Table - COMPANY:EMPLOYEES					
1	1	TController	BROATCH, ROBERT E.	1	110000
1	2	TChairman of the Board	COMPTON, RONALD E	1	
1	3	TVP	BENANAV, GARY	1	
2	1	TChairman of the Board	CLINE, ROBERT S.	1	110000
3	1	TChief Executive Office	MICHAEL, GARY	1	110000
3	2	TChief Operations Offic	CARLEY, JOHN	1	
3	3	TChief Financial Officer	OLSON, A. CRAIG	1	
4	1	TChairman of the Board	BOSSIDY, LAWRENCE	1	110000
4	2	TPresident	BURNHAM, DANIEL P	1	
4	3	TChief Financial Officer	BARTER, JOHN W.	1	
5	1	TChairman of the Board	ALLEY, WILLIAM J	1	110000
5	2	TChief Financial Officer	HENSON, ARNOLD	1	
5	3	TChief Operations Offic	HAYS, THOMAS C.	1	
6	1	TChairman of the Board	STAFFORD, JOHN R.	1	110000
6	2	TChief Financial Officer	CONSIDINE, JOHN	1	

Figure 4-25   *The EMPLOYEES Table with Further Modifications*

14. This next UPDATE command causes an error.

   UPDATE EMPLOYEES DEP_CODE= 42 WHERE POSITION IN ('TChief Operations Officer', 'COO')

   Select this UPDATE command. Choose the **Execute SQL Statement** menu option.

   The error this statement causes is based on the referential constraint created in Chapter 3. Remember that the column, *dep_code*, is a foreign key to the table, DEPARTMENT. Because of this foreign key relationship, this update is not allowed. It would cause data in the table EMPLOYEES to be out of sync with data in table DEPARTMENTS.

   The error is shown in Figure 4-26.

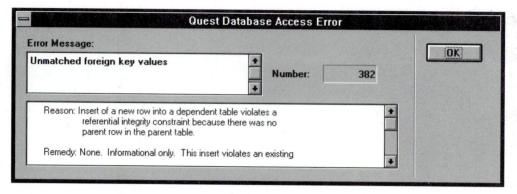

Figure 4-26 *UPDATE Command Error Caused by Referential Constraint*

15. The next UPDATE command executed is:

    UPDATE COMP SET STATE= "WHERE ZIP IS NULL

    Select this UPDATE command with your mouse. Choose the **Execute SQL Statement** menu option to execute the UPDATE command.

16. The final UPDATE command executed is:

    UPDATE COMP SET ZIP=50532 WHERE COMP_NAME LIKE '%PEPSI%'

    In this case, you may have known there was a company named Pepsi, but you may not be sure if it is Pepsi Inc. or Pepsicola Inc. or some other name.

    Select this UPDATE command with your mouse. Choose the **Execute SQL Statement** menu option to execute the UPDATE command.

17. Select the COMMIT command with your mouse. Choose the **Execute SQL Statement** menu option to execute it.

18. Choose **Close** from the File menu to close the sample database.

4.7   DELETE Command

4.7.1 DELETE Command

The DELETE command deletes one or more rows from a single table or view. All rows that satisfy the search condition are deleted either from the table or from the base table of the specified view. The DELETE command takes the form:

DELETE FROM *table-name*
WHERE *search-condition*

The search conditions for a DELETE statement are identical to the UPDATE statement search conditions, so much of what we have learned can be reused.

4.7.2 Examples

A quick example of a DELETE, where we are deleting the company named "Pepsi" from our database is:

DELETE FROM COMPANY
WHERE COMP_NAME = 'PEPSI'

Since the company name is actually 'Pepsi, Inc', we should use wildcards. For example,

DELETE FROM COMPANY
WHERE COMP_NAME LIKE 'PEPSI%'

The following command deletes from the table, EMPLOYEES, rows where the company ID is equal to 123.

DELETE FROM EMPLOYEES WHERE COMP_ID= 123

The following command deletes from the table, STOCK_PRICE, the rows where column, *symbol,* begins with R or P and where *stock_value* is a null value.

DELETE FROM STOCK_PRICE WHERE (SYMBOL = 'P%' OR SYMBOL = 'R%') AND STOCK_VALUE = NULL

4.7.3 DELETE Command Diagram

We have discussed the basics of the UPDATE command. Now, let's look at Figure 4-27, a simplified UPDATE command diagram for SQLBase.

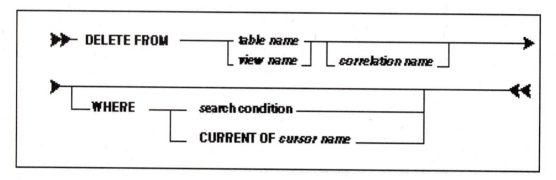

Figure 4-27 *DELETE Command Diagram*

Clauses

table name (including any qualifier) Must reference a table that exists. Any table for which the user has delete privileges can be specified. The name cannot identify a system table.

view name Any view name for which the user has delete privileges can be specified. The name cannot identify a read-only view.

WHERE search condition

Specifies the rows to be deleted based on a search condition. When this clause is used, it is called a searched DELETE.

If you do not specify a search condition, all the rows in the specified table or view are deleted.

4.8 Exercises: The DELETE Command

Exercise 4.8.1: Using the DELETE Command

In this example, you will perform simple DELETE commands.

1. Once again, make sure you are connected to the COMPANY database. If not, pull down the Utilities menu and, using the **Add** function, click on the COMPANY database.

2. Click on the **Open** button and then on the **SQL** button, as shown below.

Figure 4-28   *Opening the SQL Activity*

3. Quest prompts for a file. Choose the file c:\sqlbase\exercise\chap4\ex4-3.qsd. Click **OK**.

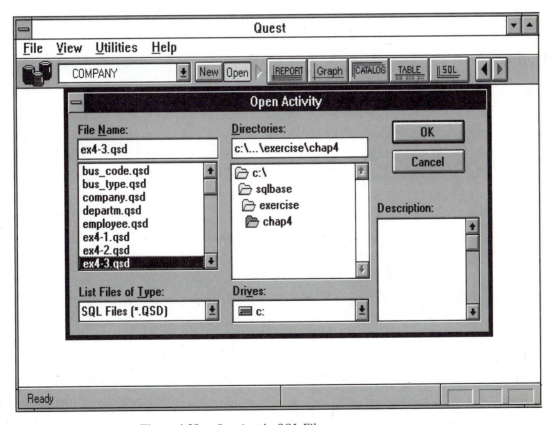

Figure 4-29   *Opening the SQL File*

4. The first DELETE command to be executed, as shown in Figure 4-30, is:

DELETE FROM COMP
WHERE COMP_NAME = 'PEPSI'

Select this DELETE statement with your mouse. Choose the **Execute SQL Statement** menu option as shown below. The objective is to step through a series of DELETE commands one at a time.

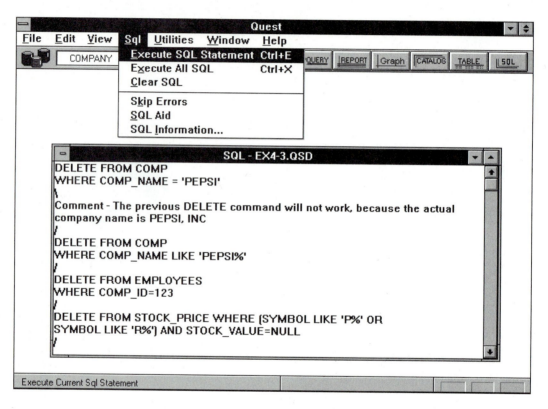

Figure 4-30   *Executing DELETE Command Examples*

Since the company name is actually 'Pepsico Inc', the first DELETE statement, while not generating an error, did not do anything. Wildcards should be used.

5. The next DELETE statement is effective:

DELETE FROM COMP
WHERE COMP_NAME LIKE 'PEPSI%'

Select this DELETE statement. Choose the **Execute SQL Statement** menu option to execute it.

6. The next DELETE Command deleted rows from the table, EMPLOYEES, where the column, *company id*, is equal to 123. Actually, there are no rows in the sample database that match this condition, but this command executes nothing very well.

DELETE FROM EMPLOYEES WHERE COMP_ID= 123

Select this DELETE statement with your mouse. Choose the **Execute SQL Statement** option from the SQL menu to execute the next DELETE command.

7. The last DELETE statement to execute deletes all rows from the table, STOCK_PRICE, that have stock symbols beginning with P or R and where the value of the stock has not yet been inserted.

DELETE FROM STOCK_PRICE WHERE (SYMBOL LIKE 'P%' OR SYMBOL LIKE 'R%') AND STOCK_VALUE = NULL

Select the DELETE statement. Again choose the **Execute SQL Statement** option.

8. Select the COMMIT command. Again choose the **Execute SQL Statement** option.

9. Choose **Close** from the File menu to close the sample database.

4.9　Summary

This chapter covered the basics of the INSERT, UPDATE, and DELETE commands. The WHERE clause is used with the UPDATE and DELETE commands. The predicates used with the WHERE clause were also covered in some detail. The WHERE clause will be used extensively throughout the next several chapters.

In Chapter 2 we designed a database. In Chapter 3, we created it. This chapter showed how to insert, modify, and delete data in the database. Chapter 5 demonstrates how to extract information from this database or query the database by means of the SELECT statement.

5   Retrieving Data:
The SELECT Statement

The ability to retrieve information in a variety of ways is a central strength
of SQL. The SELECT statement is the command used to perform this task.
This chapter specifically looks at the basic syntax of the SELECT statement.

The chapter is organized as follows:

Section 5.1 SELECT Command
Section 5.2 Using Expressions
Section 5.3 Exercises with the SELECT Command
Section 5.4 Examples: Using the SELECT Commands with UPDATE and
              DELETE
Section 5.5 Exercises with INSERT, UPDATE, and DELETE with SELECT
Section 5.6 Summary

5.1   SELECT Command

The SELECT command is used to find and retrieve data. A SELECT
statement, in its simplest form, looks like this:

    SELECT * FROM COMPANY

This SELECT statement requests all of the columns and rows in the table,
COMPANY. The "*" character is a wildcard meant to signify all columns.

A SELECT statement can also request specific columns. For example,
Figure 5-1 shows an example of a SELECT statement requesting only the

comp-name, city, and state columns from the COMPANY database and the results of that query.

SQL - EX5-2.QSD
SELECT COMP_NAME, CITY, STATE FROM COMPANY

COMP_NAME	CITY	STATE
AMERICAN STORES CO	SALT LAKE CITY	UT
AMERICAN EXPRESS CO	NEW YORK	NY
AMOCO CORP	CHICAGO	IL
ANHEUSER BUSCH COS INC	ST LOUIS	MO
APPLE COMPUTER INC	CUPERTINO	CA
ARCHER DANIELS MIDLAND CO	DECATUR	IL
ARCO CHEMICAL CO	NEWTOWN SQUARE	PA

Figure 5-1   *SQL Statement (top) and Results (bottom)*

In Figure 5-1, specific information is needed for the SELECT statement. This information is:

- The table in the database from which to find the data requested, in this case, the table COMPANY

- The conditions for the search, in this case, the columns *comp_name*, *city*, and *state*; no additional conditions are specified.

The result of a SELECT is a set of rows called a result table. A result table meets the conditions specified in the SELECT command.

SELECT DISTINCT Clause

One option used with the SELECT statement is the DISTINCT clause. This clause suppresses duplicate rows. For example, the following statement finds out in which states the companies in the table, COMPANY, are located.

SELECT DISTINCT STATE FROM COMPANY

The DISTINCT clause limits the number of results to fifty, regardless of how many rows are in our table, because there are only fifty states. No duplicate results are allowed.

Assigning Names to Expressions

Within a SELECT statement, names can be assigned as a column heading in the output. For example:

SELECT COMPANY_NUMBER=COMP_ID FROM COMPANY

Another way to accomplish the same result is to issue this SELECT statement:

SELECT COMP_ID AS COMPANY_NUMBER FROM
COMPANY

The output of this command has a heading of COMPANY_NUMBER instead of COMP_ID, as shown in Figure 5-2.

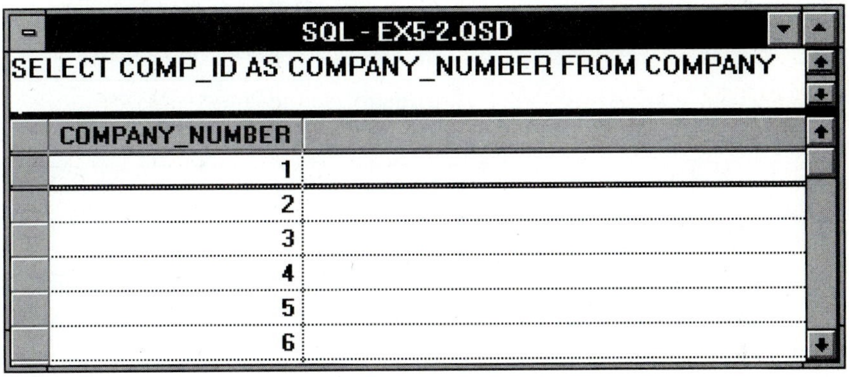

SQL - EX5-2.QSD
SELECT COMP_ID AS COMPANY_NUMBER FROM COMPANY

COMPANY_NUMBER	
1	
2	
3	
4	
5	
6	

Figure 5-2   *Assigning Names to Expressions*

5.1.1 Answering Questions

SELECT statements ask questions. With a SELECT statement, you are, in essence, asking a question and getting information back. To exemplify this, we will build a table that contains information about movies and use SELECT to help answer these questions about the table.

Here another example table, MOVIES, is introduced, having the fields shown in Figure 5-3:

Column Name	Column Description
Title	Title of the movie
Rating	Movie ratings of G, PG, PG-13, R, and NR
YR	Year that the movie was made
Type	Type of movie: Comedy, Suspense, Horror, Romance, Action/Adventure, SF, or Drama
Lead1	A leading actor
Lead2	Second leading actor
Support1	A supporting actor
Support2	Second supporting actor
Director	Director of the movie
Stars	Rating of movie on scale from 1 to 5 stars

Figure 5-3   *MOVIES Table for SELECT Searches*

With a table like that in Figure 5-3 and containing data on movies you have seen, here are just a few of the questions that might interest you:

- What are the movies to which I have given a five-star rating?
- How many movies have I seen that were rated PG?
- What movies did I see that were made between 1980 and 1985?
- What are the titles of movies I saw where I did not know who the director was?
- If at least one movie I saw was made in 1985, what are the titles and year of movies I have seen?
- What are the titles of the James Bond movies I have seen?
- What are the titles of the movies in which Audrey Hepburn or Elizabeth Taylor were leading actors?
- What were the five-star movies in which Robert Redford starred?
- Who are all the lead actors who have been in both five-star and one-star movies?

The SELECT statement will help you answer all of these questions and the thousands of variations on these questions. The flexibility of the SELECT statement when used against relational tables is, in fact, one of the chief benefits of this query language. So let's actually see this process of asking questions.

5.1.2 WHERE Clause and Predicates with the SELECT Command

The SELECT command uses the WHERE clause, just as do UPDATE and DELETE. In fact, the WHERE clause, the predicates, and search conditions covered in the last chapter can be used here exactly as they were in Chapter 4. As these are used frequently, this section reviews the use of predicates and search conditions with the WHERE clause and the SELECT statement.

The predicates and search conditions already discussed are:

- Relational Operators: <, >, <>, =, >=, <=
- BETWEEN
- NULL
- EXISTS
- LIKE
- IN
- SEARCH Conditions: AND, OR, and NOT

The example table, MOVIES, introduced in this chapter, is used as the target table to demonstrate the use of these predicates and search conditions.

Relational Predicates

Relational predicates can be used to construct a SELECT statement to answer the first question asked about our table, MOVIES, in this chapter:

What are the movies to which I have given a five-star rating?

The SELECT statement answering this question is shown below.

SQL - EX5-2.QSD
SELECT TITLE FROM MOVIES WHERE STARS = 5

TITLE
The African Queen
The Birds
Butch Cassidy and the Sundance Kid
Catch 22
Camelot
Casablanca

Figure 5-4   *SELECT with the = Operator*

The SELECT statement in this example requests only the *title* column. The relational operator, =, was used to retrieve all titles of movies with a five star-rating *equal* to five.

The second question asked about the table, MOVIES, can also be solved with relational operators. This question is:

How many movies have I seen that were not rated PG?

Figure 5-5 shows the SELECT statement that answers this question.

SQL - SELECT.QSD
SELECT COUNT(TITLE) FROM MOVIES WHERE RATING <> 'PG'

Formula1
59

Figure 5-5   *SELECT with <> Operator*

In this case, the <> operator is useful to show all movies with ratings not equal to PG. Figure 5-5 shows this SELECT statement, which returned a count of 59 movies.

The SQLBase function *Count* is used with the SELECT statement to sum the number of movie titles returned to us. This *aggregate function* is useful with the type of questions that ask "How many?"

Using the BETWEEN Predicate

The third question could also be solved with a relational operator. This question is:

What movies did I see that were made between 1980 and 1985?

Relational operators could solve this question in this way:

```
SELECT TITLE FROM MOVIES WHERE YR > 1980
AND YR < 1985
```

Although relational operators work in this case, an optimal way of answering this question is to use the BETWEEN clause, as shown in Figure 5-6.

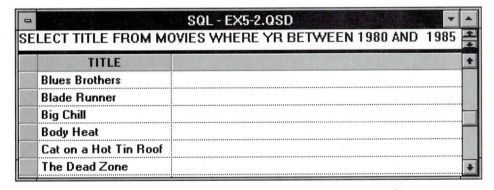

Figure 5-6 *SELECT With BETWEEN Clause*

Using the NULL Predicate

The fourth question is not easily solved by relational predicates. This question asks for the absence of a value, which can be easily solved by using a NULL predicate. The question is:

What are the titles of movies I saw where I did not know who the director was?

Figure 5-7 shows the SELECT that answers this question.

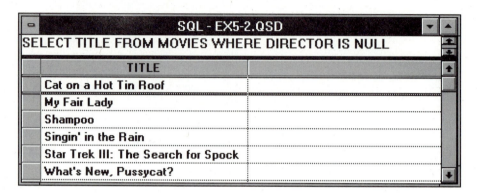

Figure 5-7   *SELECT With NULL Predicate*

Using the EXISTS Predicate

The next question from the list was:

If at least one movie I saw was made in 1985, what are the title and year of movies I have seen?

This question asks for values *only if a* condition is met, which, in this case is that at least one movie in the table, MOVIES was made in 1985. The reason a relational operator does not work well here is that the condition is based on the entire table and not on the specific row being evaluated.

The EXISTS clause, as we saw in Chapter 4, can answer such questions, but it requires a *subselect* statement. A subselect statement is a SELECT statement used within another SELECT. Subselects are very powerful and can help solve more convoluted questions. Subselects are used extensively.

The question above is solved by using a EXISTS statement, as shown in Figure 5-8.

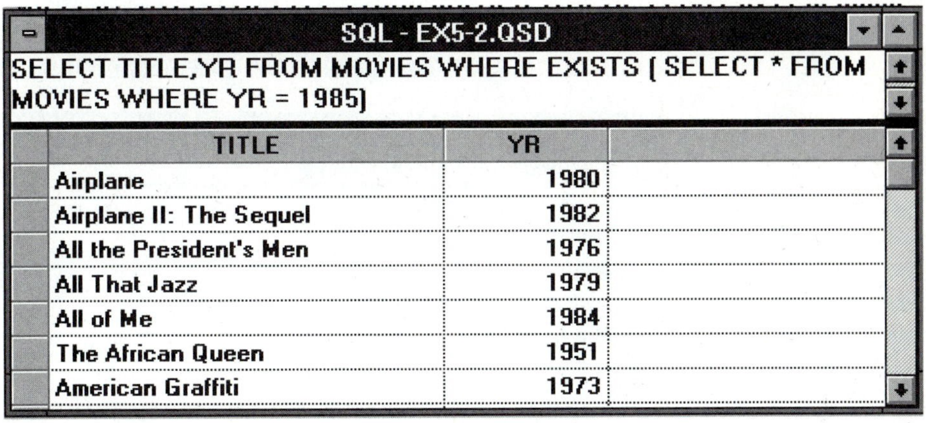

TITLE	YR
Airplane	1980
Airplane II: The Sequel	1982
All the President's Men	1976
All That Jazz	1979
All of Me	1984
The African Queen	1951
American Graffiti	1973

Figure 5-8 *SELECT with the EXISTS Predicate*

Using the LIKE Predicate

Sometimes a result set is required, and some information about the values in the column or columns requested is known. Such is the case with the question:

What are the titles of the James Bond movies I have seen?

In the case of the table, MOVIES, all James Bond movies are listed with the value "007" appended to them. Knowing this, we can use the LIKE predicate to answer the question, as shown in Figure 5-9.

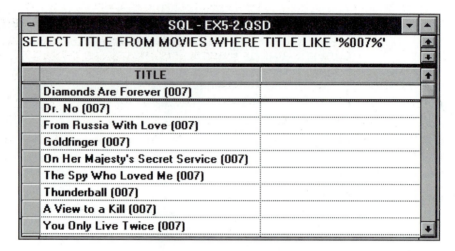

Figure 5-9   *SELECT with LIKE Predicate*

As discussed in the last chapter, the % character is a wildcard character matching one or more characters.

Using the IN Predicate

Another question asked is:

What are the titles of the movies in which Audrey Hepburn or Grace Kelly were leading actors?

This question can be answered by use of relational operators. For example:

> SELECT TITLE FROM MOVIES WHERE (LEAD1 = "Audrey Hepburn" OR LEAD1 = "Elizabeth Taylor") OR (LEAD2 = "Audrey Hepburn" OR LEAD2 = "Elizabeth Taylor")

The problem with this statement is that the number of actors you are searching for could grow and such a statement would be cumbersome. An IN predicate is useful for searching for lists of values.

This question is answered by using the IN predicate with the SELECT statement, as shown in Figure 5-10.

```
┌─┬──────────────────────────────────────────────────────────┬─┬─┐
│ ─ │                    SQL - SELECT.QSD                     │ ▼ │ ▲ │
├───┴──────────────────────────────────────────────────────────┼─┤
│ SELECT TITLE,YR, TYPE FROM MOVIES WHERE LEAD1 IN ['Elizabeth  │▲│
│ Taylor', 'Audrey Hepburn'] OR LEAD2 IN ['Elizabeth Taylor',   │ │
│ 'Audrey Hepburn']                                             │▼│
```

TITLE	YR	TYPE	
Cat on a Hot Tin Roof	1958	Drama	
Charade	1963	Suspense	
Giant	1956	Drama	
My Fair Lady	1968	Musical	

Figure 5-10 *SELECT with IN Predicate*

Search Conditions: Using AND, OR, and NOT

The combining of search conditions with AND, OR, and NOT is unavoidable. We have already done it in previous examples. Here is another question that requires combined search conditions:

What were the five-star movies in which Robert Redford starred?

The issue that calls for a combined search condition is that the actor's name could be in one of two columns, LEAD1 or LEAD2. Figure 5-11 shows the solution to this question, using a SELECT with AND and OR conditions.

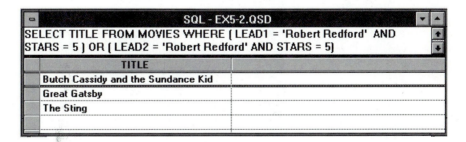

Figure 5-11 *SELECT with Combined Search Conditions*

5.1.3 SELECT Statements and Database Design

Database design has a lot to do with how easy a SELECT statement can be constructed. For example, take the question:

Who are all the lead actors who have been in both five-star and one-star movies?

The example is problematic: Two columns store leading actors - *lead1* and *lead2*. This database design is done intentionally to point out that improper database design leads to increased difficulty in information retrieval.

The question can be solved by two SELECT statements.

```
SELECT  LEAD1  FROM MOVIES WHERE STARS = 5 AND
LEAD1 IN (SELECT LEAD1, LEAD2 FROM MOVIES WHERE
STARS = 1)
```

```
SELECT  LEAD 2 FROM MOVIES WHERE STARS = 5 AND
LEAD1 IN (SELECT LEAD1, LEAD2 FROM MOVIES WHERE
STARS = 1)
```

A more correct way to treat this information would be to create separate tables for movie titles and movie actors. Having a table for movie actors would also avoid the limitation that only two leading actors can be specified in the database.

Of course, if we have more than one table from which to retrieve data, then a SELECT statement must now do a join between the tables to get the proper information.

5.1.4 Simple SELECT Command Diagram

Figure 5-12 shows a simple command diagram for the SELECT statement. The SELECT statement has many more clauses than we have covered so far; they are discussed in the next chapter.

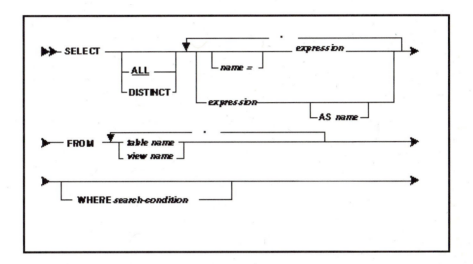

Figure 5-12   *SELECT Command Diagram*

Clauses

ALL	Retrieves *all* rows; the default for a SELECT.
DISTINCT	Suppresses duplicate rows.
	You cannot use the DISTINCT keyword to SELECT LONG VARCHAR data types.
expression	A select list that contains expressions that are separated by commas. An expression can be:

- Column name
- Constant
- Bind variable
- Result of a function
- System keyword

name = expression or **name as expression**

> Assigns a name that is used as a column heading in the output instead of the column name itself.

FROM

> Contains the names of the tables or views from which the set of resulting rows is formed. Each name must identify a table or view that exists in the database.

WHERE search condition

> Specifies a search condition for the base tables or views.
>
> With SQLBase, you cannot use a LONG VARCHAR column in a subselect search condition.

5.2   Using Expressions

An expression is:

- An item that yields a single value
- A combination of items and operators that yields a single value

An *item* can be any of the following:

- Column name
- Constant
- Bind variable
- Result of a function
- System keyword
- Another expression

The form of an expression is shown in Figure 5-13:

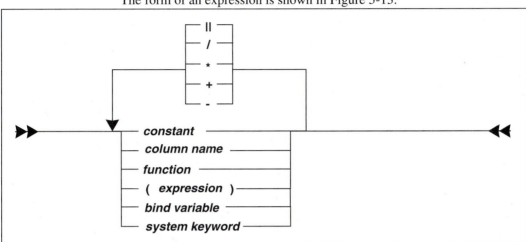

Figure 5-13   *Expression Diagram*

If you do not use arithmetic operators, the result of an expression is the specified value of the term. For example, the result of 1+1 is 2; the result of the expression AMT (where AMT is a column name) is the value of the column.

5.2.1   Null Values in Expressions

If any item in an expression contains a null value, then the result of evaluating the expression is null (*unknown* or false).

5.2.2   String Concatenation Operator (||)

The string concatenation operator (||) concatenates two or more strings:

string || string

The result is a single string.

For example, if the column PLACE contains the value "PALO ALTO," then the following example returns the string "was born in PALO ALTO."

' was born in '|| PLACE

The following example prefixes everyone's name with "Mr.":

SELECT 'Mr. '||LNAME FROM EMPLOYEES

5.2.3 Precedence

The following precedence rules are used in evaluating arithmetic expressions:

- Expressions in parentheses are evaluated first.

- The unary operators (+ and -) are applied before multiplication and division.

- Multiplication and division are applied before addition and subtraction.

- Operators at the same precedence level are applied from left to right.

5.2.4 Examples of Expressions

Table 5-1 lists some sample expressions, where the values *amount, tax, past_due, hiredate, sal,* and *bonus* are column names. **Max()** is a SQLBase-specific function, and SYSDATETIME is a system keyword for SQLBASE to provide the current system date and time.

Table 5-1   *Examples of Expressions*

AMOUNT * TAX	Column arithmetic
(CHECKS.AMOUNT * 10) - PAST_DUE	Nested arithmetic with columns
HIREDATE + 90	Column and constant arithmetic
SAL + MAX(BONUS)	Function with column arithmetic
SYSDATETIME + 4	Date/time system keyword arithmetic

An example of using an expression with arithmetic is shown below for the table, EMPLOYEES. If we had a column, *salary*, which was a yearly salary, then a monthly salary could be computed by dividing the salary by twelve as shown below:

```
SELECT EMP_ID, SALARY/12 FROM EMPLOYEES
```

5.3   Exercises with the SELECT Command

Exercise 5.3.1:   Creating the MOVIES Database

This exercise builds the MOVIES database that was used in this chapter. We will perform SELECT statements against it.

1. Open Quest, if not already open. Make sure you are connected to the COMPANY database by pulling down the Utilities menu and using the **Add** function if necessary. Click on the COMPANY database.

2. Click on the **Open** button and then on the **SQL** button as shown in Figure 5-14.

Figure 5-14   *Opening the SQL Activity*

3. Quest prompts for a file. Choose the file c:\sqlbase\exercise\chap5\ex5-1.qsd. Click **OK.**

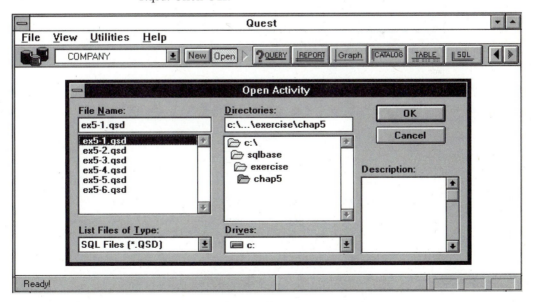

Figure 5-15   *Opening the SQL File*

4. In this step, choose **Execute All SQL**. This script creates the MOVIES database and inserts values into it.

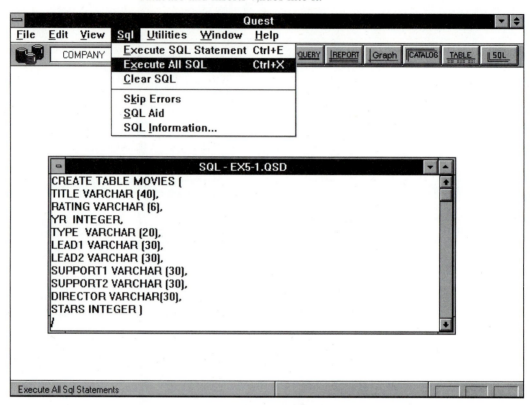

Figure 5-16 *Executing SQL on the MOVIES Database*

Exercise 5.3.2: Using the SELECT Command

In this example, you will perform updates by using predicate statements.

1. Click on the **Open** button and then on the **SQL** button.

2. Quest prompts for a file. Choose the file c:\sqlbase\exercise\chap5\ex5-2.qsd. Click **OK**.

3. Do not choose **Execute All SQL** as done in the previous exercise.

4. The first SELECT command answered the question:

What are the movies to which I have given a five-star rating?

The SELECT statement just executed is:

SELECT TITLE FROM MOVES WHERE STARS = 5

Choose this SELECT statement by clicking in the SQL activity window, pull down the SQL menu, and choose the **Execute SQL Statement** menu option as shown in Figure 5-16. The objective is to step through a series of SELECT commands one at a time.

5. The second SELECT statement answers the question:

How many movies have I seen that were rated PG?

The SELECT statement for this is:

SELECT COUNT(TITLE) FROM MOVIES WHERE RATING<> 'PG'

Choose this SELECT statement by clicking in the SQL activity window. Again, choose the **Execute SQL Statement** menu option to execute this command.

6. The third SELECT statement answers the question:

What movies did I see that were made between 1980 and 1985?

The SELECT statement for this is:

SELECT TITLE FROM MOVES WHERE YR BETWEEN 1980 AND 1985

Click on this SELECT command in the SQL activity window. Choose the **Execute SQL Statement** menu option to execute this command.

7. The fourth SELECT statement answers the question:

What are the titles of movies I saw where I did not know who the director was?

The SELECT statement for this is:

SELECT TITLE FROM MOVIES WHERE DIRECTOR IS NULL

Click on this SQL statement. Choose the **Execute SQL Statement** menu option to execute this command.

8. The fifth SELECT statement answers the question:

If at least one movie I saw was made in 1985, what are the title and years of movies I have seen?

The SELECT statement for this is:

SELECT TITLE,YR FROM MOVIES WHERE EXISTS (SELECT *
FROM MOVIES WHERE YR = 1985)

Click on this command. Choose the **Execute SQL Statement** menu option to execute this command

9. The sixth SELECT statement answers the question:

What are the titles of the James Bond movies I have seen?

The SELECT statement for this is:

SELECT TITLE FROM MOVIES WHERE TITLE LIKE '007'

Click on this command. Choose the **Execute SQL Statement** menu option to execute this command.

10. The seventh SELECT statement answers the question:

What are the titles of the movies in which Audrey Hepburn or Elizabeth Taylor were leading actors?

The SELECT statement for this is:

SELECT TITLE FROM MOVIES WHERE (LEAD1 ="Audrey
Hepburn" OR LEAD1 = "Elizabeth Taylor") OR (LEAD2 = "Audrey
Hepburn" OR LEAD2 = "Elizabeth Taylor")

Click on this SELECT statement. Choose the **Execute SQL Statement** menu option to execute this command.

11. The eighth SELECT statement answers the question:

What were the five-star movies in which Robert Redford starred?

The SELECT statement for this is:

SELECT TITLE FROM MOVIES WHERE (LEAD1 = "Robert
Redford" AND STARS =5) OR LEAD2 = "Robert Redford" AND
STARS = 5)

Click on this SELECT statement. Choose the **Execute SQL Statement** menu option to execute this command.

12. Try writing your own SELECT statements to answer one of these questions (or make up your own and try to answer them):

    How many movies were made in 1970 or 1971?

    What are the movie titles and ratings of the horror movies?

    What types of movies did Cary Grant star in? (Hint: use the DISTINCT clause to remove redundant categories.)

    Choose the **Execute SQL Statement** menu option to execute your SELECT statements.

13. To close, choose the **Close** menu option from the File menu.

5.4 Examples: Using the SELECT Commands with UPDATE and DELETE

The INSERT, UPDATE, and DELETE statements can be used in conjunction with SELECT statements. This section provides examples of using the SELECT statement with each of these commands.

5.4.1 Example with INSERT and SELECT: Copying Columns of One Database to Another

The INSERT command is very powerful when used in conjunction with the SELECT command. The following example shows how columns of a table in a database can be copied to another table.

English Translation of Example Code

Insert into a temporary table, COMPTEMP, the values of the rows *comp_id* and *comp_name* from the table, COMPANY.

The Code

First, we create the temporary table, COMPTEMP.

```
CREATE TABLE COMPTEMP(
COMP_ID INTEGER,
COMP_NAME VARCHAR(40))
```

The following code inserts the columns, *comp_id* and *comp_name*, from COMPANY into the new table.

INSERT INTO COMPTEMP(COMP_ID, COMP_NAME)
SELECT COMP_ID, COMP_NAME FROM COMPANY

5.4.2 Using UPDATE with a Subselect

An example of using a subselect with an UPDATE statement can be illustrated by using the table EMPLOYEES. If we gave everyone in the company Informix a 15% raise, the first thing that might occur to you is that the table EMPLOYEES does not have a column, *company_name*. One way to get around this is by using a subselect.

Since both the table COMPANY and the table EMPLOYEE have the column, *comp_id*, the following SQL statement will work.

UPDATE EMPLOYEES SET SALARY=SALARY*1.15 WHERE COMP_ID IN (SELECT COMP_ID FROM COMPANY WHERE COMP_NAME = "Informix")

As illustrated by this example, using a subselect is a way of getting information out of one table for use with another table.

5.4.3 Using DELETE with a Subselect

An example of using a subselect statement with a DELETE statement is illustrated by an example, in which employees in department 25 from the company, Sybase, are deleted from the EMPLOYEES table.

Here is the statement for this example:

DELETE FROM EMPLOYEES WHERE COMP_ID IN (SELECT COMP_ID FROM COMANY WHERE COMP_NAME = "Sybase")

5.5 Exercises with INSERT, UPDATE, and DELETE with SELECT

Exercise 5.5.1: Copying Columns from One Table to Another

In this exercise, the example from Section 5.4.1 is demonstrated.

English Translation of the Exercise Objective:

Insert into a temporary table, COMPTEMP, the values of the rows *comp_id* and *comp_name* from the table, COMPANY.

Exercise Steps

1. First, we create the tempory table, COMPTEMP. Click on the **Open** button and then on the **SQL** button.

2. Choose the file c:\sqlbase\exercises\chap5\ex5-3.qsd. Click **OK**.

   This file contains the statements:

   ```
   CREATE TABLE COMPTEMP(
   COMP_ID INTEGER,
   COMP_NAME VARCHAR(40))
   ```

   Choose the **Execute All SQL** menu option. You have created the table, COMPTEMP.

3. Click on the **Open** button and then on the **SQL** button.

4. Choose the file c:\sqlbase\exercises\chap5\ex5-4qsd. Click **OK**

5. The following code inserts the columns, *comp_id* and *comp_name*, from COMPANY into the new table.

   ```
   INSERT INTO COMPTEMP(COMP_ID, COMP_NAME)
   SELECT COMP_ID, COMP_NAME FROM COMPANY
   ```

   Choose the **Execute All SQL** option to perform this operation.

Exercise 5.5.2: *Using UPDATE with SELECT Command*

In this example, you will perform simple update commands.

1. Make sure you are connected to the COMPANY database by pulling down the Utilities menu and using the **Add** function. Click on the COMPANY database.

2.   Click on the **Open** button and then on the **SQL** button as shown below.

Figure 5-17   *Opening the SQL Activity*

3.   Quest prompts for a file. Choose c:\sqlbase\exercise\chap5\ex5-5.qsd.
     Click **OK**.

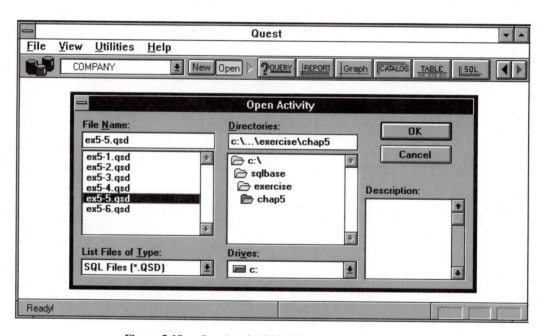

Figure 5-18   *Opening the SQL File*

4.   Choose **Execute All SQL** option from the SQL menu.

The UPDATE command executed was:

```
UPDATE EMPLOYEES SET SALARY=SALARY*1.15
WHERE COMP_ID IN (SELECT COMP_ID FROM
COMPANY WHERE COMP_NAME = "Informix")
```

Exercise 5.5.3: Using DELETE with SELECT Command

In this example, you will perform the DELETE example in Section 5.4.3.

1. Make sure you are connected to the COMPANY database by pulling down the Utilities menu and choosing the **Add** function. Click on the COMPANY database.

2. Click on the **Open** button and then on the **SQL** button.

3. Quest prompts for a file. Choose c:\sqlbase\exercise\chap5\ex5-6.qsd. Click **OK.**

4. Choose **Execute All SQL**.

   The DELETE command executed was:

   DELETE FROM EMPLOYEES WHERE COMP_ID IN (SELECT
   COMP_ID FROM COMANY WHERE COMP_NAME = "Sybase")

5.6 Summary

This chapter covered the basics of the SELECT statement, including a review of the use of predicates and search conditions. Expressions, as used in SQL statements, were examined in more detail; SELECT statements were used in conjuction with INSERT, UPDATE, and DELETE.

The tool we have been using in our exercises, Quest, is a query tool that can build SELECT statements automatically for you via a point-and-click interface. Later in this book, end-user query and report tools are discussed in more detail.

The next chapter covers more options with the SELECT statement, including GROUP BY, ORDER BY, and HAVING. Unions and joins are also common features of the SELECT statement; they are discussed in Chapter 7.

6   Functions and the Clauses ORDER BY, GROUP BY, and HAVING

This chapter adds to our knowledge of the SELECT command and introduces three new clauses: ORDER BY, GROUP BY, and HAVING. Aggregate functions are also introduced.

The chapter is organized as follows:

6.1   *ORDER BY Clause*

The ORDER BY clause specifies the ordering, or sorting, of rows in a result table. Rows can be sorted on more than one column. Figure 6-1 shows an example of sorting the columns *comp_name*, *city*, and *state* from the table, COMP, by state.

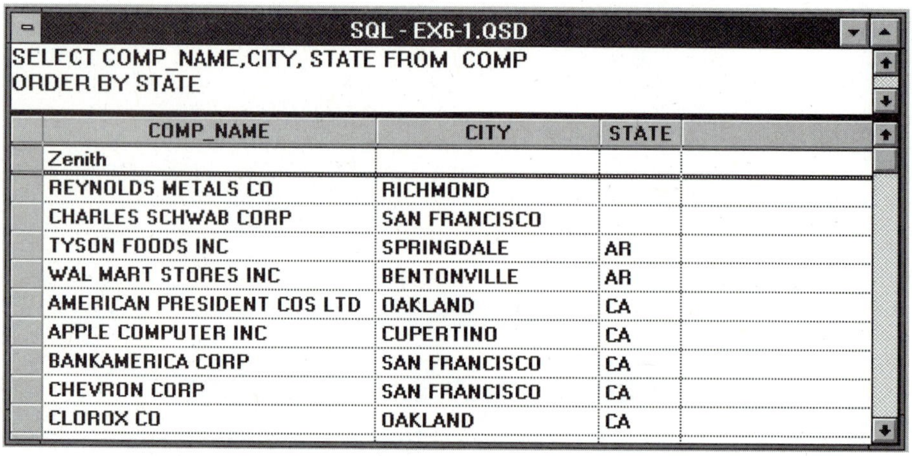

SQL - EX6-1.QSD			
SELECT COMP_NAME,CITY, STATE FROM COMP			
ORDER BY STATE			
COMP_NAME	**CITY**	**STATE**	
Zenith			
REYNOLDS METALS CO	RICHMOND		
CHARLES SCHWAB CORP	SAN FRANCISCO		
TYSON FOODS INC	SPRINGDALE	AR	
WAL MART STORES INC	BENTONVILLE	AR	
AMERICAN PRESIDENT COS LTD	OAKLAND	CA	
APPLE COMPUTER INC	CUPERTINO	CA	
BANKAMERICA CORP	SAN FRANCISCO	CA	
CHEVRON CORP	SAN FRANCISCO	CA	
CLOROX CO	OAKLAND	CA	

Figure 6-1   *Example of Sorted Columns*

Ascending or Descending Sorts

Each column name (or number) can be optionally followed by ASC or DESC for ascending or descending sort sequence. ASC is the default order. Figure 6-2 shows an example of the same sort as Figure 6-1, except that a descending sort is used.

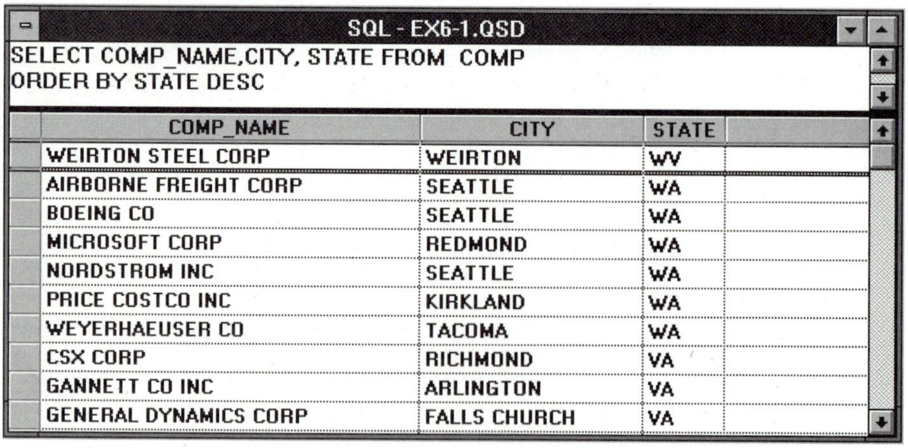

SQL - EX6-1.QSD			
SELECT COMP_NAME,CITY, STATE FROM COMP			
ORDER BY STATE DESC			
COMP_NAME	**CITY**	**STATE**	
WEIRTON STEEL CORP	WEIRTON	WV	
AIRBORNE FREIGHT CORP	SEATTLE	WA	
BOEING CO	SEATTLE	WA	
MICROSOFT CORP	REDMOND	WA	
NORDSTROM INC	SEATTLE	WA	
PRICE COSTCO INC	KIRKLAND	WA	
WEYERHAEUSER CO	TACOMA	WA	
CSX CORP	RICHMOND	VA	
GANNETT CO INC	ARLINGTON	VA	
GENERAL DYNAMICS CORP	FALLS CHURCH	VA	

Figure 6-2   *Sorted Columns, Descending Order*

More Than One Sort

You can also sort by more than one column, using the ORDER BY clause, as shown in Figure 6-3. The table, COMP, is sorted by both city and state:

```
┌─────────────────────────────────────────────────────────────┐
│ ⊟              SQL - EX6-1.QSD                      ▼  ▲      │
├─────────────────────────────────────────────────────────────┤
│ SELECT COMP_NAME,CITY, STATE FROM  COMP             ▲        │
│ ORDER BY STATE,CITY                                 ▼        │
├──────────────────────────┬────────────────┬─────────┬───────┤
│        COMP_NAME         │      CITY       │  STATE  │  ▲    │
├──────────────────────────┼────────────────┼─────────┤       │
│ WAL MART STORES INC      │ BENTONVILLE     │ AR      │       │
│ TYSON FOODS INC          │ SPRINGDALE      │ AR      │       │
│ HILTON HOTELS CORP       │ BEVERLY HILLS   │ CA      │       │
│ LITTON INDUSTRIES INC    │ BEVERLY HILLS   │ CA      │       │
│ WALT DISNEY CO           │ BURBANK         │ CA      │       │
│ LOCKHEED CORP            │ CALABASAS       │ CA      │  ▼    │
├──────────────────────────┴────────────────┴─────────┴───────┤
│ ◄                                                   ►        │
└─────────────────────────────────────────────────────────────┘
```

Figure 6-3   *Sorting by More Than One Column*

The major sort is on the first column specified in the ORDER BY clause. In Figure 6-3, the column *state* is used as the major sort. The minor sorts are on the columns specified after that. In this case, there is only one minor sort in Figure 6-3, the column *city*.

Using the ORDER BY Clause with Expressions or Functions

If the sort is on a column derived from a function or arithmetic expression, the column must be specified by an integer that signifies its relative number in the select list of the command.

The following SELECT shows an ORDER BY clause that references an expression, STOCK_VALUE*2, instead of a column:

    SELECT SYMBOL, STOCK_VALUE*2 FROM STOCK_PRICE
    ORDER BY 2

The ORDER BY clause uses the number 2 to specify the relative number in the select list where that expression is located. Figure 6-4 shows the SELECT statement and its result.

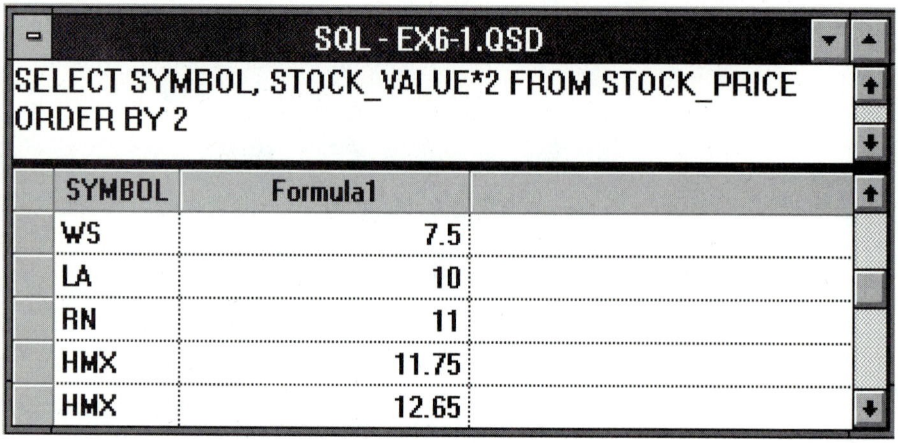

```
┌─────────────────────────────────────────────────────────────┐
│ [-]              SQL - EX6-1.QSD                    [▼] [▲]  │
├─────────────────────────────────────────────────────────────┤
│ SELECT SYMBOL, STOCK_VALUE*2 FROM STOCK_PRICE          [+]   │
│ ORDER BY 2                                                    │
│                                                        [+]   │
├─────────────────────────────────────────────────────────────┤
```

SYMBOL	Formula1	
WS	7.5	
LA	10	
RN	11	
HMX	11.75	
HMX	12.65	

Figure 6-4   *Sorting with an Expression*

Restrictions on the ORDER BY Clause

Generally, there are restrictions on the use of the ORDER BY clause. For example, some of the restrictions SQLBase has when using the ORDER BY clause are:

- You cannot use an ORDER BY clause in a subselect.

- You cannot use string functions in an ORDER BY clause. Instead, specify the string function in the select list and then use the select list column number in the ORDER BY clause.

6.2   Functions

Relational databases have a set of functions for manipulating strings, dates, and numbers. A function returns a value that is derived by applying the function to its arguments.

We used functions in previous chapters. For example, we used the Count() function in Chapter 4 to determine the number of rows in a table. The Count() function is referred to as an *aggregate* function. While all database vendors offer functions, most vendors vary in the number and type of functions they offer.

Functions can generally be classified in these groups:

- Aggregate functions
- String functions
- Date and time functions
- Logical functions
- Special functions
- Math functions
- Finance functions

An example of a time function for SQLBase is shown in Figure 6-5. A column named *stock_date* contains '18-JAN-1994 10:14:27 AM'. The following expression returns a concatenated version of this string: '18-JAN-1994':

@DATEVALUE(STOCK_DATE)

Figure 6-5 executes the following SELECT statement:

SELECT SYMBOL, @DATEVALUE (STOCK_DATE) AS STOCK_DATE, STOCK_VALUE FROM STOCK_PRICE

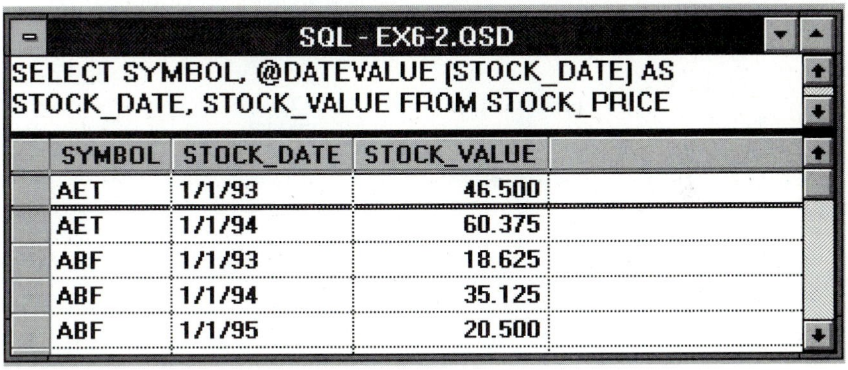

SQL - EX6-2.QSD

SELECT SYMBOL, @DATEVALUE [STOCK_DATE] AS STOCK_DATE, STOCK_VALUE FROM STOCK_PRICE

SYMBOL	STOCK_DATE	STOCK_VALUE	
AET	1/1/93	46.500	
AET	1/1/94	60.375	
ABF	1/1/93	18.625	
ABF	1/1/94	35.125	
ABF	1/1/95	20.500	

Figure 6-5   *SELECT with Time Function*

6.2.1   *Functions and Database Vendors*

Most database vendors vary in how they implement functions. While database vendors provide similar functionality and generally use the same aggregate functions, the names of functions differ widely from vendor to vendor.

This section provides a sampling of functions from Oracle, Sybase, and SQLBase.

Oracle Function Summary

Table 6-1   *Oracle Function Summary*

Function Type	Functions		Comments
Aggregate	AVG MAX SDV VARIANCE	COUNT MIN SUM	Aggregate functions compute summary values from a group of values.
String	ASCII CONCATE INSTR LENGTH LOWER LTRIM RPAD SUBSTR UPPER	CHR INITCAP INSTRB LENGTHB LPAD REPLACE RTRIM SUBSTRB	String functions return information about character data types.
Date/Time	ADD_MONTHS MONTHS_BETWEEN ROUND TRUNC	LAST_DAY NEXT_DAY SYSDATE	Date/Time functions return information about date/time data values or return a date/time result.
Math	ABS COS EXP LN MOD ROUND SIN SQRT TANH	CEIL COSH FLOOR LOG POWER SIGN SINH TAN TRUNC	Math functions take single numeric values as arguments and return numeric results.
Special	NVL CONVERT RAWTOHEX TO_CHAR TO_NUMBER	CHARTOROWID HEXTORAW ROWIDTOCHAR TO_DATE	Special functions for Oracle center around data conversion.

Sybase Function Summary

Table 6-2 *Sybase Function Summary*

Function Type	Functions		Comments
Aggregate	AVG MAX SUM	COUNT MIN	Aggregate functions compute summary values from a group of values.
String	ASCII CHARINDEX LOWER PATINDEX RTRIM SOUNDEX STR SUBSTRING	CHAR DIFFERENCE LTRIM RIGHT REPLICATE SPACE STUFF UPPER	String functions return information about character data types.
Date/Time	DATENAME DATEADD GETDATE	DATEPART DATEDIFF	Date/Time functions return information about date/time data values or return a date/time result.
Math	ABS ASIN CEILING COT EXP LOG PI RADIANS ROUND SIN TAN	ACOS ATAN COS DEGREES FLOOR LOG10 POWER RAND SIGN SQRT	Math functions take single numeric values as arguments and return numeric results.
Special	DB_NAME SUSER_NAME COL_NAME ISNULL SUSER_ID	HOST_NAME USER_NAME COL_LENGTH DB_ID USER_ID	Special functions for Sybase center around system-related information, like returning a database name or a user ID.

SQLBase Function Summary

Table 6-3 *SQLBase Function Summary*

Function Type	Functions		Comments
Aggregate	AVG MAX SDV @SDV	COUNT @MEDIUM SUM	Aggregate functions compute summary values from a group of values.
String	@CHAR @DECODE @FIND @LENGTH @MID @PROPER @REPLACE @SCAN @SUBSTRING @UPPER	@CODE @EXACT @LEFT @LOWER @NULLVALUE @REPEAT @RIGHT @STRING @TRIM @VALUE	String functions return information about character data types.
Date/Time	@DATE @DATEVALUE @HOUR @MINUTE @MONTHBEG @QUARTER @SECOND @TIMEVALUE @WEEKDAY @YEARBEG @DATEVALUE	@DATETOCHAR @DAY @MICROSECOND @MONTH @NOW @QUARTERBEG @TIME @WEEKBEG @YEAR @YEARNO @DAY	Date/Time functions return information about date/time data values or return a date/time result.
Math	@ABS @ASIN @ATAN2 @EXP @INT @LOG @PI @SIN @TAN	@ACOS @ATAN @COS @FACTORIAL @LN @MOD @ROUND @SQRT	Math functions take single numeric values as arguments and return numeric results.
Logical	@IF	@ISNA	Logical functions return a value based on a condition; the result is always 1 or 0.

Table 6-3   *SQLBase Function Summary (Continued)*

Function Type	Functions		Comments
Special	@CHOOSE @DECRYPT @HEX	@CODE @DECODE @LICS	Special functions for SQLBase.
Financial	@CTERM @PMT @RATE @SYD	@FV @PV @SLN @TERM	Financial functions for SQLBase.

A Follow Up Note On SQLBase Functions

SQLBase provides DB2-compatible functions as well as other functions. Functions that are extensions of DB2 and are *not* compatible with DB2 are prefixed with an "at (@)" sign.

In most cases, SQLBase automatically converts the value to the required data type.

In functions that perform arithmetic operations, arguments can be character data types if the value forms a valid numeric value (only digits and standard numeric editing characters).

For date/time functions, an argument can be a character or numeric data type.

6.3   Aggregate Functions

This section covers *aggregate functions* and provides an example of each. An aggregate function computes one summary value from a group of values. Aggregate functions can be applied to the data values of an entire table or to a subset of the rows in a table.

The following are common aggregate functions:

AVG
COUNT
MAX

MEDIAN
MIN
SUM
SDV

Note: The data type of the argument may be numeric, date/time, or character. If an argument is a character data type, the value must form a valid numeric or date/time value (only digits and standard editing characters). SQLBase automatically converts the value to the required data type.

Below is a brief description, diagram, and example of each of the listed aggregate functions.

6.3.1 AVG

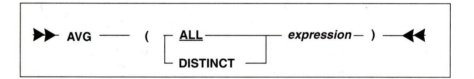

The AVG function returns the average of the values in the argument. The data type of the result is numeric.

The keyword DISTINCT eliminates duplicates. If DISTINCT is not specified, then duplicates are not eliminated.

Null values are ignored.

The example in Figure 6-6 shows a SELECT statement using the AVG function.

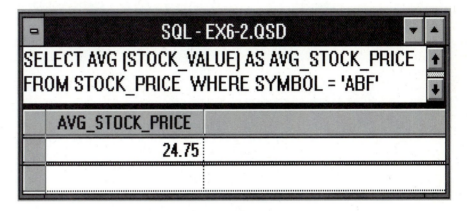

Figure 6-6   *Select with AVG Function*

6.3.2   COUNT

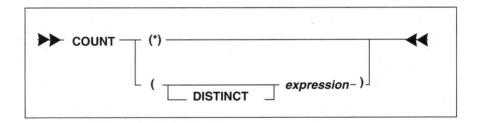

The COUNT function returns a count of items.

COUNT(*) always returns the number of rows in the table. Rows that contain null values are included in the count.

COUNT(column-name) returns the number of column values. An example of COUNT() is shown in Figure 6-7.

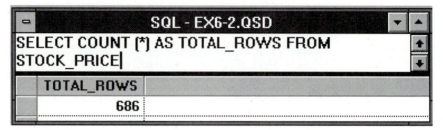

Figure 6-7   *SELECT with COUNT() Function*

COUNT(DISTINCT column-name) filters out duplicate column values. Another example is shown in Figure 6-8. The keyword DISTINCT eliminates duplicates. If DISTINCT is not specified, then duplicates are not eliminated.

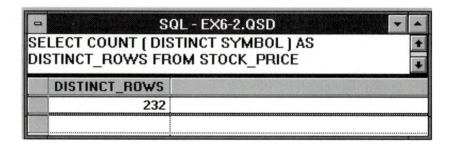

Figure 6-8   *SELECT with COUNT and DISTINCT keyword*

6.3.3 MAX

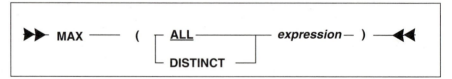

The MAX function returns the maximum value in the argument, which is a set of column values. The data type of the result is the same as the input argument. Figure 6-9 shows an example.

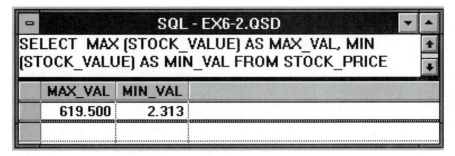

Figure 6-9   *SELECT with MAX Function*

The keyword DISTINCT eliminates duplicates. If DISTINCT is not specified, then duplicates are not eliminated.

Null values are ignored.

6.3.4   MEDIAN

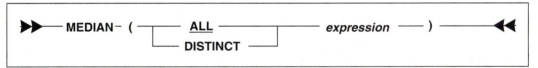

The MEDIAN function returns the middle value in a set of values. An equal number of values lie above and below the middle value.

@MEDIAN finds the middle value with this formula:

$(n + 1) / 2$

For example, if there are five items, then the middle item is the third:

$(5 + 1) / 2 = 6 / 2 = 3$

For example, if there are six items, then the middle item is between the third and the fourth:

$(6 + 1) / 2 = 7 / 2 = 3.5$

The median is the arithmetic average of the third and fourth values as shown in Figure 6-10.

The keyword DISTINCT eliminates duplicates. If DISTINCT is not specified, then duplicates are not eliminated. Be cautious when using DISTINCT, because the result may lose its statistical meaning.

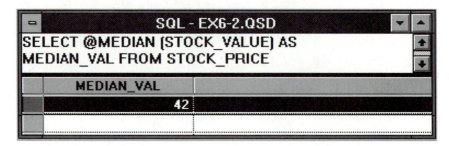

Figure 6-10 *SELECT with MEDIAN Function*

The result of our query is 42, which, as everyone knows, is the answer to everything according to the *Hitchhiker's Guide to the Galaxy*.

Null values are ignored.

6.3.5   MIN

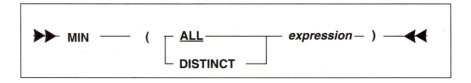

The MIN function returns the minimum value in the argument, which is a set of column values. The data type of the result is the same as the input argument.

An example of using the MIN function was shown in Figure 6-9.

The keyword DISTINCT eliminates duplicates. If DISTINCT is not specified, then duplicates are not eliminated.

Null values are ignored.

6.3.6 SUM

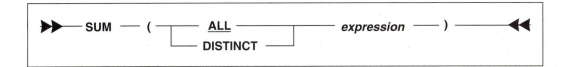

The SUM function returns the sum of the values in the argument, which is a set of column values. The data type of the result is the same as the input argument.

Figure 6-11 shows an example of using SUM.

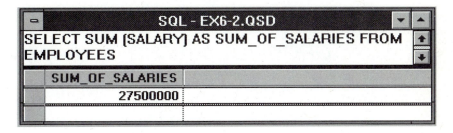

Figure 6-11   *SELECT with SUM Function*

The keyword DISTINCT eliminates duplicates. If DISTINCT is not specified, then duplicates are not eliminated.

Null values are ignored.

6.3.7 SDV

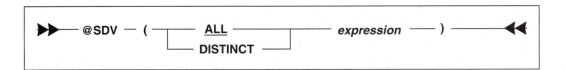

The SDV function computes the standard deviation for the set of values specified by the argument. Figure 6-12 shows an example of using the SDV function.

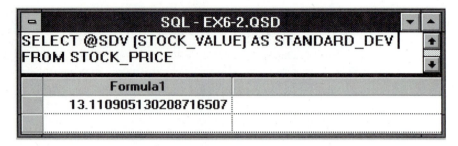

Figure 6-12   *SELECT with SDV Function*

The keyword DISTINCT eliminates duplicates. If DISTINCT is not specified, then duplicates are not eliminated.

Note that this function, for SQLBase, produces double precision, which is not the same as an integer value.

6.4   *GROUP BY, HAVING, and Aggregate Functions*

6.4.1   *GROUP BY and Aggregate Functions*

The GROUP BY clause groups the result rows of the query in sets, according to the columns named in the clause. Columns not listed in the GROUP BY clause should be aggregate functions.

In Figure 6-13, the *stock_value* rows are being "grouped" by the stock symbol name. A MAX function is being performed on *stock_value*.

```
SQL - EX6-3.QSD
SELECT SYMBOL, MAX [STOCK_VALUE] AS MAX_VALUE
FROM STOCK_PRICE GROUP BY SYMBOL
```

SYMBOL	MAX_VALUE
AAPL	59.750
ABF	35.125
ABS	50.500
ACCOB	16.750

Figure 6-13   *SELECT with GROUP BY Function (1)*

The GROUP BY clause cannot be applied to aggregate functions, since aggregates yield one value. Had we tried:

SELECT SYMBOL, MAX (STOCK_VALUE) AS MAX_VALUE
FROM STOCK_PRICE GROUP BY STOCK_VALUE

an error would be generated.

Another example of GROUP BY is shown in Figure 6-14.

```
┌─────────────────────────────────────────────────────────────┐
│ ─              SQL - EX6-3.QSD                        ▼ ▲    │
│ SELECT SYMBOL, MIN (STOCK_VALUE) AS MINIMUM  , MAX(STOCK_VALUE)  ✦ │
│ AS MAXIMUM FROM STOCK_PRICE WHERE SYMBOL LIKE 'A%'           │
│ GROUP BY SYMBOL ORDER BY SYMBOL                           ✦  │
├──────────┬─────────┬─────────┬──────────────────────────┬───┤
│  SYMBOL  │ MINIMUM │ MAXIMUM │                          │ ✦ │
├──────────┼─────────┼─────────┼──────────────────────────┤   │
│  AAPL    │  29.250 │  59.750 │                          │   │
│  ABF     │  18.625 │  35.125 │                          │   │
│  ABS     │  26.750 │  50.500 │                          │ ✦ │
└──────────┴─────────┴─────────┴──────────────────────────┴───┘
```

Figure 6-14   *SELECT with GROUP BY Function (2)*

If a GROUP BY clause is specified, then:

- Each column in the select list must be listed in the GROUP BY clause; or

- Each column in the select list must be used in an aggregate set function that yields a single value.

For example, the following command will not work because only one column, the column in the GROUP BY clause, *symbol*, should be listed in the select list:

SELECT SYMBOL, STOCK_VALUE, MIN (STOCK_VALUE)
FROM STOCK_PRICE GROUP BY SYMBOL

The column, *stock_value*, is also listed in the select list, but this is not allowed because all stock_values are being "grouped" by the symbol name and only one value is being returned.

The GROUP BY Clause has the following restriction:

If the column by which a grouping occurs is an expression (but not an aggregate function), you must specify a number that indicates its relative position in the select list. Figure 6-15 demonstrates this.

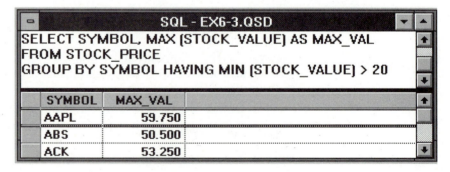

SYMBOL	DOUBLE_IT	AVERAGE
AAPL	58.5	29.250
AAPL	78	39.000
AAPL	119.5	59.750

Figure 6-15   *GROUP BY Restriction*

6.4.2 HAVING Search Condition

The HAVING clause can only be used in conjunction with the GROUP BY clause. The HAVING clause allows a search condition for a group of rows.

The following example returns stock symbols and their respective maximum stock prices where the minimum stock price is greater than 20.

```
SELECT SYMBOL, MAX (STOCK_VALUE) AS MAX_VAL
FROM STOCK_PRICE
GROUP BY SYMBOL HAVING MIN (STOCK_VALUE) > 20
```

SYMBOL	MAX_VAL
AAPL	59.750
ABS	50.500
ACK	53.250

Figure 6-16   *SELECT with HAVING Clause*

The SELECT statement from Figure 6-16 returns one row for each group, provided that the condition specified by the HAVING clause is met.

6.4.3 Expanded SELECT Command Diagram

The command diagram in Figure 6-17 below is a more complete SELECT command diagram than that shown in Chapter 5. The clauses are described below.

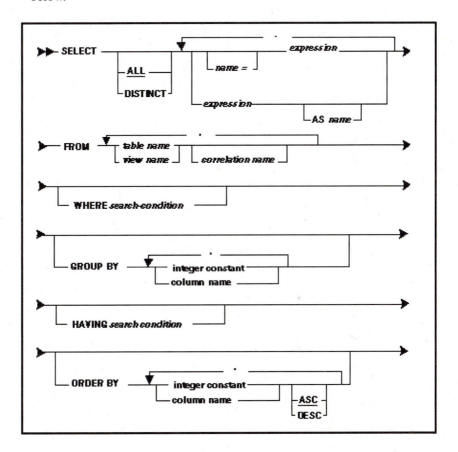

Figure 6-17 *SELECT Command Diagram*

ALL   Retrieves *all* rows; the default for a SELECT.

DISTINCT Suppresses duplicate rows.

      You cannot use the DISTINCT keyword to LONG VARCHAR data types.

expression A select list that contains expressions that are separated by commas. An expression can be a:

- Column name
- Constant
- Bind variable
- Result of a function
- System keyword

name = expression or **name as expression**

Assigns a name that is used as a column heading in the output. For example:

SELECT COMP_NAME = COMPANY_NAME FROM COMP

or:

SELECT COMP_NAME as COMPANY_NAME FROM COMP

FROM Contains the names of the tables or views from which the set of resulting rows is formed. Each name must identify a table or view that exists in the database.

A *correlation name* can be assigned for the table or view immediately preceding the name. Each correlation name in a FROM clause must be unique.

Correlation names are required when a search condition is executed more than once for the same table or view in a single SQL command (as in joining a table to itself or in correlated subqueries, described below). They provide a shorthand way to qualify column names.

In the example below, the SQL command is written using the correlation name C to designate CUSTOMER and O to designate ORDERS.

SELECT C.CUSTNO, ORDERNO FROM CUSTOMER C, ORDERS O WHERE C.CUSTNO = O.CUSTNO

WHERE search condition

WHERE clause specifies a search condition for the base tables or views.

With SQLBase, you cannot use a LONG VARCHAR column in a subselect search condition.

GROUP BY　　Groups the result rows of the query in sets according to the columns named in the clause. The select list can only contain aggregate functions when the GROUP BY clause is used or when the select list consists entirely of aggregate functions.

HAVING　　Allows a search condition for a group of rows resulting from a GROUP BY or grouping columns. If a grouping column is an expression that is *not* an aggregate function (such as SAL*10), it cannot be used in the HAVING clause.

ORDER BY　　Specifies the ordering, or sorting, of rows in a result table. Rows can be sorted on more than one column. The major sort is on the first column specified in the ORDER BY clause, and the minor sorts are on the columns specified after that.

If the sort is on a column derived from a function or arithmetic expression, the column must be specified by an integer that signifies its relative number in the select list of the command.

Each column name (or number) can be optionally followed by ASC or DESC for ascending or descending sort sequence. ASC is the default order.

6.5　Exercises with the SELECT Command

Exercise 6.5.1:　Using SELECT with the ORDER BY Clause

This exercise demonstrates the use of the ORDER BY clause with the SELECT statement.

1.　Open Quest, if it is not already open. Make sure you are connected to the COMPANY database by pulling down the Utilities menu and using the **Add** function if necessary. Click on the COMPANY database.

2. Click on the **Open** button and then on the **SQL** button.

Figure 6-18 *Opening the SQL Activity*

3. Quest prompts for a file. Choose the file c:\sqlbase\exercise\chap6\ex6-1.qsd. Click **OK**.

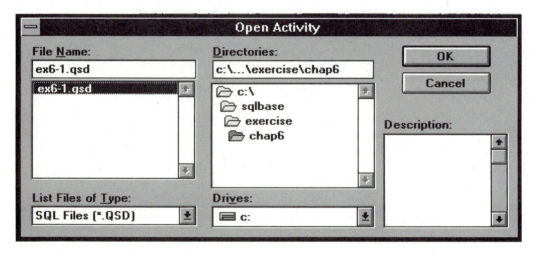

Figure 6-19 *Opening the SQL File*

4. The first SELECT command to be executed is:

   SELECT COMP_NAME,CITY, STATE FROM COMP
   ORDER BY CITY

   Select this SQL statement by clicking in the SQL activity window, pull down the SQL menu, and select **Execute SQL Statement** as shown in Figure 6-20.

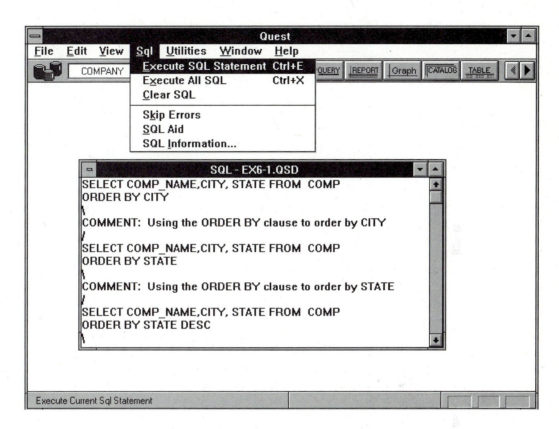

Figure 6-20   *Executing SELECT Statements With ORDER BY*

5.   The next SELECT command we execute uses the ORDER BY clause
     with the *state* column, as follows:

> SELECT COMP_NAME,CITY, STATE FROM COMP
> ORDER BY STATE

Choose this SELECT statement by clicking in the SQL Activity
window. Choose the **Execute SQL Statement** menu option.

6. The next SELECT uses the DESC option with the ORDER BY clause to order states in descending alphabetic order:

   ```
   SELECT COMP_NAME,CITY, STATE FROM COMP
   ORDER BY STATE DESC
   ```

   Choose this SELECT statement by clicking in the SQL Activity window. Choose the **Execute SQL Statement** menu option.

7. The next SELECT uses the ORDER BY clause to order by two columns: *state* and *city*, as follows:

   ```
   SELECT COMP_NAME,CITY, STATE FROM  COMP
   ORDER BY STATE,CITY
   ```

   Choose this SELECT statement by clicking in the SQL Activity window. Choose the **Execute SQL Statement** menu option.

8. The next SELECT uses the ORDER BY clause with an integer value representing the position of an expression in a select list. In this case, the expression is STOCK_VALUE*2, which cannot directly be used in an ORDER BY clause. The statement is:

   ```
   SELECT SYMBOL, STOCK_VALUE*2 FROM
   STOCK_PRICE ORDER BY 2
   ```

   Choose this SELECT statement by clicking in the SQL Activity window. Choose the **Execute SQL Statement** menu option.

9. To close, choose the **Close** option from the File menu.

Exercise 6.5.2: Using SELECT with Aggregate Functions

In this example, you will use aggregate functions.

1. Click on the **Open** button and then on the **SQL** button.

2. Quest prompts for a file. Choose the file c:\sqlbase\exercise\chap6\ex6-2.qsd. Click **OK**.

3. The first SELECT Command (time) to be executed is:

   ```
   SELECT SYMBOL, @DATEVALUE (STOCK_DATE),
   STOCK_VALUE AS STOCK_DATE FROM STOCK_PRICE
   ```

Choose this SQL statement by clicking in the SQL activity window, pull down the SQL menu, and select **Execute SQL Statement**.

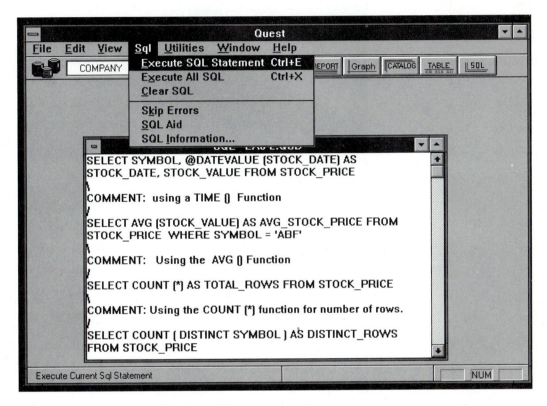

Figure 6-21 *Executing SELECT With Aggregate Functions*

4.   The next SELECT uses the AVG aggregate function to determine the average stock price for the stock, 'AAPL':

> SELECT AVG (STOCK_VALUE) AS AVG_STOCK_PRICE
> FROM STOCK_PRICE WHERE SYMBOL = 'ABF'

Choose this SELECT statement by clicking in the SQL Activity window. Choose the **Execute SQL Statement** menu option.

5. The next SELECT uses the COUNT () aggregate function to determine the number of rows in the STOCK_PRICE table:

    SELECT COUNT (*) AS TOTAL_ROWS FROM
    STOCK_PRICE

    Choose this SELECT statement by clicking in the SQL Activity window. Choose the **Execute SQL Statement** menu option.

6. The next SELECT uses the COUNT () aggregate function with the DISTINCT clause to determine the number of distinct tables in the STOCK_PRICE table:

    SELECT COUNT (DISTINCT SYMBOL) AS
    DISTINCT_ROWS FROM STOCK_PRICE

    Choose this SELECT statement by clicking in the SQL Activity window. Choose the **Execute SQL Statement** menu option.

7. The next SELECT uses the MAX () aggregate function and MIN() aggregate function to determine the maximum and minimum values of the stock symbol, 'FRD':

    SELECT MAX (STOCK_VALUE) AS MAX_VAL,
    MIN (STOCK_VALUE) AS MIN_VAL FROM STOCK_PRICE
    WHERE SYMBOL = 'FRD'

    Choose this SELECT statement by clicking in the SQL Activity window. Choose the **Execute SQL Statement** menu option.

8. The next SELECT uses the MEDIAN () aggregate function to determine the median value of the stocks in STOCK_PRICE:

    SELECT @MEDIAN (STOCK_VALUE) AS MEDIAN_VAL
    FROM STOCK_PRICE

    Choose this SELECT statement by clicking in the SQL Activity window. Choose the **Execute SQL Statement** menu option.

9. The next SELECT uses the SUM () aggregate function to determine the sum of the salaries in the EMPLOYEES table:

    SELECT SUM (SALARY) AS TOTAL_SAL FROM
    EMPLOYEES

    Choose this SELECT statement by clicking in the SQL Activity window. Choose the **Execute SQL Statement** menu option.

10. The next SELECT uses the SDV () aggregate function to determine the standard deviation of the stock values in the table STOCK_PRICE:

    SELECT @SDV (STOCK_VALUE) AS STANDARD_DEV
    FROM STOCK_PRICE WHERE SYMBOL = 'ABS'

    Choose this SELECT statement by clicking in the SQL Activity window. Choose the **Execute SQL Statement** menu option.

11. To close, choose the **Close** option from the File menu.

Exercise 6.5.3:   Using SELECT with GROUP BY and HAVING Clauses

In this example, you will use the GROUP BY and HAVING clauses with SELECT statements.

1. Click on the **Open** button and then on the **SQL** button.

2. Quest prompts for a file. Choose the file c:\sqlbase\exercise\chap6\ex6-3.qsd. Click **OK**.

3. The first SELECT command to be executed is:

    SELECT SYMBOL, MAX (STOCK_VALUE) AS MAX_VAL
    FROM STOCK_PRICE GROUP BY SYMBOL

    Select this SQL statement by clicking in the SQL activity window, pull down the SQL menu, and select **Execute SQL Statement**.

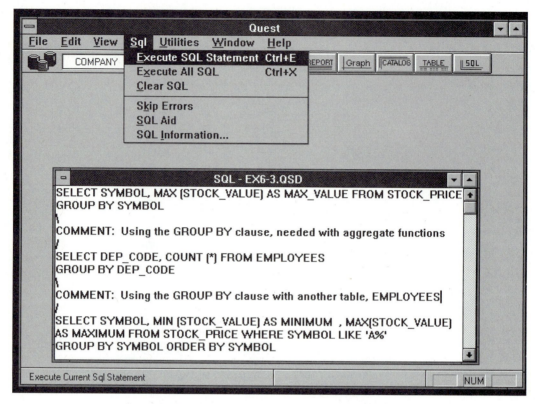

Figure 6-22 *Executing SELECT with GROUP BY and HAVING*

4. The next SELECT command demonstrates the GROUP BY clause used to total the number of employees by department. The Count () function is used for this.

```
SELECT DEP_CODE, COUNT (*) FROM EMPLOYEES
GROUP BY DEP_CODE
```

Choose this SELECT statement by clicking in the SQL Activity window. Choose the **Execute SQL Statement** menu option as shown in Figure 6-22.

5. The next SELECT command demonstrates a more complex SELECT statement, using a GROUP BY and an ORDER BY clause.

```
SELECT SYMBOL, MIN (STOCK_VALUE) AS MINIMUM,
MAX(STOCK_VALUE) AS MAXIMUM FROM
STOCK_PRICE WHERE SYMBOL LIKE 'A%'
GROUP BY SYMBOL ORDER BY SYMBOL
```

Choose this SELECT statement by clicking in the SQL Activity window. Choose the **Execute SQL Statement** menu option.

6. The next SELECT command demonstrates the use of an expression, STOCK_VALUE*2, in a select list. In this case, an integer, representing the position of the expression in the select list, is used in the GROUP BY clause.

```
SELECT  SYMBOL, STOCK_VALUE*2 AS DOUBLE_IT,
MIN (STOCK_VALUE) AS MINIMUM FROM STOCK_PRICE
GROUP BY  SYMBOL, 2
```

Choose this SELECT statement by clicking in the SQL Activity window. Choose the **Execute SQL Statement** menu option.

7. The next SELECT command demonstrates an expression, where a string, '_SYMBOL' is concatenated to the value of the SYMBOL column. Again, an integer value is required in the GROUP BY clause.

```
SELECT  SYMBOL || '_SYMBOL',   MIN (STOCK_VALUE)
AS AVERAGE  FROM STOCK_PRICE
GROUP BY  1
```

Choose this SELECT statement by clicking in the SQL Activity window. Choose the **Execute SQL Statement** menu option.

8. The next SELECT command demonstrates the use of the HAVING clause with the GROUP BY clause to limit the stock values we will look at.

```
SELECT SYMBOL, MAX (STOCK_VALUE) FROM
STOCK_PRICE GROUP BY SYMBOL
HAVING MIN (STOCK_VALUE) > 20
```

9. Choose this SELECT statement by clicking in the SQL Activity window. Choose the **Execute SQL Statement** menu option.

10. To close, choose the **Close** option from the File menu.

6.6 Summary

This chapter covered the basics of the ORDER BY, GROUP BY, and HAVING clauses of the SELECT statement. Functions and, in particular, aggregate functions were introduced as a way to extend what SQL can do by deriving new information from the data that is stored in tables. A more complete command diagram of a SELECT statement was also provided.

In the next chapter, the concepts of unions and joins are discussed to further add to your understanding of the SELECT statement. The clauses learned so far in conjunction with unions and joins shed light on the real power behind SELECT statements and the usefulness of SQL.

7   Joins and Unions

The chapter is organized as follows:

Section 7.1 Joins
Section 7.2 Unions
Section 7.3 Exercises with SELECT and Joins and Unions
Section 7.4 Summary

7.1   Joins

A *join* pulls data from different tables and compares it by matching on a common row that is in all the tables.

An example of a join can be illustrated with the COMPANY database. A company like American Express may have many locations of business in many states. If you wanted to query our database to return a list, by company name, of all the locations of a corporation, you would need to perform a join.

The example in Figure 7-3 joins two tables, COMP and LOCATIONS.

The table, COMP, Figure 7-1, looks like this:

COMP_ID	COMP_NAME	CORP_ADDR	CITY	STATE
6	AMERICAN HOME PRO	FIVE GIRALDA FARMS	MADISON	NJ
7	AMERITECH CORP	30 SOUTH WACKER D	CHICAGO	IL
8	AMERICAN PRESIDEN	1111 BROADWAY	OAKLAND	CA
9	AMERICAN STORES CO	709 EAST SOUTH TEM	SALT LAKE CITY	UT
10	AMERICAN EXPRESS C	AMERICAN EXPRESS T	NEW YORK	NY
11	AMOCO CORP	200 EAST RANDOLPH	CHICAGO	IL
12	ANHEUSER BUSCH CO	ONE BUSCH PLACE	ST LOUIS	MO
13	APPLE COMPUTER INC	20525 MARIANI AVENU	CUPERTINO	CA
14	ARCHER DANIELS MID	4666 FARIES PARKWA	DECATUR	IL

Figure 7-1   *COMP Table (for Joining)*

The primary key for the COMP table, *comp_id*, is a value that has a match in the other table we will join to it, LOCATIONS. Figure 7-2 shows the table LOCATIONS.

COMP_ID	LOCAT_ID	ADDR	CITY	STATE	ZIP
6	1	FIVE GIRALDA FARMS	MADISON	NJ	07940
6	2	685 3RD AVE	NEW YORK	NY	10017
7	1	30 SOUTH WACKER D	CHICAGO	IL	60606-7402
7	2	2000 W AMERITECH C	SCHAUMBURG	IL	60196
7	3	4650 NORTHGATE BLV	SACRAMENTO	CA	95834
8	1	1111 BROADWAY	OAKLAND	CA	94607-5500
8	2	1101 17TH ST NW	WASHINGTON	DC	20036
9	1	709 EAST SOUTH TEM	SALT LAKE CITY	UT	84102-1208

Figure 7-2   *LOCATIONS Table (for Joining)*

Figure 7-3 shows the results of a join on these two tables.

SQL - EX7-1.QSD			
SELECT COMP_NAME, LOCAT_ID, LOCATIONS.CITY, LOCATIONS.STATE FROM LOCATIONS, COMP WHERE COMP.COMP_ID = LOCATIONS.COMP_ID			
COMP_NAME	LOCAT_ID	LOCATIONS.CITY	LOCATIONS.STATE
AMERICAN BRANDS INC	1	OLD GREENWICH	CT
AMERICAN BRANDS INC	2	NEW HYDE PARK	NY
AMERICAN BRANDS INC	3	HICKORY	NC
AMERICAN HOME PRODUCTS CORP	1	MADISON	NJ
AMERICAN HOME PRODUCTS CORP	2	NEW YORK	NY
AMERITECH CORP	1	CHICAGO	IL
AMERITECH CORP	2	SCHAUMBURG	IL
AMERITECH CORP	3	SACRAMENTO	CA
AMERICAN PRESIDENT COS LTD	1	OAKLAND	CA

Figure 7-3   *COMP and LOCATION Tables Joined*

Several things should be said about this join. First, both tables, COMP and LOCATIONS, were explicitly mentioned in the FROM clause. Second, you will notice that both tables have fields, *city* and *state*. In this case, doing a SELECT on the *city* or *state* columns is ambiguous; therefore, the columns have been identified by adding the specific table name of the table from which we will get information. In this case, we specified LOCATIONS.*city* and LOCATIONS.*state*. If we had specified COMP.*city* and COMP.*state*, the result would be different, as we demonstrate in the following exercises.

The previous example of a join returned a scrollable list of all companies and the locations. If we wanted just the locations of American Express, then we could perform the join shown in Figure 7-4.

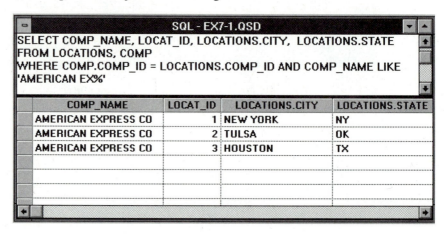

	COMP_NAME	LOCAT_ID	LOCATIONS.CITY	LOCATIONS.STATE
	AMERICAN EXPRESS CO	1	NEW YORK	NY
	AMERICAN EXPRESS CO	2	TULSA	OK
	AMERICAN EXPRESS CO	3	HOUSTON	TX

Figure 7-4   *Join for LOCATIONS Only*

In this example, we did not know if the company name was American Express or American Express Company, or American Express Inc. or some other variation, so we use the LIKE operator and the % operator.

Beware the Cartesian Product

A Cartesian product is the set of all possible rows resulting from a join of more than one table. For example, suppose we specified the previous query as shown in Figure 7-5.

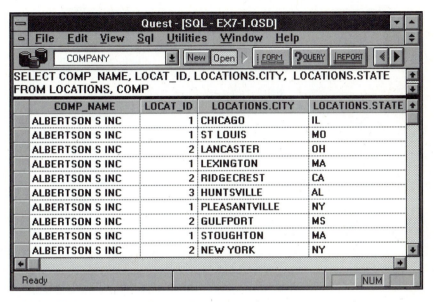

Figure 7-5 *Cartesian Product Example*

The result would be the product of the number of rows in the COMP table and the number of rows in the LOCATIONS table. COMP has 251 rows, and LOCATIONS has 475 rows, so the Cartesian product would be every possible combination, or 119,225 rows, which is probably not the desired result.

Using a WHERE clause to limit the join is almost always required.

7.1.1 Types of Joins

There are many ways to perform joins. Not all vendors perform joins in quite the same manner. Here are some of the more common types of joins:

- Equijoins
- Outer joins
- Self-joins
- Non-equijoins

7.1.2 Equijoin

The type of search condition that specifies a relationship between two tables based on an *equality* is called an **equijoin**. Figure 7-3 illustrated an equijoin on the tables COMP and LOCATIONS. This SQL statement is shown below:

```
SELECT COMP_NAME, LOCAT_ID, LOCATIONS.CITY,
LOCATIONS.CITY FROM LOCATIONS, CITY
WHERE COMP.COMP_ID = LOCATIONS.COMP_ID
```

Each result row contains the company name, location ID, and city and state of that location. If company number 1 has three locations listed, then three rows would result. The single row containing the company's name and the information from the LOCATIONS table would be joined to each of the three location rows.

The LOCATIONS rows are related to the COMPANY by use of the key column, *comp_id*, which appears in both tables.

7.1.3 Outer Join

In the previous example of the equijoin, the search condition specified a join on companies and locations. What happens if company exists in the COMP table, but no locations for that company have been entered? The example in Figure 7-6 shows what would happen.

Figure 7-6 *Outer Join Example*

In this case Zenith, with *comp_id* 252, exists, but there is no location entered for it in the LOCATIONS table. To see Zenith, an *outer join* is necessary.

An *outer join* produces a result that joins each row of one table with either a matching row or a null row of another table. The result includes *all* the rows of one table, regardless of whether they have a match with any of the rows of the table to which they are being joined.

Outer Join Semantics

In the WHERE clause, add a plus sign (+) to the join column of the table that might *not* have rows to satisfy the join condition.

The relational engine used in this book supports an outer join on only one table per SELECT statement, and it must be a *one-way* outer join. You cannot add the plus sign (+) to both sides of the join condition. You can, however, specify an outer join on more than one column of the same table, as in Figure 7-7.

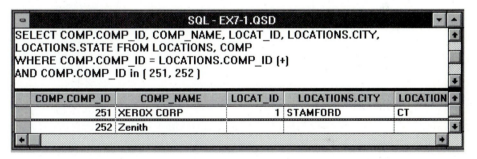

Figure 7-7 *Specifying Outer Join*

When the plus sign (+) after LOCATIONS.COMP_ID is used, an extra row containing all null values is added to the LOCATIONS table. Then, this null row is joined to rows in the COMPANY table that do not have matching orders. Therefore, all company numbers are retrieved.

Oracle Outer Join

Oracle performs outer joins a little differently. In the case of Oracle, the interpretation of null values is slightly different, as shown in Figure 7-8.

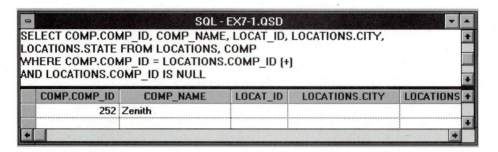

Figure 7-8   *Oracle Outer Join*

In Figure 7-8, an Oracle outer join returns only one row, for Zenith. The ANSI style shows all the rows.

7.1.4 Self-Join

A **self-join** lets you join a table to itself, as if it was two separate tables. A self-join can provide information about relationships between elements in a single table.

To treat a table as if it were two separate tables, the self-join table is given a *correlation name*. A correlation name, or alias, is a way of referencing a table by another name. It can be useful when you have a long table name and do not want to type it out.

The self-join, in Figure 7-9, starts out with:

```
SELECT A.COMP_NAME, B.COMP_NAME, A.ZIP
FROM COMP A, COMP B
```

We used the names A and B as correlation names for the table COMP so columns can be referenced by the likes of A.COMP_NAME or B.COMP_NAME instead of COMP.COMP_NAME.

The example in Figure 7-9 uses a self-join to find all pairs of companies with the same zip code.

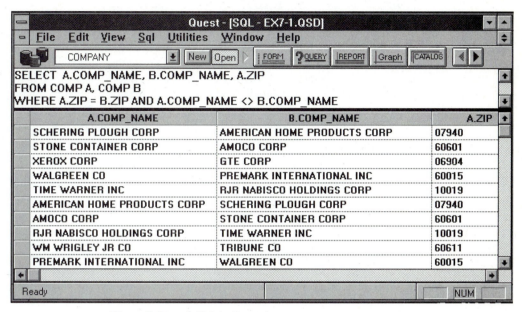

Figure 7-9   *Self-Join Example*

The COMP table is treated as two tables, using the *correlation*, or *alias* names, A and B. The company name is retrieved from correlation table A and is used as a search condition for table B.

This same information can be retrieved by means of a subquery, as shown later in the chapter.

7.1.5   Non-equijoins

A non-equijoin joins tables to one another based on comparisons other than equality. Any of the relational operators can be used (such as >, <, !=, BETWEEN, or LIKE). Figure 7-4 illustrated an non-equijoin on the tables COMP and LOCATIONS. The SQL statement in Figure 7-4 is shown below, using the LIKE operator.

```
SELECT COMP_NAME, LOCAT_ID, LOCATIONS.CITY,
LOCATIONS.CITY FROM LOCATIONS, CITY
WHERE COMP.COMP_ID = LOCATIONS.COMP_ID
AND COMP_NAME LIKE 'American EX%'
```

7.1.6 Number of Joins and Performance

Joins are often the root of performance problems. As you increase the number of joins, you increase the complexity of a query and sacrifice performance. With each table added in a join, the time needed to process the statement increases. Having many tables in a join can slow database performance considerably. In Chapter 19, data warehousing and parallel query vendors are discussed. In large part, products, such as Oracle's Parallel Query™, provide a way to dramatically speed up the performance of queries where many joins are required, but they are higher-end products.

The relational engine in this book, SQLBase, allows you to join 10 tables in a SELECT statement. Since this engine is targeted at PCs, creating more joins is often not feasible. Chapter 9 introduces views, which can be a way to decrease dependency on the use of joins, although more disk space is required.

A carefully designed database model should cut down on the need to join many tables in a statement, although in some decision-support applications, there is no getting around it.

7.2   Unions

The Union operator combines the results of two SELECT statements into a single result. The single result is all the returned records from both SELECT statements. By default, duplicate records are not returned. To return duplicate records, use the ALL keyword (UNION ALL). The form is

```
SELECT statement
UNION [ALL]
SELECT statement
```

Each result table must have the same number of columns. When the Union operator is used, the select lists for each SELECT statement must have the same number of column expressions with the same data types and must be specified in the same order.

An example of a union is shown in Figure 7-10.

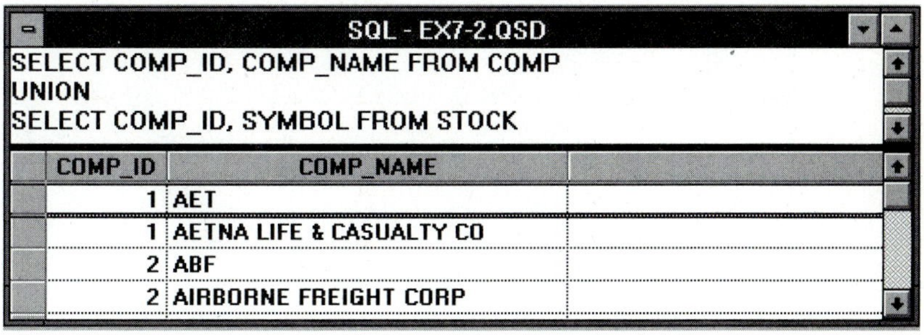

```
                    SQL - EX7-2.QSD
SELECT COMP_ID, COMP_NAME FROM COMP
UNION
SELECT COMP_ID, SYMBOL FROM STOCK
```

COMP_ID	COMP_NAME	
1	AET	
1	AETNA LIFE & CASUALTY CO	
2	ABF	
2	AIRBORNE FREIGHT CORP	

Figure 7-10   *Union Example*

This example has the same number of column expressions, and the data types match.

Restrictions on Unions

Figure 7-10 illustrates the problems of data type mismatching. While the columns *comp_name* and *symbol* are both of type VARCHAR, the first is VARCHAR (40) and the second is VARCHAR (8). This example works only because VARCHAR (40) is assumed to be the data type. (SQLBase assumes this because the column *comp_name* is referenced first.)

Now try the same UNION statement, but flip the lines, as shown below.

```
SELECT COMP_ID, SYMBOL FROM STOCK
UNION
SELECT COMP_ID, COMP_NAME FROM COMP
```

The example is not valid because the lengths of SYMBOL and COMP_NAME are different. The field is assumed to be VARCHAR (8) this time instead of VARCHAR (40) because SYMBOL is referenced first.

You will get an error, as shown in Figure 7-11.

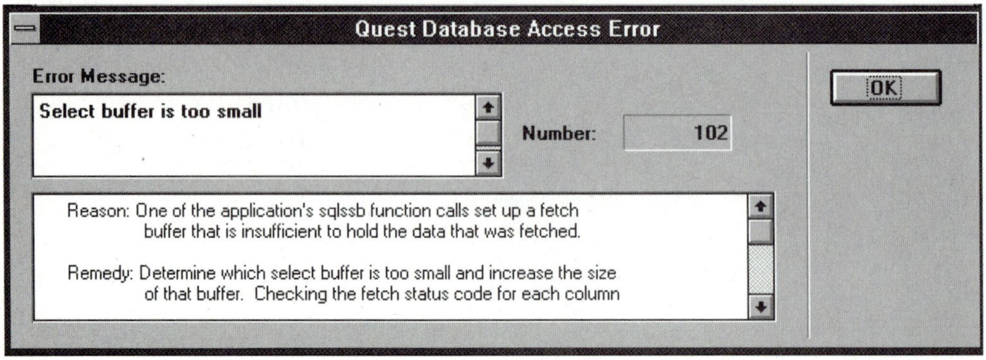

Figure 7-11 *Error from Invalid Union*

Another restriction with SQLBase for unions is that none of the columns used can be LONG VARCHAR columns.

Unions on a Single Table

Unions can be performed on a single table. For example, suppose you wanted to ask the following question:

What are the names and zip codes of companies that are located in the state of Washington or have a company ID greater than 140?

One way to answer this question is to execute this SELECT statement:

```
SELECT COMP_NAME, ZIP FROM COMP
WHERE STATE = 'WA' OR COMP_ID > 140
```

Unions can be used to perform the same result, as shown in Figure 7-12.

```
┌──────────────────── SQL - EX7-2.QSD ────────────────┬─┬─┐
│ SELECT COMP_NAME, ZIP FROM COMP WHERE STATE = 'WA'   │▼│▲│
│ UNION                                                │ │ │
│ SELECT COMP_NAME, ZIP FROM COMP WHERE COMP_ID > 140  │ │▼│
├──────────────────────────┬──────────────┬───────────┼─┤
│       COMP_NAME          │     ZIP      │           │▲│
├──────────────────────────┼──────────────┼───────────┤ │
│ AIRBORNE FREIGHT CORP    │ 98111        │           │ │
│ BOEING CO                │ 98108-4002   │           │ │
│ CHARLES SCHWAB CORP      │              │           │ │
│ MCDONALD S CORP          │ 60521        │           │ │
│ MCDONNELL DOUGLAS CORP   │ 63166-0516   │           │ │
│ MCGRAW HILL INC          │ 10020-1001   │           │ │
│ MCI COMMUNICATIONS CORP  │ 20006        │           │ │
│ MCKESSON CORP            │ 94104-5296   │           │▼│
└──────────────────────────┴──────────────┴───────────┴─┘
```

Figure 7-12   *Union on a Single Table*

Why Use Unions?

Unions can bring together similar data from one or many tables. Often similar types of data will be stored in different fields and it may be useful to bring this information together.

In Chapter 5, we created a table called MOVIES. This table was designed poorly, in that there were two fields into which a lead actor could be entered: *lead1* and *lead2*. We can use a UNION clause to put all the actors names into one field, as shown in Figure 7-13.

```
┌──────────────────── SQL - EX7-2.QSD ────────────────┬─┬─┐
│ SELECT LEAD1, title FROM MOVIES                      │▼│▲│
│ UNION                                                │ │ │
│ SELECT LEAD2, title FROM MOVIES                      │ │▼│
├──────────────────┬──────────────────────┬───────────┼─┤
│      LEAD1       │         title        │           │▲│
├──────────────────┼──────────────────────┼───────────┤ │
│                  │ Chitty Chitty Bang Bang          │ │
│ Adrian Zmed      │ Bachelor Party       │           │ │
│ Alan Arkin       │ Catch 22             │           │ │
│ Ann-Margret      │ Bye Bye Birdie       │           │▼│
└──────────────────┴──────────────────────┴───────────┴─┘
```

Figure 7-13   *Union Clause for Collating Data*

7.2.1 The *UNION Clause*

Figure 7-14 diagrams the UNION clause. Its clauses are described below.

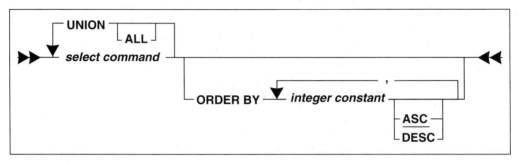

Figure 7-14   *Union Clause Diagram*

ALL   Specifies that duplicate rows will not be eliminated. The result contains all the rows selected. If ALL is used, it must be repeated for every SELECT command.

ORDER BY   Sorts the final result set of rows from the UNION of two (or more) tables. When you use an ORDER BY clause with a union, you must use an integer specifying the sequence number of the column in the select list.

7.3   *Exercises with SELECT and Joins and Unions*

Exercise 7.3.1:   *Using Joins and SELECT*

This exercise performs joins between two or more tables.

1. Open Quest, if it is not already open. Make sure you are connected to the COMPANY database by pulling down the **Utilities** menu and using the **Add** function if necessary. Click on the COMPANY database.

2. Click on the **Open** button and then on the **SQL** button.

Figure 7-15   *Opening the SQL Activity*

3. Quest prompts for a file. Choose the file c:\sqlbase\exercise\chap7\ex7-1.qsd as shown in Figure 7-16. Click **OK.**

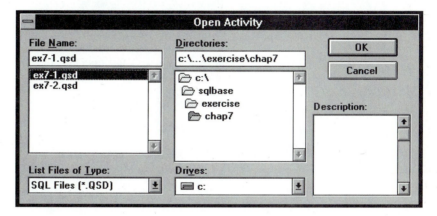

Figure 7-16   *Opening the SQL File*

4. The first SELECT command to be executed is:

> SELECT COMP_NAME, LOCAT_ID,CITY, STATE FROM
> LOCATIONS, COMP
> WHERE COMP.COMP_ID = LOCATIONS.COMP_ID

The first statement will not work because the columns, *city* and *state*, are not referenced with full names and both tables have these columns.

Choose this SQL statement by clicking in the SQL activity window, pull down the SQL menu, and select **Execute SQL Statement** as shown in Figure 7-17.

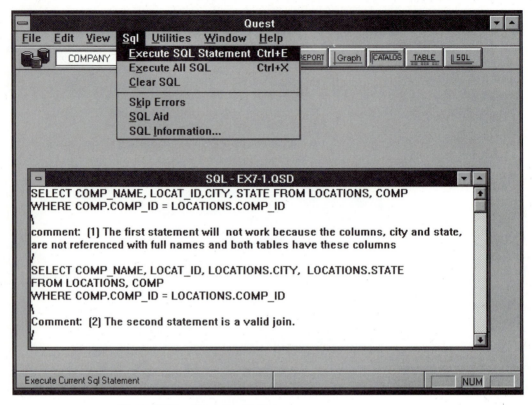

Figure 7-17   *Executing Unions*

5.   The next SELECT command correctly references column names that are used in more than one table.

> SELECT COMP_NAME, LOCAT_ID, LOCATIONS.CITY,
> LOCATIONS.STATE FROM LOCATIONS, COMP
> WHERE COMP.COMP_ID = LOCATIONS.COMP_ID

Choose this SELECT statement by clicking in the SQL Activity window. Choose the **Execute SQL Statement** menu option.

6. The next SELECT command is another join that is more specific in its query.

   ```
   SELECT COMP_NAME, LOCAT_ID, LOCATIONS.CITY,
   LOCATIONS.STATE
   FROM LOCATIONS, COMP
   WHERE COMP.COMP_ID = LOCATIONS.COMP_ID AND
   COMP_NAME LIKE 'AMERICAN EX%'
   ```

   Choose this SELECT statement by clicking in the SQL Activity window. Choose the **Execute SQL Statement** menu option.

7. The next SELECT command creates a Cartesian product, as shown in Figure 7-6. In this case, you will get 119,225 rows.

   ```
   SELECT COMP_NAME, LOCAT_ID, LOCATIONS.CITY,
   LOCATIONS.STATE
   FROM LOCATIONS, COMP
   ```

   Choose this SELECT statement by clicking in the SQL Activity window. Choose the **Execute SQL Statement** menu option.

8. The next SELECT command demonstrates a self-equijoin.

   ```
   SELECT A.COMP_NAME, B.COMP_NAME, A.ZIP
   FROM COMP A, COMP B
   WHERE A.ZIP = B.ZIP AND A.COMP_NAME <>
   B.COMP_NAME
   ```

   Choose this SELECT statement by clicking in the SQL Activity window. Choose the **Execute SQL Statement** menu option.

9. The next SELECT command demonstrates an outer join.

   ```
   SELECT COMP.COMP_ID, COMP_NAME, LOCAT_ID,
   LOCATIONS.CITY, LOCATIONS.STATE
   FROM LOCATIONS, COMP
   WHERE COMP.COMP_ID = LOCATIONS.COMP_ID (+)
   AND COMP.COMP_ID in (251, 252)
   ```

   Choose this SELECT statement by clicking in the SQL Activity window. Choose the **Execute SQL Statement** menu option.

10. The next SELECT command is used to demonstrate the difference in Oracle-style outer joins and ANSI style.

   SELECT COMP.COMP_ID, COMP_NAME, LOCAT_ID,
   LOCATIONS.CITY, LOCATIONS.STATE FROM LOCATIONS,
   COMP
   WHERE COMP.COMP_ID = LOCATIONS.COMP_ID (+)
   AND LOCATIONS.COMP_ID IS NULL

11. Choose this SELECT statement by clicking in the SQL Activity window. Choose the **Execute SQL Statement** menu option.

12. To close, choose the **Close** option from the File menu.

Exercise 7.3.2: Using Unions and SELECT

1. Click on the **Open** button and then on the **SQL** button.

2. Quest prompts for a file. Choose the file c:\sqlbase\exercise\chap7\ex7-2.qsd. Click **OK.**

3. The first union is:

   SELECT COMP_ID, COMP_NAME FROM COMP
   UNION
   SELECT COMP_ID, SYMBOL FROM STOCK

   Select this SQL statement by clicking in the SQL activity window, pull down the SQL menu, and select **Execute SQL Statement** as shown in Figure 7-18.

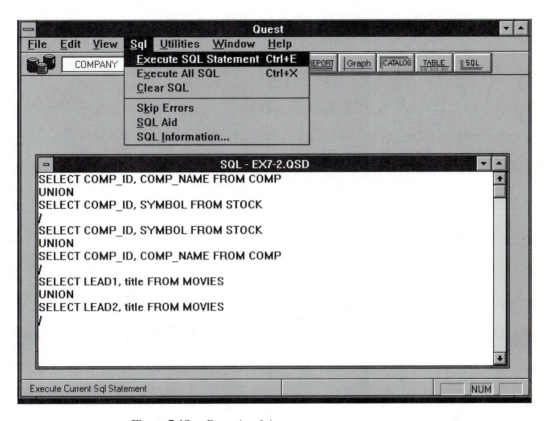

Figure 7-18   *Executing Joins*

4. The next UNION command will generate an error, as discussed in Section 7.2, because *symbol* and *comp_name* are not the same length and the shorter column is chosen for the result table length.

```
SELECT COMP_ID, SYMBOL FROM STOCK
UNION
SELECT COMP_ID, COMP_NAME FROM COMP
```

Choose this UNION statement by clicking in the SQL Activity window. Choose the **Execute SQL Statement** menu option. An error will occur.

5. The next UNION is:

```
SELECT LEAD1, TITLE FROM MOVIES
UNION
SELECT LEAD2, TITLE FROM MOVIES
```

Choose this UNION statement by clicking in the SQL Activity window. Choose the **Execute SQL Statement** menu option.

6. The next UNION is:

```
SELECT COMP_NAME, ZIP FROM COMP
WHERE STATE = 'WA'
UNION
SELECT COMP_NAME, ZIP FROM COMP WHERE
COMP_ID > 140
```

Choose this UNION statement by clicking in the SQL Activity window. Choose the **Execute SQL Statement** menu option.

7. To close, choose the **Close** option from the File menu.

7.4 Summary

This chapter has covered the use of *joins* and *unions* with SELECT statements. There is much more to learn in the use of joins and unions, but this chapter illustrates the power of the SQL language. When joins are used with the other clauses we have learned, we have the ability to answer very complicated questions.

Joins are central to decision-support systems. In order to answer business questions of today's RDBMS systems, many joins can be required. This leads to some interesting issues, because the more joins used, the more performance falls off. A specialized area of SQL users, who need to answer complex queries requiring scores of joins between tables, use technology today referred to as *Executive Information Systems* (EIS) and *data warehousing.* These technologies are discussed in Chapters 17 and 19, respectively.

8   Complex Queries and Performance

This chapter covers two subjects: the use of subqueries with SELECT statements and performance considerations.

The chapter is organized as follows:

8.1   Subqueries

SQL allows you to nest SELECT statements within other SELECT statements. Nested queries, or *subqueries*, can be used to create search conditions when information needed to create a query is not yet known.

Suppose you wanted to know the employees with the same title as an employee, John Considine. If we do not know specifically what title John Considine has, we can build a subquery to discover his title, and then issue another query to answer our initial question. The following two SELECT statements can be combined to form a single SELECT statement with a subquery.

```
SELECT POSITION, EMP_NAME FROM EMPLOYEES
WHERE EMP_NAME = 'CONSIDINE, JOHN'
SELECT EMP_NAME FROM EMPLOYEES WHERE
POSITION = 'Chief Financial Officer'
```

Figure 8-1 shows the combination of these two SELECT statements:

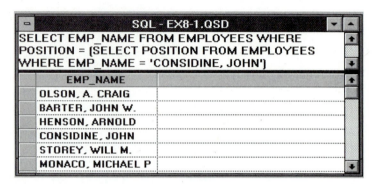

Figure 8-1   *Combining Two SELECTs with a Subquery*

The nested SELECT statement:

>SELECT POSITION, EMP_NAME FROM EMPLOYEES
>WHERE EMP_NAME = 'CONSIDINE, JOHN'

from Figure 8-1 is also referred to as an *inner query*.

8.1.1   Single Value Subqueries

Figure 8-1 showed a subquery in which the inner SELECT statement returned only one value, 'Chief Executive Officer.' In this case, the = operator was used with the subselect.

If, on the other hand, the statement:

>SELECT EMP_NAME FROM EMPLOYEES WHERE
>POSITION = (SELECT POSITION FROM EMPLOYEES
>WHERE EMP_NAME LIKE '%JOHN')

had been used, the statement would not work.

This subselect does not work because multiple values are returned by the nested SELECT statement. The top-level SELECT is expecting only one value because the = operator is used.

Subqueries using the = operator are referred to as *single value subqueries*.

Aggregate Functions and Single Value Subqueries

Aggregate functions are often used with single value subqueries. Aggregate functions are one way of ensuring that only one value will be returned within an inner query.

Figure 8-2 demonstrates the use of an aggregate function with a single value subquery. In the figure, the aggregate function, MAX (*stock_value*), ensures that only one value will be returned.

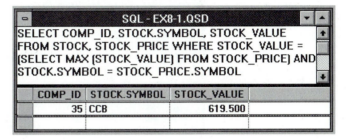

Figure 8-2 *Aggregate Function with Subquery*

Restriction on Aggregate Functions with Single Value Subqueries

If a GROUP BY clause within the inner SELECT statement had been used in Figure 8-2, we could no longer ensure that a single value is returned. The statement:

```
SELECT COMP_ID, STOCK.SYMBOL, STOCK_VALUE
FROM STOCK, STOCK_PRICE WHERE STOCK_VALUE =
(SELECT MAX(STOCK_VALUE) FROM STOCK_PRICE
GROUP BY SYMBOL) AND STOCK.SYMBOL =
STOCK_PRICE.SYMBOL
```

will not work because the GROUP BY clause allows multiple values to be returned in a subquery.

8.1.2 Multivalue Subselects

Inner SELECT statements of a subquery can return multiple values. Typically, the predicates IN and EXISTS are used in these cases.

Use of the IN Predicate for Multivalue Subselects

Suppose we ask the question: Who are the employees of companies in Chicago? This question can be answered with two SELECT statements:

SELECT COMP_ID FROM COMP WHERE
CITY = 'Chicago'

SELECT EMP_NAME FROM EMPLOYEES WHERE
COMP_ID IN (*values from first query placed here*)

Of course, the second SELECT statement requires reading the result values of the first SELECT statement and then placing them in the second. The second SELECT statement is run against our sample database; the results are shown in Figure 8-3.

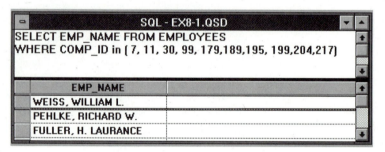

Figure 8-3   *SELECT with IN Predicate*

When the statement:

SELECT COMP_ID FROM COMP WHERE
CITY = 'Chicago'

was run against the COMPANY sample database, the result statement returned was: 7, 11, 30, 99, 179, 189, 195, 199, 204, 217. This result set was used in Figure 8-3.

This same question can be answered by combining these two statements as shown in Figure 8-4. Since the inner SELECT returns multiple values, the IN predicate is used.

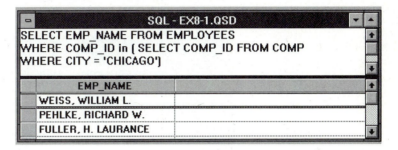

Figure 8-4   *Subquery Using IN Predicate*

Use of the EXISTS Predicate for Multivalue Subselects

The EXISTS predicate can also be used when a nested SELECT statement returns multiple values. Figure 8-5 shows an example of using the EXISTS predicate with a subquery.

```
SQL - EX8-1.QSD
SELECT  EMP_NAME, COMP_ID FROM EMPLOYEES WHERE
EXISTS (SELECT * FROM COMP WHERE CITY = 'CHICAGO')
```

EMP_NAME	COMP_ID	
BROATCH, ROBERT E.	1	
COMPTON, RONALD E.	1	
BENANAV, GARY	1	
CLINE, ROBERT S.	2	

Figure 8-5   *SELECT with EXISTS Predicate*

In Figure 8-5, if one or more companies in the database is located in Chicago, then all entries matching the condition of the top-level SELECT statement will be returned.

8.1.3 Correlated Subqueries

A *correlated subquery* is a query in which the inner SELECT statement uses a column that is referenced in the top-level SELECT statement. Figure 8-6 shows an example of a correlated subquery.

```
═  SQL - EX8-1.QSD                          ▼ ▲
SELECT  EMP_NAME, COMP_ID FROM EMPLOYEES WHERE
EXISTS (SELECT * FROM COMP WHERE CITY = 'CHICAGO'
AND COMP_ID = EMPLOYEES.COMP_ID)
```

EMP_NAME	COMP_ID	
WEISS, WILLIAM L.	7	
PEHLKE, RICHARD W.	7	
FULLER, H. LAURANCE	11	

Figure 8-6   *Correlated Subquery Example*

The SELECT statement in Figure 8-6 is a correlated subquery because the column, *comp_id*, from the EMPLOYEES table is referred to in both the inner and outer SELECT statements.

Correlated subqueries will execute an inner query many times, once for every row of the top-level query. Because of this, correlated subqueries can be tricky to use and can cause performance problems; however, correlated subqueries are also powerful to use.

Alternative Way to Write a Subquery

Subqueries can often be replaced with a join. A join could also have been used to accomplish the same end result as achieved in Figure 8-6 with a subquery. Figure 8-7 shows how a join can accomplish the same thing.

```
═  SQL - EX8-1.QSD                          ▼ ▲
SELECT EMP_NAME, EMPLOYEES.COMP_ID
FROM EMPLOYEES, COMP  WHERE CITY = 'CHICAGO'
AND COMP.COMP_ID = EMPLOYEES.COMP_ID
```

EMP_NAME	EMPLOYEES.COMP_ID	
WEISS, WILLIAM L.	7	
PEHLKE, RICHARD W.	7	
FULLER, H. LAURANCE	11	

Figure 8-7   *Using a Join Instead of a Subquery*

The fact that the SELECT statements in Figure 8-6 and Figure 8-7 accomplish the same end result leads to an interesting question: If there is more than one way to write an SQL statement to get a desired result, then which way will be faster?

The proper use of, and avoidance of, certain SQL clauses can influence the performance of queries greatly. The next section introduces some guidelines that can show you how to improve performance of SQL statements.

8.2 Performance Considerations

Performance considerations are a subject to which an entire book could be devoted. The next two sections introduce some of the fundamental issues affecting performance, such as the effects of SQL syntax variations (like those shown in Figure 8-6 and Figure 8-7) on performance.

The three areas discussed in this chapter affecting SQL performance are:

- Indexing
- Optimization of SQL statements
- Database design (discussed in Section 8.3)

NOTE! The examples shown in this section use the SQLTalk utility of SQLBase to show the time that specific queries take when run against the COMPANY sample database. The SQL Solo CD-ROM provided in this book does not have the SQLTalk utility. The SQLBase 6.0.1 Desktop Edition was used in order to show timed query results. A 33-MHz 486 IBM-compatible was used as the test machine.

8.2.1 Indexing

An *index* in a relational database is a data structure that allows rapid access to table rows, based on the value of data in one or more columns of those rows. There are only two reasons to build an index on a relational table:

- To ensure the uniqueness of the values being indexed (all primary key columns must have a unique index defined on them)

- To enhance the performance of the database

The drawback of indexes is the amount of resources they consume. Indexes requires disk space for the storage of the index tree structure. Each of these indexes also requires CPU cycles in order to be created and maintained. In particular, indexes consume processing time whenever a transaction performs an INSERT or DELETE operation against an indexed table or performs an UPDATE of a table row column that participates in one or more indexes.

The challenge for the database designer is to create indexes only for those cases where the benefits realized from the access time improvements outweigh the penalties suffered from the overhead of building and maintaining the index. While some scenarios can be identified as potentially good (or bad) candidates for an index, no irrevocable rules exist.

Example of a Good Index Choice

The SELECT statement in Figure 8-8 uses an aggregate function, MAX (*stock_value*). The column, *stock_value*, is a good choice as an index to speed this SELECT because the aggregate function performed on it requires extra computation and access to the table, STOCK_PRICE.

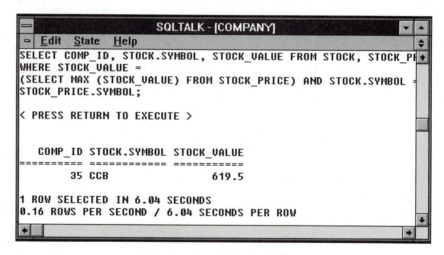

Figure 8-8   *Performance Tuning: a SELECT Without an Index*

Figure 8-8, which does not use an index on the column, *stock_value*, indicates that one row was selected in 6.04 seconds for the SELECT statement shown.

In Figure 8-9, an index is created on *stock_value*.

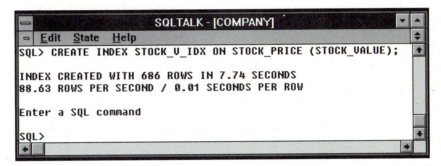

Figure 8-9 *Creating an Index*

Figure 8-10 shows the same SELECT statement shown in Figure 8-8, but now an index has been created. The timer on the SELECT statement using an index shows that one row is selected in .82 seconds!

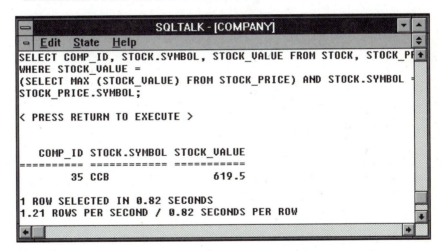

Figure 8-10 *Faster SELECT with Index*

Good Index Candidates

The following list identifies some columns that may make good index candidates:

- **Primary key columns**

  By definition, primary key columns must have unique indexes placed on them in order for the definition to be complete and to allow for the use of referential integrity.

- **Foreign key columns**

  These are usually very good index subjects because:

  - Foreign keys are often used to perform joins with their parent tables.

  - Foreign keys can be used by the system for referential integrity enforcement during delete operations against the parent table.

- **Columns that are referenced in WHERE predicates**

  Indexes on such columns can speed up these operations significantly by preventing the creation of an intermediate result table.

- **Columns that are frequently the subjects of ORDER BY or GROUP_BY clauses**

  Indexes on such columns also speed up operations by preventing the creation of an intermediate result table.

- **Any column that contains unique values**

- **Columns that are often the subject of aggregate functions (SUM, AVG, MIN, and MAX)**

- **Columns often used for validity editing in programs**.

  If an application checks for a column's existence in some table, then that column could be an index candidate.

Poor Index Candidates

The following are poor index candidates:

- **Small tables**

  The costs associated with creating and maintaining indexes on small tables, like the ones used in this book, are typically greater than the cost of performing a scan of the entire table. Of course, a unique index required to define a primary key is an exception to this rule.

- **Large batch updates**

  Tables that experience updates in large batches usually have problems with index overhead, particularly if the batches update more than 10 percent of the table. One possible way to avoid these problems while still experiencing the benefits of indexes is to drop all of the indexes on the table prior to the update, then recreate them after the update.

- **Skewness of keys**

  Another index pitfall is encountered when the index's key value distribution is significantly *skewed*. In other words, when a large percentage of rows have the same value for the index key, the index performance when accessing these rows degrades.

- **Many unknown values (nulls)**

  If there are many null values in a column, then the column has a large percentage of rows with the same value. The value distribution is skewed.

- **Frequently changing values**

  Columns that are frequently updated cause excessive index maintenance overhead. Each time the column is updated, the DBMS must delete the old value from the index tree and insert the new value.

- **Excessive length**

  Single or composite index keys that are longer than 50 bytes will cause the index to grow to a large number of levels unless the number of rows is low. Since at least one I/O is incurred for each level when searching the index, excessively long keys will degrade performance.

Composite Indexes

When an index is created on two or more columns, it is called a *composite index*. When creating composite indexes, consider the effect that the order of columns within the index has on performance. The best performance is achieved by placing, in the high order index position, the column that usually has the most restrictive selection criteria used against it. Of course, if the intended use of the index is to provide a generic search capability, then the columns that will always be fully specified must be placed first in the index or the searching capability will be lost.

One good reason to use composite indexes is to achieve *index-only access*, that is, all the data required by a query can be found within the index itself.

Example of a Composite Index

The table, STOCK_PRICE, is used by transactions to perform a lookup of stock values. Since this is done often, the DBA wants the operation to be performed with a minimum number of I/O operations. This is the SQL that is the most efficient in this case.

This is the table (slightly altered from the sample database table for effect):

```
CREATE TABLE STOCK_PRICE
(SYMBOL_ID INTEGER NOT NULL,
STOCK_VALUE DECIMAL(5,2) NOT NULL)
PRIMARY KEY(SYMBOL_ID)
```

This SELECT statement is used by transactions that perform the lookup:

```
SELECT STOCK_VALUE
FROM STOCK_PRICE
WHERE SYMBOL_ID = {integer variable here}
```

This index was required to complete the primary key definition of the table:

```
CREATE UNIQUE INDEX XPKSYM_ID
ON STOCK_PRICE (SYMBOL_ID)
```

The DBA realized that adding a new index, which includes the *stock_price* column in the low order of the key, would allow the lookup to perform *index-only access*, resulting in an I/O savings:

```
CREATE UNIQUE INDEX XSYMPRICE
ON STOCK_PRICE (SYMBOL_ID, STOCK_VALUE)
```

8.2.2   Optimizing SQL Syntax

The SQL language, like English, often offers the ability to ask a question in several ways and still get the same answer. With SQL, asking a question in one way instead of another can provide significant performance improvements.

The best way to learn how to optimize SQL statements is to try it out. There are no hard fast rules to optimizing statements. Below are three examples of ways to improve performance with syntax enhancements.

The examples demonstrate the following three rules of thumb:

- Avoid the use of the HAVING clause
- Use the IN predicate instead of the OR search condition
- Avoid ambiguous special characters with LIKE predicate

Avoid the Use of the HAVING Clause

The use of the HAVING clause in a SELECT statement can often slow a query. In Figure 8-11, the following SELECT statement is run:

```
SELECT SYMBOL, COUNT (*) FROM STOCK_PRICE
GROUP BY SYMBOL
HAVING SYMBOL LIKE 'A%P%'
```

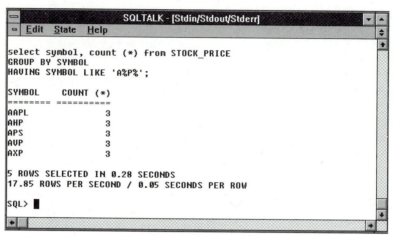

Figure 8-11 *Slow Query Because of HAVING Clause*

The HAVING clause forces extra SQL optimization that could be avoided. In this example, the SQL statement runs 5 rows in .28 seconds.

We could rewrite this statement as follows:

> SELECT SYMBOL, COUNT (*) FROM STOCK_PRICE
> WHERE SYMBOL LIKE 'A%P%'
> GROUP BY SYMBOL

Figure 8-12 shows the optimized query.

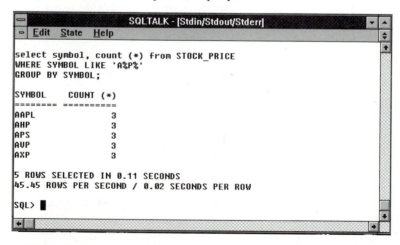

Figure 8-12 *Optimized Query*

Figure 8-12 shows that five rows can be selected in .11 seconds! This is over a 100 percent improvement in time! (Times will often vary from run to run, but this definitely shows a speedup.)

Use the IN Predicate Instead of the OR Search Condition

Figure 8-13 shows an SQL statement that makes heavy use of the OR search condition. In some cases, it can be more efficient to replace the OR search condition with an IN predicate.

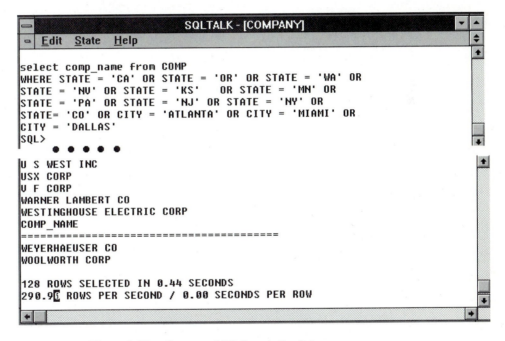

Figure 8-13 *Overuse of OR Search Condition*

Figure 8-13 shows 128 rows selected in .44 seconds. This SQL statement can be rewritten as follows:

```
SELECT COMP_NAME FROM COMP
WHERE STATE IN
('CA','OR','WA','NV', 'KS','MN','PA','NJ','NY','CO')
OR CITY IN ('ATLANTA', 'MIAMI', 'DALLAS')
```

Figure 8-14 shows an example of running this SQL statement:

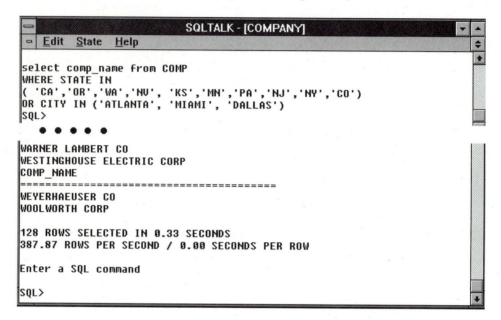

```
                    SQLTALK - [COMPANY]
 Edit   State   Help

select comp_name from COMP
WHERE STATE IN
( 'CA','OR','WA','NV', 'KS','MN','PA','NJ','NY','CO')
OR CITY IN ('ATLANTA', 'MIAMI', 'DALLAS')
SQL>
    • • • • •
WARNER LAMBERT CO
WESTINGHOUSE ELECTRIC CORP
COMP_NAME
========================================
WEYERHAEUSER CO
WOOLWORTH CORP

128 ROWS SELECTED IN 0.33 SECONDS
387.87 ROWS PER SECOND / 0.00 SECONDS PER ROW

Enter a SQL command

SQL>
```

Figure 8-14   *Increasing Performance by Replacing OR with IN Predicate*

Figure 8-14 shows that 128 rows were selected in .33 seconds. I ran this query several times and, overall, the statement is faster than the one in Figure 8-13, but not by much. Had this table been much larger, significant performance gains might have been seen.

While the rule of thumb of replacing excessive OR search conditions with an IN predicate does increase performance, you could question whether the time spent on this optimization was worth it. This case illustrates the need for trial by example.

Avoid Ambiguous Special Characters with the LIKE Predicate

You can make the LIKE clause perform more efficiently by proper placement of wildcard characters. Suppose you need information on a company, "UST INC," but are not sure how the company name is entered in the database. You can use the LIKE clause to ask the question:

What is the company name, business code ID, business description, stock symbol, and years of stock table entries for telecommunication companies?

The following SELECT statement answers this question. It performs a five-way equijoin, uses a function (@YEAR), and uses the LIKE predicate.

```
SELECT  COMP_NAME, BUS_CODES.BUS_TYPE_ID,
 BUS_DESCR, STOCK.SYMBOL, @YEAR(STOCK_DATE)
FROM COMP, BUS_TYPES, BUS_CODES,
STOCK, STOCK_PRICE
WHERE BUS_DESCR = 'Telecommunications'
AND COMP.COMP_NAME LIKE '%ST%'
AND COMP.COMP_ID = BUS_TYPES.COMP_ID
AND BUS_TYPES.BUS_TYPE_ID =
 BUS_CODES.BUS_TYPE_ID
AND COMP.COMP_ID = STOCK.COMP_ID
AND STOCK.SYMBOL = STOCK_PRICE.SYMBOL
```

Figure 8-15 shows this SQL statement executed.

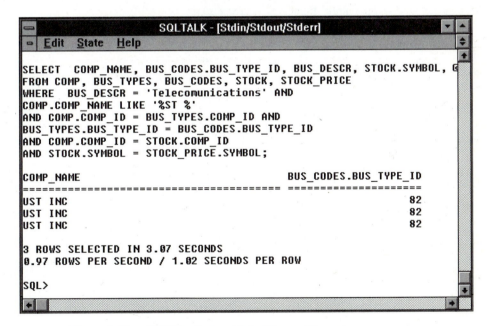

Figure 8-15 *LIKE Predicate with Ambiguous Characters*

Figure 8-15 shows that three rows were selected in 3.07 seconds. Several different ways to improve the performance were tried. Altering the LIKE predicate proved the most successful way to gain in performance.

The statement LIKE '%ST%' is problematic because the string 'ST' can appear in any position. If we had used the 'US%' instead, then we force the first two positions in the string to be 'US', eliminating any of the other alternatives.

Figure 8-16 shows the alternate SELECT with the less ambiguous LIKE predicate. Note that the statements in Figure 8-15 and Figure 8-16 will not always return the same results, although they do in this case.

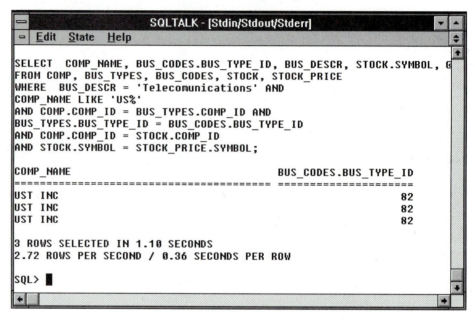

Figure 8-16   *Less Ambiguous LIKE Predicate*

The statement in Figure 8-16 runs in one-third the time!

8.3 Database Design and Performance

Database design choices can also affect performance. This section presents rules that refine database design.

These rules are typically applied in a three-step process. First, the database designer recognizes a scenario in the database that is often the subject of a particular design technique. Second, the designer then applies that technique to the database on the assumption that the benefits will be both substantial and required. Finally, the changes in database design are tested.

Database design rules do *not* offer specifically proven benefits for *every case* but represent common database design rules that are usually incorporated into physical designs by experienced DBAs.

This section discusses the following general categories of database design affecting performance:

- Database query optimizer
- Splitting tables into two or more tables
- Clustering of table rows

8.3.1 Database Query Optimizer

Databases have *query optimizers* that, based on database design, choose the optimal path for an SQL statement. The query optimization process determines the access path for all types of SQL DML statements. However, the SQL SELECT statement (a query) presents the biggest challenge to access path selection; therefore, the process is commonly referred to as *query* optimization rather than data access optimization.

Early relational database systems processed queries in a simple and direct manner without attempting to optimize either the query itself or the access path. This resulted in unacceptably long query processing times and led to the belief among some application programmers that relational database systems were not practical for real world applications. To speed query processing times and to increase the efficiency of query processing, a great deal of research and testing was carried out. Query optimization can be defined as the sum of all techniques that are employed to improve the efficiency of processing queries.

Query Optimization Steps

While the query optimizers of modern relational database systems differ in sophistication and complexity, they all follow the same basic steps in performing query optimization:

1. *Parsing* — The optimizer first breaks up the query into its component parts, checks for syntax errors, and then converts the query to an internal representation for further processing.

2. *Conversion* — The optimizer next applies rules for converting the query into a format that is syntactically optimal.

3. *Develop alternatives* — Once the query has undergone syntax optimization, the optimizer develops alternatives for processing the query.

4. *Create execution plan* — Finally, the optimizer selects the best execution plan for the query, either by following a set of rules (rule-based optimization) or by computing the costs for each alternative (cost-based optimization).

Syntax Optimization

The first progress in optimizing queries was in finding ways to restate the query so that it produced the same result but was more efficient to process. For example, consider the following query:

```
SELECT COMP_ID, BUS_DESCR
FROM BUS_TYPES, BUS_CODES
WHERE BUS_TYPES.BUS_TYPE_ID =
BUS_CODES.BUS_TYPE_ID
AND BUS_TYPES.COMP_ID = "100"
```

The most direct way to process this query is:

1. Form the Cartesian product of the vendor and product tables.

2. Restrict the resulting table to rows that meet the WHERE condition.

3. Project the two columns named in the SELECT clause.

The most direct way of optimizing this statement will not be the most efficient. The restrictions on a table should be performed as early as possible to reduce the number of rows that must be processed further. Applying this rule to the example above, we can process the query as follows:

1. Restrict the rows in the part table to those for which COMP_ID = "100".

2. Perform the join of the result to the vendor table in step 1.

The transformation described in this example is called *syntax optimization*. There are many formulas for making transformations, and all modern query optimizers use transformation rules to restate a query in a more efficient form.

The important point to realize is that *these automatic transformations free you from having to try many equivalent forms of the same query in search of the one form that yields the best performance*, because the optimizer is usually transforming all of these queries into the same final form.

Rule-based Optimization

As progress was being made in improving the processing of queries, other efforts to improve table access were taking place. These improvements included indexing techniques and hashing. However, these improvements added complexity to query processing. For example, if a table had indexes on three different columns, any one of these indexes could be used to access the table (along with sequential table access).

In addition, many new algorithms to join tables began to appear. The two most basic join algorithms are:

- **Nested Loop Join** — A row is read from the first table, called the outer table, then each row in the second table, called the inner table, is read as a candidate for the join. The second row in the first table is then read, and again each of the rows in the inner table is read, and so on until all rows in the first table are read. If the first table has M rows and the second table has N rows, M x N rows are read.

- **Merge Join** — This join method assumes that the two tables are sorted (or indexed) so that rows are read in order of the column (or columns) on which they will be joined. This allows the join to be performed by reading rows from each table and comparing the join column values until a match is found. In this way, the join is completed with one pass through each table.

The first method of dealing with this complexity was to establish heuristic rules for selecting between access paths and join methods, which is called *rule-based optimization*. With this approach, weights and preferences based on principles that are generally true, are assigned to the alternatives. Using these weights and preferences, the query optimizer works through the possible execution plans until it arrives at the best plan based on its rules. Some of the rules used by this type of optimizer are based on the placement of variable tokens, such as table or column names, within the query's syntax structure. When these names are moved, a dramatic difference in the performance of the query can sometimes be realized. For this reason, rule-based optimizers are said to be syntax sensitive. One of the methods for tuning this type of database system involves moving tokens to different positions inside a statement.

Cost-based Optimization

Cost-based optimization is similar to rule-based optimization, except that cost-based optimizers use statistical information to select the most efficient execution plan. The cost of each alternative execution plan is estimated, using statistics such as the number of rows in a table and the number and distribution of the values in a table column. The cost formulas typically consider the amount of I/O and CPU instructions required to perform the execution plan. The statistics are stored in the system catalog and maintained by the database system.

To understand how statistics can make a difference, consider the following query:

```
SELECT COMP_ID, COMP_NAME FROM COMP
WHERE STATE = "FL"
```

If an index exists on the STATE column, a rule-based optimizer would use this index to process the query. However, if 90 percent of the rows in the customer table have FL in the STATE column, using the index is actually slower than simply processing the table sequentially. A cost-based optimizer would detect that using the index would not be advantageous.

The cost-based optimization approach today represents the state of the art in query optimization techniques. Most high-quality relational database systems employ a cost-based optimizer.

8.3.2 Splitting Tables

One of the most common denormalization techniques that can be applied to a physical database design to improve performance is the vertical or horizontal splitting of tables. Vertical splitting is the process of moving some of a table's *columns* to a new table that has a primary key identical to that of the original table. Horizontal splitting is the moving of some of the *rows* of one table to another table that has a structure identical to the first. The resulting tables can be managed in ways that tailor each to its particular performance requirements. The basic motivation for performing a split is:

- The original table has some performance problem that must be solved.

- One or more subsets of the original table have significantly different performance requirements that cannot be met in combination.

Vertically Splitting Large Rows

The most common reason for vertically splitting a table to correct performance problems is that the row length of the original table is too large.

Some entities in the entity relationship diagram may contain a large number of attributes or a few unusually long attributes. When these entities are converted to a relational table, the size of a row can actually be larger than the usable database page size. Consequently, multiple physical I/O could be required to retrieve the row in a worst-case scenario. These multiple I/O operations will degrade performance. To resolve this situation, the table can be vertically split in order to reduce the row to a more manageable size.

Horizontally Splitting Tables

Horizontal splitting of a table is the moving of some of the *rows* of one table to another table that has a structure identical to the first. Horizontal splitting occurs most often to isolate current data from historical data so that the performance of accessing current data is increased.

For example, organizations must frequently store several years of order information to produce comparison and historical reports. If an organization creates several hundred thousands of orders per year, an order table that contains five years of order information might exceed one million rows. Such a large table would slow the access to current year's orders, which are probably the most frequently accessed. In this situation, the database designer might choose to horizontally split the order table(s) into two tables, one for the current year's orders and another for all other orders.

8.3.3 Clustering Table Rows

Performance can be improved by using a *clustered hashed* index, which controls the physical storage location of rows within a table. Using this indexing technique, which is actually not a physical index at all but a method of storing the underlying subject table, can enhance some aspects of database performance in particular cases. There are two major reasons why this technique should be applied to a table:

- For faster access to single table rows

- To accommodates the clustering of table rows that are often accessed together

Direct Random Access of Rows

Whenever fast direct access to a single row of a table is critical and a unique key exists to identify that row, you should consider a clustered hashed index. A unique clustered hashed index on the column can allow retrieval of a row with a single read operation, under certain conditions.

This technique would be appropriate, for example, when a high volume transaction has to access a large account table in a bank's teller system. Since the teller knows the customer account number, the program can access the account information directly with a single I/O, eliminating not only the need to traverse a large index tree, but also the I/O and locking overhead associated with that task. Since many tellers are performing similar transactions simultaneously, the overall load on the DBMS and disk subsystem is decreased through the use of a clustered hashed index. In addition, the response time for the transactions is enhanced.

Clustering Rows Together

When a fairly small number of rows of a single table are often accessed as a group, the clustered hashed indexing technique can allow for these rows to be located physically adjacent to each other. This allows the maximum database performance to be realized for a commonly accessed group of rows.

This technique is sometimes called *foreign key clustering*. It is often a foreign key within the table that defines the group of data that should be clustered. When the value of a foreign key is the same for a group of records, the RDBMS attempts to store this group of records in proximity to each other. This foreign key becomes the subject key of the *non-unique* clustered hashed index that is placed on the table.

8.4   Exercises with Complex Queries

Exercise 8.4.1:   Issuing Subqueries

This exercise steps through the use of subqueries.

1.   Open Quest, if not already open. Make sure you are connected to the COMPANY database by pulling down the Utilities menu and using the **Add** function if necessary. Click on the COMPANY database.

2. Click on the **Open** button and then on the **SQL** button.

Figure 8-17 *Opening the SQL Activity*

3. Quest prompts for a file. Choose the file c:\sqlbase\exercise\chap8\ex8-1.qsd. Click **OK**

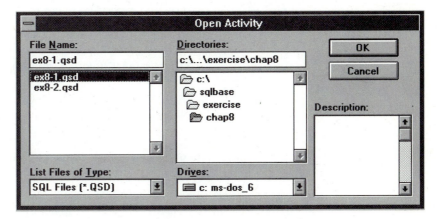

Figure 8-18 *Opening the SQL File*

4. The first SELECT command to be executed is:

    SELECT POSITION, EMP_NAME FROM EMPLOYEES
    WHERE EMP_NAME = 'CONSIDINE, JOHN'

    Select this SQL statement by clicking in the SQL activity window, pull down the SQL menu, and select **Execute SQL Statement**.

5. The next SELECT command to be executed is:

    SELECT EMP_NAME FROM EMPLOYEES WHERE
    POSITION = 'TChief Financial Officer'

    Choose this SELECT statement by clicking in the SQL Activity window. Choose the **Execute SQL Statement** menu option.

6. The previous two SELECT statements can be combined to form a subquery, as shown below.

   SELECT EMP_NAME FROM EMPLOYEES WHERE
   POSITION = (SELECT POSITION FROM EMPLOYEES
   WHERE EMP_NAME = 'CONSIDINE, JOHN')

   Choose this SELECT statement by clicking in the SQL Activity window. Choose the **Execute SQL Statement** menu option.

7. The next SELECT statement will not work because the = operator requires a single value to be returned from the SELECT statement.

   SELECT EMP_NAME FROM EMPLOYEES WHERE
   POSITION = (SELECT POSITION FROM EMPLOYEES
   WHERE EMP_NAME LIKE '%JOHN')

   Choose this SELECT statement by clicking in the SQL Activity window. Choose the **Execute SQL Statement** menu option.

8. The next SELECT statement demonstrates a single value subquery, which forces only values to be returned by using an aggregate function.

   SELECT COMP_ID, STOCK.SYMBOL,STOCK_VALUE
   FROM STOCK, STOCK_PRICE WHERE STOCK_VALUE =
   (SELECT MAX(STOCK_VALUE) FROM STOCK_PRICE)
   AND STOCK.SYMBOL = STOCK_PRICE.SYMBOL

   Choose this SELECT statement by clicking in the SQL Activity window. Choose the **Execute SQL Statement** menu option.

9. The next two SELECT statements can be combined (as shown in step 10) to form one subquery.

   SELECT COMP_ID FROM COMP WHERE CITY =
   'CHICAGO'

   SELECT EMP_NAME FROM EMPLOYEES
   WHERE COMP_ID IN (7,11,30,99,179,189,195,199,204,217)

   Choose these SELECT statements by clicking in the SQL Activity window. Choose the **Execute SQL Statement** menu option for both of them.

10. The next SELECT statement shows a subquery that returns multiple values. In this case the IN operator is used.

    ```
    SELECT EMP_NAME FROM EMPLOYEES
    WHERE COMP_ID IN (SELECT COMP_ID FROM COMP
    WHERE CITY = 'CHICAGO')
    ```

    Choose this SELECT statement by clicking in the SQL Activity window. Choose the **Execute SQL Statement** menu option.

11. The next SELECT statement demonstrates a multiple-value subquery, using the EXISTS predicate.

    ```
    SELECT EMP_NAME, COMP_ID FROM EMPLOYEES
    WHERE EXISTS (SELECT * FROM COMP
    WHERE CITY = 'CHICAGO')
    ```

    Choose this SELECT statement by clicking in the SQL Activity window. Choose the **Execute SQL Statement** menu option.

12. The next SELECT statement demonstrates a correlated subquery.

    ```
    SELECT EMP_NAME, COMP_ID FROM EMPLOYEES
    WHERE EXISTS (SELECT * FROM COMP
    WHERE CITY = 'CHICAGO' AND
    COMP_ID = EMPLOYEES.COMP_ID)
    ```

    Choose this SELECT statement by clicking in the SQL Activity window. Choose the **Execute SQL Statement** menu option.

13. To close, choose the **Close** option from the File menu.

Exercise 8.4.2:   Improving Performance

This exercise steps through examples of ways to improve performance.

1. Click on the **Open** button and then on the **SQL** button within Quest.

2. Quest prompts for a file. Choose the file c:\sqlbase\exercise\chap8\ex8-2.qsd. Click **OK.**

3. The first SELECT command to be executed is:

    ```
    SELECT COMP_ID, STOCK.SYMBOL, STOCK_VALUE
    FROM STOCK, STOCK_PRICE
    WHERE STOCK_VALUE =
    ```

(SELECT MAX (STOCK_VALUE) FROM STOCK_PRICE)
AND STOCK.SYMBOL = STOCK_PRICE.SYMBOL

Choose this SQL statement by clicking in the SQL activity window, pull down the SQL menu, and select **Execute SQL Statement**.

4. The next SELECT command to be executed creates an index on the column, *stock_price*.

CREATE INDEX STOCK_V_IDX ON STOCK_PRICE
(STOCK_VALUE)

Choose this SQL statement by clicking in the SQL activity window, pull down the SQL menu, and select **Execute SQL Statement**.

5. Re-execute the SELECT statement in step 3. While SQL Solo has no timing function, this SELECT statement will execute faster.

6. The next SELECT command to be executed is:

SELECT SYMBOL, COUNT (*) FROM STOCK_PRICE
GROUP BY SYMBOL
HAVING SYMBOL LIKE 'A%P%'

Choose this SQL statement by clicking in the SQL activity window, pull down the SQL menu, and select **Execute SQL Statement**.

7. The next SELECT command to be executed rewrites the SQL statement in step 6 in order to avoid the use of the HAVING clause.

SELECT SYMBOL, COUNT (*) FROM STOCK_PRICE
WHERE SYMBOL LIKE 'A%P%'
GROUP BY SYMBOL

Choose this SQL statement by clicking in the SQL activity window, pull down the SQL menu, and select **Execute SQL Statement**.

8. The next SELECT command to be executed is:

SELECT COMP_NAME FROM COMP
WHERE STATE = 'CA' OR STATE = 'OR' OR STATE = 'WA'
OR STATE = 'NV' OR STATE = 'KS'   OR STATE = 'MN' OR
STATE = 'PA' OR STATE = 'NJ' OR STATE = 'NY' OR
STATE= 'CO' OR CITY = 'ATLANTA' OR CITY = 'MIAMI' OR
CITY = 'DALLAS'

Choose this SQL statement by clicking in the SQL activity window, pull down the SQL menu, and select **Execute SQL Statement**.

9. The next SELECT command to be executed replaces the use of the OR search conditions in step 8 with the IN predicate.

    ```
    SELECT COMP_NAME FROM COMP
    WHERE STATE IN
    ('CA','OR','WA','NV', 'KS','MN','PA','NJ','NY','CO')
    OR CITY IN ('ATLANTA', 'MIAMI', 'DALLAS')
    ```

    Choose this SQL statement by clicking in the SQL activity window, pull down the SQL menu, and select **Execute SQL Statement**.

10. The next SELECT command to be executed is:

    ```
    SELECT  COMP_NAME, BUS_CODES.BUS_TYPE_ID,
    BUS_DESCR, STOCK.SYMBOL, @YEAR(STOCK_DATE)
    FROM COMP, BUS_TYPES, BUS_CODES, STOCK,
    STOCK_PRICE
    WHERE BUS_DESCR = 'Telecommunications' AND
    COMP.COMP_NAME LIKE '%ST%'
    AND COMP.COMP_ID = BUS_TYPES.COMP_ID AND
    BUS_TYPES.BUS_TYPE_ID =
    BUS_CODES.BUS_TYPE_ID
    AND COMP.COMP_ID = STOCK.COMP_ID
    AND STOCK.SYMBOL = STOCK_PRICE.SYMBOL
    ```

    Select this SQL statement by clicking in the SQL activity window, pull down the SQL menu, and select **Execute SQL Statement**.

11. The next SELECT command to be executed changes the LIKE predicate used in step 10 to cut down the number of string searches performed. Again, this will improve performance; however, the statement is not identical to the one in step 10.

    ```
    SELECT  COMP_NAME, BUS_CODES.BUS_TYPE_ID,
    BUS_DESCR, STOCK.SYMBOL, @YEAR(STOCK_DATE)
    FROM COMP, BUS_TYPES, BUS_CODES, STOCK,
    STOCK_PRICE
    WHERE BUS_DESCR = 'Telecommunications' AND
    COMP.COMP_NAME LIKE 'US%'
    AND COMP.COMP_ID = BUS_TYPES.COMP_ID AND
    ```

BUS_TYPES.BUS_TYPE_ID =
BUS_CODES.BUS_TYPE_ID
AND COMP.COMP_ID = STOCK.COMP_ID
AND STOCK.SYMBOL = STOCK_PRICE.SYMBOL

Select this SQL statement by clicking in the SQL activity window, pull down the SQL menu, and select **Execute SQL Statement**.

12. To close, choose the **Close** option from the File menu.

8.5 Summary

In this chapter, we covered two main topics: subqueries and performance considerations.

First, we discussed the use of subqueries, or SELECT statements that are nested with other SELECT statements. *Single value*, *multiple value,* and *correlated subqueries* were covered. Various examples of creating subqueries were provided.

Second, we covered performance considerations and discussed three ways of improving performance:

- Indexing

- Altering SQL syntax

- Altering initial database design

The concept of the database query optimizer was introduced. Modern RDBMS apply many optimization techniques to improve queries.

Subqueries and performance issues are both advanced topics of SQL and merit a great deal more discussion; however, in this chapter, we provided a basic introduction to both subjects.

The next chapter introduces the concept of *views*, which will continue to extend our knowledge of the SQL language.

9 Views

This chapter provides an overview of views. Views provide ways to control access to tables and SQL statements. Views are also a way to control how data is presented.

The chapter is organized as follows:

9.1 Introduction to Views

Views are an alternative way of looking at the data from database tables. While tables control how data is stored, views provide a unique way of presenting data to users in a manner not bound to the physical table restrictions.

A view is basically a query that is permanently stored in the database and is assigned a unique name of its own. The view appears as if it is a table in the database.

9.1.1 Examples of Using a View

The following statement creates a view called COMP_VIEW.

```
CREATE VIEW  COMP_VIEW (COMP_ID, COMP_NAME,
CORP_ADDR, CITY, STATE, ZIP)  AS
SELECT * FROM COMP
```

The above view contains the same results as the COMP table. The main difference between COMP_VIEW and COMP is that whereas the latter is defined as a physical table in the database and contains real data, COMP_VIEW does not actually exist in the database except as a name assigned to a query. When the view is invoked in a subsequent query, the underlying query that constitutes COMP_VIEW is executed and the resultant table is used to retrieve the desired data.

If we wanted to restrict the data in COMP so only companies in California could be accessible, we could create a view called COMP_CAVIEW as shown below:

```
CREATE VIEW  COMP_CAVIEW (COMP_ID, COMP_NAME,
CORP_ADDR, CITY, STATE, ZIP)  AS
SELECT * FROM COMP WHERE STATE = 'CA'
```

You can use the result set of the view table just as you use a regular database table. You can execute queries against it, perform joins with other tables and queries, create reports, and so on.

In Figure 9-1, we select the company names of all the companies with zip codes starting with 9. Instead of using the COMP table, we use the view, COMP_CAVIEW.

SQL - EX9-1.QSD

SELECT COMP_NAME, CITY, STATE FROM COMP_CAVIEW
WHERE ZIP LIKE '9%'

COMP_NAME	CITY	STATE	
AMERICAN PRESIDENT COS LTD	OAKLAND	CA	
APPLE COMPUTER INC	CUPERTINO	CA	
BANKAMERICA CORP	SAN FRANCISCO	CA	
CHEVRON CORP	SAN FRANCISCO	CA	
CLOROX CO	OAKLAND	CA	
CONSOLIDATED FREIGHTWAYS INC	PALO ALTO	CA	
WALT DISNEY CO	BURBANK	CA	

Figure 9-1   *Using a View Instead of a Table*

Now the same query is executed against the table COMP in Figure 9-2. The results are a superset of company names from COMP_CAVIEW.

SQL - EX9-1.QSD			
SELECT COMP_NAME, CITY, STATE FROM COMP			
WHERE ZIP LIKE '9%'			
COMP_NAME	**CITY**	**STATE**	
AIRBORNE FREIGHT CORP	SEATTLE	WA	
AMERICAN PRESIDENT COS LTD	OAKLAND	CA	
APPLE COMPUTER INC	CUPERTINO	CA	
BOEING CO	SEATTLE	WA	
BANKAMERICA CORP	SAN FRANCISCO	CA	
CHEVRON CORP	SAN FRANCISCO	CA	
CLOROX CO	OAKLAND	CA	

Figure 9-2   *Table COMP as a Comparison to COMP_CAVIEW*

VIEWS and INSERTS, UPDATES, AND DELETES

Views can be updated, deleted from, or inserted into, but there are restrictions. Here are some restrictions:

- Views can contain the name of only one table in the FROM clause if they are to be updated, deleted, or inserted into.

- A view cannot contain any derived columns based on GROUP BY functions or arithmetic expressions.

- You can modify tables through a view only if the view references a single table name in the FROM clause of the SELECT command, and the view columns are not derived from a function or arithmetic expression.

- If you create the view from a table join or it has derived columns, it is read-only and you cannot update the underlying tables through it.

- To create a view, you must possess the corresponding SELECT privileges on the columns of the base tables that constitute the view.

The following view contains all the rows and columns in the EMPLOYEES table:

```
CREATE VIEW EMP_VIEW AS
SELECT * FROM EMPLOYEES
```

Because only one table is involved in the creation of EMP_VIEW, the view can be updated.

Use of WITH CHECK OPTION with Views

EMP_VIEW could have been specified as updatable with a WITH CHECK OPTION. This means that if an UPDATE, DELETE, or INSERT operation is performed on the view, the system checks to see that the view definition is not violated as a result of this operation. The WITH CHECK OPTION on this view enforces *referential integrity*.

In the following example, EMP_VIEW is dropped and redefined by using the WITH CHECK OPTION.

```
DROP VIEW EMP_VIEW

CREATE VIEW EMP_VIEW AS
SELECT * FROM EMPLOYEES
WHERE COMP_ID IN
(SELECT COMP_ID FROM COMP)
WITH CHECK OPTION
```

The example view, EMP_VIEW, has an integrity constraint. No employee record in EMP_VIEW can be inserted, updated, or deleted unless the *comp_id* field in EMPLOYEES exists in the COMP table. In other words, if company ID 1001 does not exist in the COMP table, then you cannot insert a record into EMP_VIEW with that company ID.

Since the contents of EMP_VIEW are identical to the contents of the EMPLOYEES table, inserting a record into EMPLOYEES is the same as inserting it into EMP_VIEW, with one added benefit: There is an integrity constraint that ensures the validity of *comp_id*.

The following INSERT statement will be checked to see if it has a valid *comp_id*.

```
INSERT INTO EMP_VIEW (EMP_ID,EMP_NAME,
COMP_ID) VALUES (22, 'Frank Johnson', 101)
```

DROPPING A VIEW

The first view we created was COMP_VIEW. To drop this view, you simply use the following DROP VIEW command:

```
DROP VIEW COMP_VIEW
```

9.1.2   Why Use a View?

We have already hinted at some good reasons to use views. Two of the most compelling reasons to use views are:

- Views are a good way of presenting a constant unchanging appearance of the database to the world.

- Views can be used to perform queries that simply cannot be done by using one SQL statement alone.

Views Present a Constant Unchanging Appearance

Section 9.2 discusses "hiding" the physical database design. It is a common technique to have applications access views and not physical tables directly. If views are accessed instead of the physical tables, the underlying table structure can change without anyone ever realize it.

Performing Queries That Can Only Be Done With Views

Views can be used to perform queries that simply cannot be done with one SQL statement alone. For example, suppose we want to know company names, business descriptions, stock symbols, and the maximum stock values for companies in the telecommunications industry. This example is shown in Figure 9-3.

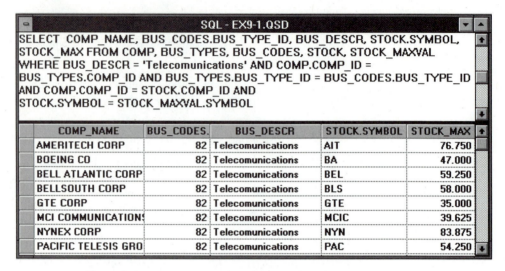

Figure 9-3 *Performing Advanced Query Using a View*

The query in Figure 9-3 cannot be done in one SELECT statement without the use of views. Because of limitations on how aggregate functions are used, this SQL statement would be rejected without a view.

Notice that the view, STOCK_MAXVAL, is referenced in Figure 9-3. To allow an aggregate function to appear as a regular column, the following SQL view, STOCK_MAXVAL, is created:

> CREATE VIEW STOCK_MAXVAL (SYMBOL, STOCK_MAX) AS
> SELECT SYMBOL, MAX (STOCK_VALUE) FROM
> STOCK_PRICE GROUP BY SYMBOL

This view treats the results of an aggregate function as a column. STOCK_MAXVAL is then joined with four other tables to get the desired result.

9.1.3 Disadvantages of Using Views

Views are clearly useful, but there are drawbacks. Here are several disadvantages to using views:

- **Increased Database Size**

  Views can significantly increase the size of your database.

- **Slower Queries**

  A view is basically the same as a query (even though it looks like a table). Quest must still execute the query commands to obtain the data for the view. The more complex the view, the longer it will take to display.

- **Administrative Overhead**

  The primary costs incurred by the extensive use of views fall into two administrative areas. The impact on the database administration area is the overhead of creating and managing the many views that will exist. The second impact is on the task of security administration, since more authorizations will need to be managed to ensure that all database access is through views instead of base tables.

9.2   CREATE VIEW and DROP VIEW Command Diagrams

The command diagrams for the CREATE VIEW and the DROP VIEW commands are illustrated in this section.

9.2.1 CREATE VIEW Command Diagram

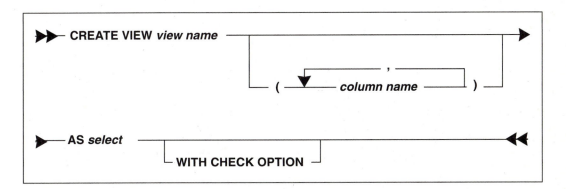

Clauses

view name	Must not be the name of an existing view or table in the database.

column name Specify column names if you want to give different names to the columns in the view. If you do not specify column names, the columns of the view have the same names as those of the result table of the SELECT command.

If the results of the SELECT command have duplicate column names (as can occur with a join) or if a column is derived from a function or arithmetic expression, you must give names to all the columns in the view. The new column names have to appear in parentheses after the view name.

SELECT Defines the view. The view has the rows that would result if the SELECT command were executed. See the description of SELECT for an explanation of this clause.

You cannot use the ORDER BY clause in a view definition.

Relational databases will often have restrictions on views. For example, with SQLBase, a view is considered read-only and cannot be updated if its definition involves any of the following:

- FROM clause that names more than one table or view
- DISTINCT keyword
- GROUP BY clause
- HAVING clause
- Aggregate function

WITH CHECK OPTION

Causes all inserts and updates through the view to be checked against the view definition and rejected if the inserted or updated row does not conform to the view definition. If the clause is omitted, then no checking occurs.

9.2.2 DROP VIEW Command Diagram

The command diagram for the DROP VIEW command is very simple, with only one clause: the view name.

▶▶ **DROP VIEW** *view name* ◀◀

Clauses

view name Removes the view from the system catalog. Any views whose definition depends either partially or wholly on the dropped view are also dropped. All privileges on the views are also removed.

9.3 Creation of an External Schema

Views can present a constant unchanging appearance of a database to the world. Creating a set of views that map directly to physical tables can be referred to as the creation of an *external schema*.

Table structures and database organizations can change greatly over time. External schemas isolate data views from internal implementations. Applications that access the database can remain unaffected by changes if views are used.

Examples of physical schema-level database changes that can be hidden by views include the following:

- Object owners changes
- Column names changes; the view definitions can map the old column names to the new names, thereby making column name changes invisible to users' views
- Table names changes, which can be handled in the same way as column names
- Table column additions, since these new columns need not be added to existing views
- Table column reordering; views can explicitly order their columns independently of the underlying table's column ordering
- The combination of two or more tables into one, assuming that the primary keys of the two tables are the same

9.3.1 Creating an External Schema

Here are the suggested steps to create an external schema.

- We can create a "mirror" view of base tables, so that the underlying physical table are not seen.
- We can create additional views to represent different representations of data.

- We can use an evolutionary process to hone the data design into the most efficient form. This often requires a lengthy period of time to create the data design.

9.3.2 Creating a Mirror View of Base Tables

The creation of an initial external schema starts by creating a view that mirrors each base table in the physical table. The name of each view should reflect the fact that it is a view of the underlying base table, such as COMP for the mirror view of the base table COMP_T (where _T signifies a base table).

The following example appends _T to base tables in the COMPANY database and creates the mirror views of the base tables:

```
ALTER TABLE COMP RENAME TABLE COMP_T
ALTER TABLE EMPLOYEES RENAME TABLE EMPLOYEES_T
ALTER TABLE DEPARTMENTS RENAME TABLE
DEPARTMENTS_T
ALTER TABLE REVENUE RENAME TABLE REVENUE_T
ALTER TABLE BUS_TYPES RENAME TABLE BUS_TYPES_T
ALTER TABLE BUS_CODES RENAME TABLE BUS_CODES_T
ALTER TABLE LOCATIONS RENAME TABLE LOCATIONS_T
ALTER TABLE STOCK RENAME TABLE STOCK_T
ALTER TABLE STOCK_PRICE RENAME TABLE
STOCK_PRICE_T

CREATE VIEW COMP
AS SELECT COMP_ID, COMP_NAME, CORP_ADDR,
CITY, STATE, ZIP FROM COMP_T

CREATE VIEW EMPLOYEES
AS SELECT COMP_ID, EMP_ID, EMP_NAME, POSITION,
DEP_CODE FROM EMPLOYEES_T

CREATE VIEW DEPARTMENTS
AS SELECT DEP_CODE, DEP_NAME FROM
DEPARTMENTS_T

CREATE VIEW REVENUE
AS SELECT COMP_ID, REVENUE_YR, GROSS_REV,
NET_REV, FISCAL_YR FROM REVENUE_T
```

```
CREATE VIEW BUS_TYPES
AS SELECT COMP_ID, BUS_TYPE_ID FROM BUS_TYPES_T

CREATE VIEW BUS_CODES
AS SELECT BUS_TYPE_ID, BUS_DESCR FROM
BUS_CODES_T

CREATE VIEW LOCATIONS
AS SELECT COMP_ID, LOCAT_ID, ADR, CITY, STATE, ZIP,
PHONE FROM LOCATIONS_T

CREATE VIEW STOCK
AS SELECT SYMBOL, EXCHANGE, COMP_ID FROM
STOCK_T

CREATE VIEW STOCK_PRICE
AS SELECT SYMBOL, STOCK_DATE, STOCK_VALUE FROM
STOCK_PRICE_T
```

9.3.3 Creating Additional Views

Additional views can be created for programs that perform database queries when the data requirements of the program are fully documented. Also, views for ad hoc database users can be created when their data requirements have been adequately described.

We will add two views. The first view is STOCK_MAXVAL, which we needed earlier to perform the SELECT statement in Figure 9-3.

```
CREATE VIEW STOCK_MAXVAL (SYMBOL, STOCK_MAX)
AS SELECT SYMBOL, MAX (STOCK_VALUE) FROM
STOCK_PRICE GROUP BY SYMBOL
```

The second view we will add is BUS_TYPE_VIEW. In Chapter 2, the tables BUS_TYPES and BUS_CODES were created during our data normalization process. In reality, the two tables will almost always be joined to find business description names that correspond to companies listed in the COMP table. This view will be:

```
CREATE VIEW BUS_TYPE_VIEW (COMP_ID, COMP_NAME,
BUS_TYPE_ID, BUS_DESCR) AS
SELECT COMP_T.COMP_ID, COMP_NAME,
BUS_TYPES_T.BUS_TYPE_ID, BUS_DESCR FROM
COMP_T, BUS_TYPES_T, BUS_CODES_T
WHERE COMP_T.COMP_ID = BUS_TYPES_T.COMP_ID
AND BUS_TYPES_T.BUS_TYPE_ID =
BUS_CODES_T.BUS_TYPE_ID
```

We created a third view to avoid some confusion you may have already encountered. Remember, in Chapter 3, the table name COMPANY was altered to COMP. We now create an additional view, called COMPANY, that is identical to COMP, so that either name will access the table COMP_T.

```
CREATE VIEW COMPANY
AS SELECT COMP_ID, COMP_NAME, CORP_ADDR,
CITY, STATE, ZIP FROM COMP_T
```

9.3.4 Evolving the External Schema

While these CREATE VIEW statements build the initial external schema view of the database, this task is best viewed as an evolutionary process. As additional information requirements become known, additional views will be added to the external schema to satisfy these requirements in an efficient and flexible manner. To facilitate the administration of the external schema's DDL, these views should be kept together in a subdirectory where they can be conveniently accessed and reexecuted, should the need arise.

No programs or queries need be written to access the base tables, either by the DBAs or by anyone else.

9.4 Exercises with Views

Exercise 9.4.1: Using CREATE VIEW and DROP VIEW

This exercise shows examples of creating and dropping views.

1. Open Quest, if it is not already open. Make sure you are connected to the COMPANY database by pulling down the Utilities menu and using the **Add** function if necessary. Click on the COMPANY database.

2. Click on the **Open** button and then on the **SQL** button.

Figure 9-4   *Opening the SQL Activity*

3. Quest prompts for a file. Choose the file c:\sqlbase\exercise\chap9\ex9-1.qsd. Click **OK.**

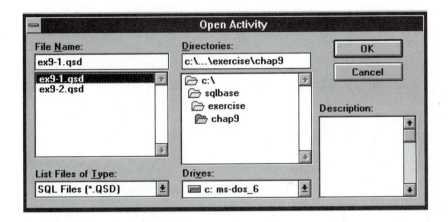

Figure 9-5   *Opening the SQL File*

4. The first CREATE VIEW command to be executed is:

    CREATE VIEW COMP_VIEW (COMP_ID, COMP_NAME,
    CORP_ADDR, CITY, STATE, ZIP) AS
    SELECT * FROM COMP

    Choose this SQL statement by clicking in the SQL Activity window, pull down the SQL menu, and select the **Execute SQL Statement** menu option.

5. The next CREATE VIEW command to be executed is:

    CREATE VIEW COMP_CAVIEW (COMP_ID,
    COMP_NAME, CORP_ADDR, CITY, STATE, ZIP) AS
    SELECT * FROM COMP WHERE STATE = 'CA'

Choose this SQL statement by clicking in the SQL Activity window, pull down the SQL menu, and select the **Execute SQL Statement** menu option.

6. We now execute a SELECT command against the view COMP_CAVIEW.

   SELECT COMP_NAME, CITY, STATE FROM
   COMP_CAVIEW
   WHERE ZIP LIKE '9%'

   Choose this SQL statement by clicking in the SQL Activity window, pull down the SQL menu, and select the **Execute SQL Statement** menu option.

7. We now execute a SELECT command against the table COMP, which will give us a superset of the result from step 5:

   SELECT COMP_NAME, CITY, STATE FROM COMP
   WHERE ZIP LIKE '9%'

   Choose this SELECT statement by clicking in the SQL Activity window, pull down the SQL menu, and select the **Execute SQL Statement** menu option.

8. Here, the view, EMP_VIEW is created.

   CREATE VIEW EMP_VIEW AS
   SELECT * FROM EMPLOYEES

   Choose this CREATE VIEW statement by clicking in the SQL Activity window. Choose the **Execute SQL Statement** menu option.

9. We now execute an INSERT command against the view EMP_VIEW.

   INSERT INTO EMP_VIEW (EMP_ID,EMP_NAME,
   COMP_ID) VALUES (22,'Frank Johnson',1001)

   Choose this INSERT statement by clicking in the SQL Activity window. Choose the **Execute SQL Statement** menu option.

10. The EMP_VIEW view is dropped:

    DROP VIEW EMP_VIEW

Choose this DROP VIEW statement by clicking in the SQL Activity window. Choose the **Execute SQL Statement** menu option.

11. We now execute a CREATE VIEW command for view EMP_VIEW with a WITH CHECK OPTION clause.

```
CREATE VIEW EMP_VIEW AS
SELECT * FROM EMPLOYEES
WHERE COMP_ID IN
(SELECT COMP_ID FROM COMP)
WITH CHECK OPTION
```

Choose this CREATE VIEW statement by clicking in the SQL Activity window. Choose the **Execute SQL Statement** menu option.

12. We now execute the INSERT command to the view EMP_VIEW done previously.

```
INSERT INTO EMP_VIEW
(EMP_ID, EMP_NAME, COMP_ID)
```

Choose this INSERT statement by clicking in the SQL Activity window. Choose the **Execute SQL Statement** menu option. This command generates the error shown in Figure 9-6.

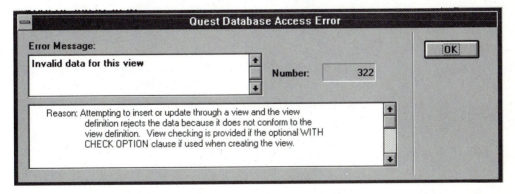

Figure 9-6   *Error Condition on INSERT into View*

13. The DROP VIEW command is used to drop the COMP_VIEW view.

```
DROP VIEW COMP_VIEW
```

Choose this DROP VIEW statement by clicking in the SQL Activity window. Choose the **Execute SQL Statement** menu option.

14. We now execute the CREATE VIEW command to create the view STOCK_MAXVAL, which uses the result of an aggregate function as a column.

    CREATE VIEW STOCK_MAXVAL (SYMBOL, STOCK_MAX)
    AS SELECT SYMBOL, MAX (STOCK_VALUE) FROM
    STOCK_PRICE GROUP BY SYMBOL

    Choose this CREATE VIEW statement by clicking in the SQL Activity window. Choose the **Execute SQL Statement** menu option.

15. Here ia a SELECT command that makes use of the STOCK_MAXVAL view:

    SELECT COMP_NAME, BUS_CODES.BUS_TYPE_ID,
    BUS_DESCR, STOCK.SYMBOL, STOCK_MAX FROM
    COMP, BUS_TYPES, BUS_CODES, STOCK,
    STOCK_MAXVAL
    WHERE BUS_DESCR = 'Telecommunications' AND
    COMP.COMP_ID = BUS_TYPES.COMP_ID AND
    BUS_TYPES.BUS_TYPE_ID =
    BUS_CODES.BUS_TYPE_ID AND
    COMP.COMP_ID = STOCK.COMP_ID AND
    STOCK.SYMBOL = STOCK_MAXVAL.SYMBOL

    Choose this SELECT statement by clicking in the SQL Activity window. Choose the **Execute SQL Statement** menu option.

16. We now execute the COMMIT command to commit the changes we have made to our database. Choose this COMMIT statement by clicking in the SQL Activity window. Choose the **Execute SQL Statement** menu option.

17. To close, choose the **Close** option from the File menu.

Exercise 9.4.2:   Creating an External Schema

This exercise will create a very simple external schema, as demonstrated in Section 9.3. Note that the view, STOCK_MAXVAL, has already been created in the last exercise and so is not in this one.

1. Click on the **Open** button and then on the **SQL** button.

2. Quest prompts for a file. Choose the file c:\sqlbase\exercise\chap9\ex9-2.qsd. Click **OK**.

3. Choose the **Execute All SQL** menu option, as shown below:

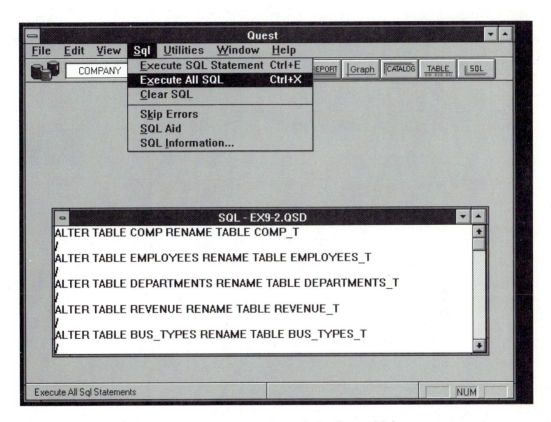

Figure 9-7   *Executing Script to Create External Schema*

4. An external schema is created! Try some SELECT statements of your own on this database. The views do not significantly change our database design, but they insulate the physical design from end users.

5. To close, choose the **Close** option from the File menu.

9.5   Summary

This chapter covered the basics of using views. Both the advantages and disadvantages of using views were discussed. We used views to create an *external schema,* a means by which the physical table is hidden from end users in order to control design changes. In the next chapter, we discuss another method to provide access control to tables: privileges. Whereas views are a way to control how data is presented, privileges are a way to control what SQL statements are used.

10 Privileges and Use of GRANT and REVOKE

Privileges provide ways to control access to tables and SQL statements. This chapter discusses the SQL commands that grant and revoke privileges: the GRANT and REVOKE commands.

The chapter is organized as follows:

10.1   Privileges and the GRANT Command

The entire book has so far assumed the presence of a single user. So far, you have not needed to know much about users because, by default, the exercises have been performed assuming that you are the creator of the database. The original creator of a database is allowed unrestricted access to all the tables in the database. This original creator (who has the name SYSADM in the SQLBase relational engine included with this book) can create and destroy new tables without any limitations. Clearly, not all users should have unlimited access to a database.

Multiple users can be created with different levels of access authority to the database. This section discusses the GRANT statement, the SQL command that allows you to add users and to select which privileges you want them to have.

10.1.1 Adding Users

The following command adds a new user, Michele, identified by the password MIKI.

```
GRANT CONNECT
TO MICHELE
IDENTIFIED BY MIKI
```

More than one user can be added in a single GRANT command. For example:

```
GRANT CONNECT
TO JAMES, MORT, BRIAN
IDENTIFIED BY COBRA, ALPHA, BLUE
```

Adding new users is as easy as this! We have added the users, Michele, James, Mort, and Brian. The CONNECT privilege was given to these users.

10.1.2 Granting Table and Authority-Level Privileges

Adding a new user is only one function of the GRANT command. In general, the GRANT command can grant privileges in two specific categories:

- Authority levels
- Table privileges

Authority Levels

Authority level means the types of operations a user can perform (such as logging on, creating tables, or creating users). This form of the GRANT command assigns users of the database and assigns their authority level.

Authority levels are common to all SQL implementations, but there are many extensions from vendor to vendor. For SQLBase, the authority levels listed in Table 10-1 can be granted by SYSADM:

Table 10-1 *SQLBase Authority Levels*

Authority	Description
CONNECT	Must be granted before any other. It allows the user to log on to the database and exercise any of the privileges assigned for specific tables. The IDENTIFIED BY clause is required for granting CONNECT.
RESOURCE	Gives a user the right to create tables, to drop those tables, and to grant, modify, or revoke privileges to those tables for valid users of the database. Users with RESOURCE authority automatically have all privileges on tables that they have created.
DBA	Automatically assigns all privileges on any table in the database to a user, including the right to grant, modify, or revoke the table privileges of any other user in the database. However, a DBA cannot create new users or change a password or authority level of an existing user. These privileges are restricted to SYSADM.

Oracle and SQLBase both have the authorities CONNECT, RESOURCE, and DBA. Oracle also has the concept of user defined *Roles*. There are user-defined groups of privileges, or Roles, that can be granted to users as a block. Sybase has the concept of system administration authorities, but Sybase also creates a level of privileges based on database operators.

Table Privileges

Table privileges are privileges assigned to users giving the right to use SQL commands against certain tables. Generally, the creator of the table has the right to grant these privileges, unlike authority privileges that must be given by the original creator of a database.

Table 10-2 lists the standard table privileges for the GRANT command.

Table 10-2   *GRANT Command Privileges*

Privilege	Description
SELECT	Select data from a table or view.
INSERT	Insert rows into a table or view.
DELETE	Delete rows from a table or view.
UPDATE	Update a table and (optionally) update only the specified columns.
INDEX	Create or drop indexes for a table.
ALTER	Alter a table.
ALL	Exercise all of the above for a table.

10.1.3 Examples of GRANT and Authority Levels

This section demonstrates the three authority levels of SQLBase: CONNECT, RESOURCE, and DBA.

Only SYSADM can use the GRANT command to provide authority levels. SYSADM can create new users and change the authority levels and table privileges of existing users. This is the highest authority level, and it is preassigned by SQLBase to SYSADM.

Connect Authority

We have already used the CONNECT authority to create the users Michele, Brian, Mort, and James. For SQLBase, the user name SYSADM is already predefined. The user name SYSADM cannot be changed, and there can only be one SYSADM for a database. The only thing that can be changed for SYSADM is the password.

The CONNECT authority simply means that the specified user is a valid user and can connect to the database (in this case, COMPANY) and access any tables to which he has been granted specific privileges.

At this point, Michele has only been granted CONNECT authority. She does not have specific privileges to any of the tables in the database. The statement:

> SELECT * FROM COMPANY

will not work for Michele until we grant her the privilege to use SELECT.

Resource Authority

The following examples illustrate how to grant RESOURCE authority. Note that since Michele was assigned a password (MIKI) when she was granted CONNECT authority, no password needs to be specified in the following command.

> GRANT RESOURCE TO MICHELE

Michele can now issue CREATE TABLE and DROP TABLE commands as well as GRANT and REVOKE commands on tables that she creates.

DBA Authority

Sometimes, the original creator of a database may want to grant authority to a user to access, modify, or drop not only his or her own tables but also to do so with all other tables in the database.

This is known as DBA authority and is similar to RESOURCE authority. The only difference is that DBA authority does not allow a user to create new users or to change their existing authority levels. The only person who can do that is the original creator of the database (i.e., with RESOURCE authority).

The following command grants DBA authority to James.

> GRANT DBA TO JAMES

Note that if you GRANT a user the RESOURCE or DBA authority, the permission does not take effect until the next time the user connects.

10.1.4 TABLE Privileges and the GRANT Command

This form of the GRANT command gives a user one or more specified privileges for a table or view. Table privileges can be granted by any user who has the authority to do so.

- A user with DBA authority can grant privileges on any tables or views in the database.

- A user with RESOURCE authority (but without DBA authority) can grant privileges only on tables created by him or on views that are based completely on tables created by him.

- A user with only CONNECT authority cannot grant privileges. Nor does he have privileges to any tables or views unless he is explicitly granted such privileges with a GRANT command.

This section provides examples of these table privileges: SELECT, INSERT, DELETE, UPDATE, INDEX, ALTER, and ALL.

Examples of Granting Table Privileges

The following set of GRANT commands provide the different privileges for the users Michele, James, Mort, And Brian. Here are the privileges that we will give our four users:

NAMES/ TABLE PRIVILEGES	Michele	James	Mort	Brian
SELECT	Yes	Yes	Yes	
INSERT	Yes		Yes	Yes
UPDATE	Yes		Yes	
DELETE	Yes			
INDEX	Yes			Yes
ALTER	Yes			Yes
ALL (all above checked)	Yes			

Note that the privileges are granted for specific tables. For example, Brian is granted privileges on table COMP_T, whereas Michele is granted privileges on the views, COMP and EMPLOYEES, created in the last chapter.

All table privileges are given to user Michele as shown here:

```
GRANT ALL ON COMP, EMPLOYEES TO MICHELE
```

The user James is granted the privilege to query the COMP table:

```
GRANT SELECT ON COMP TO JAMES
```

The user Mort is granted SELECT, INSERT, and UPDATE:

```
GRANT SELECT, INSERT, UPDATE
ON COMP TO MORT
```

The user Brian is granted INDEX and ALTER permissions for the table COMP_T.

```
GRANT INDEX, ALTER ON COMP_T TO BRIAN
```

Note that you cannot grant the INDEX or ALTER privileges for a view. You should grant these privileges directly on the base tables.

If we had an additional user, Kristi, with the same privileges as Brian, we could issue the following command to grant privileges to both users at once:

```
GRANT INDEX, ALTER ON COMP_T TO BRIAN, KRISTI
```

Note that since Brian already had INDEX and ALTER privileges on COMP, repeating the privilege in another GRANT command had no additional effect for that user.

Granting UPDATE Privileges on a Specific Column

UPDATE privileges may be granted to a user on specified columns within a table.

The following command grants the UPDATE privilege to Mort and Brian on the EMP_NAME and POSITION columns of the EMPLOYEES table.

```
GRANT UPDATE (EMP_NAME, POSITION)
ON EMPLOYEES TO MORT, BRIAN
```

Granting Privileges to All Users

We might have more users we need to add, like Dan and Sarah. Rather than listing individual users, you can use the keyword PUBLIC to signify all users. The following GRANT gives all table privileges to all users for the tables STOCK and LOCATIONS.

GRANT ALL ON STOCK, LOCATIONS TO PUBLIC

Restrictions on Table Privileges

User privileges may include all SQL statements except CREATE and DROP TABLE. A user granted only the CONNECT authority to a database may not create or drop tables. A user must be granted RESOURCE authority to CREATE his own tables. Such a user may also DROP tables that he or she has created. He automatically has all access privileges (SELECT, INSERT, DELETE, UPDATE, INDEX and ALTER) on any tables that he creates.

10.1.5 A Quick Note on Synonyms

Synonyms can be used to simplify references to tables. The following scenario shows the usefulness of synonyms.

In Section 10.5, an exercise asks you to log on to the COMPANY database as user MORT. Consider the following command:

UPDATE COMP SET COMP_ID = 900
WHERE COMP_NAME LIKE '%PEPSI%'

Until now, this command has worked, but we have been executing commands under the user SYSADM. When we log on as the user MORT, this command does not work, because the table we are updating, COMP, has to be referenced by the creator of this database, SYSADM. The following command will work:

UPDATE SYSADM.COMP SET COMP_ID = 900
WHERE COMP_NAME LIKE '%PEPSI%'

Referencing tables in this manner can be cumbersome. You may want to use a *synonym*. For example, the table, SYSADM.COMP, can be referenced by another name, in this case, "C." The following command creates a synonym called C.

CREATE SYNONYM C
FOR SYSADM.COMP

Now the UPDATE command we just executed can be referenced as:

UPDATE C SET COMP_ID = 900
WHERE COMP_NAME LIKE '%PEPSI%'

Any future commands can now reference SYSADM.COMP as C. For example:

SELECT * FROM C

Note that a synonym is only valid for the person who created it. No other user can use it. Another user could, however, create an identically named synonym.

10.2   GRANT Command Diagrams

Two command diagrams for the GRANT command are shown below:

- GRANT (table privileges)

- GRANT (database authority)

10.2.1 GRANT (Database Authority) Command Diagram

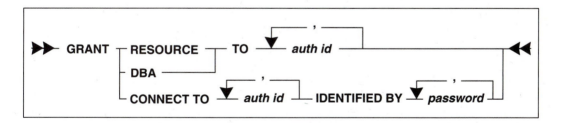

Clauses

authorization id

> The username that gives a user authorization to connect to a database. The authorization-ID SYSADM is preassigned by the system and reserved for the SQLBase superuser.

IDENTIFIED BY password

> Required *only* when granting CONNECT authority to a user; the phrase used to introduce the new user's password.

password   Any valid SQL short identifier. To change the password of a user, grant that user CONNECT authority with the new password.

> When a database is first created, the original creator of the database (SYSADM) is always identified by the password SYSADM. The owner of the database can change the password to a private password before granting authority to any other user.

10.2.2 GRANT (Table Privileges) Command Diagram

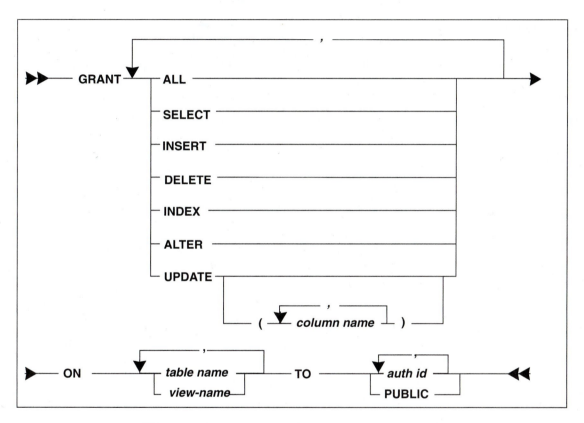

Clauses

table name	Must identify a table that exists in the database.
view name	Must identify a view that exists in the database.
column name	A column in the table or view specified in the ON clause. Each column name must be unqualified, and each column name must be in every table or view identified in the ON clause.
auth id	Must refer to a user who has been granted at least CONNECT authority to the database.

PUBLIC   Granting a privilege to PUBLIC means that all current and future users have the specified privilege on the table or view.

10.3   Privileges and the REVOKE Command

So far, we have seen examples only of how to grant privileges and authority levels to users. The table privileges and authority levels may be selectively revoked through the REVOKE command.

For each GRANT command option, there is a corresponding REVOKE option. The next two sections show examples of using REVOKE to take away the authority level and table privileges granted previously.

10.3.1 Examples of the REVOKE Command and Database Authority Privileges

This form of the REVOKE command removes the authority level of a user who has previously been granted authority for a database. Here are some rules on who may use the REVOKE command with authority level privileges:

- A SYSADM can revoke any of the authorities granted to a user (including CONNECT authority).
- A DBA can revoke any privileges of any user of the database (but not change authority levels).
- The creator of a table (RESOURCE authority) can revoke any privileges he previously granted to a user.

Below are examples of using REVOKE with CONNECT, RESOURCE, and DBA privileges.

Revoking Connect Authority

The following command removes Michele's privileges from our database:

    REVOKE CONNECT FROM MICHELE

If the privileges granted Michele are not removed first, this command will not be allowed. Order of issuing REVOKE command is important.

Revoking RESOURCE Authority

The following command removes RESOURCE authority from the user
James:

REVOKE RESOURCE FROM JAMES

Revoke DBA Authority

The following command strips DBA authority from Mort:

REVOKE DBA FROM MORT

If you revoke a user's RESOURCE or DBA authority, the revocation does
not take effect until the next time the user connects.

10.3.2 Examples of REVOKE and Table Privileges

This form of the REVOKE command revokes privileges previously granted
to users for a table or view.

Any user with the appropriate GRANT (table privileges) authority for a
table can revoke the privileges for the corresponding tables or views. The
creator of a table can revoke privileges on it.

Examples of Revoking Table Privileges

The following set of REVOKE commands revoke all the privileges that were
granted in Section 10.1.4 to the users Michele, James, Mort, and Brian.

The following command revokes all privileges from the user Michele:

REVOKE ALL ON COMP FROM MICHELE

The next command revokes the privilege to query the COMP table from the
user James.

REVOKE SELECT ON COMP FROM JAMES

The following command revokes SELECT, INSERT, and UPDATE from the
user Mort.

REVOKE SELECT, INSERT, UPDATE, DELETE
ON COMP FROM MORT

INDEX and ALTER privileges are revoked from the user Brian for the table COMP with this command:

REVOKE INDEX, ALTER ON COMP_T FROM BRIAN

Revoking UPDATE Privileges on a Specific Column

UPDATE privileges can be removed from a user on specified columns within a table.

The following command revokes the UPDATE privilege from users Mort and Brian on the *emp_name* and *position* columns of the EMPLOYEES table.

REVOKE UPDATE (EMP_NAME, POSITION)
ON EMPLOYEES FROM MORT, BRIAN

Revoking Privileges of All Users

Rather than listing individual users, use the keyword PUBLIC to signify all users. The following REVOKE command removes all table privileges of all users for the tables EMPLOYEES and LOCATIONS.

REVOKE ALL ON EMPLOYEES, LOCATIONS
FROM PUBLIC

10.4   REVOKE Command Diagrams

Two command diagrams for the REVOKE command are shown in this section:

- REVOKE (database authority)
- REVOKE (table privileges)

10.4.1 REVOKE (Database Authority) Command Diagram

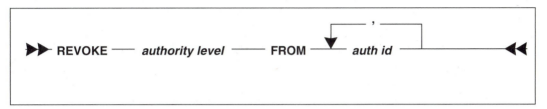

Clauses

authority level

DBA, RESOURCE and CONNECT can be revoked by SYSADM.

FROM auth id

Must refer to a valid user who currently has the privileges that are being revoked.

10.4.2 REVOKE (Table Privileges) Command Diagram

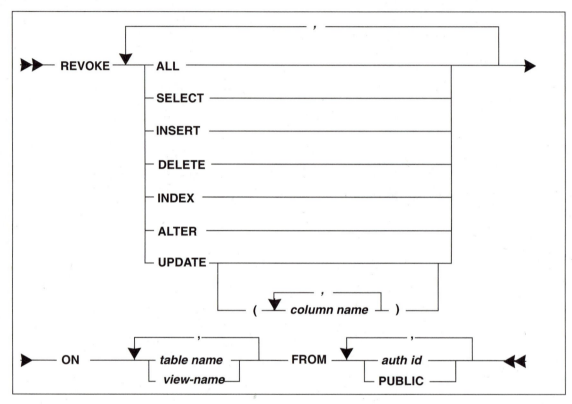

Clauses

ON table name Must identify a table that exists in the database.

ON view name Must identify a view that exists in the database.

column name If you specify more than one table or view and UPDATE privileges are revoked for selected columns, then each column named must be in the specified tables or views.

FROM auth id Must refer to a valid user who currently has the privileges that are being revoked.

FROM PUBLIC
Revoking a privilege from PUBLIC means that all current users have the specified privilege revoked.

10.5 Exercises with GRANT and REVOKE

Exercise 10.5.1: Using the GRANT Command

This exercise uses the GRANT command to set the privileges discussed in Section 10.1.

1. Open Quest, if it is not already open. Make sure you are connected to the COMPANY database by pulling down the Utilities menu and using the **Add** function if necessary. Click on the COMPANY database.

2. Click on the **Open** button and then on the **SQL** button, as shown below:

Figure 10-1   *Opening the SQL Activity*

3. Quest prompts for a file. Choose the file c:\sqlbase\exercise\chap10\ex10-1.qsd, as shown below. Click **OK.**

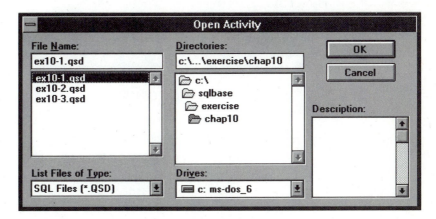

Figure 10-2   *Opening the SQL File*

4. Pull down the SQL menu and select **Execute All SQL** statement, as shown in Figure 10-3.

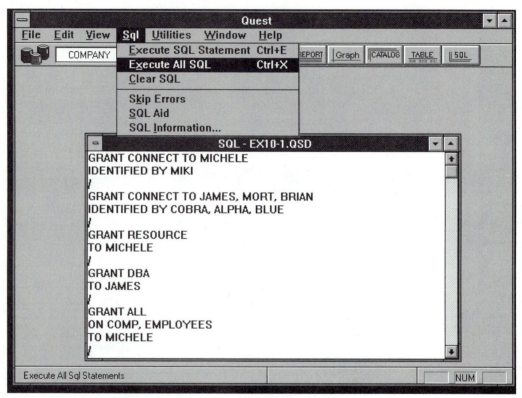

Figure 10-3   *Executing GRANT Commands*

5. The GRANT commands executed were discussed in detail in Section 10.1.1. They were:

    GRANT CONNECT TO MICHELE IDENTIFIED BY MIKI

    GRANT CONNECT TO JAMES, MORT, BRIAN
    IDENTIFIED BY COBRA, ALPHA, BLUE

    GRANT RESOURCE TO MICHELE

    GRANT DBA TO JAMES

    GRANT ALL ON COMP, EMPLOYEES TO MICHELE

GRANT SELECT ON COMP TO JAMES

GRANT SELECT, INSERT, UPDATE ON COMP TO MORT

GRANT INDEX, ALTER ON COMP_T TO BRIAN

GRANT UPDATE (EMP_NAME, POSITION)
ON EMPLOYEES TO MORT, BRIAN

GRANT ALL ON STOCK, LOCATIONS TO PUBLIC

COMMIT

6. To close, choose the **Close** option from the File menu.

Exercise 10.5.2: Connecting Through Quest as Different Users

This exercise will configure Quest so that you can connect to a RDBMS as different users. In this case, we will log into the database as user MORT and demonstrate restrictions on SQL commands. Try logging in as different users on your own to demonstrate the restrictions each user has.

1. Pull down the Utilities menu option in Quest, choose the **Database** option, then choose the **Configure** option on the cascading menu, as shown below:

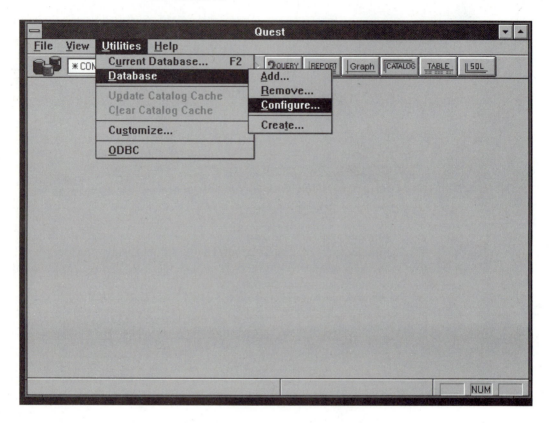

Figure 10-4 *Configuring Quest for Different Users*

2. Select the check box **Prompt for User/Password on first connect,** as shown in Figure 10-5:

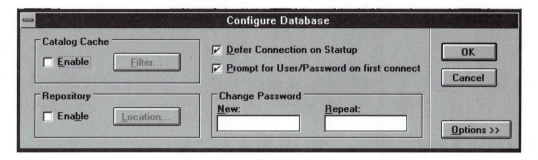

Figure 10-5 *The Configure Database Window of Quest*

3. Completely exit from Quest. Make sure on log out that the box **Save workspace?** is checked, as shown below:

Figure 10-6 *Exiting Quest to Save Options*

4. Reopen Quest. Click on the **Open** button and then on the **SQL** button.

5. Quest prompts for a file. Choose the file c:\sqlbase\exercise\chap10\ex10-2.qsd. Click **OK**.

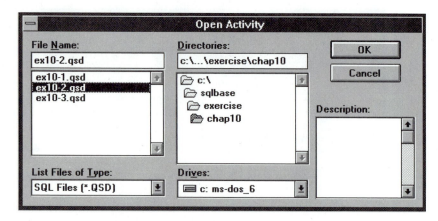

Figure 10-7 *Opening a SQL File*

6. You will be prompted for a user name. Type in **mort** as the user and **alpha** as the password. Click **OK**.

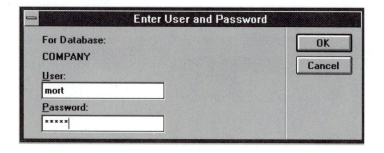

Figure 10-8 *Logging in Under a User Name*

7. You should now see the open SQL Activity. Select the first UPDATE statement in the window. The user MORT was granted UPDATE privilege in Exercise 10.5.1, so this command will work:

```
UPDATE SYSADM.COMP SET COMP_ID = 900
WHERE COMP_NAME LIKE '%PEPSI%'
```

Choose this UPDATE statement by clicking in the SQL Activity window. Choose the **Execute SQL Statement** menu option.

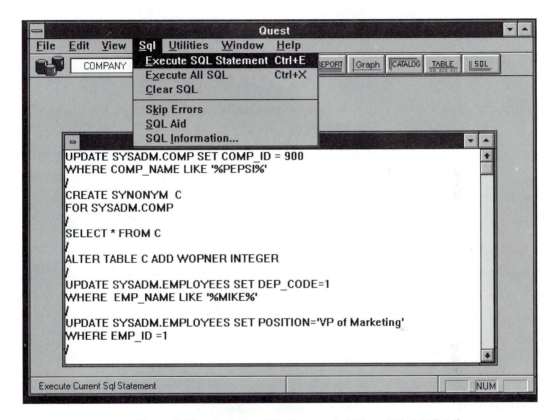

Figure 10-9 *Executing SQL Commands Without SYSADM Privileges*

8. We can create a synonym for SYSADM.COMP. The second command in the SQL Activity windows uses the CREATE SYNONYM command to do this:

```
CREATE SYNONYM  C
FOR SYSADM.COMP
```

Choose this statement by clicking in the SQL Activity window. Choose the **Execute SQL Statement** menu option.

9. The next SELECT statement shows the use of the synonym C in place of SYSADM.COMP:

    SELECT * FROM C

    Choose this SELECT statement by clicking in the SQL Activity window. Choose the **Execute SQL Statement** menu option.

10. The next command attempts to issue an ALTER command:

    ALTER TABLE C ADD WOPNER INTEGER

    Mort does not have ALTER privileges for the table COMP, so this command will not work. There is another problem with this command. In Chapter 9, COMP was created as a view. You cannot alter views, so the error message shown in Figure 10-10 is displayed.

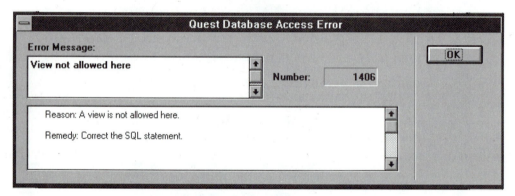

Figure 10-10   *View Error Message*

Choose this SELECT statement by clicking in the SQL Activity window. Choose the **Execute SQL Statement** menu option.

11. The next command to execute is:

    UPDATE SYSADM.EMPLOYEES SET POSITION='VP of Marketing' WHERE EMP_ID =1

    This command should work, since user MORT was given UPDATE privileges on the columns, POSITION and EMP_name, from the EMPLOYEES table.

Choose this statement by clicking in the SQL Activity window. Choose the **Execute SQL Statement** menu option.

12. The next command to execute is:

UPDATE SYSADM.EMPLOYEES SET DEP_CODE=1
WHERE EMP_NAME LIKE '%MIKE%'

Mort does not have UPDATE privileges on this column. You will see the error shown in Figure 10-11:

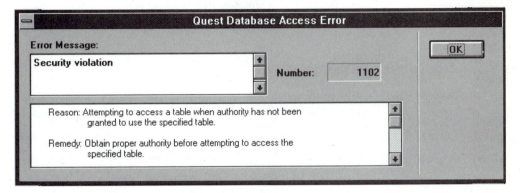

Figure 10-11 *Security Violation Error*

Choose this statement by clicking in the SQL Activity window. Choose the **Execute SQL Statement** menu option.

13. The next command to execute is:

DELETE FROM SYSADM.EMPLOYEES
WHERE COMP_ID = 145

This command will not work because Mort does not have DELETE privileges. You will see the same error shown in Figure 10-11.

Choose this statement by clicking in the SQL Activity window. Choose the **Execute SQL Statement** menu option.

14. The next command to execute is:

CREATE TABLE TESTER2
(COL1 INTEGER)

This command will not work because Mort does not have the RESOURCE or DBA authorities needed.

Choose this statement by clicking in the SQL Activity window. Choose the **Execute SQL Statement** menu option.

15. The next command to execute is COMMIT.

Choose this COMMIT statement by clicking in the SQL Activity window. Choose the **Execute SQL Statement** menu option.

16. You can exit Quest, start it back up again, and then replay this exercise as different users. The results will differ depending on which user you log in as.

Exercise 10.5.3: Revoking Privileges

This exercise will use the REVOKE command to revoke the privileges granted in Exercise 10.5.1:

1. Completely exit Quest and open it up again. Click on the **Open** button and then on the **SQL** button.

2. Quest prompts for a file. Choose the file c:\sqlbase\exercise\chap10\ex10-2.qsd. Click **OK**.

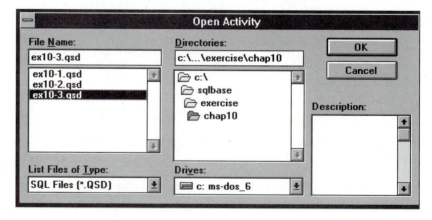

Figure 10-12 *Opening the SQL File*

3. You are prompted for a user, as shown below. Type in **sysadm** as the user and **sysadm** as the password. Click **OK**.

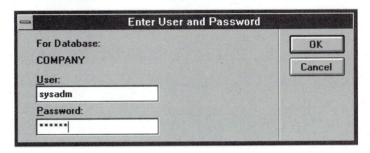

Figure 10-13 *Logging into Quest*

4. Pull down the **SQL** menu and select **Execute All SQL** statement, as shown below:

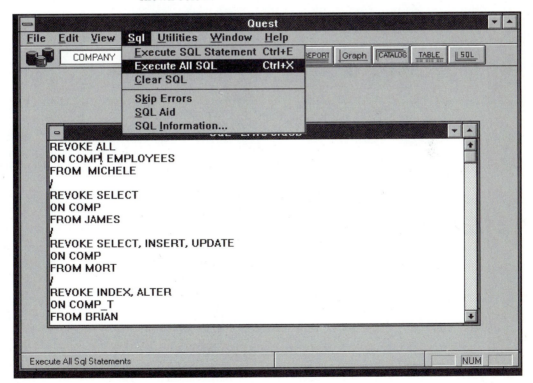

Figure 10-14 *Executing the REVOKE Command*

5. These are the REVOKE commands discussed in Section 10.3:

   REVOKE ALL ON COMP, EMPLOYEES FROM MICHELE

   REVOKE SELECT ON COMP FROM JAMES

   REVOKE SELECT, INSERT, UPDATE ON COMP
   FROM MORT

   REVOKE INDEX, ALTER ON COMP_T FROM BRIAN

   REVOKE UPDATE (EMP_NAME, POSITION)
   ON EMPLOYEES FROM MORT, BRIAN

   REVOKE ALL ON STOCK, LOCATIONS FROM PUBLIC

   REVOKE DBA FROM JAMES

   REVOKE CONNECT FROM JAMES, MORT, BRIAN

   REVOKE RESOURCE FROM MICHELE

   REVOKE CONNECT FROM MICHELE

   COMMIT

   The order of these commands is important. For example, if you tried to issue the REVOKE CONNECT FROM MICHELE command before revoking the privileges granted her, the statement would not work.

6. To close, choose the **Close** option from the File menu.

10.6   Summary

This chapter covered the use of GRANT and REVOKE commands. Two forms of privileges were discussed in this chapter: authority level and table privileges. Authority-level privileges covered granting and revoking rights to execute the following types of commands:

- DROP TABLE and CREATE TABLE
- GRANT and REVOKE

Table-level privileges control commands performed on existing tables. They include the following SQL commands:

- SELECT
- INSERT, UPDATE, and DELETE
- CREATE INDEX
- ALTER TABLE

In this chapter we created four users. Each user was given different privileges, allowing us to maintain security. Security is maintainable in this manner.

11 System Tables and Stored Procedures

System tables describe the structure and data within a database. Stored procedures are a way to enable an RDBMS to execute complex operations. This chapter discusses both these subjects together for a specific reason: System tables and stored procedures are two areas in which relational database vendors do not find common ground. Neither system tables nor stored procedures are uniform from vendor to vendor. While this chapter introduces both subjects, to really learn about either, you will need to focus on a specific relational database.

The outline is organized as follows:

Section 11.1 Introduction to System Tables
Section 11.2 How Vendors Vary System Tables
Section 11.3 Exercises with System Tables
Section 11.4 Stored Procedures and Triggers
Section 11.5 Summary

11.1 Introduction to System Tables

Information about database objects is maintained in *system tables*. For example, we ask the question: What are the columns for the table COMP? System tables can be used to query for this information. System tables are also referred to as a *system catalog* or as *data dictionaries*.

All vendors vary in their implementation of system tables. Our goal is not to cover these tables in complete detail, but to introduce the concepts of tables that describe the structure and relevant information about database objects.

The most basic function of a system table is to describe the structure of a database. Figure 11-1 executes a SELECT statement, using SQLBase to discover what columns are in the table COMP.

SQL - EX11-1.QSD		
SELECT NAME, TBCREATOR, TBNAME		
FROM SYSCOLUMNS WHERE TBNAME = 'COMP'		

NAME	TBCREATOR	TBNAME
CITY	SYSADM	COMP
COMP_ID	SYSADM	COMP
COMP_NAME	SYSADM	COMP
CORP_ADDR	SYSADM	COMP
STATE	SYSADM	COMP
ZIP	SYSADM	COMP

Figure 11-1   *SELECT to List Columns in COMP*

The command in Figure 11-1 identifies the column names, the table creator, and the table name for the table COMP. The system catalog has a table, SYSCOLUMNS, that was used in this example. SYSCOLUMNS contains information about the name of all columns in a database, the creator of all columns, and the table name that those columns belong to.

If we issued a similar SELECT statement by using SQL Server, the same table, SYSCOLUMNS, exists. Oracle, however, would require the use of a view, USER_TAB_COLUMNS.

Other Examples of Using System Tables

System tables can also be used to discover what tables exist in a database. Figure 11-2 shows a SELECT statement for SQLBase, using the table SYSTABLES, which provides both the names of existing tables and the creator of these tables.

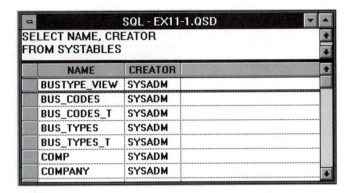

Figure 11-2   *SYSTABLES Table Example*

Figure 11-3 shows a SELECT statement that finds the name, the creator, and the column names of all columns in a database.

NAME	TBCREATOR	TBNAME	
BUS_TYPE_ID	SYSADM	BUS_TYPES_T	
COMP_ID	SYSADM	BUS_TYPES_T	
CITY	SYSADM	COMP	
COMP_ID	SYSADM	COMP	
COMP_NAME	SYSADM	COMP	
CORP_ADDR	SYSADM	COMP	
STATE	SYSADM	COMP	

```
SQL - EX11-1.QSD
SELECT NAME, TBCREATOR, TBNAME
FROM SYSCOLUMNS
```

Figure 11-3   *SYSCOLUMNS Table Example*

Figure 11-4 shows a SELECT statement that returns information about system indexes.

NAME	CREATOR	TBNAME
XPKCOMPANY	SYSADM	COMP_T
XPKBUS_TYPE	SYSADM	BUS_TYPES_T
XPKBUS_CODES	SYSADM	BUS_CODES_T
XPKEMPLOYEES	SYSADM	EMPLOYEES_T
XPKREVENUE	SYSADM	REVENUE_T
XPKSTOCK_VAL	SYSADM	STOCK_PRICE_T
XPKDEP_CODE	SYSADM	DEPARTMENTS_T

SELECT NAME, CREATOR, TBNAME FROM SYSINDEXES

Figure 11-4   *SYSINDEXES Table Example*

More Examples: System Tables and Privileges

In addition to the above three tables, the SQLBase system dictionary contains other tables that contain information about users, their authority levels, and privileges. These are the SYSUSERAUTH, SYSTABAUTH, and SYSCOLAUTH tables.

The SYSUSERAUTH table contains the name of each user to whom a CONNECT (or higher) authority has been granted. Figure 11-5 shows an example of using SYSUSERAUTH. The passwords (encrypted) and indications whether a user has RESOURCE or DBA authority are two other fields of information contained in SYSUSERAUTH.

SELECT * FROM SYSUSERAUTH

NAME	RESOURCEAUTH	DBAAUTH	PASSWORD
SYSADM	G	G	FFCBBIEFCDNFAPMH
SYSSQL			IEHCOAFBFNMMFJKA
MICHELE	Y		IICPCOJJBMLOPJDO
JAMES	Y	Y	GCEDCCMLKKHFKEGD
MORT			HJBBHOALJADCNLDP
BRIAN			HNKHNEADJEFAMCDJ

Figure 11-5   *SYSUSERAUTH Table Example*

Now let us look at the SYSTABAUTH table (Figure 11-6) for the entries relating to the COMP and EMPLOYEES tables. This table shows authorities granted to users on specific tables. The table also shows whether the users added in Chapter 10 have privileges to use the ALTER, DELETE, INSERT, and UPDATE commands.

SQL - EX11-1.QSD					
SELECT GRANTEE, TTNAME, ALTERAUTH, DELETEAUTH, INSERTAUTH, UPDATEAUTH FROM SYSTABAUTH WHERE TTNAME IN ['COMP','EMPLOYEES']					
GRANTEE	**TTNAME**	**ALTERAUTH**	**DELETEAUTH**	**INSERTAUTH**	**UPDATEAUTH**
JAMES	COMP				
MORT	COMP			Y	Y
MICHELE	COMP		Y	Y	Y
MORT	EMPLOYEES				Y
BRIAN	EMPLOYEES				Y
MICHELE	EMPLOYEES		Y	Y	Y

Figure 11-6 *SYSTABAUTH Table Example*

Figure 11-7 shows the use of the system table, SYSCOLAUTH, which shows privileges granted on the column authority.

SQL - EX11-1.QSD			
SELECT * FROM SYSCOLAUTH WHERE TNAME IN ['COMP','EMPLOYEES']			
GRANTEE	**CREATOR**	**TNAME**	**COLNAME**
BRIAN	SYSADM	EMPLOYEES	POSITION
BRIAN	SYSADM	EMPLOYEES	EMP_NAME
MORT	SYSADM	EMPLOYEES	POSITION
MORT	SYSADM	EMPLOYEES	EMP_NAME

Figure 11-7 *SYSCOLAUTH Table Example*

11.2   How Vendors Vary System Tables

In this section, we will look at system catalogs of three RDBMS systems: Oracle, Sybase SQL Server, and SQLBase. The idea of this section is not to cover system tables for all vendors in detail, but rather to serve as an introduction. If you desire to learn about system tables for a specific database, consult the manuals of that specific database.

11.2.1 Oracle's System Tables

One interesting feature about Oracle's catalogs is that most objects in the system catalog begin with one of four names: USER, ALL, and DBA or V$. Information in USER views corresponds to objects relating to the user performing the query. Information in ALL views includes USER information as well as information granted to PUBLIC. Information in DBA views includes all information available about database objects. Views beginning with V$ are tables for the system statistic tables.

Master Catalog (A View Named DICTIONARY)

The view named DICTIONARY describes all the other views in the system catalogs. If you wanted to know what other views are available in Oracle's system catalog. You could issue the following SELECT statement:

SELECT Table_Name, Comments FROM DICT

The view, DICTIONARY, is also referred to as the synonym, DICT.

A Look at USER Level Oracle System Tables

Table 11-1 lists some of the USER level Oracle system tables. There are many more USER system catalogs, but this is a representative list.

Table 11-1   *USER-Level Oracle System Tables*

View Name	Description
USER_AUDIT_CONNECT	Entries of logon and logoff for audit purposes
USER_AUDIT_OBJECT	Records on all objects (tables, views, indexes,...) for audit purposes
USER_AUDIT_SESSION	User records for audit purposes
USER_CATALOG	Tables, views, and synonyms for a user
USER_COL_COMMENTS	Comments for user tables and views
USER_COL_GRANTS	Grants for columns where a user has ownership or some grant privilege
USER_ERRORS	Errors for stored objects for a user
USER_INDEXES	Indexes owned by a user
USER_OBJECTS	Objects owned by a user
USER_OBJECT_SIZE	Size of PL/SQL objects
USER_ROLE_PRIVS	Group-level privileges, or Roles, for a user
USER_SOURCE	Source of stored objects available to a user
USER_SYNONYMS	Private synonyms available to a user
USER_SYS_PRIVS	System privileges granted to a user
USER_TABLES	Information for a user's table
USER_TAB_COLUMNS	List of comments for user's tables and views
USER_VIEWS	All user views

A Look at System Tables Beginning With ALL

Table 11-2 lists some of the system tables beginning with ALL.

Table 11-2   *Oracle ALL System Tables*

View Name	Description
ALL_CATALOG	All views, synonyms, and tables available for a user
ALL_COL_COMMENTS	Comments on all tables and views available to a user
ALL_COL_GRANTS	All grant privileges available to a user
ALL_INDEXES	All indexes available to a user
ALL_IND_COLUMNS	All columns used in indexes available to users
ALL_OBJECTS	Information on all objects available to a user
ALL_SOURCE	Available source code on stored objects for a user
ALL_SYNONYMS	All synonyms available to a user
ALL_TABLES	All tables available to a user
ALL_TAB_COLUMNS	All table columns available to a user
ALL_TAB_COMMENTS	Comments on all tables available to users
ALL_USERS	All users of a database
ALL_VIEWS	All views available to a user

A table like ALL_TABLES describes tables accessible to all users (those tables where privileges for all users have been granted).

A Look at DBA-Level Tables

Table 11-3 lists some DBA level tables; there are more DBA tables than this.

Table 11-3   *Oracle DBA-Level Tables*

View Name	Description
COLUMN_PRIVILEGES	Column privileges
DICT_COLUMNS	Descriptions of columns in the system tables and views
DBA_TABLES	Description of all tables in the database
DBA_AUDIT_CONNECT	Entries of logon and logoff for audit purposes
DBA_TABLESPACES	All table spaces
ROLE_ROLE_PRIVS	A convoluted one! Lists role privileges granted to roles or groups of privileges
TABLE_PRIVILEGS	All table privileges

Many of these tables have to do with privileges, which are system administration issues. The difference for tables like USER_TABLES and ALL_TABLES versus DBA_TABLES is simply the number of tables that are viewable by the instigator of the query using these views.

V$ Tables for System Performance

Tables beginning with V$ are system statistics tables. Table 11-4 lists specific V$ tables. Again, there are many V$ parameters; this is a representation.

Table 11-4   *Oracle V$ Tables*

View Name	Description
V$ACCESS	Sessions that are accessing objects and the objects that are locked
V$ARCHIVE	Archive log status
V$BACKUP	Backup status for data

Table 11-4   *Oracle V$ Tables (Continued)*

View Name	Description
V$DATABASE	Database information from a control file
V$ENABLEDPRIVS	Enabled privileges
V$FILESTATE	File input and output statistics
V$LOADCSTAT	Load statistics for a load
V$LOG	Log status
V$LOGFILE	Log file descriptions
V$NLS_PARAMETERS	Current native language support
V$PROCESS	Status for currently active processes
V$SESSION	Information about current session
V$SYSSTAT	System-wide statistics
V$TIMER	Time, at a granular level
V$VERSION	Version numbers of database components

11.2.2 Sybase System Tables

Sybase SQL Server system tables vary a great deal from Oracle system tables. With SQL Server, there are two catalogs:

- Tables for a master database
- Tables relating to each database

Sybase System Catalogs (Tables for Master Database)

Table 11-5 lists tables in the SQL Server master database.

Table 11-5 *Sybase Tables in SQL Server Master Database*

Table Name	Description
sysconfigures	User configuration options
syscurconfigs	Shows the current values for configuration options.
sysdatabases	Details all databases for SQL Servers.
sysdevices	Provides definitions for all disks and other devices of a database.
syslocks	Lists all active locks.
syslogins	Details server login information.
sysmessages	Lists all server error messages and nonfatal warnings.
sysprocesses	Lists active Sybase processes.
sysusages	Provides information for disk resources assigned to databases.

System Catalogs Stored in Each Database

Table 11-6 lists tables that store information about each individual table:

Table 11-6 *Sybase System Catalogs*

Table Name	Description
sysalternates	Provides server login names to database aliases.
syscolumns	Contains table and view column details and parameters for stored procedure.
syscomments	Lists all defaults, triggers, rules, stored procedures, and views.
sysdepends	Defines dependency relationships between stored procedures and trigger, as well as views and other database objects.

Table 11-6   *Sybase System Catalogs (Continued)*

Table Name	Description
sysindexes	Defines all table indexes.
syskeys	Details primary and foreign key information.
syslogs	Stores database transaction log information.
sysobjects	Provides information on all objects.
syssegments	Lists defined disk segments.
systypes	Describes user-defined and system types.
sysusers	Provides information about users of the database.

11.2.3 SQLBase System Catalogs

Table 11-7 lists tables in the SQLBase data dictionary.

Table 11-7   *SQLBase Data Dictionary Tables*

Table Name	Description
SYSCOLAUTH	Each user's column update privileges
SYSCOLUMNS	Each column of every table
SYSCOMMANDS	All the stored command and procedures
SYSEVENTS	All the system timer events
SYSEXECUTEAUTH	Authority levels of users for executing stored procedures
SYSFKCONSTRAINTS	Each foreign key constraint
SYSINDEXES	Each table's indexes
SYSKEYS	Each column in every index

Table 11-7   *SQLBase Data Dictionary Tables (Continued)*

Table Name	Description
SYSPKCONSTRAINTS	Each primary key constraint
SYSROWIDLISTS	Information about saved result sets
SYSSYNONYMS	All table and view synonyms
SYSTABAUTH	Each user's table privileges
SYSTABCONSTRAINTS	Each table constraint
SYSTABLES	Each table or view
SYSTRGCOLS	Each column on which an UPDATE trigger exists
SYSTRIGGERS	Each trigger
SYSUSERAUTH	Each user's database authority level
SYSVIEWS	Text of each view

11.3   Exercises with System Tables

Exercise 11.3.1: Exercises with System Tables for SQLBase

This exercise examines system tables.

1. Open Quest, if it is not already open. Make sure you are connected to the COMPANY database by pulling down the Utilities menu and using the **Add** function if necessary. Click on the COMPANY database.

2. Click on the **Open** button and then on the **SQL** button.

Figure 11-8   *Opening the SQL Activity*

3. Quest prompts for a file. Choose the file
   c:\sqlbase\exercise\chap11\ex11-1.qsd. Click **OK.**

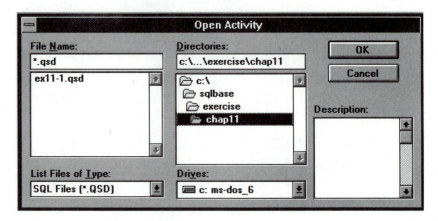

Figure 11-9 *Opening The SQL File*

4. The first SELECT command shows the name of all columns for the table
   COMP, using the system table, SYSCOLUMNS.

   SELECT NAME, TBCREATOR, TBNAME
   FROM SYSCOLUMNS WHERE TBNAME = 'COMP'

   Choose this SQL statement by clicking in the SQL Activity window. Pull
   down the SQL menu and select **Execute SQL Statement.**

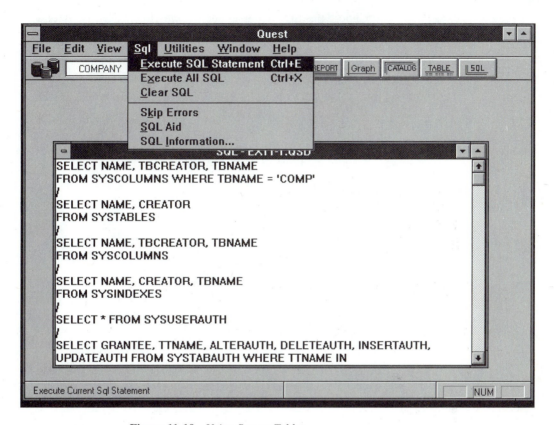

Figure 11-10 *Using System Tables*

5. The next SELECT command shows the name and creator of all tables in the system table, SYSTABLES:

   SELECT NAME, CREATOR
   FROM SYSTABLES

   Choose this SQL statement by clicking in the SQL activity window. Pull down the SQL menu and select **Execute SQL Statement**.

6. The next SELECT command lists all columns for our database as well as the creator and table name of those columns.

   SELECT NAME, TBCREATOR, TBNAME
   FROM SYSCOLUMNS

Choose this SQL statement by clicking in the SQL Activity window. Choose the **Execute SQL Statement** menu option.

7. Now, execute a SELECT command against the system table, SYSINDEXES, to return all defined system indexes.

   SELECT NAME, CREATOR, TBNAME
   FROM SYSINDEXES

   Choose this SELECT statement by clicking in the SQL Activity window. Choose the **Execute SQL Statement** menu option.

8. Now, execute a SELECT command against the system table, SYSUSERAUTH, which will list all privileges.

   SELECT * FROM SYSUSERAUTH

   Choose this SELECT statement by clicking in the SQL Activity window. Choose the **Execute SQL Statement** menu option.

9. This SELECT command provides information on table privileges for the tables COMP and EMPLOYEES, using the system table SYSTABAUTH.

   SELECT GRANTEE, TTNAME, ALTERAUTH,
   DELETEAUTH, INSERTAUTH, UPDATEAUTH FROM
   SYSTABAUTH WHERE TTNAME IN
   ('COMP','EMPLOYEES')

   Choose this SELECT statement by clicking in the SQL Activity window. Choose the **Execute SQL Statement** menu option.

10. Now, execute a SELECT command against the system table, SYSCOLAUTH, which will list all column level privileges.

    SELECT * FROM SYSCOLAUTH
    WHERE TNAME IN ('COMP','EMPLOYEES')

    Choose this SELECT statement by clicking in the SQL Activity window. Choose the **Execute SQL Statement** menu option.

11. To close, choose the **Close** option from the File menu.

11.4 Stored Procedures and Triggers

A *stored procedure* is code that is stored in a relational database. A stored procedure can be stored both in text format and compiled format (for optimal performance). It can also receive input arguments and can return results. Stored procedures are used by programmers to implement what are commonly referred to as application *business rules*.

Programmers who develop applications often use stored procedures as a way to run pieces of code from their application on a server, where it will run faster.

Stored procedures, like system catalogs, vary greatly from vendor to vendor. Oracle has a stored procedural language called PL/SQL (for stored procedures as well as for stored functions and triggers). Sybase has a procedure language, using their SQL implementation, TransAct SQL. SQLBase uses the programming language from SQLWindows (SAL) to write stored procedures.

11.4.1 Advantages of Stored Procedures

Stored procedures are used for a variety of reasons:

- Stored procedures increase performance.

- Stored procedures can be run on database servers, offloading code from client machines (which most often are slower).

- Stored procedures can simplify business logic. For example, one stored procedure can be used by Visual C++, Visual Basic, and SQLWindows applications. You do not have to reimplement the same logic three times!

- Stored procedures can allow a database administrator to write code that allows users to perform tasks that they would not normally be able to do.

- Database vendors often add functionality by providing prebuilt stored procedures for users, illustrated below in our discussion of implementations by Oracle and Sybase.

We have seen many reasons for using stored procedures! There are, of course, disadvantages. For example, stored procedures are not generic. Therefore, application developers often shy away from stored procedures so that their applications can be used against multiple relational database engines.

11.4.2 Triggers

Triggers are similar to stored procedures. As with stored procedures, pieces of code are stored in a database; however, whereas stored procedures are called programmatically or interactively, triggers are tied to the occurrence of events. For example, triggers can be activated before or after an INSERT, UPDATE, or DELETE of a row.

Figure 11-11 is an example of how a trigger could be created in Oracle, triggering the execution of code based upon an INSERT, UPDATE, or DELETE.

```
CREATE TRIGGER  OUR_TRIGGER
   BEFORE INSERT OR UPDATE OR DELETE ON COMP
   FOR EACH ROW
DECLARE
   < place varibles here >
BEGIN
   <place PL/SQL here >
END;
```

Figure 11-11 *Creating Trigger in Oracle*

This example is the basis by which a trigger, created in Oracle, would cause PL/SQL code to be executed *before* an INSERT, UPDATE, or DELETE is executed.

Whenever a table is modified in any way, a trigger can perform auditing or checking of the changes. Triggers are often used to check the integrity of data as it is inserted, updated, or deleted.

11.4.3 Vendors' Stored Procedures

The next four sections briefly discuss implementations of stored procedures by Oracle, Sybase, Centura, and the ANSI standard for stored procedures.

Oracle Stored Procedures

Oracle uses the PL/SQL procedural language to create stored procedures and triggers, as well as what Oracle refers to as stored functions.

An example of creating a stored procedure, NEW_STOCK, with Oracle is shown in Figure 11-12.

```
CREATE PROCEDURE NEW_STOCK (SYM  IN VARCHAR2)
AS
   BEGIN
       INSERT INTO STOCK
           (SYMBOL, EXCHANGE, COMP_ID)
       VALUES
           (SYM, NULL, NULL);
   END;
/
```

Figure 11-12 *Creating Stored Procedure with Oracle*

Once the procedure NEW_STOCK has been created, we can grant the right for a user to use it. For example, if the user James were to use it, we could issue the statement:

GRANT EXECUTE ON NEW_STOCK TO JAMES

Now, James can add a stock symbol in Oracle by interactively or programmatically executing the following command:

EXECUTE NEW_STOCK ('PIXAR')

Oracle Packages

A unique feature of Oracle PL/SQL is *packages*. Packages are bundles of stored procedures and triggers. Oracle comes with several packages, including the subset listed in Table 11-8.

Table 11-8   *Some Oracle Packages*

Package	Description
dbms_alert	Notifies when events occur within the database.
dbms_describe	Contains a stored procedure that lists information about stored procedure.
dbms_lock	Contains commands to lock a database. There are five stored procedures in this package.
dbms_output	Contains stored procedures used for debugging, including disable, enable, get_line, get_lines, new_line, and put_line.
dbms_pipe	Contains commands to create and use pipes (which are similar to pipes used in the UNIX® operating system).
dbms_session	Commands to change parameters during a user's session (using the ALTER SESSION command).
dbms_snaphot	Allows for manipulation of snapshots. Snapshots in Oracle are equivalent to read-only copies of data used for data duplication.
dbms_transaction	Contains procedures allowing COMMIT and ROLLBACK.
dbms_utility	Contains a whole set of utilities that developers may need.

Sybase Stored Procedures

TransAct SQL has been used as a stored procedural language for both Sybase and Microsoft. Microsoft SQL Server has made several modifications to this language, including the ability to call compiled application code from languages like C and C++ from within stored procedures.

An example of creating a stored procedure for SQL Server is shown in Figure 11-13.

```
CREATE PROCEDURE LS_COMP_COLUMNS
AS
    SELECT * FROM COMP

GO
```

Figure 11-13 *Creating Stored Procedure for SQL Server*

Sybase comes with many prebuilt stored procedures. You may have noticed that Oracle has many more system tables than does Sybase. Sybase compensates for this by providing stored procedures that accomplish many of the things you would expect of system tables. Table 11-9 is a partial list of stored procedures provided for users by Sybase.

Table 11-9   *Some Sybase Stored Procedures*

Stored Procedures	Description
sp_addalias	Grants access, using aliases to get access to a database.
sp_addgroup	Adds groups to a database.
sp_adduser	Adds a user to a database.
sp_changeddbowner	Changes database owners.
sp_dboption	Sets database options.
sp_depends	Lists table dependencies that views may have.
sp_defaultlanguage	Sets default language settings used by a user.
sp_dropalias	Drops an alias.
sp_dropgroup	Drops a group.
sp_dropuser	Drops a user.

Table 11-9 *Some Sybase Stored Procedures (Continued)*

Stored Procedures	Description
sp_foreignkey	Displays information about foreign key relationships between tables.
sp_help	Lists information on objects and their owners.
sp_helpgroup	Displays information on groups.
sp_helpindex	Displays information on indexes.
sp_helplog	Displays log information.
sp_helpjoins	Displays information on columns that can be used as joins.
sp_helpprotect	Displays information for determining privileges on objects and users.
sp_helpsort	Displays information on character sets.
sp_helptest	Displays text that was used to create objects.
sp_helpuser	Displays user information.
sp_index	Displays index information on tables.
sp_primarykey	Declares a primary key of a table.
sp_rename	Allows renaming of objects.
sp_renamedb	Allows renaming of database.
sp_who	Displays the users that are logged on to a database.

SQLBase Stored Procedures

After release 6.0, SQLBase provides stored procedures. The CD supplied with this book does not have a SQLBase engine with stored procedures. SQLBase also has the concept of stored commands, or single SQL statements that are stored by the relational engine. You can create a stored command as follows:

```
STORE MYCOMMAND
UPDATE COMP
SET COMP_ID= 100
WHERE CITY= :1
```

The above command was stored in the database as COMMAND1. It may now be executed for a specific value of the column *city* as follows (from the SQLTalk utility):

```
EXECUTE MYCOMMAND
\
Portland
/
```

SQLBase uses the SQLWindows Application Language (SAL) as its procedural language. Procedures for SQLBase can be created by means of the SQLWindows development tool and then cut and pasted into SQLBase with the administration tool, SQLConsole.

ANSI Standard Stored Procedures

ANSI has made an attempt to define a standard process to create a generic stored procedural language. The Watcom database has an ANSI standard procedural language; however, it is hard to have a standard with only a few adherents.

11.4.4 Vendors That Generate Stored Procedural Language

It is likely that vendors will offer generic ways to cross the bridge between different implementations of stored procedures. One interesting attempt comes from Logicworks, as discussed in Chapter 2.

Logicworks, with the ERwin tool, provides a way to generically write ANSI-style stored procedures. They advertise the ability to create the various stored procedure implementations for you. Write a stored procedure once and implement it across multiple platforms!

As technology like this matures, it will go a long way toward making SQL more generic.

11.5   Summary

This chapter introduced the concepts of system tables and stored procedures. This chapter serves only as an introduction. To properly discuss the implementations of stored procedures or system tables of the major RDBMS vendors is a task more ambitious than I would attempt in an introductory SQL book.

Stored procedures and system tables are a major stumbling block to a common, standardized SQL language, but they both are powerful pieces of relational databases and should not be ignored.

12   Data Integrity and Constraints

So far, this book has covered important concepts concerning referential integrity. In Chapter 2, we discussed primary and foreign keys and created them in Chapter 3. We have discussed data integrity throughout this book; however, there is still more to cover. There are no exercises in this chapter; instead, this chapter focuses on data integrity issues not previously discussed. Transaction analysis is also covered, since it affects data integrity, but it could have been covered in the sections concerning performance.

The chapter is organized as follows:

Section 12.1   Data Integrity
Section 12.2   Foreign Keys: More on Delete Rules
Section 12.3   Foreign Key Guidelines
Section 12.4   Implications for SQL Operations
Section 12.5   Transaction Analysis and Integrity
Section 12.6   Summary

12.1   Data Integrity

Section 12.1.1 reviews integrity concepts covered in previous chapters. Section 12.1.2 outlines the new data integrity concepts.

12.1.1   Referential Integrity Review

Referential integrity ensures that all references from one table to another are valid. Referential integrity prevents problems from occurring when changes in one table are not reflected in another. The following points review key data integrity features discussed so far.

Primary Keys and Unique Index

The exercises in Chapter 3 created primary keys for the COMPANY database. Unique indexes for each primary key value were also created. These primary keys enforce the uniqueness of all rows. Note that not all relational database engines require the explicit creation of a unique index. A primary key, by definition, is a unique value.

In a Chapter 4 exercise, we attempted to INSERT a nonunique value into a primary key value. We learned that this INSERT violated a referential constraint. All primary key values must be unique.

NOT NULL

When we created tables in Chapter 3, we created columns by using the NOT NULL clause. For example,

```
CREATE TABLE TESTER
(TESTCOL INTEGER NOT NULL)
```

The NOT NULL used with column *testcol* requires that columns always contain a value. Without the use of the NOT NULL clause, it is possible for foreign keys to contain NULL values. The NOT NULL clause enforces data integrity by requiring data to exist in certain columns.

Creating Foreign Keys

Chapter 3 also showed the following command to generate a foreign key:

```
ALTER TABLE EMPLOYEES FOREIGN KEY (DEP_CODE)
REFERENCES DEPARTMENTS ON DELETE RESTRICT
```

REFERENCES DEPARTMENTS ON DELETE RESTRICT was used without much further explanation. This chapter elaborates on this clause, which can be referred to as a delete rule.

Using the CREATE TABLE to Create a Foreign Key

Although not covered previously, a foreign key can be created by using a CREATE TABLE command, as follows:

```
CREATE TABLE EMPLOYEES
(COMP_ID INTEGER NOT NULL,
```

```
EMP_ID INTEGER NOT NULL,
TITLE VARCHAR (50),
EMP_NAME VARCHAR (40) NOT NULL,
DEP_CODE INTEGER NOT NULL,
PRIMARY KEY (COMP_ID,EMP_ID),
FOREIGN KEY (DEP_CODE)
 REFERENCES DEPARTMENTS ON DELETE RESTRICT))
```

Views and WITH CHECK OPTION

In Chapter 10, we used a data integrity feature; we created views with the WITH CHECK OPTION clause. This provided a level for data integrity by enforcing that checks be made on INSERT, UPDATE, and DELETE.

12.1.2 Data Integrity Concepts

The following concepts are discussed in the subsequent sections:

- **Foreign keys: more on delete rules**

  Both primary and foreign keys have already been discussed, but, foreign keys are much trickier than primary keys. They define relationships among tables; therefore, more needs to be said about foreign keys and their delete rules.

- **Foreign key guidelines**

  Guidelines for use of foreign keys with SQLBase are discussed.

- **Implications of SQL commands**

  When primary and foreign keys are used, SQL commands like INSERT, UPDATE, and DELETE are affected. This section discusses the implications of data integrity on SQLBase commands.

- **Transaction analysis and data integrity**

  The decision was made to discuss transaction analysis as a component of data integrity; however, transaction analysis is not only critical to data integrity, it is also critical for performance and proper database design.

12.2   Foreign Keys: More on Delete Rules

This section elaborates on delete rules for foreign keys, but first, we introduce a few concepts important to understanding data integrity and foreign key/ primary key relationships.

12.2.1 Concepts Important to Data Integrity and Foreign Keys

Before we discuss delete rules, we discuss these concepts:

- Parent and child tables
- Self-referencing table/rows
- Delete-connected tables

Parent and Child Tables

Together, the primary key and foreign key create a *parent/child* relationship. The table containing the primary key is the *parent table*; the table containing the foreign key is a *child table*. A child of a child is called a *descendant*.

A *foreign key* references a primary key in either the same or another table. The *dep_code* column of the DEPARTMENTS table is an example of a primary key. The *dep_code* column of the EMPLOYEES table is an example of a foreign key, as shown in Figure 12-1.

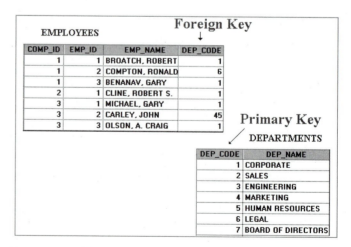

Figure 12-1   *Foreign Key Example*

Before creating a foreign key, you must first create the primary key it references and, as required by some RDBMS vendors, you may also create a unique index on that primary key.

Issues with Parent/Child Relationship and Foreign Keys

The following example demonstrates referential integrity. First, an entry in EMPLOYEES table is inserted.

```
INSERT INTO EMPLOYEES (COMP_ID, EMP_ID,
EMP_NAME, DEP_CODE) VALUES
(400,'Dan Hawley',50,'Chief Executive Officer', 30)
```

There's nothing inherently incorrect about this statement. However, if department 30 does not exist in the DEPARTMENTS table, this record could potentially corrupt the data integrity.

Every *dep_code* value in the EMPLOYEES table should be a valid department code in the DEPARTMENTS table. This rule is called a *referential integrity constraint.*

Note that a valid reference is not the same as a correct reference. Referential integrity does not correct a mistake such as assigning an employee to the *wrong* department; it only verifies that the department actually exists.

Self-Referencing Tables and Rows

A table can be a child of itself. This is called a *self-referencing table.* A self-referencing table contains both a foreign and primary key with matching values within the same table.

An example of a self-referencing table is the ENGINEERS table, in which the foreign key MGR (MANAGER) references the primary key EMPL_NUM, as shown in Figure 12-2.

EMP_NUM	REP_OFF	NAME	TITLE	HIRE_DATE	MANAGER
101	10	BROATCH, ROBERT	MANAGER	1988-02-01	
102	20	COMPTON, RONALD	SEN. ENG	1992-09-05	103
104	30	BENANAV, GARY	SEN. ENG	1991-01-07	109
105	10	CLINE, ROBERT S.	ENGINEER	1985-04-12	101
110	20	MICHAEL, GARY	QA	1994-03-10	100
111	21	CARLEY, JOHN	SEN. ENG	1984-03-03	100
123	30	OLSON, A. CRAIG	QA	1989-07-08	109

Figure 12-2   *Self-Referencing Table Example*

Delete-Connected Tables

Tables are *delete-connected* if deleting a row in one table affects the other table. For example, deleting an office from the DEPARTMENTS table affects the EMPLOYEES table, since each employee is associated with a department. Any table that is involved in a delete operation is delete-connected.

The following definitions apply to delete-connected tables:

- A self-referencing table is delete-connected to itself.

- A child table is always delete-connected to its parent table, no matter what DELETE rule you specify.

- A table is delete-connected to its grandparent and great-grandparent tables when the delete rules between the parent and grandparent, or the grandparent and the great-grandparent, are set to cause what is known as a cascading effect.

Figure 12-3 illustrates this concept.

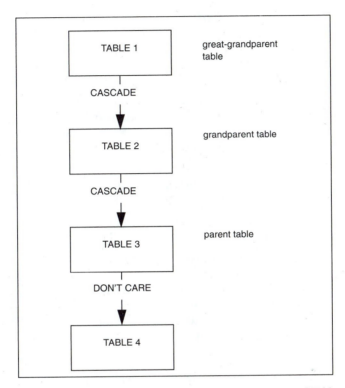

Figure 12-3   *Cascading Effect in Delete-Connected Tables*

In Figure 12-3, TABLE 4 is delete-connected to its grandparent table, TABLE 2, since the delete rule between TABLE 2 and TABLE 3 is set so that any effect to the ancestor will *cascade* to the descendants. TABLE 4 is also delete-connected to its great-grandparent table, TABLE 1, since the delete rule between TABLE 1 and TABLE 2 is also set to cause the cascading effect. The delete rules between TABLE 4 and its parent, TABLE 3, do not affect these delete-connections.

12.2.2 Delete Rules

When you try to delete a row from the parent table, you can specify one of three delete rules:

- RESTRICT
- CASCADE
- SET NULL

DELETE RESTRICT

The RESTRICT rule prevents you from deleting a row from the parent table if the row has any child rows. You can delete a row if there are no child rows.

For the sample COMPANY database, a DELETE RESTRICT rule is appropriate for the relationship between the EMPLOYEES table and the DEPARTMENTS table. You should not be able to delete departmental information from the database if there are still employees that are part of that department. The following example, which you have seen before, shows the DELETE RESTRICT rule.

```
ALTER TABLE EMPLOYEES FOREIGN KEY (DEP_CODE)
REFERENCES DEPARTMENTS ON DELETE RESTRICT
```

If you do not specify a DELETE rule, then RESTRICT is the default because it has the least potential for damage.

DELETE CASCADE

The CASCADE rule specifies that when a parent row is deleted, all of its associated child rows are automatically deleted from the child table(s). Deletions from the parent table *cascade* to the child table. If any part of the delete fails, the whole delete operation fails. The delete is also propagated to descendant tables.

A DELETE CASCADE rule is appropriate for the relationship between DEPARTMENTS and EMPLOYEE tables if, when a department code is deleted, you want all associated employees to be deleted, too. The following code shows a DELETE CASCADE.

```
ALTER TABLE EMPLOYEES FOREIGN KEY (DEP_CODE)
REFERENCES DEPARTMENTS ON DELETE CASCADE
```

Be careful when using the CASCADE rule because it can delete an extensive amount of data if it is used incorrectly.

DELETE CASCADE does not delete a parent row if a child or descendant row has a DELETE RESTRICT rule.

For a self-referencing table, CASCADE is the only DELETE rule allowed.

DELETE SET NULL

The DELETE SET NULL rule specifies that when a parent row is deleted, the foreign key values in all of its child rows should automatically be set to NULL.

In this example with the DELETE SET NULL clause, if a department is deleted, any employee's department code is set to NULL.

ALTER TABLE EMPLOYEES FOREIGN KEY (DEP_CODE)
REFERENCES DEPARTMENTS ON DELETE SET NULL

For a foreign key, you can use the SET NULL option only if at least one of the columns of the foreign key allows null values. The default is RESTRICT.

12.3   Foreign Key Guidelines

All RDBMS have foreign key guidelines. Here, we use SQLBase as an example. SQLBase obeys the following rules:

- **Matching columns.** A foreign key must contain the same number of columns as the primary key. The data types of the foreign key columns must match those of the primary key on a one-to-one basis, and the matching columns must be in the same order.

  However, the foreign key can have different column names and default values. It can also have null attributes. If an index is defined on the foreign key columns, the index columns can be in ascending or descending order, which may be different from the order of the primary key index.

- **Using primary key columns.** A column can belong to both a primary and foreign key.

- **Foreign keys per table.** A table can have any number of foreign keys.

- **Number of foreign keys.** A column can belong to more than one foreign key.

- **Number of columns.** A foreign key cannot contain more than 16 columns.

- **Parent table.** A foreign key can reference a primary key only in its parent table. This parent table must reside in the same database as the foreign key.

- **Null values.** A foreign key column value can be null. A foreign key value is null if any column in the foreign key is null.

- **Privileges.** You must grant ALTER authority on a table to all users who need to define that table as the parent of a foreign key.

- **System catalog table.** The foreign key cannot reference a system catalog table.

- **Views.** A foreign key cannot reference a view.

- **Self-referencing row.** In a self-referencing row, the foreign key value can be updated only if it references a valid primary key value.

Foreign Key Indexes

SQLBase does not require an index on a foreign key, but an index can increase database performance. A join with primary and foreign keys is fairly common. Creating an index on the foreign key can improve the performance of these joins.

Foreign Keys and Null Values

A foreign key column can have a null value, unlike a primary key column. Even though a null value does not match any value in a primary key, it satisfies the referential integrity constraint. This is also true for a multiple-column foreign key that contains part null/non-null values; SQLBase regards a foreign key value as null if any of its column values is null. (SQLBase represents null values as NULL.)

It is strongly recommended that you do not allow a foreign key to have partial null/non-null values. Either all foreign key columns should allow null values, or none at all. The following example with the DEPARTMENTS and EMPLOYEES tables demonstrates the problems with partial null foreign keys.

The composite key *dep_code* is a primary key in the DEPARTMENTS table. The key dep_code is a foreign key in the EMPLOYEES table referencing the DEPARTMENTS table.

Assume that the EMPLOYEES table allowed null values for the *dep_code* column, as shown below:

```
INSERT INTO EMPLOYEES VALUES
(200,44,'Miles Fowler','Senior VP',NULL)
```

As a result, the row contains a foreign key value that does not match any primary key value in the DEPARTMENTS table, as shown in Figure 12-4.

comp_id	emp_id	emp_name	position	dep_code
200	44	Miles Fowler	Senior VP	NULL

Foreign key

Primary key

dep_code	DESCRIPTION
1	Corporate
44	Aerospace Unit

Figure 12-4 *Foreign Key Value Without Primary Key Match*

12.4   Implications for SQL Operations

Referential constraints have special implications. In this section, we outline the implications of referential constraints for SQLBase operations. This section describes how referential integrity affects the INSERT, UPDATE, DROP, SELECT, and DELETE commands.

Views share the referential constraints of their base tables.

12.4.1 INSERT

SQLBase enforces the following rules when you insert data into a table with one or more foreign keys:

- Each non-null value you insert into a foreign key column must match a value in the primary key.

- If any column in the foreign key is null, SQLBase regards the entire foreign key as null. SQLBase does not perform any referential checks on an INSERT statement with a null foreign key.

- You cannot insert values into a parent or child table if the parent table is no longer complete (for example, if you dropped the primary index).

You can insert data into the parent table at any time without affecting the child table. For example, adding a new office to the DEPARTMENTS table does not affect the EMPLOYEE table.

12.4.2 UPDATE

If you are updating a child table, every non-null foreign key value that you enter must match a valid primary key value in the parent table. If the child table references multiple parent tables, the foreign key values must all reference valid primary keys.

The only UPDATE rule that can be applied to a parent table is RESTRICT. This means that any attempt to update the primary key of the parent table is restricted to cases where there are no matching values in the child tables.

SQLBase enforces the following rule on an UPDATE statement:

- An UPDATE statement that assigns a value to a primary key *cannot* specify more than one record.

12.4.3 DELETE

As discussed in Section 12.2, you can specify a delete rule for each parent/child relationship created by a foreign key in a SQLBase application. The delete rule tells SQLBase what to do when a user tries to delete a row from the parent table. You can specify one of three delete rules:

- RESTRICT
- CASCADE
- SET NULL

12.4.4 DROP

Dropping a table drops both its primary key and any foreign keys. When you drop a parent table or its primary key, the referential constraint is also dropped.

Before you drop a primary or foreign key, consider the effect this will have on your application programs. Dropping a key drops the corresponding referential relationship. It also drops the delete rule for a foreign key. In addition, the primary key of a table is a permanent, unique identifier of the entities it describes, and some of your programs might depend on it. Without a primary or foreign key, your programs must enforce these referential constraints.

Note that dropping a primary or foreign key is not the same as deleting its value.

Use the ALTER TABLE statement to drop a primary or foreign key.

Dropping a Primary Key

If you have ALTER privilege on both the parent and child tables, you can drop a primary key. The following example drops a primary key:

ALTER TABLE DEPARTMENTS DROP PRIMARY KEY

This statement drops the primary key of the DEPARTMENTS table. It also drops the parent/child relationship with the EMPLOYEES table.

If a user has ALTER privilege on a table, you cannot revoke this privilege if he has already created a foreign key that references that table.

Dropping a primary key does not drop the primary index. The index remains a unique index on the former primary key's columns.

Dropping a Primary Index

Dropping a primary index results in an incomplete table. To create a complete table definition, create another unique index on the columns of the primary key.

Referential constraints remain even if you drop the primary index.

Dropping a Foreign Key

The following SQL statement drops the foreign key DEP_CODE from the EMPLOYEES table:

ALTER TABLE EMPLOYEES DROP FOREIGN KEY
DEP_CODE

To drop a foreign key, you must have ALTER privilege on both the parent and dependent tables.

12.4.5 SELECT

Because a SELECT statement does not change actual data values, it is not affected by referential integrity.

12.5   Transaction Analysis and Integrity

Database transactions usually involve *multiple* database accesses. For example, consider the banking transaction of withdrawing $1000 from a savings account and depositing the funds into a checking account. This transaction entails two separate database operations: subtracting $1000 from the savings table and adding $1000 to the checking table. If either one of these database operations successfully completes but the other does not, the account balances would be wrong. Both of these operations must complete successfully or neither of them should complete successfully.

Thus, a database transaction is a logical unit of work that causes the database to advance from one consistent state to another. In other words, a transaction moves the database from one state that does not violate the data integrity requirements of the database to another state that does not violate the data integrity requirements of the database. In addition, a database transaction is a grouping of logically related database operations, so that all of the database accesses should complete successfully or none of them should be applied to the database. Otherwise, if only some of the database accesses complete successfully, the database is left in an inconsistent state.

So, in order to ensure the integrity of the database, it is necessary to rigorously define the database transactions. This section describes how to define transactions and identifies the information that is typically included in transaction definitions.

Hence, well-defined transactions are a prerequisite for physical database design. Without this information, the database designer has no rule to guide in the selection of physical database constructs. For example, the database designer will be unable to determine whether a clustered or nonclustered table will result in better performance. A similar argument can be made for index selection.

12.5.1 Defining Transactions

Transaction definitions can take many forms. Some organizations may possess a CASE tool with a transaction definition facility as part of a data repository. Other organizations may choose to define transactions by using paper-based or automated forms. Regardless of the media, all good transaction definitions include several key ingredients. Each of these is discussed below.

Transaction Name, Number, and Description

The first step in defining transactions is to uniquely identify each database transaction. This is accomplished by assigning a name and unique identifier to each transaction.

In addition, a short narrative should be composed, referred to as the transaction description, which describes the transaction in business terms:

- The description should specify what the transaction accomplishes for the user rather than how it is accomplished.

- The description should be understandable by users (it should not include technical jargon).

The purpose of transaction names and descriptions is to provide users and MIS staff with a means for distinguishing one transaction from another.

Example: Transaction Number: 001

Example: Transaction Name: Transfer Funds

Example: Transaction Description: The Transfer Funds transaction verifies that sufficient funds exist in the account to be debited. If sufficient funds exist, the transaction debits the account by the specified amount and credits the other account for the same amount.

In OnLine Transaction Processing (OLTP) systems, the database transactions are known ahead of time. For these types of systems, a one-to-one relationship exists between the transaction definitions and the actual transactions submitted to SQLBase.

In Decision Support Systems (DSS), transactions are not known ahead of time. These systems are characterized by ad hoc and exception reporting. Therefore, it is not possible to describe each and every transaction. With these systems, the transaction definitions are illustrative of the actual transactions that will be submitted to SQLBase once the system is implemented. DSS systems require the database designer to predict the type of transactions the users will likely run.

Transaction Type and Complexity

Frequently, transaction definitions also categorize transactions in terms of type and complexity. For example, transactions may be defined as either "Batch" or "Online" and given a complexity rating of either "High," "Medium," or "Low." This information is useful for producing listings or totals of like transactions. For example, management may require an estimate of the time required to complete physical database design. To accomplish this, one might need to know how many low, medium, and high complex transactions a system has. The database for a system with a large percentage of high-complexity transactions would take longer to design than a system with mostly low-complexity transactions.

The complexity rating is a matter of judgment but should be based on the degree of difficulty the database designer is likely to have meeting the performance requirements for the transaction (see below). A transaction of high complexity has at least two of the following characteristics:

- Contains many SQL statements (more than 10)
- Contains WHERE clauses with many predicates (for example, three or more table joins or subqueries)
- The SQL statements affect many rows (more than 100)

On the other hand, a low-complexity transaction has the following characteristics:

- Contains few SQL statements (three or fewer)
- Contains WHERE clauses with only one or two predicates
- The SQL statements affect few rows (fewer than 25).

Transaction Volumes

Transaction definitions must also include volume information. This typically includes the average and peak frequency of each transaction. For example, a branch bank might estimate that the funds transfer transaction described in the introduction of this section will occur 50 times an hour with peak loads reaching 65 transactions per hour.

The transaction volume statistics are extremely important for physical database design; consequently, care should be taken to be as accurate as possible. For example, the database designer will handle a transaction that occurs 1000 times per hour quite differently from one that occurs only once per hour.

If the new computer system is replacing an existing system, it may be possible to derive transaction volumes from the existing system. On the other hand, new systems rarely duplicate the transaction logic of their predecessors, so these differences should be considered.

Typically, the hardest situation in which to deduce accurate transaction volumes is one in which no automated or manual predecessors exist. These situations occur when organizations enter new lines of business. In this case, volume statistics may be no more than educated guesses.

Transaction Performance Requirements

The transaction definitions should also document the performance requirements of each transaction. As mentioned, the transaction performance requirements are the basis of physical database design. During physical database design, the database designer chooses the physical constructs from among the various options provided by SQLBase, such that all transactions meet or exceed their transaction performance requirements. Without specifying performance requirements, the database designer has no means by which to evaluate whether the database performance is acceptable.

Some organizations prefer to specify exact performance requirements for each transaction. The performance requirements typically take the form of number of execution seconds. For example, one requirement might state that the transfer funds transaction must complete in three seconds or less.

Relative Priority

Transaction definitions also should rank each transaction in terms of relative priority, which describe how important to the business one transaction is compared to all other transactions. Physical database design ensures that each transaction meets or exceeds its performance requirements. Consequently, the transactions must be evaluated one at a time. The relative priority of each transaction provides the sequence in which transactions are evaluated. This ensures that the most important transactions receive the most attention.

Transaction SQL Statements

Each transaction definition must also specify the SQL statements that perform the necessary database operations. These SQL statements are either UPDATE, INSERT, DELETE, or SELECT commands, which are known collectively as SQL DML (data manipulation language). The SQL statements are required during physical database design to forecast the execution times of the transactions. In addition, a detailed understanding of the database design and significant experience with SQL is required to accurately code many SQL statements. Therefore, it is sometimes preferable for the database designer to provide the SQL statements for the application programmers rather than allowing them to code the SQL themselves. However, the database designer and the application programmers must coordinate their efforts closely to ensure that the SQL statements support the program's data requirements.

The transaction definitions should also include, for each SQL statement, a brief (nontechnical) narrative explaining:

- What the command accomplishes
- Why it is required (if it is not obvious)
- Number of rows in the database affected by the command

The number of rows affected means either the number of rows returned (in the case of a SELECT command) or the number of rows inserted, updated, or deleted. The performance of any SQL command depends on the number of database rows affected. For example, it would take longer to read 10,000 customer rows than 1 customer row. Hence, the number of records affected by each SQL command is an important element of physical database design.

Once coded and described, each SQL command should be validated for accuracy. To accomplish this, it will be necessary to construct a small test database. Many users find it useful to build a SQLTalk script containing all the transactions' SQL commands for this purpose.

Also, keep in mind that the DML should be coded against the external, rather than the internal, schema. The initial external schema created in Chapter 4 will probably contain many of the views needed to support the transactions.

12.6   Summary

This chapter covered new concepts regarding referential integrity and introduced transaction analysis. We addressed specific issues involving the implications of using foreign keys. For example, when DELETE commands are used there are several delete rules applied to foreign keys that will affect the behavior of this SQL command.

Good database design, transaction analysis, and referential integrity are very much intertwined. Good application developers will spend time up-front to design a data structure and analyze table relationships before beginning the development of an application.

13   SQL Variations

This chapter discusses the differences among the leading relational database products currently on the market that utilize the SQL language for their data language. We compare Centura Software's SQLBase, used throughout this book, with IBM's DB2, Sybase's SQL Server, Microsoft's SQL Server, Oracle from Oracle Corporation, and Informix from Informix Corporation. These products together form the large majority of the market for client-server relational database software.

The chapter is organized as follows:

Section 13.1 Differences in SQL
Section 13.2 Differences in Database Systems
Section 13.3 SQL Language Variations
Section 13.4 SQL Statement Elements
Section 13.5 Summary

13.1   Differences in SQL

Sometimes you may hear someone criticize SQL for "being neither structured nor a query language." In the same way, it is easy to be critical of what many people call "standard SQL," because no vendor actually sells a product that implements the true, plain vanilla standard for SQL. Of course, neither of these criticisms is really fair. Much of the SQL language syntax is oriented towards querying data (which is reasonably well structured); the rest is merely needed in order to create and maintain the data resource. But after all, without strong, flexible ways to get data out of a database, what value would the database have?

13.1.1 Why Variations Exist

Similarly, variations of SQL have developed for reasons that enhance the value of their associated database systems. Furthermore, the first implementations of SQL were not developed by a standards committee. Rather, they were developed by computer scientists working at a variety of software corporations, who were attempting to create a new way of accessing database systems. These scientists had no way of knowing that their work would eventually be in such high demand that it would be adopted by virtually every leading database system on the market. At the time, other data access languages, such as Quel, were also being developed and promoted for adoption in the marketplace. SQL just happened to be the one that caught on.

Only after the initial products using SQL achieved success in the marketplace did the American National Standards Institute (ANSI) become involved in building a consensus for a fully standardized syntax. This consensus was developed by a committee on which sat representatives of major database software vendors, and leading computer scientists. Much of their activity until recently has been to attempt to negotiate a common language set that is contained within the leading product offerings. As such, the ANSI standard for SQL is often viewed as "the lowest common denominator" of SQL available.

But if ANSI SQL forms the lowest common denominator, then what is contained in the leading vendor's products? Usually, a dialect of SQL that the vendor feels offers significant advantages to ANSI standard SQL and expects will cause customers to select his product over competitors'. Some of the underlying causes of these variations are:

- Performance improvement
- Implementation of a new capability that has not yet been the subject of a standard
- Ability to run on a specific hardware or software platform
- Greater ease of use
- Ease of interface with the vendor's other products
- Upward compatibility with previous versions

As you can see, these are all good reasons. No vendor has ever decided to introduce SQL variations into his product merely to confuse and confound developers and users, although sometimes you may feel that way. Behind every difference is some causal factor that may serve to differentiate that particular database system from others on the market. Realizing this is one technique you can use to evaluate competing database products. Of course, there are numerous other factors that should influence a purchasing decision as well.

13.1.2 Amounts of Variation

You may wonder how much work is involved in learning more than one SQL offering. After all, I'm sure you're making a significant effort to get through this book to learn the SQLBase implementation of SQL; when you finish you may not feel like tackling another. Be assured that the variations are not *that* extreme. The first time you learn SQL, you have to learn many new statements, as well as what clauses must appear where, which ones are mandatory or optional, and which may be repeated. And that's not even mentioning the hardest part, which is how to make the jump from conceptualizing your needs to knowing what SQL statements and clauses are required! But you'll find that once you get good at that hard part, it is equally applicable to all the SQL you'll ever need to work with, because while the syntax of various implementation varies, the conceptual purpose behind the various statements and clauses remains the same.

When you complete this book, you'll have a good understanding of the SQL implemented by Centura Software in the SQLBase product. This is a particularly good database to learn on, because it adheres closely both to the ANSI standards and to industry trends and doesn't have a lot of embellishments that add unusual features or capabilities. You'll discover that other implementations of SQL will build upon the base of knowledge you've acquired from this book. As you'll see, all leading SQL implementations follow the same basic set of verbs and command structures. To become a multilingual SQL expert, all you have to do is try to remember the deviations from common practices that each product you use may have. Don't worry: When you forget, the product will remind you, usually with some sort of message saying "INVALID SYNTAX."

13.1.3 Benefits of Knowing Variations

You may wonder why you would want to learn more than one SQL offering in any case? The main reason, of course, is to enhance your own capabilities. For the moment, working with SQLBase may allow you to do everything you want to accomplish. Maybe this will always be true, but don't bet on it. There are a lot of copies of the other leading database management systems out there, and eventually you'll probably run into at least one of them.

If your use of database management systems is to get information from them (what is often called an "end user"), then you may be at the mercy of your employers. You get to become an expert at whatever database system they choose to buy! Of course, maybe you'll have a say in the choice, but either way, you have to make the best use of the final selection that you can. If you should switch employers, you may well end up switching SQL dialects when you discover your new employer uses a different database than the one you have been familiar with.

If you're a data processing professional, then your use of database management systems is probably through some role that you play in the development of programs and applications that make use of the DBMS as their storage mechanism. You are what is referred to as a "developer," which may be a programmer, a DBA, a project leader, or some other similar position. You are in a more complex situation than the end user, since you may have to deal with multiple DBMSs *simultaneously*.

Sometimes developers work in a corporation that has not adopted just one database management system but has managed to somehow acquire several of them. You may now find yourself involved in developing a system that has to make use of more than one of these existing databases, so that you must be prepared to use the appropriate SQL syntax with each one of them.

Alternatively, developers sometimes find themselves building a system that is supposed to be able to run on one of any number of DBMSs. This is usually the case if you work for a company that builds and markets software. They usually don't want to restrict their potential market to only those customers who only own one particular DBMS. They would prefer that anyone owning any SQL-compliant DBMS be able to buy and run their software. Therefore, they will want you to develop their product in a manner that will allow it to run under different database management systems with either no or minimal modification. To do this, you will need to write your code very close to the ANSI SQL standard, the lowest common denominator of database systems. You may also find yourself using some middleware software that eases the task of writing non-product-specific SQL, such as Microsoft's ODBC drivers.

13.2   Differences in Database Systems

Although on the surface most relational database management systems seem quite similar, there are significant differences lying under the covers. While this chapter deals mainly with the variations in the SQL syntax of the leading products, there are a few other significant items you need to be aware of.

13.2.1 Storage Structure Differences

Probably the most significant variation in relational database implementations is the way that data is structured and stored on external disk devices. The number of data files and their types vary between virtually all systems. Don't assume that because you may know some tricks about manipulating the external environment for one database system, they will apply to any other database system. Each software company has adopted whatever external storage mechanisms they thought best at the time they originally designed their system, and most don't make major changes in these areas because of the high impact such modifications would have throughout their product's code.

Another corollary aspect to these differences is the way vendors implement various access mechanisms such as indexes. While most products support some type of binary tree index structure, many have also chosen to implement other techniques. Some of these underlying physical differences show up as variations in SQL syntax, either at the major statement or the clause level. For instance, in the CREATE INDEX statement, specifying CLUSTERED in DB2 will cause the rows in the subject table to be placed physically in order by the index key, as well as building a b-tree index structure. In the same statement in SQLBase, specifying the CLUSTERED HASHED clause will not build any physical index structure at all but will cause the space for the table to be preallocated and the rows to be subsequently inserted according to a hash function that is applied to the subject index key.

While the details of all the variations in physical storage structures of RDBMSs is well beyond the scope of this book, be aware that there are significant differences. If you ever have to port an actual database between different systems, you will need to spend some time studying these implementation details before you will be ready to analyze the impact of moving the database.

13.2.2 Query Optimization Differences

Another area of wide variation between relational database management systems is that of the query optimizer. This is a software component of all relational systems whose function it is to determine, for any given SQL statement, how that statement should actually be processed. The optimizer does this by converting the request into a standardized format, then evaluating the table(s) involved to determine what possibilities exist for satisfying the requirements of the statement. It then performs some sort of logic in an attempt to choose one of the alternatives. In this way, the optimizer is the component that frees the users of the database from having to describe *how* to get the data they want; all they have to do is describe *what* data is needed through the SQL syntax.

In most relational implementations, the optimizer bases its selection of the access technique on statistical analysis of the contents of the database. The goal of this analysis is generally to attempt to determine the quickest, most efficient access technique possible. For this reason, the decisions made by the optimizer have a major impact on how quickly the database software performs. Also, each database system has some method that controls when and how these statistics are gathered. This is typically either a nonstandard SQL statement or a utility program supplied with the software. You need to find out how to keep these statistics reasonably up to date in order to provide the optimizer with accurate information. Doing this will allow the optimizer to select access techniques that will allow your database software to perform at its best possible level.

Another important consequence of these query optimizer variations is that the same SQL may produce very different performance results on different RDBMSs. Because of differences in the internal form of the SQL, the kinds of statistics, and the various physical options available to each optimizer, the techniques selected to satisfy a particular SQL statement by one system may be (and probably will be) completely different from the selection made by another system for the exact same statement.

Because of this, if you intend to do things like moving an application between different database management systems, you should be prepared to deal with a difference in performance after making the move. Take the time to validate the performance of your application on each individual database management system it will run on by thoroughly system-testing it in each environment. Only by doing this will you be able to feel comfortable that your database design and programs perform adequately in each kind of database system that they may run on.

13.3   SQL Language Variations

This section covers the detailed differences in the SQL implemented by the leading relational database management systems:

- SQLBase
- DB2
- Sybase SQL Server (which I'll call Sybase)
- Microsoft SQL Server (which I'll call SQL Server)
- Oracle
- Informix
- SQL II is also shown for the purpose of illustrating the standard statement. This is from the ANSI SQL-92 standard.

First, we cover the differences in name and identifier limitations implemented by each system, since these variations apply equally across all types of SQL statements. Then, we examine the statements within each area of SQL separately, noting the syntax differences of each. We first cover DQL, since the SELECT statement is the most complex SQL. Then, we move on to DML and the INSERT, UPDATE, and DELETE statements. Finally, we briefly cover DDL, mostly discussing differences in the CREATE statement for those clauses that are common across all implementations. Not covered are details on particular implementation-specific DDL that affects features unique to each product.

The following conventions are used in the syntax definitions that make up the remainder of this chapter:

- { | }   Choose one from the list.

- [|]   Choose one of the optional features.

- [|]...   Choose one of the optional features multiple times, separated by space.

- { , }   Choose multiple from the list separated by comma.

- [,]   Choose multiple from optional list, separated by comma.

- CAPS   Required text.

- x_y   Possible definition available or terminal.

13.3.1 Names and Identifiers

Table Name

> *base_table | view*

All systems allow base table or view names to be used interchangeably in DQL or DML. Note that DDL generally requires the base table name, except when defining views.

Base Table or View

DB2:

> [*auth_id.*] *identifier*

In DB2 the owner qualifier is called an authid.

In all systems, identifier has a maximum length of 18 characters. It is made up of:

> { A - Z | @ | # | $ } *followed by*
> [{ A - Z | 0 - 9 | @ | # | $ | _ }]...

SQL Server and Sybase:

> [[*database.*] *owner.*] *identifier*

The database name above contains the name of the system containing the object.

Oracle:

> [*schema .*] *identifier*

Oracle calls the owner qualifier, or authid, a schema name.

Column Names

> [*column_qualifier .*] *column*

SQLBase 5.2:

Maximum column name length is 18 characters with a maximum of 253 columns in a table.

Column name composition is:

> [a-z] *followed by*
> [a-z | # | @ | $]...

Column_qualifier is the table name format for the appropriate system.

DB2:

Maximum column name length is 18 characters, with a maximum of 255 columns in a table. There is also a limit on row width, which is that the sum of all column bytes must be less than 4005.

Oracle:

Maximum column name length is 30 characters, and there is a maximum of 254 columns in a table.

13.3.2 Data Query Language

SQL II Standard SELECT

```
SELECT [ DISTINCT ] select_item_commalist
[ INTO host_variable_commalist ]
FROM table_ref_commalist
[ WHERE search_condition ]
[GROUP BY { table_alias | column_ref_commalist } [ HAVING
        search_condition ] ]
[ { UNION | INTERSECT | EXCEPT } [ ALL ] [
        CORRESPONDING [ BY ( column_ref_commalist ) ]
        query_spec | TABLE table | table_constructor ]
[ ORDER BY sort_item_commalist ]
```

TABLE table is:

SELECT * FROM *table*

The UNION operation is defined so that a given row appears only if it appears in at least one of the result sets created by a select statement. No duplicates are allowed.

The INTERSECT operation is defined so that a given row appears only if it appears in all of the result sets created by the SELECT statement. Again, no duplicates are allowed.

The EXCEPT operation is defined so that a given row appears in the result only if it appears in the first result set and not in the second.

ALL qualifies an operation so that duplicates are allowed in the final result set. In UNION, it appears as the sum of its appearance in the result sets. In EXCEPT, it appears as the difference of its appearance in the result sets.

CORRESPONDING qualifies an operation so that it restricts the operation to columns whose name and data type are comparable in each of the select clauses. If no *column_ref_commalist* is specified, all the columns that have the same name and comparable data type are used. Only those columns used will be output.

SQLBase SELECT:

    SELECT [ALL | DISTINCT] *select_item_commalist*
    FROM *table_ref_commalist*
    [WHERE *search_condition*]
    [GROUP BY *column_ref_commalist* [HAVING *search_condition*
        ]]
    [UNION [ALL]]
    [ORDER BY *sort_item_commalist*]
    [FOR UPDATE OF *column_commalist*]

DB2 SELECT:

    SELECT [ALL | DISTINCT] *select_item_commalist*
    FROM *table_ref_commalist*
    [WHERE *search_condition*]
    [GROUP BY *column_ref_commalist* [HAVING *search_condition*]
        ]
    [UNION|EXEPT|INTERSECT [ALL] *query_spec*]
    [ORDER BY *sort_item_commalist*]
    [FOR UPDATE OF *column_ref_commalist*]
    [FOR FETCH ONLY]

The FOR FETCH ONLY option specifies that no UPDATE or DELETE statements will be issued against this cursor. Creating a cursor that will never be updated can improve performance.

Sybase SELECT:

    SELECT [ALL | DISTINCT] *select_list_commalist*
    [INTO *base_table*]
    [FROM *table_ref_commalist*
    [WHERE *search_conditions*]
    [GROUP BY [ALL] *aggregate_free_expression_commalist*
        [HAVING *search_conditions*]]
    [UNION [ALL] *query_spec*]
    [ORDER BY *sort_item_commalist*

        [COMPUTE *aggregate_function_commalist* [BY
               column_commalist]]
        [FOR {READ ONLY I UPDATE [OF *column_commalist*]}]
        [FOR BROWSE]

SQL Server SELECT:

        SELECT [ALL I DISTINCT] *select_item_commalist*
        [INTO *base_table*]
        [FROM *table_ref_commalist*]
        [WHERE *search_conditions*]
        [GROUP BY [ALL] *aggregate_free_expression_commalist*
               [HAVING *search_conditions*]]
        [UNION [ALL] *query_spec*]
        [ORDER BY *sort_item_commalist*]
        [COMPUTE *aggregate_function_commalist* [BY
               column_commalist]]
        [FOR BROWSE]

The FOR BROWSE option functions like the FOR FETCH ONLY as
mentioned for DB2.

Oracle SELECT:

        SELECT [ALL I DISTINCT] *select_item_commalist*
        FROM *table_ref_list*
        [WHERE *search_condition*]
        [[START WITH *search_condition*] CONNECT BY
               search_condition]
        [GROUP BY *scalar_exp_commalist* [HAVING *search_condition*]
               ...]
        [{ UNION [ALL] I INTERSECT I MINUS } *query_spec*]
        [ORDER BY *sort_item_commalist*]
        [FOR UPDATE [OF *column_commalist*]
        [NOWAIT]

The NOWAIT option in Oracle avoids the long wait for a lock. Control is
returned immediately with the appropriate error code. Note that the START
WITH clause allows control over the determination of which table in a join
is in the outer loop.

Informix SELECT:

        SELECT [ALL I DISTINCT I UNIQUE] *select_item_commalist*

FROM *table_ref*
[WHERE *search_condition*]
[GROUP BY { *column_ref_commalist* | *integer* }[HAVING
         search_condition]]
[UNION *query_spec*]
[ORDER BY *sort_item_commalist*]
[INTO TEMP *base_table* [WITH NO LOG]]

Notice that Informix allows the immediate creation of a temporary table, which can be built without the overhead of logging.

13.3.3 Data Manipulation Language

SQL II Standard INSERT

INSERT INTO *table*
[(*column_commalist*)]
insert_item

SQLBase, Sybase, SQL Server, and Oracle INSERT:

INSERT INTO *table*
[(*column_commalist*)]
insert_item

Note that these systems conform exactly to the standard.

DB2 INSERT:

INSERT [INTO] *table*
[(*column_commalist*)]
insert_item

DB2 does not require the INTO portion of the statement.

Informix INSERT:

INSERT INTO { *table* | *synonym* }
[(*column_commalist*)]
insert_item

SQL II Standard UPDATE

UPDATE *table*
SET *assignment_commalist*
[WHERE *search_condition*]

SQLBase UPDATE:

> UPATE *table_ref*
> SET *assignment_commalist*
> [WHERE *search_condition*]
> [CHECK EXISTS]

The CHECK EXISTS option causes an error code to be returned if no rows meet the WHERE criteria to be updated.

DB2, Oracle, and Informix UPDATE:

> UPDATE *table*
> SET *assignment_commalist*
> [WHERE *search_condition*]

Sybase and SQL Server UPDATE:

> UPDATE *table_ref*
> SET *assignment_commalist*
> [FROM *table_ref_commalist*]
> [WHERE *search_conditions*]

These systems allow data in a table to be updated, using values from another table, by implementing the FROM clause.

SQL II Standard DELETE

> DELETE FROM *table*
> [WHERE *search_condition*]

SQLBase, DB2, Oracle, and Informix DELETE:

> DELETE FROM *table*
> [WHERE *search_condition*]

This command deletes zero-to-multiple rows of data from a table without using a cursor.

Sybase and SQL Server DELETE:

> DELETE { [FROM] *table* | *table* [FROM *table_commalist*] }
> [WHERE *search_conditions*]

These systems allow rows from one table to be deleted, based on criteria that apply to multiple tables, such as a join.

13.3.4 Data Definition Language

SQL II Standard CREATE TABLE

CREATE [{ GLOBAL | LOCAL } TEMPORARY] TABLE
    base_table
(*base_table_element_commalist*)
[ON COMMIT { DELETE | PRESERVE } ROWS]

The ON COMMIT option can be used only with temporary tables. The
GLOBAL | LOCAL options have to do with the level of distributed schema
definition to which the table applies.

SQLBase CREATE TABLE:

CREATE TABLE *table*
(*base_table_element_commalist*)
[IN {[*database_name.*]*tablespace* | DATABASE *database* }]
[PCTFREE *integer*]

The IN clause is provided for compatibility with DB2 but is ignored by
SQLBase. The PCTFREE parameter does apply to SQLBase physical
storage.

DB2 CREATE TABLE:

CREATE TABLE *base_table*
(*base_table_element_commalist*)
[IN {[*database_name.*]*tablespace* | DATABASE *database* }]

As with most variations on the CREATE TABLE, the DB2 differences are
oriented toward specifying where the table will be physically located.

Sybase and SQL Server CREATE TABLE:

CREATE TABLE *base_table*
(*base_table_element_commalist*)
[ON *segment_name*]

Oracle CREATE TABLE:

CREATE TABLE *base_table*
(*base_table_element_commalist*)
[[PCTFREE *integer*], [PCTUSED *integer*], [INITRANS *integer*
    ], [MAXTRANS *integer*], [TABLESPACE *tablespace*], [

STORAGE *storage_clause*] [CLUSTER *cluster* (
  column_commalist)]]
[ENABLE { { UNIQUE (*column_commaiist*) | PRIMARY KEY |
  CONSTRAINT *constraint* } using_index_clause | ALL
  TRIGGERS}]
[DISABLE { { UNIQUE (*column_commalist*) | PRIMARY KEY |
  CONSTRAINT *constraint* } CASCADE | ALL
  TRIGGERS}]
[AS *query_spec*]

Oracle has a lot of physical space allocation parameters that can be set in the CREATE TABLE statement. Also, a number of constraints can be defined and can either use indexes built explicitly or can implicitly create their own indexes. Furthermore, the table can be populated as part of the CREATE TABLE by specification of a query statement in the AS clause.

Informix CREATE TABLE:

CREATE [TEMP] *table_name*
(*base_table_element_commalist*)
[WITH NO LOG]
[IN *dbspace* [EXTENT *first_kbyte* NEXT *next_kbyte*]
[LOCK MODE PAGE | ROW]]

The WITH NO LOG clause can be used only with temporary tables. Note that the lock granularity for the table can be set at create time.

SQL II Standard CREATE VIEW

CREATE VIEW *view* [(*column_commalist*)]
AS SELECT *statement*
[WITH [CASCADED | LOCAL] CHECK OPTION]

The WITH CHECK OPTION specifies that view predicates will be checked on UPDATEs and INSERTs. CASCADED means that view predicates are checked for underlying views. The default of LOCAL checks only predicates contained in this view.

SQLBase and Sybase CREATE VIEW:

CREATE VIEW *view* [(*column_commalist*)]
AS *query_spec*
[WITH CHECK OPTION]

DB2, SQL Server, and Informix CREATE VIEW:

    CREATE VIEW *view* [(*column_commalist*)]
    AS *query_spec*

CREATE INDEX

There is no ANSI SQL standard syntax for creating an index, presumably because the statement is implementation dependent.

SQLBase CREATE INDEX:

    CREATE [UNIQUE] [CLUSTERED HASHED]
    INDEX *index*
    ON *table*
    (*column_name*{ASC|DESC}
    [,*column_name* {ASC|DESC}] ...)
    [PCTFREE *integer*]
    [SIZE *integer* ROWS]

The PCTFREE default is 10%.

DB2 CREATE INDEX:

    CREATE [UNIQUE] INDEX *index*
    ON *base_table*
    (*column_name*{ASC | DESC}
    [,*column_name* {ASC|DESC}] ...)

Sybase and SQL Server CREATE INDEX:

    CREATE [UNIQUE] [CLUSTERED | NONCLUSTERED]
    INDEX *index*
    ON *base_table* (*column_ref_commalist*)
    [WITH {FILLFACTOR = *integer*, IGNORE_DUP_KEY,
        SORTED_DATA, [IGNORE_DUP_ROW |
        ALLOW_DUP_ROW]}]
    [ON *segment_name*]

FILLFACTOR specifies free space in each index node and defaults to zero. The SORTED_DATA option eliminates the sort. Upon creation, each row is checked to ensure that it is already sorted. If this fails, CREATE INDEX fails. If IGNORE_DUP_KEY is not set, then UPDATE or INSERT of duplicate keys will fail.

Oracle CREATE INDEX:

CREATE INDEX [*schema.*] *index*
ON *base_table*
(*column_name*{ASC|DESC}
[,*column_name* {ASC|DESC}]...)
[[INTRANS *integer*], [MAXTRANS *integer*], [TABLESPACE
    tablespace], [STORAGE *storage_clause*], [PCTFREE
    integer]]

[NOSORT]

The main difference in the Oracle syntax is the addition of their standard physical storage specification clause. As with SQL Server and Sybase, they also provide the option to avoid a sort.

Informix CREATE INDEX:

CREATE [UNIQUE | DISTINCT] [CLUSTER] INDEX *index*
ON *base_table*
(*column_name*{ ASC | DESC }
[, *column_name* { ASC | DESC }] ...)

Informix considers UNIQUE and DISTINCT to be synonyms.

SQL II Standard ALTER TABLE

ALTER TABLE *table*
{ ADD [COLUMN] *column_def* } |
{ ALTER [COLUMN] *column* { SET DEFAULT *default* | DROP
    DEFAULT } |
DROP [COLUMN] *column* { RESTRICT | CASCADE } |
ADD *base_table_constraint_def* |
DROP CONSTRAINT *constraint* { RESTRICT | CASCADE } }...

The standard ALTER allows either columns or constraints to be added or removed from a table. Not all vendors have implemented this much flexibility in their products.

SQLBase ALTER TABLE:

ALTER TABLE *base_table*
{ DROP *column_commalist* |
ADD *column_def*... |
RENAME { *column newname*... | TABLE *newname* } |

> MODIFY *column* [*data_type* (*length*)] [[NOT] NULL [WITH
>   DEFAULT]... |
> { ADD | DROP } { PRIMARY KEY *column_commalist* |
>   *foreign_key_def* , }

Views that reference dropped, modified, or renamed columns or tables are automatically dropped. Columns that cannot be dropped are those that are indexed or belong to a primary or foreign key. You can modify a column to increase the length, but not to decrease the length. You cannot change data type or length of numeric columns.

DB2 ALTER TABLE:

> ALTER TABLE *base_table*
> { ADD *column data_type* { FOR BIT DATA | NOT NULL WITH
>   DEFAULT | *column_constraint_def* } |
>   *base_table_constraint_def* |
> DROP PRIMARY KEY |
> DROP FOREIGN KEY *constraint* }...}

Sybase ALTER TABLE:

> ALTER TABLE *base_table*
> { ADD *column_def* |
> ADD *base_table_constraint_def* |
> DROP CONSTRAINT *constraint* |
> REPLACE *column* DEFAULT { *scalar_exp* | USER | NULL } }

The *scalar_exp* is used as a default value for a column. You cannot include the name of any columns or other database objects, but you can include built-in functions that do not reference database objects. This default value must be compatible with the data type of the column. You cannot add columns of bit types or user-defined types that are based on bit. REPLACE changes the default value of a column.

SQL Server ALTER TABLE:

> ALTER TABLE *base_table*
> ADD { *column data_type* NULL, }

SQL II Standard DROP TABLE

> DROP TABLE *table*
> { CASCADE | RESTRICT }

The CASCADE option causes any referencing view definitions and integrity constraints to be dropped with the table. Alternatively, the RESTRICT option means that if the table is referenced in any view definition or integrity constraint, the drop will fail.

SQLBase, DB2, and Informix DROP TABLE:

DROP TABLE *base_table*

Sybase and SQL Server DROP TABLE:

DROP TABLE *base_table_commalist*

These systems allow you to drop more than one table in a single statement.

SQL II Standard DROP VIEW

DROP VIEW *view* { CASCADE | RESTRICT }

The CASCADE and RESTRICT options function the same as for the DROP TABLE statement.

All Systems DROP VIEW:

DROP VIEW *view*

There are no variations in the implementation of this statement.

All Systems DROP INDEX:

DROP INDEX *base_table.index*

There are no variations in the implementation of this statement.

13.4   SQL Statement Elements

In this section, the elements referred to throughout the previous section are explained in detail. This information is stripped out of the basic statement syntax in order to make the statements easier to read. There are variations among the different database management systems in this area, too.

Note that if an element is not designated for a particular database management system, then that system either uses the general definition or has no reference to that type of element whatsoever.

13.4.1 Basic Statement Elements

Assignment

> column_name = { scalar_exp | NULL | DEFAULT }

SQLBase, DB2, Sybase, and SQL Server Assignment:
> column_name = {scalar_exp | NULL }

Oracle Assignment:
> { (column_commalist) = (query_spec) | column = { scalar_exp |
> query_spec } }

Informix Assignment:
> { (column_commalist) | * = scalar_exp | query_spec } | { column
> = { scalar_exp | query_spec } , } }

SQLBase Sort Item:
> { column_ref | integer } [ASC | DESC]

DB2 Sort Item:
> column_ref

Sybase Sort Item:
> { table | column_ref | integer | scalar_exp } [ASC | DESC]

SQL Server Sort Item:
> { table | column_ref | integer | alias | scalar_exp } [ASC | DESC]

Oracle Sort Item:
> scalar_exp | integer [ASC | DESC]

Informix Sort Item:
> integer | alias | column_ref [ASC | DESC]

Insert Item

> { query_spec | VALUES (row_constructor_list) | DEFAULT
> VALUES }

Insert Item

> { *query_spec* | VALUES (*row_constructor_list*) }

Select Item

> *scalar_exp* [[AS] *alias*] | [*table.* *]

Where table .* is a comma list of all columns in that table.

SQLBase Select Item:

> *alias* = *scalar_exp* | *scalar_exp* [AS *alias*] | [*table.*]. * | *column*
> FROM *table*

DB2 Select Item:

> *scalar_exp* [*alias*] | [*table.* *]

Sybase Select Item:

> * | { *alias* = { *column* | IDENTITY (*precision*) } | *column* [AS]
> *alias* } | *column_commalist* | *scalar_exp* | @ *variable* =
> *scalar_exp*

The IDENTITY (precision) operation allows you to create a column that has identity properties.

SQL Server Select Item:

> * | { *alias* = *column* | *column alias* } | *column_commalist* |
> *scalar_exp* | @ *variable* = *scalar_exp*

Oracle and Informix Select Item:

> [{ *table* | *synonym* }.] * | *scalar_exp alias*

Table Reference

> *table* [[AS] *alias* [(*column_commalist*)]] | (*query_spec*) [AS
>] *alias* [(*column_commalist*)] | *join_table_exp*

SQLBase, DB2, and Oracle Table Reference:

> *table alias*

Sybase Table Reference:

> *table* { *alias* | { HOLDLOCK | NOHOLDLOCK } [SHARED] } }

The HOLDLOCK | NOHOLDLOCK [SHARED] options can be used only in a SELECT statement.

SQL Server Table Reference:

> *table* { *alias* | HOLDLOCK }

The HOLDLOCK option can be used only in a SELECT statement.

Informix Table Reference:

> { *table* | *synonym* } [AS] [*alias*] | *join_table_exp*

Join Table Expression

> *table_ref* [NATURAL] [*join_type*] JOIN *table_ref* [ON
>   *search_condition* | USING (*column_commalist*)] |
>   *table_ref* CROSS JOIN *table_ref*

Informix Join Table Expression:

> *join_type* [( ] *table_ref_commalist* [ )] [AS] [*alias*]

Join Type

> INNER | LEFT [OUTER] | RIGHT [OUTER] | FULL [OUTER] |
> UNION

SQLBase, DB2, ,Sybase, and Oracle Base Table Element:

> *column_def* | *base_table_constraint_def*

SQL Server and Informix Base Table Element:

> *column_def*

Column Definition

> *column* { *data_type* | *domain* } [*default_def*] [
>   *column_constraint_def_list*]

SQLBase and SQL Server Column Definition:

> *column data_type* [*default_def*]

DB2, Sybase, Oracle, and Informix Column Definition:

> *column data_type* [*default_def*] [*column_constraint_def_list*]

Base Table Constraint Definition

[CONSTRAINT *constraint*] { *candidate_key_def* |
foreign_key_def | *check_constraint_def* } [*deferrability*]

SQLBase and DB2 Base Table Constraint Definition:

candidate_key_def | *foreign_key_def*

Sybase Base Table CONSTRAINT Definition:

[CONSTRAINT *constraint*] { *candidate_key_def* |
foreign_key_def | *check_constraint_def* }

Candidate Key Definition

{ *primary_key_def* | *unique_key_def* } (*column_commalist*)

SQLBase and DB2 Candidate Key Definition:

primary_key_def (*column_commalist*)

Sybase Candidate Key Definition:

{ *primary_key_def* | *unique_key_def* } [CLUSTERED |
NONCLUSTERED] (*column_commalist*)

PRIMARY KEY Definition

PRIMARY KEY

Note that the standardized usage of a primary key does not allow null values.

UNIQUE Key Definition

UNIQUE

The difference between a unique key and a primary key is that a unique key allows null values.

FOREIGN KEY Definition

FOREIGN KEY (*column_commalist*) *references_def*

SQLBase FOREIGN KEY Definition:

FOREIGN KEY *constraint* (*column_commalist*) *references_def*

Note that the constraint must be named only if the foreign key column names are longer than eight characters.

DB2 FOREIGN KEY Definition:

FOREIGN KEY [*constraint*] (*column_commalist*)
references_def

Sybase Foreign Key Definition:

references_def

REFERENCES Definition

REFERENCES *base_table* [(*column_commalist*)] [MATCH {
FULL | PARTIAL }] [ON DELETE *referential_action*] [
ON UPDATE *referential_action*]

SQLBase REFERENCES Definition:

REFERENCES *base_table* [ON DELETE *referential_action*]

In order for the definition to be effective, the base table must have a unique index explicitly created on the primary key.

DB2 REFERENCES Definition:

REFERENCES *base_table* { [ON DELETE *referential_action*] [
ON UPDATE RESTRICT] | [ON UPDATE RESTRICT [
ON DELETE *referential_action*] }

Sybase REFERENCES Definition:

REFERENCES *base_table* [(*column_commalist*)]

Oracle REFERENCES Definition:

REFERENCES *base_table* [(*column_commalist*)] [ON
DELETE *referential_action*]

Referential Action

NO ACTION | CASCADE | SET DEFAULT | SET NULL |
RESTRICT

The default is RESTRICT.

SQLBase and DB2 Referential Action:

RESTRICT | CASCADE | SET NULL

CHECK Constraint Definition

CHECK (*search_cond*)

Column CONSTRAINT Definition

[CONSTRAINT *constraint*] { NOT NULL I PRIMARY KEY I
    UNIQUE KEY I *references_def* I CHECK (*search_cond*)
    } [*deferrability*]

SQLBase and DB2 Column CONSTRAINT Definition:

[*constraint*] *references_def*

Sybase Column CONSTRAINT Definition:

[{ *identity_col* I [NULL] NULL }] [CONSTRAINT *constraint*] { {
    PRIMARY KEY I UNIQUE KEY } [CLUSTERED I
    NONCLUSTERED] [WITH FILLFACTOR = *integer*] [
    ON *segment_name*] I *references_def* I CHECK (
    search_cond) }

Oracle Column CONSTRAINT Definition:

[CONSTRAINT *constraint*] { [NOT] NULL I PRIMARY KEY I
    UNIQUE I *references_def* I CHECK (*search_cond*) } [
    using_index_clause I DISABLE]

Informix Column CONSTRAINT Definition:

CONSTRAINT *constraint*

USING INDEX Clause

USING INDEX [PCTFREE *integer* I INITRANS *integer* I
    MAXTRANS *integer* I TABLESPACE *tablespace* I
    STORAGE *storage_clause*]... [EXCEPTIONS INTO
    base_table]

Storage Clause

(INITIAL *integer* { K I M } I NEXT *integer* { K I M } I MINEXTENTS
    integer I MAXEXTENTS *integer* I PCTINCREATE *integer*
    I OPTIMAL { *integer* { K I M } I NULL } I FREELIST
    integer I FREELIST GROUPS *integer* ...)

K refers to kilobyte and M refers to megabyte.

Deferrability

[INITIALLY { DEFERRED | IMMEDIATE }] [NOT]
DEFERRABLE

Note that INITIALLY DEFERRED and NOT DEFERRABLE are mutually
exclusive. Also, if INITIALLY [DEFERRED | IMMEDIATE] are not specified,
then INITIALLY IMMEDIATE becomes the default. If INITIALLY
IMMEDIATE is specified and DEFERRABLE is not specified, then NOT
DEFERRABLE becomes the default. INITIALLY specifies the initial mode of
the constraint at creation and start of every SQL transaction. DEFERRED
specifies whether constraint checking can be deferred. DEFERRABLE means
that the constraint is checked immediately or at the end of the transaction.
NOT DEFERRABLE means that the constraint is checked after every
statement.

DEFAULT Definition

DEFAULT { *literal* | *niladic_function_ref* | NULL }

SQLBase DEFAULT Definition:

NOT NULL [WITH DEFAULT]

DB2 DEFAULT Definition:

NOT NULL [WITH DEFAULT][PRIMARY KEY]

The WITH DEFAULT option assigns zero (numeric data type), current
date/time (date/time data type), or spaces (character data type) upon
INSERT.

Sybase DEFAULT Definition:

DEFAULT { *literal* | USER | NULL } [{IDENTITY | NULL | NOT
NULL}]

Each table in a database can have one IDENTITY column with a type of
numeric and scale zero. IDENTITY columns are not updateable and do not
allow nulls. The IDENTITY value uniquely identifies each row in a table.

SQL Server Default Definition:

NOT NULL | NULL

Oracle DEFAULT Definition:

DEFAULT *scalar_exp* | NULL | *pseudocolumn* | *sequence* |
ROWLABEL | *scalar_function*

Informix Default Definition:

NOT NULL | UNIQUE

Pseudocolumn

LEVEL | ROWID | ROWNUM

Sequence

CURRVAL | NEXTVAL

Collation Source

EXTERNAL ('*translation*') | *collation* | DESC (*collation*)
DEFAULT | TRANSLATION *translation* [THEN
COLLATION *collation*]

Translation Source

EXTERNAL ('*translation*') | IDENTITY | *translation*

13.4.2 Search Conditions

Search Condition

[( ] [NOT] { *comparison_cond* | *between_cond* | *like_cond* |
in_cond | *match_cond* | *all_or_any_cond* |
existence_cond | *unique_cond* | *null_cond* |
overlaps_cond } [{ AND | OR } *search_condition*] [ )] [
IS [NOT] *truth_value*]

SQLBase and DB2 Search Condition:

[( ] [NOT] { *comparison_cond* | *between_cond* | *null_cond* |
in_cond | *match_cond* | *all_or_any_cond* |
existence_cond } [{ AND | OR } *search_condition*] [ )]

Sybase Search Condition:

> [( ] [NOT] { *comparison_cond* I *between_cond* I *like_cond* I
> *null_cond* I *in_cond* I *existence_cond* I *all_or_any_cond* I
> } [{ AND I OR } *search_condition* [ )]

SQL Server Search Condition:

> [( ] [NOT] { *comparison_cond* I *like_cond* I *between_cond* I
> *in_cond* I *all_or_any_cond* I *null_cond* } [{ AND I OR }
> *search_condition*] [ )]

Truth Value

> TRUE I FALSE I UNKNOWN

Comparison Condition

> *row_constructor comparison_operator row_constructor*

Comparison Operator

> = I <> I < I <= I > I >= I != I !> I !<

SQL Server and Sybase Comparison Operator:

> = I <> I < I <= I > I >= I != I !> I !< I *= I =*

The *= I =* operators cause an outer join on the left or right side.

Between Condition

> *row_constructor* [NOT] BETWEEN *row_constructor* AND
> *row_constructor*

Sybase LIKE Condition:

> *character_string_exp* [NOT] LIKE '*pattern*' [ESCAPE
> *character_string_exp*]

The pattern can contain:

- (_)   Any single character
- (%)   Any sequence of zero or more characters
- [ ]   Any single character in specified range ([a-f] I [abcdef])
- [^]   Any character not in specified range ([^a-f] I [^abcdef])

SQLBase and SQL Server LIKE Condition:
> *character_string_exp* [NOT] LIKE '*pattern* '

Pattern

> *character_string_exp* | [*character_string_exp*] [% | _] [*pattern*]

Where :

- (_)   Any single character
- (%)   Any sequence of zero or more characters

SQLBase Pattern:
> USER | *character_string_exp* | [*character_string_exp*] [_ | %] [*pattern*]

Where:

- (_)   Any single character
- (%)   Any sequence of zero or more characters

SQL Server Pattern:
> *character_string_exp* | [*character_string_exp*] [% | _ | [ ] | [^]] [*pattern*]

Where:

- (_)   Any single character
- (%)   Any sequence of zero or more characters
- [ ]   Any single character in specified range ([a-f] | [abcdef])
- [^]   Any character not in specified range ([^a-f] | [^abcdef])

NULL Condition

> *row_constructor* IS [NOT] NULL

IN Condition

> *row_constructor* [NOT] IN (*query_spec*) | *scalar_exp* [NOT] IN (*scalar_exp_commalist*)

SQLBase IN Condition:

scalar_expression [NOT] IN (*query_spec* |
scalar_exp_commalist)

DB2 IN Condition:

scalar_expression [NOT] IN (*query_spec* | (
row_constructor_commalist) | *scalar_expression*

SQL Server IN Condition:

scalar_expression [NOT] IN (*query_spec* |
scalar_exp_commalist)

MATCH Condition

row_constructor MATCH [UNIQUE] [PARTIAL | FULL] (
query_spec)

DB2 ALL or ANY Condition:

row_constructor comparison_operator [ALL | ANY | SOME] (
query_spec)

SQL Server & SQLBase ALL or ANY Condition:

row_constructor comparison_operator [ALL | ANY] (*query_spec*
)

Existence Condition

EXISTS (*query_spec*)

OVERLAPS Condition

(*scalar_exp, scalar_exp*) OVERLAPS (*scalar_exp, scalar_exp*)

13.4.3 Data Types

Data Type

fixed_length_character | *variable_length_character* | *datetime* |
fixed_length_national_character |
variable_length_national_character | *integer* | *decimal* |
float | *fixed_length_bit_string* | *variable_length_bit_string*

SQLBase Data Type:
> *integer* | *float* | *fixed_length_character* |
> *variable_length_character* | *long_text* | *datetime*

DB2 Data Type:
> *fixed_length_character* | *variable_length_character* | *datetime* |
> *integer* | *decimal* | *float* | *fixed_length_bit_string* |
> *variable_length_bit_string* | *long_text* | *long_text_bit*

Sybase Data Type:
> *fixed_length_character* | *variable_length_character* | *datetime* |
> *fixed_length_national_character* | *money* |
> *variable_length_national_character* | *integer* | *decimal* |
> *float* | *fixed_length_bit_string* | *variable_length_bit_string*

SQL Server Data Type:
> *integer* | *float* | *fixed_length_character* |
> *variable_length_character* | *long_text* |
> *fixed_length_bit_string* | *variable_length_bit_string* |
> *datetime* | *money* | *sysname*

Fixed-Length Character

> CHAR[ACTER] [(*length*)]

DB2 maximum length is 254 bytes.

Sybase maximum length is 255 bytes.

SQLBase maximum length is 254 bytes.

SQL Server Fixed-Length Character:
> CHAR (*length*)

SQL Server maximum length is 255.

Variable-Length Character

> VARCHAR (*length*) CHARACTER SET (*character_set* |
> *form_of_use*) | CHAR[ACTER] VARYING (*length*)

SQLBase, DB2, and SQL Server Variable-Length Character:

VARCHAR (*length*)

DB2 maximum length <= 4000.

SQL Server maximum length <= 255.

SQLBase maximum length <= 254.

Sybase Variable Length Character:

VARCHAR (*length*) I CHAR[ACTER] VARYING (*length*)

Maximum length <= 255.

SQLBase Integer:

INT[EGER] I SMALLINT I NUMBER

INTEGER is 31 bits.

SMALLINT is 15 bits, .5 precision.

NUMBER is 15 digit, 23 precision.

DB2 Integer:

INT[EGER] I SMALLINT

INTEGER is 31 bits.

SMALLINT is 15 bits.

Sybase Integer:

INT I { SMALLINT I INTEGER } I TINYINT

INT is 31 bits.

SMALINT is 15 bits.

TINYINT is 8 bits (0 —— 255).

SQL Server Integer:

INT I SMALLINT I TINYINT

INT is 31 bits.

SMALINT is 15 bits.

TINYINT is 8 bits (0—— 255).

Decimal

NUMERIC [(*precision* [, *scale*])] | DEC[IMAL] [(*precision* [, *scale*])]

For Sybase, NUMERIC and DECIMAL can have a maximum of 17 bytes for storage.

For DB2, maximum is 31 digits with default precision = 5 and scale = 0 if both are unspecified.

SQLBase DECIMAL:

DEC[IMAL] [(*precision* [, *scale*])

A maximum of 15 digits. Default precision = 5 and scale = 0 if both are unspecified.

FLOAT

{ FLOAT | DOUBLE PRECISION } [(*precision*)] | REAL

For SQLBase, the precision is single if (1 < =precision < = 21), or double if (22 <= precision <= 53).

REAL is single precision.

For Sybase, FLOAT is either 4 or 8 bytes, DOUBLE PRECISION is 8 bytes, and REAL is 4 bytes.

For DB2, FLOAT is 64 bits.

For SQL Server, FLOAT is 64 bits, 15 digit precision, and REAL is 32 bits, 7 digit precision.

Datetime

date | time | timestamp

Sybase and SQL Server Datetime:

timestamp

Date

DATE

Time

TIME (precision) [WITH TIME ZONE]

SQLBase and DB2 TIME:

TIME

TIMESTAMP

TIMESTAMP (*precision*) [WITH TIME ZONE]

SQLBase and DB2 TIMESTAMP:

TIMESTAMP

Sybase TIMESTAMP:

DATETIME | SMALLDATETIME

SQL Server TIMESTAMP:

DATETIME | SMALLDATETIME | TIMESTAMP

INTERVAL

INTERVAL *interval_qualifier*

Fixed-Length Bit String

BIT(*length*)

DB2 Fixed-Length Bit String:

CHAR[ACTER] [(*length*)] FOR BIT DATA

Sybase and SQL Server Fixed-Length Bit String:

BIT | BINARY (*length*)

BIT columns cannot be null or have an index on them. BINARY has a maximum length of 255.

Variable-Length Bit String

BIT VARYING(*len*)

DB2 Variable-Length Bit String:

VARCHAR (*length*) FOR BIT DATA

Sybase and SQL Server Variable-Length Bit String:
VARBINARY (*length*)

The maximum length allowed is 255. Storage size is the actual size of data.

Interval Qualifier

range_field | *single_field*

Range Field

{ YEAR | DAY | HOUR | MINUTE } [(*precision*)] TO { YEAR | MONTH | DAY | HOUR | MINUTE } | SECOND [(*precision*)]

Single Field

{ YEAR | DAY | HOUR | MINUTE } [(*precision*)] | SECOND [(*leading_precision* [, *frac_precision*])]

DB2 Long Text:
LONG VARCHAR

DB2 has a maximum length of 32700 bytes.

Sybase and SQL Server Long Text:
TEXT

SQL Server and Sybase both have a maximum size of 2 raised to the 31 power -1 characters.

SQLBase Long Text Binary:
LONG [VARCHAR]

DB2 Long Text Binary:
LONG VARCHAR FOR BIT DATA

Sybase and SQL Server Long Text Binary:
IMAGE

Same length restriction as for long text.

SQL Server Money:
MONEY | SMALLMONEY

MONEY is 64 bits long with an accuracy of four places. SMALLMONEY is 42 bits long, also with a four-place accuracy. MONEY is rounded to two places when displayed.

13.5 Summary

The most important concepts from this chapter are summarized by the following points:

- Although there is a standard for SQL, all relational database management systems implement their own particular dialect.

- Even though SQL syntax varies among systems, conceptually, the statements all perform similar functions.

- Because of differences between physical implementations and optimization techniques of various databases, the same SQL statements may perform differently on different systems.

- It is worth being versed in more than one database management system in order to be more versatile.

- Detailed SQL syntax diagrams are horrible to read.

In this chapter, we covered the differences between various implementations of leading database management systems.

14   Writing Applications Using SQL

We have been issuing commands interactively from an SQL Activity window within Quest. When you want to use SQL from a program you have written, you will have to use SQL in an extended form, known as embedded SQL. This chapter focuses on embedded SQL with 3GL languages. For example, the languages of C, C++, Fortran, Pascal, or COBOL are 3GLs. Chapter 15 looks specifically at 4GL languages.

The chapter is organized as follows:

14.1   Introduction to Embedded SQL

Embedded SQL can be defined as SQL commands that are embedded within a program and that are prepared during the precompilation and compilation process before the program is executed. After an SQL command is prepared, the command itself does not change (although values of host variables specified within the command can change). Embedded SQL is also referred to as static SQL.

14.1.1 How Does Embedded SQL Work?

Relational database vendors all specify an application programmatic interface (API) to their database. The most direct way for a client application to access a database server is to code to the database vendor's own API through embedded SQL. For example, Oracle has an API referred to as OCI or Open Call Interface™. If you buy Oracle's Open Client developer's software, this API, along with sample applications showing how to use embedded SQL, are provided.

Alternatively, you can use a router or gateway product to translate from one vendor's API to another vendor's API. Centura Software's SQLRouter™ and SQLGateway™ products provide such a service. You can write, using embedded SQL, to Centura Software's SQL/API (using COBOL, C, C++, or SQWindows) and then use SQLNetwork "routers," which support IBM's DB2, DB/400™, Oracle, SQL Server, Informix, and CA-Ingres, among others.

The ODBC standard provides yet another alternative for application developers. ODBC is a published standard API that many vendors have agreed to support. While Microsoft has controlled the ownership and direction of the ODBC interface, almost every relational database vendor offers some sort of ODBC solution. ODBC relies on third-party database drivers or access tools that conform to the ODBC specification to translate the ODBC standard API calls. The ODBC calls generated by the client application are directly mapped into the database vendor's proprietary API calls. (Some database vendors use the ODBC interface as their native interface, like Quadbase or Microsoft SQL Server 6.0.)

14.1.2 Why Use Embedded SQL?

SQL commands are useful to define, manipulate, control, and query data in a relational database. However, SQL is not a programming language. Using the API functions to call SQL commands gives you the following features that plain SQL commands do not:

- Procedural logic
- Extensive data typing
- Variables

Using the API functions to develop a client application that uses SQL enables you to use SQL without giving up the power and flexibility of the programming language.

14.1.3 Database Access Cycle

The following steps describe a process of accessing data in a database through a series of embedded SQL statements. While not all RDBMS databases require all the same steps or do them in quite the same way, these steps give you a fundamental understanding of the process of issuing an SQL statement within an application.

1. A client *connects* to the server by passing a string that contains the name of a database, a user name, and a password. The SQL/API returns to the client a handle that identifies the connection. The client uses this connection in subsequent commands.

2. At the *prepare* phase (also called the *compile* phase), the client sends a command string to the server requesting an action.

    For EARLY describe: The client may not know the data types or lengths of the items that command returns. It can call an EARLY describe function asking the server to return information that describes the command's output. For operations other than SELECT, only a status code is returned.

3. If appropriate, the client tells the SQL/API about *bind* variables (input data) for the command. The SQL/API on the client machine buffers these requests and sends them to the server in one message with the execute request in the *execute* phase.

4. The client asks SQLNetwork to *execute* the command. When appropriate, the input items from the bind phase are sent with the execute request.

    For LATE describe: The client may not know the data types or lengths of the items that the command returns. It can call a LATE describe function asking the server to return information that *describes* the command's output. For operations other than SELECT, only a status code is returned.

5. When processing a SELECT command, the client *fetches* the output. The server may return as many rows as possible in one message, which the API stores in a buffer. The client fetches each row or number of rows from the API with a fetch function.

6. When a database is actually changed, in order to cause that data to be permanently part of the physical database, a *commit* command is

executed. In the event of an error, the change can be reversed if a *rollback* command is issued before the commit.

7.   When the client is finished processing, it *disconnects*. If a client disconnects without committing, any changes are now saved.

Steps 2 through 7 are repeated for as many commands as the client application has to process.

CONNECT Statement

When an application passes a connect request to the database, it is usually done with a database name, a user name, and a password. The CONNECT statement is usually done on the first request for an SQL *handle*, or *cursor*, in the application. A *cursor* is returned to identify the particular database connection. Context is established for that SQL *handle*. The application uses the handle for all subsequent commands, unless a separate SQL handle is required for simultaneous SQL statements. In the case of simultaneous SQL statements, a CONNECT request will be issued from within the application, but the API will determine whether or not a new cursor/context can be established upon the same connection or if a new connection to the database is required.

The advantage of using the same connection is that the time required to establish the SQL handle is significantly less than that required to establish a new connection.

Prepare (Compile)

Precompilation involves processing of a program containing SQL commands or procedures that take place before compilation. SQL commands are replaced with statements that are recognized by the host language compiler. Output from precompilation includes source code that can be submitted to the compiler.

An application sends an SQL command string to the server or RDBMS requesting some action:

*   If the command is for a SELECT statement, the application may not know the data types for the requested data fields; a describe function will be called by the application to receive the data type information (if available from the RDBMS).

*   All other commands return only a status code.

Bind Data

A bind variable is a variable used to associate data to an SQL command. Bind variables can be used:

- In the VALUES clause of an INSERT command
- In a WHERE clause
- In the SET clause of an UPDATE command

Bind variables are the mechanism to transmit data between an application work area and SQLBase. A bind variable is also referred to as an "into variable" or a "substitution variable."

Binding data is a process of indicating that data from within an application variable is to be bound to a data variable in a prepared or compiled SQL statement each time the statement is to be executed. Bind variables are also known as program variables, host variables, or parameter markers.

Sybase and Microsoft SQL Server have, until recently, not had the notion of bind variables. This architecture changed with Sybase System 10, which more closely follows the ANSI standard of bind variables.

Execute

The client application needs to request the server to execute the previously compiled SQL command. If bind variables are used, then the input data from the bind phase is sent with the execute request.

Fetch

If the previously compiled and executed SQL command was a SELECT, an application will need to fetch the output. The server may return as many rows as possible in one message, which can be stored in a client buffer. The application fetches each row with a fetch function.

Commit and/or Rollback

A *commit* is a process that causes data changed by an application to become part of the physical database. Before changes are committed, unchanged data still is stored by the database server and new, modified data is stored in temporary buffers. Changes are stored with a commit. Data can be restored to its prior state before a commit by a *rollback*.

A rollback cancels a transaction and undoes any changes that it made to the database. All locks are freed unless cursor-context preservation is set to on.

A relational database will ensure the consistency of data by verifying either that all the data changes made during a transaction are performed or that none of them are performed. A transaction begins when the application starts or when a commit or rollback is executed. The transaction ends when the next commit or rollback is executed. This is called logical unit of work.

Three other concepts that are used with commits and rollbacks are rollforwards, savepoints, and autocommit. *Rollforwards* reapply changes to a database. The transaction log contains the entries used for rollforward. A *savepoint* is an intermediate point within a transaction to which a user can later rollback (to cancel any subsequent commands) or commit (to complete the commands).

The *autocommit* feature allows you to commit an SQL statement after it is executed. This provides a level of transaction reliability.

If the program continues to perform database calls after the execution of a commit or rollback, a new transaction is considered to have begun.

A rollback of the transaction may occur for a variety of reasons besides program request (as indicated through the program issuing the rollback command) including:

- Program failure
- System failure
- Environmental failure (e.g., power failure)

If any of these events occur, then a relational database must ensure that all noncommitted transactions are rolled back so that the database never appears to have been affected by them.

Disconnect

When the application has processed all SQL requests, a disconnect should be issued to end the connection with the server. If multiple SQL handles were used within the application, all handles should be disconnected explicitly.

Examples of Embedded SQL Functions for SQL Server, ODBC, and SQL/API

The database access cycle of different vendors varies a good deal. Sybase's DB-Library is one of the most singular. Table 14-1 below shows calls for separate APIs: Sybase's DB-Library, ODBC, and Centura Software's SQL/API.

Table 14-1 *Embedded SQL Function Examples*

Activity	ODBC Function	DB-Library Function	SQLWindows Function
Connect	SQLConnect() SQLDriverConnect()	dbopen & dbuse	SqlConnect()
Prepare/Compile	SQLPrepare()	N/A	SqlPrepare()
Execute	SQLExecute() SQLExecDirect()	dbsqlexec	SqlExecute()
Fetch	SQLFetch SQLExtendedFetch	dbnextrow	SqlFetch()
Disconnect	SQLDisconnect	dbclose	SqlDisconnect()

14.2 Definition of Terms

In the next few pages, we discuss a number of terms used with embedded SQL:

- Cursor, connections, and context
- Cursor context preservation (CCP)
- Error messages
- Front-end result sets (FERS)
- Isolation levels
- Time-out (lock time-out)

14.2.1 Cursor, Connections, and Context

A *cursor* is used for select statements to point to result sets. Cursors are used for data pointers to data structures on servers so that multiple cursors or SQL handles can be opened at one time to the same database. There may be only one physical connection (not all databases support this). Each cursor represents a *context*. A context can be thought of as a thread into a database.

Databases such as Oracle, Sybase, Informix, SQLBase, and Ingres can support multiple connections to multiple servers from multiple applications. If you think this can get confusing, you are right. How application developers manage cursors, connections, and context is an area that frequently causes performance problems.

With Sybase's SQL Server "Streams"- based type of processing, there is an exclusive (single) context for each DBProcess established by the client application. Therefore, a commit or rollback affects only the DBProcess on which it was issued. SQLBase uses multiple contexts with a single transaction.

14.2.2 Cursor-Context Preservation (CCP)

CCP is a programmatically definable setting that allows applications to maintain active front-end result sets (FERs) after a commit.

Informix, Oracle, Sybase System 10, and SQLBase have methods of cursor context preservation after a commit statement. Sybase SQL Server's DB-Library uses something called MapGti/cursors to simulate this.

CCP after a rollback is a more restricted functionality, but several databases support this.

14.2.3 Error Messages

Handling error messages is one of the trickier aspects of programming with embedded SQL.

Function calls, or API calls, have return codes that can be translated to tell not only the success or failure of a call, but possible reasons for any error. For example, the following is C code that does error handling on a database function call (call, sqlcnc(), from Centura Software's SQL/API).

```
if (rcd = sqlcnc (&cur, dbname, 0))
{
    printf("FAILURE ON CONNECT%d\n",rcd);
    exit(1);
}
else
    printf("Connection Established \n");
```

This code segment attempts to connect a cursor to a database. A return code, rcd, is returned. If the return code is not successful, it can be used for diagnosis of a problem. When the SQL/API is used for SQLBase, a file, error.sql, is used as a lookup table of return code errors.

14.2.4 Front-end Result Sets (FERs)

Front-end result sets (FERs) are the rows fetched from the server and delivered to the client (front end). By taking a snapshot of the result set at the time of the fetch and sending it to the client, SQLNetwork provides backward and forward scrolling access to fetched data, even when the database does not. This powerful feature provides a great deal of flexibility to client applications but also can have performance and resource implications. Developers should understand the way their databases handle connections and cursors.

Figure 14-1 illustrates how some databases support scrolling result sets. The user browsing on the client application moves forward and backward through the result set on the server.

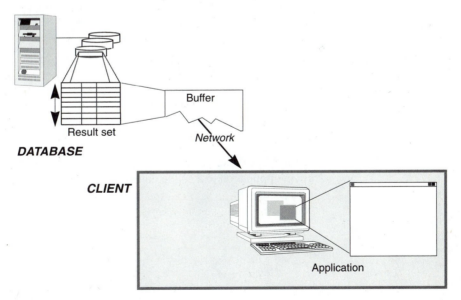

Figure 14-1   *Scrolling Result Sets*

14.2.5 Isolation Levels

The protocols that are used by a database to perform locking operations on behalf of a transaction are called *isolation levels*. These define how long locks will be held and how an RDBMS will pass data to the transaction via the message buffer.

Isolation levels control how access to the tables in a database by one user affects other users accessing the same tables on that database. These isolation levels are controlled by locks. The isolation level you choose depends on the application's requirement for:

- **Consistency**
  Uncommitted updates, deletes, and inserts are not seen by other transactions. High consistency guarantees that all data encountered by a transaction does not change for a specified duration (usually the scope of the transaction) and only the application can change the data it selects; everyone else is "locked" out.

- **Concurrency**
  How many users can access data at the same time is influenced by lock granularity, duration, and exclusion mode. High concurrency allows multiple users to execute database transactions simultaneously without interfering with each other.

Isolation levels you set apply to *all* cursors connecting an application to a single database. Changing isolation levels causes an implicit commit that destroys compiled commands for *all* cursors that the application has connected to a single database; however, specifying the same isolation level as the current level, with a set isolation command, does not cause an implicit commit.

Figure 14-2 illustrates how Isolation levels apply to all cursors connecting a client application to a single database. The cost of high concurrency is low consistency.

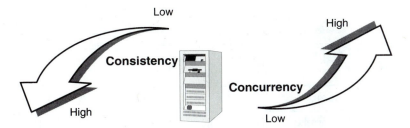

Figure 14-2   *Isolation Level Considerations*

CA-Ingres

CA-Ingres servers do not support isolation levels. You can use SET LOCKMODE to set different types and levels of locks. The CA-Ingres default lock is Shared for read (or select) and Exclusive for write (delete and update) until the end of a transaction.

ODBC

Although the positioned update clause is defined at the ODBC SQL conformance core level, some ODBC drivers and their data sources are not able to support this feature if the ODBC driver supports only the minimum level of SQL grammar.

Oracle

Oracle's OCI does not support isolation levels.

SQL Server

DB-Library does not support the concept of isolation levels.

Isolation Levels at a Glance

Table 14-2 summarizes isolation level equivalents for several vendors.

Table 14-2   *Isolation Levels at a Glance*

Data Source	Isolation Level Equivalents			
SQLBase	Read repeatability	Cursor stability	Read-only	Release Locks
AS/400	*ALL	*CS	*NONE	*CHG
Informix-Online (not SE)	Repeatable read	Cursor stability	Dirty Read	Committed read
CA-Ingres	N/A	N/A	N/A	N/A
ODBC	SQL_TXN_ SERIALIZABLE	SQL_TWN_ REPEATABLE_ READ	SQL_TXN_ READ_ UNCOMMITTED	SQL_TXN_ READ_ COMMITTED
Oracle	N/A	N/A	N/A	N/A
SQL Server	with HOLDLOCK	Default	N/A	N/A

14.2.6 Time-out (Lock Time-out)

To temporarily restrict other users' access to data, a database can issue a *lock*. Locking prevents data from being modified by more than one user at a time and prevents data from being read while being updated. A lock serializes access to data and prevents simultaneous updates that might result in inconsistent data.

A situation when two transactions, each having a lock on a database page, attempt to acquire a lock on the other's database page is called a *deadlock*. One type of deadlock occurs when each transaction holds a shared lock on a page and each wants to acquire an exclusive lock. A deadlock is also called a deadly embrace. Deadlocks can be difficult to get out of and can be hard to detect.

14.3 Examples of Embedded SQL Using SQL API

Centura Software supplies the following example program with their SQL/API for use with the C programming language. This program demonstrates how to open a cursor to a database, compile a string of SQL commands, and execute those commands. The SQL commands compiled and executed are:

- To create a table called COMMAND
- To create a table called EMP with columns *emp_name, emp_no, and emp_dob*

14.3.1 The Code

```
#include "sql.h"
#include <stdio.h>
/*---------------------------------------------------------------------*/

/*  Example of compiling an SQL statement and then executing it.*/

/*---------------------------------------------------------------------*/

main()

{
  SQLTCUR   cur;/* SQLBASE cursor number  */
  SQLTRCD   rcd;/* return code  */

  staticchar   ctbcmd[] =/* CREATE TABLE COMMAND   */
"CREATE TABLE EMP (EMP_NAME CHAR(20), EMP_NO
NUMBER, EMP_DOB DATETIME)";

/* CONNECT TO THE DATABASE */
  if (rcd = sqlcnc(&cur, "DEMO", 0))
  {
    printf("FAILURE ON CONNECT %d\n",rcd);
    return(1);
  }
```

```
/* COMPILE CREATE TABLE SQL STATEMENT */

if (rcd = sqlcom(cur, ctbcmd, 0))

{
  printf("FAILURE ON COMPILE, rcd = %d\n",rcd);
  sqldis(cur);
  return(1);
}


/* EXECUTE CREATE TABLE SQL STATEMENT */

if (rcd = sqlexe(cur))
  printf("CANNOT CREATE TABLE, rcd = %d\n",rcd);
else
  printf("TABLE SUCCESSFULLY CREATED \n");

/* DISCONNECT FROM THE DATABASE */

if (rcd = sqldis(cur))
  printf("FAILURE ON DISCONNECT %d\n",rcd);
}
```

14.3.2 The Application

The sample code above shows four stages necessary to executing an SQL command:

- Connection to a database (using the sqlcnc() function call)
- Compilation of an SQL statement (using the sqlcom() function call)
- Execution of an SQL statement (using sqlexe() function call)
- Disconnection from the database (using the sqldis () function call)

The C code shown in the examples needed three variables:

- **cur**
  Variable for the cursor connection to the database

- **rcd**
  Variable for the return code of a function call used for error handling

- **ctbcmd**
  String variable containing the SQL command

After each function call is executed, a level of error handling was programmed.

The SQL statement that was executed, (stored in the string variable, ctbcmd) was:

```
CREATE TABLE command;
CREATE TABLE EMP (EMP_NAME CHAR(20),
EMP_NO NUMBER, EMP_DOB DATETIME);
```

14.4 ODBC Overview

The Microsoft Open Database Connectivity (ODBC) standard is an application programming interface (API) specification written by Microsoft. The ODBC API relies on third-party database drivers or access tools that conform to the ODBC specification. These drivers and access tools translate the ODBC standard API calls generated by the client application and make requests of many database vendor's RDBMs.

In theory, once a program is written by using ODBC, various ODBC drivers can be used with the program and that program can connect to many different databases. In reality, all drivers vary at some level, and databases do not all have generic SQL calls, so no API can truly be generic; however, ODBC is widely available and more easily reused than many other solutions.

ODBC is an effort to standardize the way in which front-end products access database servers from different vendors. Chapter 15 discusses several of the more prominent vendors who are working with the ODBC standard and offering ODBC products for resale. This chapter also discusses ODBC in more detail.

For a complete discussion of ODBC for application developers, check Microsoft's *ODBC 2.0 Programmer's Reference and SDK Guide* from Microsoft Press. Microsoft also provides the ODBC API, with sample programs, through their developer's program.

14.5 Using ODBC with Embedded SQL

Table 14-3 lists some of the more significant ODBC functions. The list is incomplete. More functions are added all the time, but the list is a start. Notice that Microsoft has defined Core, Level 1, Level 2, and increasingly advanced levels of compliance to this API. As a developer, one must know what level of ODBC calls are supported by certain vendors. For example, one vendor may support fifteen Level-2 ODBC API calls; another vendor may support eight Level-2 ODBC API calls. Both vendors may be ODBC compliant because not all API calls are mandatory.

Table 14-3   *ODBC Functions with Embedded SQL*

Function	Description
Core Functions	
SQLAllocConnect	Gets a connection handle.
SQLAllocEnv	Gets an environment handle.
SQLAllocStmt	Allocates a statement handle.
SQLBindCol	Assigns storage for a result column and specifies the data type.
SQLCancel	Cancels an SQL statement.
SQLColAttributes	Describes the attributes of a column in the result set.
SQLConnect	Connects to a specific driver by data source name, user ID, and password.
SQLDescribeCol	Describes a column in the result set.
SQLDisconnect	Closes a database connection.
SQLError	Returns additional error or status information.
SQLExecDirect	Executes a statement.
SQLExecute	Executes a prepared statement.
SQLFetch	Fetches a row.
SQLFreeConnect	Releases the connection handle.
SQLFreeEnv	Releases the environment handle.
SQLFreeStmt	Ends statement processing and closes the associated cursor, discards pending results, and, optionally, frees all resources associated with the statement handle.

Table 14-3 *ODBC Functions with Embedded SQL (Continued)*

Function	Description
SQLGetCursorName	Returns the cursor name associated with a statement handle.
SQLNumResultCols	Returns the number of columns in the result set.
SQLPrepare	Prepares an SQL statement for later execution.
SQLRowCount	Returns the number of rows affected by an INSERT, UPDATE, or DELETE request.
SQLSetCursorName	Specifies a cursor name.
SQLSetParam	Assigns storage for a parameter in an SQL statement.
SQLTransact	Commits or rolls back a transaction.
Level-1 Functions	
SQLColumns	Returns the list of column names in specified tables.
SQLDriverConnect	Connects to a specific driver by connection string or requests that the Driver Manager and driver display connection dialogs for the user.
SQLGetConnectOption	Returns the value of a connection option.
SQLGetData	Returns part or all of one column of one row of a result set. (Useful for long data values).
SQLGetFunctions	Returns supported driver functions.
SQLGetInfo	Returns information about a specific driver and data source.
SQLGetStmtOption	Returns the value of a statement option.

Table 14-3   *ODBC Functions with Embedded SQL (Continued)*

Function	Description
SQLGetTypeInfo	Returns information about supported data types.
SQLParamData	Returns the storage value assigned to a parameter for which data will be sent at execution time. (Useful for long data values).
SQLPutData	Sends part or all of a data value for a parameter. (Useful for long data values).
SQLSetConnectOption	Sets a connection option.
SQLSetStmtOption	Sets a statement option.
SQLSpecialColumns	Retrieves information about the optimal set of columns that uniquely identifies a row in a specified table, and the columns that are automatically updated when any value in the row is updated by a transaction.
SQLStatistics	Retrieves statistics about a single table and the list of indexes associated with the table.
SQLTables	Returns the list of table names stored in a specific data source.
Level-2 Functions	
SQLBrowseConnect	Returns successive levels of connection attributes and valid attribute values. When a value has been specified for each connection attribute, connects to the data source.
SQLDataSources	Gets a list of available data sources.

Table 14-3 *ODBC Functions with Embedded SQL (Continued)*

Function	Description
SQLMoreResults	Determines whether there are more result sets available and, if so, initializes processing for the next result set.
SQLNativeSQL	Returns the text of an SQL statement as translated by the driver.
SQLNumParams	Returns the number of parameters in a statement.

14.6   Summary

This chapter discussed the subject of embedded SQL and including SQL in an application. The fundamentals of a database access cycle were covered, including the following steps:

- Connect to a database
- Prepare a statement to compile
- Execute a statement
- Fetch data for a select
- Commit or rollback
- Disconnect from a database

Not all databases follow the same access steps, nor do they have the same concepts; nevertheless, embedded SQL concepts such as cursors, cursor context preservation (CCP), and front-end result sets were also covered.

We paid special attention to ODBC, which has market popularity. We also discussed other embedded SQL languages, including SQL Server's DB-Library and Centura Software's SQL API. This chapter is by no means an inclusive discussion of vendors' embedded SQL APIs; Chapter 16 discusses many other vendors who provide APIs with their connectivity products.

The next chapter shows how 4GL application development environments help hide levels of complexity that are encountered when embedded SQL is used.

15   Fourth Generation Languages

In Chapter 14, we looked at the issues of embedded SQL within applications written in third-generation languages, or 3GLs. 3GLs include languages like C, C++, Pascal, Fortran, and COBOL. While 3GLs have historically offered powerful and high-performance environments for application development, they also require a high degree of expertise and effort to complete tasks.

In this chapter, we look at *fourth generation languages*, or *4GLs*, which, unlike their 3GL counterparts, offer an extremely fast way to develop applications. Fourth generation languages make the use of SQL a relatively painless process compared to what it was even two years ago. We also discuss several of the rapid application development environments in the market today and demonstrate the construction of a simple Microsoft Windows application.

The chapter is organized as follows:

Section 15.1 Past, Present, Future
Section 15.2 4GL (Rapid Application Development) Vendors
Section 15.3 4GL Checklist
Section 15.4 Exercises
Section 15.5 Summary

15.1   Past, Present, Future

The following assumptions, both positive and negative, have usually been made about 4GLs:

- 4GLs are graphically oriented.
- By using them, one can develop an application quickly.

- 4GLs contain built-in functionality to connect to SQL databases.
- They run pseudo-code and therefore are slower than their 3GL counterparts, which run binary code.
- They are not as portable as 3GLs.
- 4GLs provide another layer of abstraction on top of 3GLs.

While these statements have been true, it is also true that 4GL technology has been developing at a lightning-fast pace, in conjunction with the arrival of more powerful hardware. For example, several 4GLs can now compile code into binary for major performance gains. Moreover, many 4GL tools are developing impressive portability stories.

Many publications and consultants refer to 4GLs as Rapid Application Development, or *RAD*, tools. What will be done with RAD tools in the future may surprise you. In fact, discussing existing functionality of today's 4GL vendors would likely make this chapter out of date in three months.

Some of the things you can expect for all 4GL vendors to provide in the future:

- Full compilation of code to binary, equaling the speed of 3GLs!
- Prebuilt object components, making application development resemble the creation of plug-and-play building blocks!
- Three-tier computing, allowing for application partitioning, distributed computing (through technologies like OLE and DCE).
- Integrated design, testing, and team development capabilities.
- Ability to create complete, robust, applications without writing a single line of code.

Many of these features are available today.

The rest of this chapter discusses some of the leading vendors in this market (there are many) and provides a detailed list of the features to evaluate when looking at a 4GL. We then demonstrate an application developed to access the database we created in the previous chapters.

15.2   4GL (Rapid Application Development) Vendors

Following is a list of RAD tool vendors in the market today. This list is by no means complete, but is meant to represent the more dominant players. All products are trademarks or registered trademarks of their respective companies.

Blythe Software, Inc. (Omnis 7)
989 E. Hillsdale Blvd #400
Foster City, CA 94404
(415) 571-0222

PRODUCT: Omnis 7

PLATFORMS: Windows, Windows 95, Windows NT, Macintosh, OS/2, UNIX

POSITION: Omnis 7 is a client/server development tool with a template-driven prototyping capability. Omnis 7 is now a multiplatform development environment that connects to a wide variety of back ends. Omnis 7 has native, ODBC, and DAL (Data Access Language) access to relational database vendors. Blythe provides design tools as well as automated maintenance tools. SQL Express is a query, reporting, and development tool. Graph-It provides an extensive graphing tool.

Borland International, Inc. (Delphi)
100 Borland Way
Scotts Valley, CA 95066-3249
(800) 233-2444; (408) 431-1000

PRODUCT: Delphi Desktop Edition, Delphi Client/Server Edition

PLATFORMS: Windows, Windows 95, Windows NT

POSITION: Delphi is a 16-bit and 32-bit object-oriented client/server development tool, with many out-of-the-box components. Delphi is based on an Object Pascal language, which is a cross between Turbo Pascal and a 4GL scripting language. The benefit of the Object Pascal language is that it can be compiled into binary for great performance and yet offers traditional 4GL advantages. Delphi includes Borland's ReportSmith reporting tool and the Borland Database Engine (BDE) that provides access to remote or local database engines, including Borland's own relational engine, Interbase and dBASE.

Centura Software Corp. (SQLWindows, Centura)
1060 Marsh Rd
Menlo Park, CA 94025
(415) 321-9500

PRODUCT: SQL Solo, SQLWindows Desktop, SQLWindows Network Edition, SQLWindows Corporate Edition, Centura

PLATFORMS: Windows, Windows 95, Windows NT, Sun Solaris

POSITION: SQLWindows is a 16-bit, graphical, object-oriented client/server development tool that boasts QuickObjects, advanced team development, object orientation, and a published, low-level interface to enable third parties to develop components to work with the development environment. QuickObjects are prebuilt components that allow application development with very little coding, including QuickObject interfaces to E-Mail and Lotus Notes.

With the release of Centura Developer, Centura Software offers a 32-bit big brother to the SQLWindows product line, including advanced team development capabilities, Internet connectivity, three-tier computing, application partitioning, and replication capabilities. Centura has a compiler option to compile objects into binary code.

IBM Corp. (VisualAge)
Old Orchard Road
Armonk, NY 10504
(914) 765-1900

PRODUCT: VisualAge

PLATFORMS: Windows, Windows 95, Windows NT, and OS/2

POSITION: VisualAge is a graphical application tool, based on IBM SmallTalk. It boasts class libraries and a set of prebuilt components for such things as data access, transaction processing, and multimedia. VisualAge comes in a single user and team development pack. The product was created as IBM's central client/server development tool for OS/2, with optimized links to the DB2 family as well as connectivity to a wide range of other databases. VisualAge's object library and library management support enhance team development support.

Informix Software, Inc. (INFORMIX-NewEra)
4100 Bohannon Dr
Menlo Park, CA 94025
(415) 926-6300

PRODUCT: INFORMIX-NewEra

PLATFORMS: Windows, Windows 95, Windows NT, Sun Solaris, HP-UX, and IBM AIX

POSITION: NewEra is an object-oriented, visual development tool with reusable class libraries. NewEra has five modules: Application Builder, Window Painter, ViewPoint Pro, Debugger, and Repository Browser. ViewPoint Pro is a point-and-click tool for query, reporting, and form generation as well as a schema generation tool. NewEra builds SuperViews, which define and manage database modeling informations. NewEra also has application repositories for team programming.

Microsoft Corp. (Visual Basic)
One Microsoft Way
Redmond, WA 98052
(206) 882-8080

PRODUCT: Visual Basic, Visual Basic Professional Editions

PLATFORMS: Windows, Windows 95, Windows NT

POSITION: Visual Basic is a 16-bit and 32-bit application development tool with component capability. Visual Basic Standard Edition is the market leader for rapid application development for single-user systems. Visual Basic Standard Edition has object components, once called VBXs but now called OCXs (OCXs comply with Microsoft's OLE standard). Visual Basic is a clear leader for its ease of use as well as .... well it's from Microsoft. With the Professional Edition of Visual Basic, source-code management through Source-Safe, application partitioning through OLE servers, and a copy of SQL Server 6.0 desktop edition for SQL access are added. The Crystal Reports report writer is also included with Visual Basic.

Oracle Corp. (Power Objects)
500 Oracle Parkway
Redwood Shores, CA 94065
(415) 506-7000

PRODUCT: Power Objects

PLATFORMS: Windows, Windows 95, Windows NT, Macintosh, OS/2

POSITION: Power Objects is a client/server development environment based on the Visual Basic scripting language and enhanced with object-oriented structures. Programmers build master objects, which will be used on forms to create programs. Oracle touts this approach as portable across platforms.

Power Objects is a relative newcomer in the market. Oracle also has Designer/2000, an analysis and designer toolkit, and Developer/2000, which is a forms-based development tool.

Powersoft Corp. — Sybase Tools Division (PowerBuilder)
561 Virginia Rd.
Concord, MA 01742
(508) 287-1500

PRODUCT: PowerBuilder Desktop, PowerBuilder Team/ODBC, PowerBuilder Enterprise

PLATFORMS: Windows, Windows 95, Windows NT, Sun Solaris, Macintosh

POSITION: PowerBuilder is a 16-bit and 32-bit graphical client/server development tool that has gained wide acceptance for ease of use and for features such as DataWindows, the Data Pipeline, and full-featured reporting capabilities. DataWindows are data-aware controls that can be embedded within each other. The Data Pipeline is a tool to move information from one table or database to another. PowerBuilder's reporting includes a cross-tabular report generation dialog box and the inclusion of InfoMaker, which has PowerViewer, a querying tool, and PowerMaker, which is for forms generation and reporting. PowerBuilder also now ships with S-Designer, a logical modeling tool Sybase acquired. PowerBuilder also has application partitioning and Watcom, their relational engine, which was renamed to SQL Anywhere.

Progess Software Corp. (Progress)
14 Oak Park
Bedford, MA 01730
(617) 280-4000

PRODUCT: Progress

PLATFORMS: Windows, Windows 95, Windows NT, Macintosh, most UNIX variations

POSITION: The Progess system has six components: Progress 4GL with the User Interface Builder (UIB), Data Dictionary, Progress Help System, Procedure Editor, Compiler, and Progress relational database engine. Progress has traditionally had a strong presence in the UNIX market. Progress touts the ability to dynamically connect and disconnect to multiple databases simultaneously.

15.3   4GL Checklist

The following is a feature list of 4GL capabilities. 4GLs have historically been oriented towards the graphical access of data from relational database vendors, but this is changing. With the rapid expansion of the World Wide Web, the type of information available to the public will increase dramatically. 4GLs will serve as tools to integrate widely disparate information. Therefore, when such tools are evaluated, a variety of criteria should be examined.

Some of the main items on which to evaluate 4GL tools are:

- Ease of use and documentation
- Connectivity
- Performance and scalability
- Team development
- Debugging
- Forms, query, and reporting
- Components and third-party applications
- Object orientation
- Three-tier strategy
- Language support and extensions

15.3.1 Ease of Use and Documentation

As with query tools, ease of installation, documentation, and support can easily outweigh increased functionality. Often the best, newest, greatest features are the same ones that are not documented and are the most confusing to use. The following is a list of criteria to evaluate ease of use and documentation for 4GLs.

- Ease of installation
- Context-sensitive help
- Prebuilt components
- Rapid application development
- Documentation

Ease of Installation

Initial installation should be straightforward; however, when remote connectivity to relational engines on back-end servers is involved, there is a potential for difficulty in getting all the components together.

Context-sensitive Help

During coding, how easy is it to get on-line documentation of function calls? Tools like Visual Basic and SQLWindows allow you to select a function call, press a key, and see the help for that function appear. This is known as *context-sensitive help*.

Prebuilt Components

Without coding, can applications be quickly built for database tasks such as SELECT, INSERT, UPDATE, and DELETE? Many tools today incorporate wizards that will quickly create such applications. The question is, How many components have been built in? With Microsoft pushing OLE components in the form of OCXs, many components will be commercially available. 4GL vendors are increasing bundling such components with their tools. For example, if you are adding Lotus Notes® or "e-mail" to your application, you should not have to write code. Wizards exist to do this work for you.

Rapid Application Development

How fast can you develop an application? While stand-alone programs are nice to piece together, a better test of RAD for SQL applications is to build applications that connect over a network to back-end database servers.

Complex applications can be built in hours, using object-oriented coding. One major key to RAD that is often neglected is the availability of off-the-shelf class object libraries. Many such libraries provide capabilities that would require months of coding to recreate, even for experienced developers.

Documentation

Clearly, Visual Basic has a mountain of books and documentation written about it. But as your requirements for advanced, client/server applications to RDBMs increase, the amount of documentation and the clarity of the documentation diminishes. Most tools have Computer Based Training (CBT) available, and most have books about them published. With the popularity of CD-ROMs, documentation is now often on-line, like the software included with this book.

15.3.2 Connectivity

Chapter 17 briefly discusses many of the connectivity vendors in the market. Here are some criteria for looking at connectivity for 4GLs.

- Native connectivity support to relational databases
- Level of ODBC support
- ODBC vendors supported
- Access to Xbase databases and spreadsheets
- OLE support
- E-mail enabled
- Internet

Native Connectivity Support to Relational Database

Does a 4GL provide native connectivity to an environment? ODBC connectivity to databases is the most generic way to connect to a relational database. Every relational vendor supports some level of native connectivity. For example, the native connectivity for Oracle is the Oracle Connectivity Interface. This is the fastest, most optimized way to access Oracle. For Sybase System 11, Sybase's CT Library provides the fastest connectivity. Microsoft has made ODBC the native interface to SQL Server 6.0.

Level of ODBC Support

ODBC drivers available today are getting faster. As described in Chapter 14, ODBC connectivity has many levels of compliance. There are also many vendors who provide ODBC drivers, so when using this criterion for connectivity, remember that not all ODBC drivers are created equal. The ODBC compliance levels will also continually progress. As long as Microsoft controls the standard, it is important to be aware of the compliance features they are adding to this standard.

ODBC Vendors

Let's say that you want to connect to a DB2 database on an AS/400. There are ODBC drivers from Starware, IBM, Showcase, and other vendors. Intersolv sells a library of ODBC drivers to database vendors. ODBC drivers vary from vendor to vendor. Many vendors supply their own ODBC drivers. Are they all the same? Not likely. Awareness of this point will help avoid many headaches.

Access to Xbase Databases and Spreadsheets

Most 4GLs not only access SQL today, but personal databases and spreadsheets as well. Does a 4GL support Access™, Paradox™, dBASE™, FoxPro™, as well as Lotus 1-2-3® or Microsoft Excel™? This is a fairly common feature of 4GLs today. All products have different levels of support.

OLE Support

OLE is an architecture Microsoft developed for creating component-based computing. This is a powerful concept, and one that is likely to be pervasive. Most 4GLs that run on a Windows-based environment should support OLE. As Microsoft advances this standard, vendors will offer different levels of compliance. Be careful of the use of the word OLE. Microsoft has many meanings for this word, which can be very confusing. For example, a 4GL can incorporate an OLE object into its own environment. In this case, the 4GL is an *OLE control*. The objects you embed in an application are OLE enabled, or *OCXs*. Also, a 4GL application could be called from other applications to run an OLE object. In this case, a 4GL allows an application to be an *OLE server*. If you can programmatically access an OLE object, you are using *OLE automation*. If you are interested in OLE, I suggest you read up on the subject in one of the many books Microsoft Press has published.

E-mail Integration

Objects can be written to enable an application to integrate e-mail without any code. SQLWindows provides e-mail QuickObjects to do this. There are many vendors who provide e-mail protocols, including Novell, IBM/Lotus, and Microsoft. Support for e-mail-enabled components does not necessarily imply all protocols are supported; this is a checklist item to be aware of.

Internet

Here are just a few of the features soon to be commonplace with 4GL tools:

- Access to SQL over the World Wide Web from a web server
- Use of a web browsers within an application,
- Integration with the Java™ language with RAD development for Internet-enabled applications

Internet technology is advancing at a lightning-fast pace. Java is a programming language that is becoming a standard for use with the World Wide Web. All the major relational database vendors are extremely active with this technology.

15.3.3 Performance and Scalability

Optimizing SQL applications involves many aspects, including application performance, network performance, and server RDBMS performance. Here is a list of a few performance features that you should look for in a RAD tool:

- Compilation to binary
- Optimized connectivity
- Three-tier computing

Compilation to Binary

4GLs today are moving from running pseudocode to binary code in products like Delphi, SQLWindows, and PowerBuilder. Binary compilation will dramatically speed up client performance. With SQL database access, however, performance may be more an issue of network connectivity than of how a client application performs.

Optimized Connectivity

Some 4GLs supply connectivity optimizations, like buffers that store retrieved information from SQL queries. These are also referred to as front-end result sets. Data compression is another mechanism used to speed up performance. Most vendors will have a list of connectivity optimization features.

Three-Tier Computing

If code runs slow for an application, there is always an opportunity to run that code on a server. The process of running code elsewhere is referred to as *three-tier computing*. Three-tier computing is a major component of what the industry often calls second generation client/server application development.

Code can be run remotely in a variety of ways. For example, a database can run code in the form of stored procedures. An *application server* could be used, where an application can call another application on another machine that specializes in running predefined functions.

Vendors offer three-tier computing in a number of ways:

- Remote OLE
- Remote procedure calls (RPC))
- Distributed Computing Environment (DCE), an RPC implementation
- Stored procedures
- Transaction monitors (like Tuxedo™ from Novell)

15.3.4 Team Development

There is a wide variance in how well 4GLs support team development. Here are a few concepts to consider for team projects:

- Version control and security
- Single integrated repository to manage data definitions and source code
- Project management, reporting, and documentation
- Impact Analysis
- Consistent coding standards
- On-Line communication ability
- Integration with logical and object modeling tools

Version Control and Security

When an application is being developed, many versions will be written over time. Many questions arise in this situation, including the following:

- How well can a tool offer application branch revisions off a single source tree?
- Can a tool easily merge code from different versions?
- What happens when multiple users check out specific components of a version?

- As code is checked out, how well is this code protected?
- Are versions protected by passwords?
- Can only one user write to an object at one time?

These issues can be complex, and version control could be the subject of its own book. For large applications, this should be a major criterion for RAD tool selection.

Single Integrated Repository to Manage Data Definitions and Source Code

If a team of developers is creating an application, the components of the application should be stored in an agreed-upon location or *repository*. That repository is usually an RDBMS. If it is open, you are not required to use one vendor's database over another. A repository should be able to store all types of data, including code, bitmaps, logic diagrams, and documents.

Project Management, Reporting, and Documentation

Most team development tools have set ways to perform project management as well as generate status reports and feature documentation. The process of project management of a RAD tool should be understood. Often a RAD tool will integrate with a third-party project management tool. In that case, the level of integration is at issue.

Impact Analysis

When a physical database is changed via the ALTER command, applications may very well be impacted. For example, a column an application uses may be deleted from a physical database. Impact analysis is the process of evaluating the impact of database design changes on applications.

Consistent Coding Standards

Some tools dictate the coding standards you should use when programming. Other tools allow you to define you own. Windows, Windows 95, OS/2, Macintosh, and UNIX all have coding guidelines. How a RAD tool promotes coding standards should be examined.

On-Line Communication Ability

Application developers doing joint development should have ways to communicate with each other, including check-in and check-out logs, code change comments, and activity records. Many tools make this easy to do and remind developers to do it; others do not.

Integration with Logical and Object Modeling Tools

As described in Chapter 2, logical model diagrams are frequently used before an application is developed. Many tools provide integration between logic model diagrams and team repositories. In fact, vendors like Logic Works generate application code for leading RAD tools. Logic Works also integrates with team development repositories.

There are object model tools that design databases through object diagrams. Object models can be used to model business processes and manage team development of objects.

15.3.5 Debugging

For RAD tools, ease of installation, documentation, and support can easily outweigh increased functionality. New features are only as good as they can be used and understood. Debugging capabilities will often indicate how robust a tool is. Some debugging features to consider are:

- Tracing bugs
- Code step-through
- Exception handling on SQL errors
- QA tools

Tracing Bugs

RAD tools should have a way to open a development environment so that when an operating system error occurs, there are methods to trace what happened.

Code Step-Through

Some tools have automated code step-through processes. Debuggers should have features like code playback, breakpoints to halt an application at certain points, and command sets to see values stored in variables.

Exception Handling on SQL Errors

All back-end RDBMS handle errors differently and generate different error messages. A RAD tool should have an easy method for handling SQL and RDBMS errors. SQL errors should be treated differently than operating system errors. For RAD tools, some class libraries have very complex error handling code for databases like Oracle, Sybase, Informix, CA-Ingres, DB2, and other RDBMs. Much coding time is involved in writing such error handling mechanisms.

QA Tools

Many developers try to write their own test routines and to automate this process themselves. Off-the-shelf QA tools do exist. Such tools are invaluable for larger projects. Products like QA Partner™ from Segue Software, and SQA Teamtest™ by SQA, Inc. are designed to help track software testing through all cycles of application development.

15.3.6 Forms, Query, and Reporting

4GLs all include query and report capabilities. The most common requirement an end user will have of a relational database is to query for information and build a report with the results. Chapters 17 and 18 are devoted to query and reporting capabilities, since these are so fundamental both to relational databases and to 4GL tools.

15.3.7 Components and Third-Party Applications

Component-based computing is the wave of the future. With object component standards emerging, like OCXs from Microsoft, the building of applications will resemble a plug-and-play, building-block assembly of best-of-breed tools. Here is a view of the components and third-party applications that complement RAD tools.

- OLE OCXs and VBXs
- Help controls
- CASE vendor integration
- Logical modeling tool set
- Middleware vendors
- Component development

OLE OCXs and VBX Integration

VBXs are Visual Basic components that can be used in other environments. OCXs are the extension of these components through the OLE standard. Tools like Visual Basic, Delphi, and SQLWindows can incorporate OCXs today, which means applications like Microsoft Word, which is OLE enabled, can be linked directly into an application with no coding or very little coding. Generating your own OCXs through such tools is another feature to look for. Another useful feature is calling an OCX over a network to run on another machine. (You can run an SQL report on an NT computer, run your application on a Windows client, and connect to a relational database on a Sun® server. This is a strategy for three-tier computing.)

Many vendors offer OCX component kits with features that include graphing, reporting, and developing new user interfaces.

Help Controls

To develope help utilities in an application, a RAD tool should either have mechanisms to automate help systems or have good third-party tools for it. For Microsoft Windows environments, tools like RoboHELP™ from Blue Sky Software and Help Magician Pro™ by Software Interphase, Inc., provide inexpensive, robust help-authoring systems.

CASE Vendor Integration

CASE (Computer Aided Software Engineering) tools take a much broader view of application development than do RAD tools. However, to tap into the "quick and easy" application development environment that RAD tools promote, CASE vendors often provide integrating tools that coexist with RAD tools. It may be interesting to look at such tools for large application development projects. For example, Rational Rose integrates their object modeling tool with RAD tools to help generate object classes. A list of some leading CASE tool vendors include:

- Bachman Information Systems Inc., Burlington, MA
- CASE Systems, Inc., Norcross, CA
- CSA Research, Quebec City, Quebec, Canada
- Evergreen CASE Tools, Redmond, WA
- LBMS, Inc., Houston, TX
- Logic Works, Inc., Princeton, NJ
- Popkin Software & Systems, New York, NY
- Rational Software Corp., Santa Clara, CA

Logic Modeling Tools

Chapter 2 discussed the subject of logic modeling tools. Logical modeling tools offer varying levels of integration with RAD tools. For example, Logic Works has integrated packages for some RAD tools, i.e., ERwin for Visual Basic, ERwin for PowerBuilder, and ERwin for SQLWindows. The level of integration with logical model tools is important because logical model tools today can help generate physical databases from scripts as well as code for applications.

Middleware Vendors

Chapter 16 discusses middleware vendors in the relational database market. RAD tools will integrate with middleware vendors to add increased connectivity to many database platforms as well as to increase performance.

Component Development

Some RAD tools excel in how easily they make their internal scripting language available to integrate components into the environment. With OLE, tools have a mechanism to create components that integrate with many environments. Some vendors extend this capability. For example, SQLWindows contains a Component Developer's Kit that allows C++ and SQLWindows developers to easily integrate components within SQLWindows 4GL.

15.3.8 Object Orientation

Object-oriented programming, OOP, is much ballyhooed by every RAD tool. Some tools are clearly more object-oriented than others. For example, IBM's VisualAge is based on SmallTalk, a true object oriented (OO) language. The most important feature of OO languages is the ability to deliver on the promise of code reuse by means of:

- Encapsulation
- Inheritance
- Polymorphism
- Object reusability and class libraries

Encapsulation

In object-oriented programming, an application is composed of objects. These objects contain data, information about the current state or condition of the object, and actions, or methods, that the object can perform. An object-oriented language supports an interface to these objects, and the internal structure of the object is hidden, or *encapsulated*.

You can almost view this as a black box approach to programming. For example, we build an object, called BalanceInquiry, which contains functions to get financial information about my bank account. Once the object is created, the only thing I need to do to get my checking balance is make a call to the object. The encapsulated function code and data in the object, BalanceInquiry, need not concern an application developer as long as we know how to get the information requested.

Inheritance

Suppose you want to create the software equivalent of a teller machine, an object called Tmachine. Since a teller machine performs balance inquiries, you may want to reuse the code from the object BalanceInquiry that we just described. The object Tmachine can *inherit* the functionality of the object BalanceInquiry.

When an object inherits functionality from multiple objects, that case is referred to as *multiple inheritance*. Not all 4GLs support multiple inheritance. It is a definite advantage if a development tool has multiple inheritance.

Polymorphism

The object BalanceInquiry has a function, or method, called GetCheckingBalance. *Polymorphism* is a way that a function, like GetCheckingBalance, can be called by using different data types (like integers, real numbers, and floating-point numbers). The function will correctly interpret the function despite having different data types passed to it. This example is also referred to as *overloading* a function.

Object Reusability and Class Libraries

The last three items discussed are features of object-oriented programming. What really matters in OOP is how well you can create and reuse objects. The number and power of prebuilt class libraries a RAD tool has will often indicate its usefulness. Class libraries are code that is supplied before compilation.

Visual Basic has many OCX components, but these are compiled and usually written in Visual C++, an object-oriented 3GL.

PowerBuilder has commercially available class libraries like PowerTOOL™ from PowerCerv Corp., and PowerClass™, PowerLock™, and PowerObjects™ from ServerLogic Corp.

SQLWindows has commerically available class libraries like Building Blocks™ from Front End Systems, and ClassIQ™ from Metex. Such libraries can save months of code development when developing RDBMS-related applications.

15.3.9 Language Support and Extensions

A common requirement of application developers is the ability to easily translate their application into other languages. Oracle has an Oracle Translation Manager, or OTM, that translates application text into multiple languages. Informix provides a class library for translation into other languages. Some features to look for in multiple language support are:

- Native language support
- Double-byte character set

Native Language Support

If a RAD tool does not have direct native language support, there are commercially available products to help, like Power Resource™ from Soft Approach. Often, application developers store different text strings in a database for many different languages and load the proper text string into their application for the language being used.

Double-byte Character Set

Asian languages require more bits of information to represent their character set. In order to support Asian languages, double-byte character sets are required. This is fairly standard today.

15.4 Exercises

The first exercise, Exercise 15.4.1, shows how far application vendors have come toward automating the process of application development. This exercise opens a SQLWindows application designed to display the information stored in our Fortune 500 database. The application, comp.app, took less than two hours to write!

Exercise 15.4.2 shows how to access the tutorial and sample applications for learning SQLWindows contained in the CD-ROM included with this book. It is not the purpose of this book to cover 4GLs in extensive detail. For further reading, see the Prentice Hall book by Rajesh Lalwani, *Power Programming with SQLWindows*, which discusses SQLWindows development.

Exercise 15.4.1: Creating a Simple Application

Before You Start

In the directory, c:\sqlbase\exercise\chap15, there is a file, company.dbs, which is a copy of the database as it should be if all the previous exercises were completed. If you have not finished all the exercises, you can still view this application by copying this file into c:\sqlbase\company directory.

Compiling the Application

1. Open the SQLWindows application. Click on the SQLWindows icon shown below.

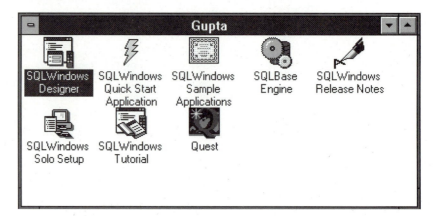

Figure 15-1 *SQLWindows Designer*

2. You are asked if you want to create a QuickForm, as shown in Figure 15-2. Because you will be loading a prebuilt application, press **Cancel**.

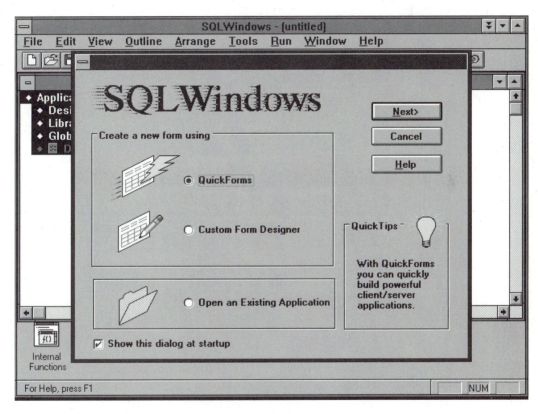

Figure 15-2 *Opening SQLWindows*

3. Pull down the File menu and choose the **Open** menu option.

4. You are prompted for an application to open. Choose the file: c:\sqlbase\exercise\chap15\comp.app. Click **OK**.

Figure 15-3 *Opening the SQLWindows Application*

5. Once the application is loaded, you can compile it by pressing the **F7** key on your keyboard (the shortcut method!). Press **F7**. Wait a few seconds and the application will be up and running!

Running the Application

6. Choose the company, American Stores Co and press **OK** as shown in Figure 15-4.

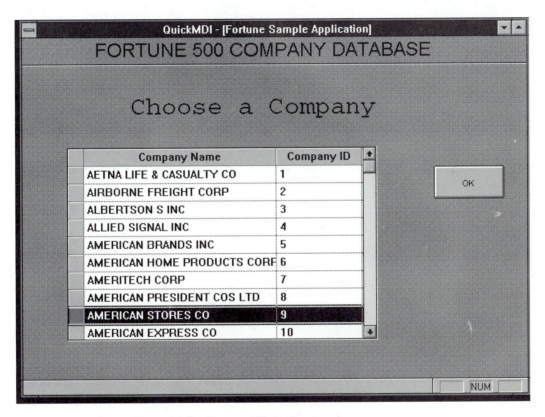

Figure 15-4 *Fortune 500 Application*

7. Go to the form shown below.

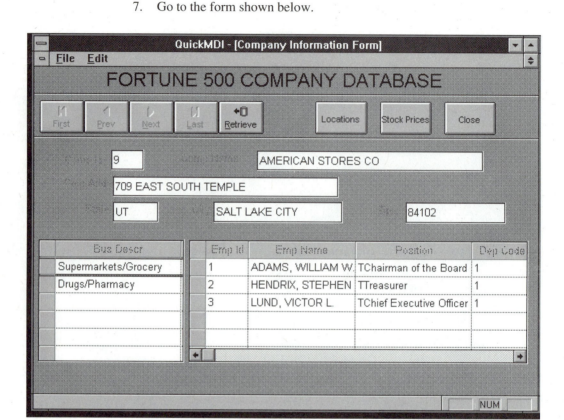

Figure 15-5 *Company Information Form*

The screen contains information about the specific company chosen. Note that four tables from the COMPANY database had to be used to get the information on the screen: COMP, EMPLOYEES, BUS_TYPES, and BUS_CODES.

8. There are three buttons at the top right-hand corner of the screen, Company Information Form, shown in Figure 15-5.

Choose the **Locations** button; the Location Information screen shown below is displayed. Choose the **Clos**e button in the upper-right hand corner to return to the screen shown in Figure 15-5.

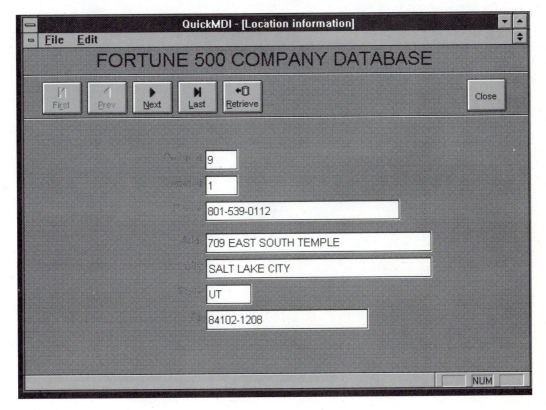

Figure 15-6 *Location Information Screen*

9. Choose the **Stock Prices** button; the Stock Information screen is displayed.

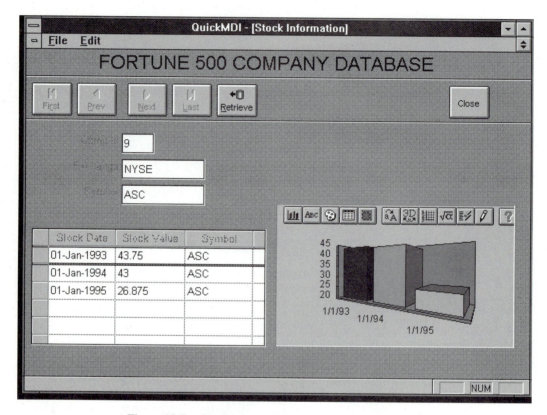

Figure 15-7 *Stock Information Screen*

10. Choose the **Close** button to return to the main screen. If you want information about another company, choose another entry and do it again!

11. To exit, click on the top-left icon shown in Figure 15-4 and choose the **Close** menu option.

This application can be modified or compiled to an executable. The next exercise points to a tutorial that allows you to learn the 4GL in more detail.

Exercise 15.4.2: Learning a 4GL

The following figure shows the program group for the installed software from the CD-ROM in the back of this book.

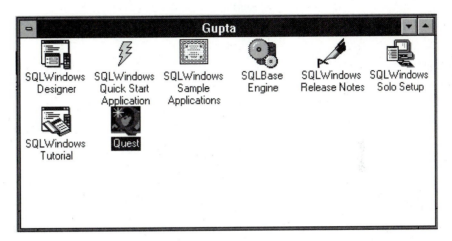

Figure 15-8 *The SQLWindows Tutorial and SQLWindows Sample Application Icons*

1. For a tutorial on SQLWindows, click on the **SQLWindows Tutorial** icon.

2. For a look at sample applications, open the **SQLWindows Sample Application** icon.

3. It is not our intention to provide an in-depth discussion of this 4GL product. The software contained in this CD-ROM has context-sensitive help as well as on-line documentation.

15.5 Summary

This chapter covered general functionality of 4GLs and introduced several of the leading vendors in this market. The major direction of this market is the componentization of prebuilt controls. In the application development market of the future, people will offer best-of-breed components. The OLE technology by Microsoft, Opendoc technology by Apple, and the DCE technology supported by OSF and UNIX vendors define such a world of distributed, component-based application development.

Components exist today that make talking to SQL back-end RDBMS relatively painless. The differences of the SQL vendors and their varieties of error handling, as well as the issues of synchronizing data between them, can easily be handled by prebuilt controls. Small component "applets" can be developed in one environment and shared in another.

16   Database Middleware

In Chapter 14, we discussed the specifics of embedded SQL within an application. Connectivity solutions today provide much more than connectivity to an RDBMS through embedded SQL; They also provide features like transparent access of data across multiple databases, client/server connectivity across many different network protocols, and easy access to nonrelational data. These solutions can loosely be defined as *database middleware*.

This chapter is organized as follows:

Section 16.1   Overview of Database Middleware
Section 16.2   Direct, Proprietary Access to RDBMS
Section 16.3   Multidatabase Connectivity
Section 16.4   Gateways and Vendors
Section 16.5   Extended Middleware Connectivity
Section 16.6   Summary

16.1   *Overview of Database Middleware*

Database middleware is sold under an abundance of names, including gateways, routers, drivers, and connectivity toolkits. The term "database middleware" is akin to the term "open systems": It is both loosely defined and frequently misused. Database middleware acts as an intermediary between front-end applications and remote data. Because of the number of database vendors, network protocols, and connectivity providers, understanding can be hopelessly complex. Database middleware also relies on a network layer of hardware and software that is often taken for granted.

For example, when you buy an ODBC driver today, an assumption is made that you already have networking software in place to connect a client to a back-end database.

This chapter divides middleware solutions into separate categories:

- Direct proprietary APIs
- Multidatabase API solutions
- Gateway products
- Extended middleware

These categories are meant to simplify the discussion of connectivity solutions; however, they are used loosely. For example, Sybase sells a native API to Sybase, an ODBC driver, a gateway product, and extended middleware software solutions. (To correctly categorize these products depends on how Sybase, or any other vendor, decides to bundle their software, i.e., ODBC is frequently bundled with a vendor's native API.)

Advancements of Today's Middleware Solutions

Having discussed the difficulties of middleware, it is only fair to discuss the advancements of today's technology. Middleware technology has progressed rapidly within the last few years. A few of the advancements are:

- Most middleware solutions have eliminated the problems associated with programming to each of the different network protocols (and the endless onslaught of newer versions and software patches); for example, TCP/IP, SPX/IPX, NetBIOS, LU6.2, AppleTalk®.

- Middleware can "open" applications to allow interchanging of database vendors without major rewrites. While the ODBC interface does not solve all problems, it does go a long way toward standardizing a common method of accessing all relational databases.

- Middleware has progressed to the point where some vendors can transparently provide data movement between relational and nonrelational data. Many solutions perform error handling as well as data replication functions.

- Layers have been built on top of complex APIs to simplify application development, using embedded SQL. Many vendors offer class libraries that provide generic interfaces to all major back-end databases.

16.2 *Direct, Proprietary Access to RDBMS*

In Chapter 14, we looked at APIs to use with embedded SQL. In particular, we discussed SQL/API and ODBC. These can be viewed as the API component of middleware. Relational database vendors have historically defined their own proprietary APIs. For example, Oracle corporation has the Oracle Call Interface (OCI), and Sybase relies on DB-Library (Sybase System 10.x and 11.x) and Client Library (SQL Server 4.x). If you want your client application to access a database server, the most direct alternative is to write to the database vendor's native API.

The benefits of writing to a vendor's native API are:

- Performance
- Use of database specific features that other solutions do not provide

You could choose to write to Oracle and Sybase by using ODBC, but there are still functionality trade-offs to doing so. Below, we discuss the native connectivity packages for Oracle, Sybase, and Informix. Although there are many native software packages that could be discussed here, these are three of the most interesting given market acceptance.

Direct Access Solutions

Most vendors offer their own native API for programmatic connectivity to their database. Listed below are three popular vendors and their APIs. All products are trademarks or registered trademarks of their respective companies.

Informix Software, Inc. (INFORMIX-Net)
4100 Bohannon Dr
Menlo Park, CA 94025
(415) 926-6300

PRODUCT: INFORMIX-Net for UNIX, INFORMIX-ESQL/C with INFORMIX-Net for Windows, NT, Macintosh, and OS/2

PLATFORMS: Windows, Windows NT, Macintosh, OS/2, leading UNIX variations

POSITION: INFORMIX-ESQL/C is Informix's own embedded SQL solution for C (and COBOL), portable across an array of platforms. INFORMIX-Net allows communication between client and server machines, across most network protocols, but most commonly TCP/IP, as this is a de facto standard in the UNIX market.

Oracle Corp. (SQL*Net)
500 Oracle Parkway
Redwood Shores, CA 94065
(415) 506-7000

PRODUCT: SQL*Net

PLATFORMS: Runs on most hardware platforms

POSITION: Supports Oracle's native API, called OCI, to allow embedded SQL calls. SQL*Net also includes an ODBC driver for those who prefer it. Oracle's SQL*Connect product can be used with SQL*Net to allow remote data access to other databases, including DB2, SQL/DS, and Tandem NonStop SQL. SQL*Net runs over all major network protocols, including AppleTalk, Banyan Vines, DECnet, LU6.2, Named Pipes, NetBIOS, OSI, SPX/IPX, TCP/IP, and X.25.

Sybase, Inc. (Open Client/ C Developers Kit)
6475 Christie Ave
Emeryville, CA 94608
(510) 596-3500

PRODUCT: Open Client/ C Developers Kit

PLATFORMS: Includes Windows, Macintosh, OS/2, DOS, most UNIX implementations, IBM MVS/CICS

POSITION: Supports multiple APIs, including Sybase Embedded SQL, Sybase Client Library, Sybase DB-Library, and ODBC. Sybase Client Library is the native API to SQL Server 4.x databases. Sybase DB-Library is the native API to Sybase System 10 and 11 databases. Sybase Open Server is available to connect to mainframe databases. Open Client runs over all major network protocols, including AppleTalk, LU6.2, Named Pipes, NetBIOS, OSI, SPX/IPX, TCP/IP, and X.25.

16.3   Multidatabase Connectivity

You can use a router or gateway product to translate from one vendor's API to another vendor's API. Centura Software's SQLRouter and SQLGateway products provide such a service. They sit between a SQLWindows or Quest client application and a non-SQLBase database server and translate API calls into non-SQLBase API calls. Centura Software has SQLNetwork products that support IBM's DB2, AS/400, and Database Manager, Oracle, SQL Server, Informix, Ingres, and more.

16.3.1 ODBC

In 1991, Microsoft Corporation announced the Open Database Connectivity (ODBC) application programmatic interface (API) for use with Microsoft Windows, among other platforms.

Many APIs existed prior to ODBC. What made ODBC attractive was its "open" interface and its base on the call-level interface (CLI) defined by the SQL Access Group (SAG). SAG is a consortium of industry leaders in the DBMS market. Microsoft was the first to write a series of drivers to work with their ODBC API; many vendors have followed. Microsoft has developed a Software Developer's Kit (SDK).

Adding Capability

Microsoft added extensions to ANSI/ISO standard CLI. CLI is core-level ODBC. There are two other levels of ODBC compliance, Level 1 and Level 2.

- Core level — Defines basic embedded SQL operations like:
  - connecting to a database
  - preparing and executing SQL statements
  - fetching data from result sets
  - commit and rollback statements
  - basic error handling

- Level 1 — Superset of the core level. It adds functionality such as:
  - getting and setting connection parameters
  - obtaining information about an ODBC driver
  - obtaining catalog information from a database

- Level 2 — Superset of Level 1. It adds functionality like:
  - retrieving queries in an array format
  - obtaining privileges, keys, and stored procedures from a catalog
  - getting native SQL from a database
  - providing translation ability
  - scrollable cursors

Caveat

Not all ODBC drivers are the same. Not all ODBC drivers meet Level 1 or Level 2 specifications completely. To be ODBC compliant, you merely have to provide core-level functionality. For another, Microsoft permits vendors to implement DBMS-specific extensions to ODBC. In the case of stored procedures, no vendors do quite the same thing.

Another thing to be aware of is that beyond the ODBC specification, describing three levels of conformance (core, Level 1, and Level 2), there is also a *grammar-level compliance*. Grammar-level compliance is a Pandora's box. For example, data types are not the same for all databases and are not well defined in most ODBC drivers today.

Grammar-level compliance is described as minimum, core, and extended. Here is a basic outline of grammar-level compliance:

- Minimum — Includes support for CREATE and DROP table and a baseline level of support for the SELECT, INSERT, UPDATE, and DELETE statements. Fixed-length character data is the only data type required for minimum compliance.

- Core — Superset of minimum grammar, which includes CREATE and DROP index statements, GRANT and REVOKE commands, the ability to do subqueries and perform aggregate functions. Core level adds eight data types for numeric data and variable-length character data.

- Extended — Superset of core grammar, which includes SELECT statements within UPDATE statements, UNION, and outer joins. Ten more data types are defined in this grammar level for logical, binary data types as well as "extended types" like time variables and more abstract data.

For information on implementing ODBC, refer to Microsoft's *ODBC 2.0 Programmer's Reference and SDK Guide* available from Microsoft Press.

Market Momentum

ODBC's main attraction is the sheer number of vendors who have implemented it. It is the most generic way to program to a back-end database available today.

It would be hard to count the number of vendors who now have ODBC-compliant drivers. Intersolv, owner of Q+E, one of the leaders in ODBC driver development, touts over 30 drivers to many different databases, including Xbase databases like dBASE, Paradox, and Btrieve. Microsoft provided Visigenic the exclusive rights to provide an ODBC SDK on non-Windows environments.

Future

The ODBC standard will be enhanced by Microsoft. ODBC 3.0 is in the works at Microsoft. The manner in which ODBC is used today will change. Microsoft would like to replace ODBC with an OLE container that can provide database access. They are wrapping the ODBC interface in an OLE object. In reality, the market has adopted the ODBC standard. The marketplace will likely move ahead with the standard more slowly than Microsoft would wish.

16.3.2 Vendors with ODBC Drivers

Following is a list of the leading providers of ODBC solutions. Almost every RDBMS vendor and database middleware provider has developed or acquired an ODBC technology. They are usually specific to their own technology. The vendors below supply general ODBC connectivity to multiple data sources. All products are trademarks or registered trademarks of their respective companies.

Intergraph Corp. (ODBC Drivers)
One Madison Industrial Park
Huntsville AL 35894
(205) 730-2000

PRODUCT: ODBC Drivers

PLATFORMS: Windows, Windows NT, Sun Solaris, SCO, and other UNIX variants

POSITION: Intergraph offers a set of ODBC Drivers to access the major relational database vendors, including Oracle, CA-Ingress, Informix, Microsoft SQL Server, and Sybase SQL Server.

Intersolv, Inc. (Q+E ODBC Pack)
3200 Tower Oaks Blvd
RockVille MD, 20852
(301) 230-3200

PRODUCT: Q+E ODBC Pack, Q+E Database Library, Multilink/VB

PLATFORMS: ODBC Pack runs on Windows, Windows 95, OS/2, Sun Solaris, and Windows NT. They have support for over 30 databases, including ALLBase, Btrieve, Clipper, DB2, DB2/2, DB2/6000, dBASE, Excel.XLS files, FoxBase, SQLBase, Informix, CA-Ingres, Microsoft SQL Server, NetWare SQL, Oracle, Paradox, PROGRESS, SQL/400, SQL/DS, Sybase System 10, Sybase SQL Server 4.x, Teradata, text files, and XDB. Also supports gateways, including IBM DDCS/2 and DDCS/6000, MDI Gateway, SQLHost, and Sybase-10 OmniSQL Gateway.

POSITION: In May 1994, Intersolv acquired Q+E software. The company has gained a leadership role in supplying ODBC-compliant drivers and has formed strategic relationships with companies, including INFORMIX and Centura Software. Intersolv has created ODBC 2.0, 32-bit versions of their drivers, and continues to add functionality rapidly. Intersolv does a lot of work to add specific support for different databases, including stored procedures.

Microsoft Corp. (ODBC SDK)
One Microsoft Way
Redmond, WA 98052
(206) 882-8080

PRODUCT: ODBC 2.0 SDK, ODBC Driver Kit

PLATFORMS: Windows, Windows 95, Windows NT. Microsoft's Driver Kit includes support for Access, FoxPro, Excel, Btrieve, dBASE, Paradox, and text files, as well as Microsoft SQL Server.

POSITION: Microsoft's ODBC driver technology continues to move forward with ODBC 3.0. A new direction of OLE database access (encapsulated ODBC) is in the works. Most features of ODBC 1.0 and 2.0 will likely become part of the ANSI/ISO standard for database access. Microsoft formed a strategic alliance with Simba Technologies, Inc., to supply drivers for Microsoft applications in its desktop driver kit.

Openlink Software, Ltd. (ODBC Drivers)
15 Cherry Orchard Rd
Croydon CR9 6BB, United Kingdom
44-81-681-7701

PRODUCT: ODBC Drivers

PLATFORMS: Windows, Macintosh, UNIX, OS/2, Windows NT, DEC
VMS, and Novell. Supports many databases, including DB2, Oracle,
Informix SE & Online, Progress, Sybase SQL Server 4.X, Sybase System
10, UNIFY 2000, CA-Ingres, MS SQL Server, RDB

POSITION: Openlink stresses their high-performance ODBC drivers. A
quote from their marketing literature reads, "high-performance database
independent communication technology... delivers blistering performance."
Openlink replaces the standard communication layer to a database to deliver
the performance, which gains them other enhanced features as well. Other
features Openlink stresses are:

- ODBC 1.0/2.0 (Core + Level 1 + Level 2) compliance
- 16-bit and 32-bit mode
- Synchronous and asynchronous behavior
- Concurrent access to heterogeneous databases from one driver
- Enhanced security, using simplexed or duplexed data encryption

Simba Technologies, Inc. (ODBC Pack)
2125 Western Ave. Ste 301
Seattle, WA 98121
(206) 441-0340

PRODUCT: Microsoft ODBC Driver Pack

PLATFORMS: Windows, Windows 95, Windows NT. Microsofts Driver Kit
(supplied by Simba, formerly PageAhead) includes support for Access,
FoxPro, Excel, Btrieve, dBASE, Paradox, and text files, as well as Microsoft
SQL Server

POSITION: Simba changed their name from PageAhead. Simba
Technology has worked with Microsoft for development of ODBC drivers
and has forged relationships with several other key vendors.

Syware, Inc. (Dr. DeeBee)
P.O. Box 91, Kendall Station
Cambridge, MA 02142
(617) 497-1376

PRODUCT: Dr. DeeBee Tools (Check, Info, Peek, Test, Timer, Spy, Replay, Super Bundle)

PLATFORMS: Windows, Windows 95, Windows NT

POSITION: Syware, with Dr. DeeBee, has positioned itself as a leading provider of powerful ODBC testing tools. For a developer of ODBC applications, tools to analyze and trace ODBC calls, to time performance, to replay coding sequences, and to perform diagnostics are critical.

Visigenic Software, Inc. (ODBC SDK)
951 Mariner's Blvd. Ste. 460
San Mateo, CA 94404
(415) 286-1900

PRODUCT: ODBC SDK

PLATFORMS: Sun Solaris, HP-UX, IBM AIX, SCO, Macintosh, and OS/2

POSITION: Visigenic has exclusive rights from Microsoft to license and port ODBC to all non-Windows platforms. Roger Sippl, a founder of Informix, is CEO of Visigenic. Both IBM and Apple licensed Visigenic technology in May of 1995 to bundle ODBC developer's kits in their environments.

16.3.3 Vendors with Multidatabase APIs

All products are trademarks or registered trademarks of their respective companies.

Apple Computer, Inc. (DAL)
One Infinite Loop
Cupertino, CA 95014
(408) 966-1010

PRODUCT: DAL

PLATFORMS: Macintosh, Windows clients to VAX/VMS, A/UX, AS/400, MVS, VM, UNIX, and PC-LAN

POSITION: Although Apple has for some time offered its own access method to relational databases through DAL, Apple has also licensed Visigenic's ODBC solutions as a generic SQL access method. Apple has third parties offering DAL interfaces, for example, Independence Technologies, which offers a ODBC/DAL driver that bridges the two middleware technologies.

Borland International, Inc. (IDAPI)
100 Borland Way
Scotts Valley, CA 95066
(408) 431-1000

PRODUCT: IDAPI

PLATFORMS: Windows, Windows 95, Windows NT

POSITION: In 1992, Borland, IBM, Novell, and WordPerfect announced plans for their own open API called the Integrated Database Application Programming Interface, or IDAPI. Like ODBC, IDAPI is based on the call-level interface of the SQL Access Group.

IDAPI was positioned by Borland to be a direct competitor to the ODBC standard. IDAPI has not enjoyed the market acceptance of ODBC, and while Borland still provides the IDAPI interface today, they have stated a much more harmonious existence with the ODBC standard. Writing to the IDAPI API does not lock you in. As both IDAPI and ODBC were based on the ANSI/ISO CLI specification, they are both adaptations of an evolving industry standard.

Centura Software Corp. (SQLNetwork API)
1060 Marsh Rd.
Menlo Park, CA 94025
(415) 321-9500

PRODUCT: SQL/API

PLATFORMS: Windows, Windows NT. Supports multiple RDBMS with the SQL/API including Oracle, Informix, Sybase, DB2, DB2/400, CA-Ingres, HP Allbase, Cincom Supra, and SQLBase

POSITION: Centura's SQL/API offers a generic way to access multiple back-end relational databases; it existed long before the ODBC standard evolved. Because Centura wrote "routers" or adapters to the native client connectivity of database vendors like Oracle, Sybase, IBM, CA-Ingres, and Informix, they have native solutions for connectivity, which has historically offered better performance than do more generic solutions. Centura Software now offers users the choice of using an ODBC-compliant API or their own.

Information Builders, Inc. (EDA/SQL)
1250 Broadway
New York, NY 10001
(212) 736-4433

PRODUCT: EDA/SQL and EDA API/SQL

PLATFORMS: Client access includes Windows, OS/2, and Macintosh, HP-UX, SCO UNIX, DEC VAX, IBM mainframe, AS/400, AIX, Sun Solaris

POSITION: Information Builders provides an API that allows users to access most major databases through its subroutine libraries. EDA/SQL adds many functions to enhance connectivity, including access to nonrelational data (particularly on mainframe), support for parallel processing, for parallel query processing, and copy management tools to move data between heterogeneous data sources.

TechGnosis, Inc. (SequeLink)
5 Burlington Woods Dr, Suite 202
Burlington, MA 01803
(617) 229-6100

PRODUCT: SequeLink

PLATFORMS: Client access includes Windows, OS/2, and Macintosh, and many UNIX variants to a wide variety of host machines, supporting a wide variety of protocols.

POSITION: TechGnosis has licensed middleware solutions to thousands of companies, providing direct access to host data. TechGnosis also offers an ODBC-compliant interface to access their middleware through Windows.

16.4   Gateways and Vendors

In the field of network communications, gateways are defined as hardware and/or software that connects two computer networks of different architectures. Almost always, gateways are talked about in conjuction with facilitating connectivity to mainframe systems, e.g., DB2 or SQL/DS on an IBM mainframe. Many relational vendors today provide gateways to legacy or mainframe systems. Usually, gateways are extensions to a broader connectivity strategy. For example, Information Builders EDA/SQL Database gateways are extensions of their EDA/SQL and EDA API/SQL, so that anyone using their connectivity has a solution for accessing legacy data on a mainframe. Products like MDI's OmniSQL™ and Centura Software's SQLHost behave similarly.

Gateways differ from more direct solutions in that there usually is a hardware component between the client and server machines that acts as the physical "gateway." Usually, additional software is required on the server to process requests. Figure 16-1 illustrates a diagram of a gateway that acts as the intermediary between multiple PC clients and a mainframe machine.

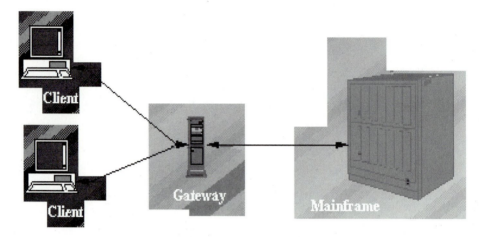

Figure 16-1 *Gateway Connectivity*

Gateway machines do not have to be large systems but can be Intel processor-based servers with operating systems like OS/2, Novell NetWare®, and Microsoft Windows NT. OS/2, with IBM's distributed Database Connection Services (DDCS), provides protocol conversion between the PC networking environments and IBM mainframe protocol. Novell NetWare is also a convenient gateway. Novell offers NetWare for SAA, which is a software suite that connects client networks with mainframe environments. Microsoft is moving strongly into this arena with its BackOffice connectivity for SNA.

Gateway Vendors

Below is a list of vendors with gateway products. All products are trademarks or registered trademarks of their respective companies.

Centura Software Corp. (SQLHost)
1060 Marsh Rd.
Menlo Park, CA 94025
(415) 321-9500

PRODUCT: SQLHost and SQLGateway

PLATFORMS: Client access through Windows, Windows 95, and Windows NT.

POSITION: If you write to the SQL API, or ODBC, Centura Software will allow you to connect to mainframe data through their gateway products. The application services component of this product enables developers to create CICS applications on a mainframe and access them with static SQL, or to access nonrelational databases like IMS and data repositories in VSAM.

SQLNetwork for DB2 comprises three separate components: SQLHost, SQLGateway, and SQLRouter. SQLHost is the mainframe resident software. SQLGateway is the pathway from client to server, providing several methods of accessing a mainframe: through TCP/IP (with TCP/IP loaded on a mainframe), through an OS/2 gateway using DDCS, through a NetWare gateway, using Novell for SAA). SQLRouter is client-based software to translate the ODBC or Centura Software's SQL/API calls.

Computer Associates, Inc. (CA-Ingres Gateways)
One Computer Associates Plaza
Islandia, NY 11788
(516) 543-3010

PRODUCT: CA-Ingres/Gateways

PLATFORMS: Likely to change as of this writing.

POSITION: The CA-Ingres gateway products are extensions of the CA-Ingres middleware solutions, CA-Ingres/STAR, CA-Ingres/Net. These gateways access mainframe-based data, including DB2, SQL/DS, and IMS.

IBM Corp. (DDCS)
Old Orchard Rd
Armonk, NY 10504
(914) 765-1900

PRODUCT: Distributed Database Connection Services (DDCS)

PLATFORMS: Runs on OS/2, IBM AIX, HP-UX, Sun Solaris. Client access from DOS, Windows, OS/2, and UNIX systems

POSITION: DDCS resides on a server (OS/2, AIX, HP-UX, or Sun Solaris system) which enables client systems to access data in any DRDA-enabled server. IBM's DRDA, or Distributed Relational Database Architecture, is a middleware layer that provides a method of data access to IBM database products regardless of location. Once a mainframe, AS/400 system, or RS/6000 system is DRDA enabled, a client can request a gateway, through DDCS, to access back-end data.

Information Builders, Inc. (Database Gateways)
1250 Broadway
New York, NY 10001
(212) 736-4433

PRODUCT: EDA/SQL DB2 Gateway, EDA SQL/DS Gateway

PLATFORMS: Clients include Windows, OS/2, Macintosh, and UNIX machines

POSITION: Information Builders Gateways access DB2, SQL/DS, as well as a host of other mainframe databases, not all of which are relational, such as IMS and IDMS. The gateway product is an extension of their EDA/SQL product line, which also offers EDA/SQL enabled products like Lotus 1-2-3, as well as their EDA API/SQL for embedding SQL in applications. Informix supports the EDA/SQL suite of products with their own INFORMIX-Enterprise Gateway.

MDI - a Sybase Company (OmniSQL)
3035 Center Green Dr.
Boulder, CO 80301
(303) 443-2706

PRODUCT: OmniSQL Gateway

PLATFORMS: Gateway runs on Windows NT, UNIX systems, and DEC VAX

POSITION: OmniSQL is an extension of Sybase's middleware connectivity strategy to non-Sybase databases. OmniSQL is a transparent way for users to access relational data without knowledge of the actual location of a data source. OmniSQL connects into more than 20 data sources, including DB2, SQL/DS, as well as nonrelational data, like IMS and VSAM.

Oracle Corp. (Transparent Gateway for DRDA, Open Gateway Technology)
500 Oracle Parkway
Redwood Shores, CA 94065
(415) 506-7000

PRODUCT: Oracle Transparent Gateway, Open Gateway Technology

PLATFORMS: Gateways include OS/2 and RS/6000; clients include UNIX systems, DEC VAX, OS/2, Windows, Macintosh

POSITION: Oracle's gateway strategy is an extension of their connectivity through SQL*Net. The Open Gateway technology opens database access to DB2, SQL/DS, IDMS, IMS, among others. Oracle provides an Oracle Transparent Gateway Developer's Kit (for writing data interface routines), as well as an Oracle Procedural Gateway Developer's Kit (for writing with Oracle's PL/SQL RPC in order to use Oracle's stored procedure methodology with non-Oracle data sources).

16.5   Extended Middleware Connectivity

Software vendors are not always easy to categorize. The solutions they provide offer unique features not seen elsewhere. Many middleware vendors offer extended features and integrated solutions for relational databases that go beyond what we have discussed so far. Vendors that have such product offerings are described in this section. More than likely, what are considered extended features today will be standard in future products; however, the category does provide a convenient way to describe such products.

Being a middleware vendor is like being a lineman on a football team: while both are critical to success, neither gets much recognition. Companies like Attachmate, Wall Data, and Platinum Technologies have concentrated on supplying middleware solutions for connecting disparate computer systems. None of the three would be considered household names.

Extended Middleware Vendors

The list below discusses some of the more unique middleware solutions on the market today, providing solutions in the SQL relational database market. All products are trademarks or registered trademarks of their respective companies.

Attachmate Corp. (SELECT! Professional 5.0)
3617 131st Ave., SE
Bellevue, WA 98006
(206) 644-4010

PRODUCT: SELECT! Professional

PLATFORMS: Windows and OS/2 clients

POSITION: Provides a simplified GUI interface to facilitate database access, query and analysis features, data transfer from heterogeneous databases, and data transfer from database servers into client-based applications. SELECT! supports native connectivity as well as ODBC and DRDA. Some of the supported SQL databases include DB2, SQL/DS, Microsoft SQL Server, Sybase SQL Server, and Oracle.

Cincom Systems, Inc. (ObjectHub)
2300 Montana Ave
Cincinatti, OH 45211
(800) 543-3010

PRODUCT: Total ObjectHub

PLATFORMS: Windows client; works with RUMA APPC, NetWare for SAA, IBM PC AS/400 support, and Microsoft SNA Server. Connectivity to major database vendors, including Oracle, Sybase, Rdb, Informix, Supra Server, CA-Ingres, and more.

POSITION: Cincom has taken an object-oriented approach to relational database management. Their software allows the end users a single view and access to nonrelational, relational, and object-oriented databases.

Informix Software, Inc. (INFORMIX-Star)
4100 Bohannon Dr
Menlo Park, CA 94025
(415) 926-6300

PRODUCT: INFORMIX-Star for UNIX

PLATFORMS: Leading UNIX variations

POSITION: INFORMIX-Star is an extended middleware solution that allows database users to view multiple Informix databases as if they were a single database, regardless of where they are on the network. A main benefit of this product is that you no longer have to rely on a single, centralized database server. Databases at branch sites can be incorporated into the central corporate data without a long development and deployment cycle.

MDI — a Sybase Company (InfoPump)
3035 Center Green Dr.
Boulder, CO 80301
(303) 443-2706

PRODUCT: InfoPump

PLATFORMS: OS/2

POSITION: Can be used in conjunction with the MDI OmniSQL to access midrange, mainframe, and DB2 databases. Used to transfer data heterogeneously to multiple back ends.

Platinum Technology, Inc. (Integrator)
1815 S Meyers Rd.
Oakbrook Terrace, IL 60181
(708) 620-5000

PRODUCT: Integrator

PLATFORMS: Windows, OS/2 client

POSITION: Gives users access to data on the mainframe, including DB2, IMS, IDMS, and VSAM.

Techsmith Corp. (Remote NetLib)
3001 Coolidge Rd, Ste 400
East Lansing, MI 48823
(517) 333-2100

PRODUCT: Remote NetLib

PLATFORMS: DOS, Windows, Windows 95

POSITION: Allows users to access SQL data from remote sites. It is a fast, protocol-independent connectivity solution that, used in tandem with TechSmith's Enterprise Wide product, allows users to remotely execute application software via a dedicated PC gateway as if connected locally.

VMARK Software, Inc. (HyperSTAR)
50 Washington St
Westboro, MA 01581
(508) 366-3888

PRODUCT: HyperSTAR

PLATFORMS: Clients on Windows, Windows 95, Windows NT, Macintosh, and UNIX operating systems

POSITION: VMARK has created an object-oriented SQL middleware API (STAR/C) based on compliance with the Object Management Group (OMG). Low-level database access to multiple back ends (including Oracle, Informix, Sybase, CA-Ingres, DB2, and uniVerse) is simplified, eliminating other middleware or gateway products. A key feature is that any data access method can be supported by an object-oriented paradigm. This product makes use of native capabilities of the different database back ends and also offers high performance by supporting an asynchronous execution feature.

Wall Data, Inc. (RUMBA)
11332 NE 122nd Way
Kirkland, WA 98034
(206) 814-9255

PRODUCT: RUMBA for Database Access

PLATFORMS: Windows users

POSITION: Gives Windows users direct access to IBM host databases, including DB2 and SQL/DS, as well as OS/400 on AS/400 platform. Users do not have to have any gateway product.

16.6   Summary

Database middleware vendors today have solved the problem of heterogeneous database access through ODBC and other solutions outlined in this chapter; however, these solutions continue to suffer not only from ease of use problems, but also from a performance standpoint.

When application developers want to access a relational database, chances are they will have to evaluate the trade-offs of more open, generic solutions versus higher-performing, but more constraining, technologies for specific database vendors.

It stands to reason that database access will continue to become automated until the trade-offs of generic vs. fast performance will no longer be an issue. At this point, there will likely be a consolidation of all the data access technologies available today.

17   A Look at Query Tools

Learning the SQL language or how to use embedded SQL for application development is not always required; end users may desire nothing more than the ability to query a database for specific information and/or generate graphs and reports. Query tools exist that automate the process of building SQL statements for you to provide such functionality. This chapter looks at such query tools, discussing the classes of end-user query tools and decision support query tools (or executive information systems, EIS). The chapter then steps through the use of a query tool and discusses the specific features this class of tools offers.

This chapter is organized as follows:

17.1   Query Tools

A plethora of end-user query and reporting tools are available today. Most query tools will accomplish fairly complex tasks without any required knowledge of the SQL language on a user's part. This book has been using a query tool, Quest, throughout this book to facilitate the lab exercises. All the exercises we have done so far, using the SQL Activity in Quest, could have been done by using point-and-click methodology without you knowing anything about the SQL language.

17.1.1 Components of Query Tools

Although query tools may differ in overall look, there are several components that are common to these tools. We discuss each of these components in more detail later in the chapter. These features are:

- **GUI query interface**

  A query tool provides data access through an easy and intuitive graphical interface for accessing corporate databases. There is no need to know SQL to retrieve data. Query tools can allow a user to create a query by example by generating a list of possible values as well as conditions to assist in query generation. Simply by pointing and clicking, a user should be able to access data.

- **Reporting capability**

  Once data access has been accomplished through a specific query, end users commonly want to generate a report based on the information retrieved. They may also want to format the data in a structured manner and perform summations and totals on the data they have retrieved. Reporting tools provide this capability and more.

  Most query products are really both a query and a report tool; many tools are designed for one or the other task separately. We discuss report-generating tools in Chapter 18; however, a good query tool should provide some form of reporting.

- **Forms capability**

  Forms provide an intuitive interface for accessing and updating data. Using forms, data entry operators can view and enter data in screens that resemble the paper forms they are familiar with. Forms can be created and distributed to other end users.

- **Graphing**

  Data can many times be best represented by graphs. Users often want to transform data they retrieve into charts and graphs. A query tool should be able to link query output directly to a graph.

- **Data management ability**
  Users want the power to manage their database tables and views with a simple point-and-click interface. Some query tools make database catalogs available so that a user can change them. Data management ability is an advanced ability that not all end users should have. Query tools are often offered in versions: one that has data management ability and one that does not.

- **Remote connectivity capability**
  Query tools should offer connectivity to many back ends. With the proper connectivity, queries can be made against many back-end servers. For example, with Quest you can connect to Sybase, Oracle, Informix, DB2, or SQLBase, and you would not know the difference.

17.1.2 EIS Tools

There exists a class of query tools designed for decision support. This class of query tool is characterized as part of an *Executive Information System,* or *EIS*. EIS systems require query capabilities, but they differ from end-user query tools in how they use their information. EIS systems concentrate on on-line analytical processing (OLAP). An EIS system is also referred to by many as a *decision support system*, or *DSS*.

EIS or DSS tools concentrate on large amounts of data over long time frames. They also require more complex query statements. Because the same data can be represented differently during different time snapshots, this data is often characterized as *multidimensional*.

Section 17.4 examines EIS tools more closely.

17.2   End-User Query Vendors

Query tools are advancing rapidly. Some of the vendors below are now positioning themselves in the more niche-oriented EIS market as well. Three of the vendors listed — Natural Language, Trinsic, and Powersoft — have been acquired by other companies while this book was being written. All products are trademarks or registered trademarks of their respective companies.

Andyne Computing, Ltd (GQL)
552 Princess St., 2nd
Fl. Kingston, ON, CD K7L 1C7
(800) 267-0665

PRODUCT: GQL

PLATFORMS: Windows, Windows 95, Macintosh, and most major UNIX versions, including Sun Solaris, HP-UX, and IBM AIX

POSITION: Andyne's Graphical Query Language (GQL) query tool consists of four separate applications: GQL/Admin, GQL/User, GQL/Update, and GQL/Design. GQL/User is the end-user query application, with integrated WYSIWYG reporting built in and with support for popular word processors and spreadsheets. GQL/Update is a superset of the GQL/User application, allowing end users to add, modify, and delete data from the connected SQL engine. GQL/Admin provides database administrators with added administrative functionality, like the ability to create a data model. GQL/Design is a tool for prototyping and creating new databases.

Andyne has EIS features incorporated with this product. They sell another product, Pablo, for more full-featured decision support. That product is discussed in Section 17.4, under EIS tools.

Blythe Software, Inc. (True Access)
989 East Hillsdale Blvd.
Foster City, CA 94404
(415) 571-0222

PRODUCT: True Access

PLATFORMS: Windows, Windows 95, and Macintosh

POSITION: Blythe is a relative newcomer in the query tool business. One interesting feature of the product is a notion of a "SmartVar," which is a named variable that can have a default value, as well as values for individual end users.

Brio Technology, Inc. (BrioQuery)
444 Castro St., Ste. 700
Mountain View, CA 94041
(800) 486-2746

PRODUCT: BrioQuery, DataPrism, DataPivot

PLATFORMS: Windows, Windows 95, and Macintosh

POSITION: BrioQuery is a full-package, end-user query tool. It is the combination of three modules for querying, reporting, and analysis. Brio also sells the components: DataPrism and DataPivot. DataPrism is the reporting module and DataPivot adds reporting and analysis tools. BrioQuery is sold in three configurations: Designer, Navigator, and Explorer. BrioQuery Designer allows developers and IS groups to create queries and data models. BrioQuery Navigator allows users to build queries from data models that are prebuilt (where access control and ease of use are critical). BrioQuery Explorer provides a direct way to access tables and views without the data models that the other two products require.

Brio positions itself as designed for access to data warehouses. BrioQuery could be classed as a general query tool or a more specialized EIS system for decision support.

Business Objects, Inc. (BusinessObjects)
20813 Stevens Creek Blvd., Ste. 100
Cupertino, CA 95014
(408) 973-9300

PRODUCT: BusinessObjects

PLATFORMS: Windows, Windows 95, Macintosh, UNIX

POSITION: BusinessObjects is a decision-support tool for client/server environments. BusinessObjects has a query and reporting tool and gives MIS departments in corporate America centralized control. BusinessObjects is sold as server components, the key ones being the User Module and the Manager Module. BusinessAnalyzer is an additional component that allows multidimensional reporting, which is important in decision support.

Centura Software Corp. (Quest)
1060 Marsh Rd.
Menlo Park, CA 94025
(800) 584-8782; (415) 321-9500

PRODUCT: Quest and Quest Reporter

PLATFORMS: Windows, Windows 95

POSITION: Centura Software provides two query tool configurations: Quest and Quest Reporter. Quest is targeted at data administrators and users who require access to database system catalog information as well as the ability to alter tables and views. Quest Reporter is a read-only version of Quest for end users. Both Quest and Quest Reporter provide query, reporting, graphing, and forms generation to the end user. Quest (which has been used in this book) adds views of systems catalogs, direct access to altering database tables, and the ability to directly enter SQL. Centura Software bundles its query and reporting tools with SQLBase.

Cognos Corp. (Impromptu)
67 S. Bedford St., Ste. 200 W.
Burlington, MA 01803-5164
(800) 4-COGNOS; (800) 267-2777

PRODUCT: Impromptu

PLATFORMS: Windows, Windows 95

POSITION: Impromptu 2.0 is Cognos Corporation's second release of their end-user reporting tool for Windows. Two editions of the product are available directly from Cognos: the Administrator Edition and the Enterprise Edition. Impromptu adopts a DBA end-user approach to data access. The Impromptu Administrator Edition allows the DBA to build "catalogs" of database tables that simplify data access by mimicking business models and relationships. The catalogs don't replace the database tables but instead store the information about the tables. Similar in design to database views, columns from different tables can be defined as a single catalog, with the table joins determined by the administrator. The administrator can also prebuild reports to run against these catalogs. The Enterprise Edition of Impromptu (the end-user version) then lets end users access these catalogs and reports to retrieve data or build custom reports.

Computer Associates International, Inc. (CA -Visual Express)
One Computer Associates Plaza
Islandia, NY 11788-7000
(800) CALL-CAI; (516) 342-5224

PRODUCT: CA-Visual Express

PLATFORMS: Windows, Windows 95

POSITION: CA-Visual Express comes bundled with a relational engine to act as a repository. It offers both query and reporting capability. Servers are available for access to mainframe nonrelational data sources, like IMS and VSAM. While most query tools offer some sort of ODBC support, CA-Visual Express comes bundled with over 20 ODBC drivers.

Information Builders, Inc. (Business Intelligence Suite)
1250 Broadway, 30th Fl.
New York, NY 10001-3782
(800) 969-INFO; (212) 736-4433

PRODUCT: Business Intelligence Suite works with Focus Reporter for Windows products

PLATFORMS: Windows, Windows 95

POSITION: The Business Intelligence Suite is a set of three add-on modules to Information Builders report-generation tool, Focus for Windows. WinViz is a module for a multidimensional visualizer of data. GUI Statistics is a module that provides statistical operations on results. Power Import/ Export is a data exchange mechanism to move data between Focus, the modules, and other PC applications.

IntelligenceWare, Inc. (Iconic Query)
55933 W. Century Blvd., Ste. 900
Los Angeles, CA 90045
(800) 888-2996; (310) 216-6177

PRODUCT: Iconic Query

PLATFORMS: Windows, Windows 95

POSITION: Iconic Query presents a user interface to querying different from that of other competing products. Users work in a drag-and-drop, icon-oriented interface. Pop-up interfaces are used to select values and conditions to query on. There is an ability to perform natural language queries. The tool comes with report utilities as well as SQL Editor, a tool for saving and entering SQL calls. Iconic Query supports standard SQL databases and also has a stand-alone version that talks to dBASE and Paradox.

Intersolv, Inc. (Q+E)
53200 Tower Oaks Blvd.
Rockville, MD 20852
(800) 547-4000; (301) 230-3200

PRODUCT: Q+E

PLATFORMS: Windows, Windows 95

POSITION: Intersolv's Q+E query tool gained popularity as the query tool that was bundled with Microsoft Excel (now replaced by MS Query). With Q+E's leadership in the ODBC driver business, Q+E boasts over 30 ODBC drivers to back-end databases. Q+E has added chart building, reporting, forms generation, scripting capability, a query edit window that opens to an SQL text window, and analysis and presentation tools for reports.

IQ Software Corp. (IQ, IQ Access)
3295 River Exchange Dr., Ste. 550
Norcross, GA 30092-9909
(800) 458-0386; (404) 446-8880

PRODUCT: IQ and IQ access

PLATFORMS: Windows, Windows 95, and UNIX platforms

POSITION: IQ sells two products: IQ and IQ Access. IQ is an end-user query tool with reporting capability. IQ Access is a data access and reformatting tool used for data transfer. A user wanting to move data into desktop packages like Lotus 1-2-3, Excel, Microsoft Word, dBASE, or other such tools could use IQ Access. IQ has designed their tool to work with both relational and nonrelational databases. Some of their main features are the WYSIWYG interface to reporting, which provides extensible formatting capability, native connectivity to databases for performance, and support for over 25 databases.

Microsoft Corp. (Access and MSQuery)
One Microsoft Way
Redmond, WA 98052
(206) 882-8080

PRODUCT: Microsoft Access and MSQuery

PLATFORMS: Windows, Windows 95

POSITION: While Microsoft Access and MSQuery have been geared for the single-user Windows environment, they have added features to connect to the relational back ends, including a Microsoft "Wizard" to transfer Access data to a Microsoft SQL Server RDBMS. MSQuery is the end user query portion of Access. Access has a database engine, referred to as the Jet engine. Access's Jet engine was not originally designed to be an SQL-based relational engine, but ODBC support provides an SQL front end.

Oracle Corp. (Oracle Data Query, Oracle Forms, and Oracle Reports)
500 Oracle Parkway
Redwood Shores, CA 94065
(415) 506-7000

PRODUCTS: Oracle Data Query, Oracle Forms, and Oracle Reports

PLATFORMS: MS-DOS, Windows, Windows 95, OS/2, Macintosh, most UNIX versions, and VAX/VMS

POSITION: Oracle's Data Query, Forms, and Reports products, like Oracle's RDBMS, run on many platforms. Because of Oracle's position in enterprise-level computing, they pay attention to the issues of control and ability to maintain database security and to restrict query capability that may affect overall network performance. Oracle offers WYSIWYG reporting and forms generation as well as both a graphical and a character mode interface to querying. Oracle's tools have many performance-enhancing characteristics, especially when going to an Oracle back-end RDBMS.

Powersoft Corp. — Subsidiary of Sybase (PowerViewer, PowerMaker)
561 Virginia Rd.
Concord, MA 01742
(508) 287-1500

PRODUCT: PowerMaker, and PowerViewer

PLATFORMS: Windows, Windows NT

POSITION: PowerViewer is marketed as Powersoft/Sybase's personal query, reporting, and graphing tool. This product is bundled with ODBC connectivity and comes with a runtime-only copy of the Watcom SQL database. The product was introduced in August, 1993.

PowerMaker is marketed as Sybase's personal multidatabase application development tool. In addition to the query, reporting, and graphing of PowerViewer, PowerMaker can build simple forms and offers some database manipulation functionality.

Software AG of North America, Inc. (Esperant)
11190 Sunrise Valley Dr
Reston, VA 22091
(703) 860-5050

PRODUCT: Esperant

PLATFORMS: Windows, Windows 95, and Macintosh

POSITION: This end-user and reporting tool offers the ability to access two RDBMS simultaneously. The ability to do heterogeneous joins is hard to do properly, and Esperant offers a good solution. Other features offered by Software AG include batching and scheduling reports and embedded graphs in reports.

Trinzic Corp. — Subsidiary of Platinum Technology (Forest & Trees)
101 University Ave
Palo Alto, CA 94301
(800) 952-8779

PRODUCT: Forest & Trees

PLATFORMS: Windows, Windows 95

POSITION: Forest & Trees connects to over 25 relational and nonrelational databases as well as to Microsoft Excel and Lotus 1-2-3. Forest & Trees offers query and reporting. Platinum Technologies, at the time of this writing, is in the process of acquiring Trinzic and integrating this technology with their own.

17.3   Checklist

Query tools are advancing rapidly. If this book were to compare all specific features of each query tool against every other, it would be out of date by the time of publication. Rather than take this approach, we discuss the specific features of a query tool and what should be evaluated if you are in the market for a good tool. The features are:

- Usability
- Querying
- Forms
- Graphing

- Reports
- Database management
- Connectivity
- Bells and whistles

17.3.1 Usability

Ease of installation, documentation, and support can easily outweigh increased functionality. Often the best, newest, greatest features are the same ones that are not documented and are the most confusing to use. Very few magazine articles on query tools emphasize documentation and support as much as they should.

Having said this, functionality varies greatly among the query tool vendors and should not be taken for granted. For example, Microsoft Access is one of the easiest query tools to install and one of the best documented; it is also more suited for stand-alone PCs than for client/server, SQL-based, networked solutions.

The following is a list of check-off items for usability:

- Installation and setup
- Support
- Documentation
- Inclusion of relational engine
- Security
- WYSIWYG

Installation and Setup

A query tool should be easy to set up. Initial installation is probably the easiest check-off item to gauge. The configurability of the query product, specifically for network solutions, is often the most complex item to evaluate. In client/server solutions, networking greatly affects performance of one product over another and should be weighed heavily.

Support

Every software vendor offers different levels of support. Support mechanisms can make a huge difference in usability. Many companies have forums through on-line services through the Internet, Prodigy®, CompuServe®, and other networks. These paths often are the most direct ways to reach developers.

Telephone support is another item to consider. It may be purchased at various levels. Often, consulting and classes are available, as well as computer-based training (CBT).

Documentation

Quality of the documentation often indicates the quality of the query tool. Tools that have been out in the market longer, and therefore are more stable, tend to be better documented. In some cases, there are books published on these tools.

Inclusion of Relational Engine

Products like Quest, PowerMaker, and Impromptu include an SQL-based relational engine. The ability to pull down remote data and work on it locally is of great value. If a tool does not include a database engine, you may need to purchase one. Plan on working from data that is always on a server or transfer the data to spreadsheet tools like Lotus 1-2-3 or Microsoft Excel. With laptops far more common today, disconnected computing is becoming more fashionable. The need for a local relational engine is becoming increasingly important.

Security

In a corporate setting, the ability to retain control over the system and provide safeguards from end users is a critical factor. Many of the tools mentioned offer end-user and administrator versions of their query tools.

WYSIWYG

WYSIWYG (what you see is what you get) computing generally means that an application has graphical interfaces to allow easy formatting and configuration of reports, graphs, and forms. Most tools today have added such functionality, but there are exceptions.

17.3.2 Query Features

Some companies, like Iconic Query and Natural Language, offer unique methods of building queries, but for the most part, queries have been built by means of graphical user interfaces. Specifically, vendors use menus, pop-up dialog boxes, list boxes, and drag-and-drop capability to build queries. In evaluating such tools, the questions to answer are: How easy are these queries to build? How much functionality do they provide? For GUI-driven query builders, the following are some of the most important criteria for answering these questions:

- Point-and-click selection of columns in a table
- Building tables and joining them graphically
- Intuitive query conditions builder
- Automatic generation of criteria values
- Visual display of outer joins
- Scroll capability for viewing retrieved, multipaged data
- Automatic fetching after query is defined
- Ability to cancel query fetching
- Query estimator to estimate number of rows to be retrieved
- Ability to build templates for queries
- Ability to interactively enter SQL statements
- Ability to create and save SQL scripts for reuse
- Formula editor and native back-end functions

Point-and-Click Selection for Columns in a Table

Is it easy to build queries? The goal in providing end users access to data is to deliver a simple way for these users to retrieve the data they need from corporate databases. A significant amount of training or learning should not be necessary. A suitable end-user data retrieval tool should do everything it can to make data access as simple as possible.

Building Tables and Joining Them Graphically

Novice users may not understand database table joins. A query tool should simplify the necessary actions for a join by automatically linking multitable queries. You should not have to manually specify the links. A query tool should have the ability to look up the foreign key/primary key relationship or search for common column names to determine the links. A query tool should also be able to store predefined table joins. Each time tables are selected for data retrieval, a query tool could use the defined links.

Intuitive Query Conditions Builder

Building queries should be simplified by allowing a user to point and click on tables and columns. An end user should not have to learn SQL or database architecture to obtain the needed data. Another feature of a good query tool is the ability to interactively build ranges and sets for query conditions. This feature involves graphically building conditions based on SQL operator statements.

Automatic Generation of Criteria Values

The ability to look up values in a database to build query conditions can be a very valuable feature for a query tool. For example, a user who wants to retrieve all the sales invoices for royal-blue cotton shirts may not know whether this color is not a value that the back-end database records; the database may not distinguish shades of blue. This confusion arises when a query tool does not generate a list of these values for users to pick from. As a result, the user must first run a separate query to determine valid shirt colors, pick the wanted color, then start the query. This added work makes a seemingly trivial query more involved than it should be and reduces the user's productivity by making him perform additional tasks. The user should simply select the color royal blue from a list of values retrieved from the database. He does not have to run a preliminary query to determine what data he should retrieve. In the end, he does less work to get the same information.

Visual Display of Outer Joins

When joining tables, a query tool should graphically show the links between the tables. Microsoft Access has one of the better interfaces for this. Without the heuristic diagram, links, like outer joins, can get very complex.

Scroll Capability for Viewing Retrieved, Multipaged Data

Scrolling result sets, while fundamentally simple to understand, is a capability that is not always provided by query tools, or it is provided inefficiently. For tools where data can be updated, the ability to modify a row, scroll past the row and off the page, and then scroll back to the correctly modified row is an advanced functionality that not all query tools support.

Automatic Fetching After Query Is Defined

Query tools often have an Auto Execute feature, which allows you to execute a query immediately after a change is made. While this is useful, you should be able to disable it and explicitly execute a query only when you manually issue an execute command.

Ability to Cancel Query Fetching

You should be able to halt a running query at any time by clicking on the STOP button. Long-running queries can be terminated should you decide to change the query criteria or find out that the query is incorrect and is retrieving too many rows. Once again, excessive data fetching from the database is prevented.

Query Estimator to Estimate Number Of Rows to Be Retrieved

Before executing your query, the unique query estimator shows you the number of rows that will potentially be returned. It also warns you if an incorrect join will return all the rows in the tables (a Cartesian join). With this information, you can make changes to your query before reexecuting it. The database will not be brought to a grinding halt because an unspecific query fetched thousands of rows.

Ability to Build Templates for Queries

A query tool should provide the ability to build query templates that contain the necessary tables, table links, columns, and sort orders, then distribute it to other users. This frees those users from the tasks of having to define a query from the ground up. Novice users can use the templates as defined or change the selection criteria in one easy step to personalize the query.

Ability to Interactively Enter SQL Statements

The SQL Activity window in Quest, which we have used throughout this book, is an example of a window within a query tool that allows you to directly type in SQL statements. If a tool shows the SQL statements you graphically build, it is also possible to cut and past SQL statements into such an activity. For quick-and-dirty results, this type of functionality is useful.

Create and Save SQL Scripts for Reuse

The exercises in this book were based on Quest's ability to save an SQL script to be executed at a later time. SQL scripts, reports, queries, forms, and graphs should all be reusable.

Formula Editor and Back-End Database Functions

A formula editor is an editor that allows you to perform summations and other useful analytical functions against your result data.

With many query tools, users who are familiar with their Oracle or Sybase functions must relearn the equivalents for the query tool they are using, a time-consuming process. Tools like Quest have built-in functions (70+ for Quest) that range from string and date manipulation to financial (present value, amortization) and scientific (sine, logarithms) as well as the ability to see the functions of the database they are connected to. A formula editor should incorporate all native functions of the server database to maximize the data manipulation capabilities that are available.

17.3.3 Forms

Not all query tools have form-creation capability. In the case of a tool like Oracle Forms, forms capability is offered as an add-on product. This is clearly an area where the end users decide if forms are necessary. For example, an order entry administrator prefers to view invoice data in a display that resembles a paper invoice. This user wants related data tables displayed together in one form for easy inspection and navigation. A familiar screen reduces the learning curve, making him or her more productive. Here are some criteria to look at when evaluating forms:

- Creation of simple table forms
- Creation of multiple table forms
- Ability to use check boxes, radio buttons, list boxes
- Creation of bitmaps
- Creation of multiline text fields
- Graphical definition of table relationships
- Creation of data lookup fields
- Integration with e-mail

Creation of Simple Table Forms

A form generator should create displays that resemble paper forms. Data should be easily retrievable from the form. You should simply enter the data you are searching for directly onto the display to retrieve it. No step-by-step manual query building should be necessary.

Creation of Multiple Table Forms

A forms tool should allow master-detail relationships among tables. For example, if a user has a table with a column called *customer number*, and another detail table listing all the items that customer has ordered (where the second table is dependent on the customer number column), this is a master-detail relationship. A form should be able to define such a relationship and display it on the screen.

Ability to Use Check Boxes, Radio Buttons, List Boxes

A form should have display capability that includes check boxes, radio buttons, and list boxes. Users can quickly come up to speed and be more productive.

Creation of Bitmaps

Bitmaps on a form provide a more professional look as well as provide a more intuitive look. A form should allow you to import bitmaps.

Creation of Multiline Text Fields

Forms usually need data fields for multiline text to provide the end user a way to add documentation. Multiline text fields provide this mechanism.

Graphical Definition of Table Relationships

When building a form, display table relationships graphically for a more intuitive forms building process.

Creation of Data Lookup Fields

A forms tool should allow your users the ability to enter and modify database information. For example, forms for order entry systems should allow users to enter new orders or change existing ones.

Integration with E-mail

Forms, as a "paperless" alternative, are conveniently sent via electronic mail systems. A forms-based tool should be integrated with e-mail for expediency.

17.3.4 Graphing Capability

A graph can dramatically cut down the complexity of understanding data by presenting it in a more obvious format. Below are some criteria for looking at graphing capability:

- Creation of pie, bar, line, area, and log-line graphics
- Graphing multidimensional data
- Ability to save graphs in file for reuse
- Ability to link graphs to existing queries
- Advanced charting options

Creation of Pie, Bar, Line, Area, and Log-line Graphics

A graphing tool should be able to present your data as bar, line or pie charts, in 2-D and 3-D.

Graphing Multidimensional Data

More advanced query tools, especially EIS tools discussed later, offer graphing of more than two dimensions of data. Data is represented in a *multidimensional* manner.

Ability to Save Graphs in File for Reuse

After you define a graph, a graphing tool should allow you to save it as a template and reuse it later to display the same or different sets of data. You should not have to redefine the graph types, options, or colors for each piece of data you chart.

Ability to Link Graphs to Existing Queries

After building a query, you should be able to look at that data as colorful and informative graphs with one click of the mouse. Just click on the Graph button to create a graph from your query data.

Advanced Charting Options

A graphing tool should allow a user to alter a variety of graphing options. For example, a user may want to change a color from a palette of colors to customize the graph. Also, a user may want to enter titles and axis headings to identify the different pieces of information displayed. A user may want to augment a graph with average value, minimum/maximum or best fit linear regression lines for quick inspection of data trends.

17.3.5 Reports

Chapter 18 discusses reports in more detail. Most query tools today offer some form of reporting. Here are some criteria for report generation:

- Quick default reports
- Inclusion of images in reports
- Inclusion of graphs in reports
- Creation of two-pass reports
- Drill-down ability
- Creation of matrix/cross-tab reports
- Creation of reports for reuse

- Ability to link reports to different data sets
- Providing template reports: mail, form, cross-tab
- Formula editor capabilities
- Scripting capability

17.3.6 Database Management Features

Query tool vendors often provide separate tools for end users and for administrators of multiuser database systems. Database administrators may require different functionality than do end users and may be worried about different things. For example, a database administrator may wish to change a system catalog for a database; he may never want an end user to do this, for obvious reasons. Here is a list of database management features:

- Optimization for network traffic
- Ability to view system tables
- Management of tables, views, and indexes
- Mass updates on table data
- Ability to copy existing column definitions to create a new table
- Modification of existing views
- Ability to limit / give read-only privileges and to limit access to certain activities
- Controls to set the maximum number of rows retrieved

Optimization for Network Traffic

Network and database performance are always key concerns for the database manager. Users want to access their data quickly, and database managers constantly need to tune their database systems to provide extra speed. A simple solution to enhancing data access performance, especially across remote databases, is to reduce the amount of network traffic. In processing a typical query, a data access tool needs information from the database system catalogs about the data it is to retrieve. This information is sent back and forth across the network before the query is even started. Network traffic is increased, and the query takes longer to complete. A data access tool that is enterprise-friendly should be able to reduce the amount of network traffic needed to prepare a query, consequently enhancing system performance.

Some query tools provide catalog cache, that is, a copy of the remote database's system catalogs is saved on the user's local hard drive. Since this information is stored locally, there is no need to access the remote database across the network; the extraneous network activity required to prepare a query is removed. The catalog cache significantly reduces performance bottlenecks by regulating the amount of network traffic that is required to complete a query process.

Ability to View System Tables

System tables are tables defined by the database vendor. Access to these tables is needed for administrators and some database developers, whereas end users would rather not see them. Query tools should give you different configurations so that you can view or not view these tables, depending on your need.

Management of Tables, Views, and Indexes

Managing database tables, views, and indexes should be automated, using an easy point-and-click interface. A database manager may or may not want an end user to create, modify, and drop table definitions, or to create and drop new views and indexes. Having a local database can ease the burdens of an administrator by allowing end users some privileges while not causing major changes to a production database. To maintain database security, the granting of the ability to modify tables only on local databases should be available. This leaves the corporate databases free from unwanted modifications.

Mass Updates on Table Data

The ability to perform mass updates on data allows an end user to change many rows of information at one time. Using a table search-and-replace feature to modify an entire set of rows in a single action, without having to make changes to each row individually, is a great benefit to an administrator. For an end user, this ability can be undesirable. Query tool vendors often have two different versions of their tool, and this functionality is best kept as an administrative function.

Ability to Copy Existing Column Definitions to Create a New Table

A graphical interface that allows a user to create a new table based on the column definitions of existing tables saves time when performing schema changes and data merges between two database tables.

Modification of Existing Views

System administrators often wish to modify existing views to gain performance or because a data schema has changed. A graphical interface for this task greatly simplifies the process.

Ability to Limit / Give Read-Only Privileges or to Limit Access

Restriction of users to read data but not write data to the database is critical to many multiuser environments. Not every user should be allowed to edit data in the corporate database. In many circumstances, administrators do not want to allow querying, reporting, and charting activities. These activities allow changes to data, so restricting access ensures that users do not inadvertently delete potentially sensitive and important information.

Controls to Set the Maximum Number of Rows Retrieved

A administrator should be able to restrict the maximum number of rows that can be retrieved by a user. For example, a query that fetches more than a limit of 7,000 rows will be terminated once the 7,000th row is retrieved.

17.3.7 Connectivity

Connectivity from a query tool to an RDBMS can be a complex issue, especially if you are connecting to a mainframe database. To achieve highest performance, native connectivity links are preferred. For example, Oracle supports an OCI-level call interface to their database. If a query tool supports a native OCI link to Oracle, the query tool is likely to have better performance. All query tools listed here support some form of ODBC support as well as native connectivity. Criteria for looking at connectivity are:

- Native connectivity support to relational databases
- Level of ODBC support
- ODBC vendors supported
- Access to Xbase databases and spreadsheets
- Extras to connect to a desired platform
- OLE support
- E-mail enabled

Native Connectivity Support to Relational Databases

Most query tools will tout native connectivity to leading database vendors such as Oracle, Informix OnLine, Sybase SQL Server, Microsoft SQL

Server, IBM DB2, and CA-Ingres. There are a host of others that they may or may not support natively.

Level of ODBC Support

As discussed in Chapter 15, there are several levels of ODBC support: core, Level 1, and Level 2 — with extensions likely to follow. There are also three grammar levels that are supported with ODBC. So, to say all ODBC is created equal is an exaggeration, at the least. An end user must also find out what databases a query tool supports through ODBC.

ODBC Vendors Supported

Many vendors provide support for ODBC, including Microsoft, Intersolv, Visigenics, and database vendors like Oracle and Informix, who also offer native connectivity. ODBC vendors were discussed in Chapter 15, but there are likely to be a great number of other vendors in the future. Query tools are likely to be certified with a wide variety of ODBC vendors.

Access to Xbase Databases and Spreadsheets

With ODBC support, you can fetch data from both PC and SQL databases. This gives you a wide range of databases from which you can store and retrieve data — Access, dBASE, Paradox, Btrieve, FoxPro, and others. Most query tool vendors have access solutions to spreadsheets to transfer data to and from them. For instance, Lotus 1-2-3 (or IBM 1-2-3) offers an ODBC solution.

Extras Required to Connect to Desired Platform

Unless you connect to a local database with a query tool, there is more software involved and, depending on the back-end platform, it can get complex. For example, if you are connecting to an IBM mainframe with DB2, then you may need a gateway product, as well as networking hardware and software, to get there.

OLE Support

Object Linking and Embedding will continue to grow in popularity as solutions using this technology spread, as they likely will. While its use has been more a check-off item in the past, it will become a pervasive technology. For example, Object Linking and Embedding provides a mechanism to directly connect with many personal programs, like an OLE-enabled Excel spreadsheet (or other OLE-enabled application). Every time the data changes in the database, the information in your spreadsheet is automatically updated to reflect those changes. You always have up-to-date data.

E-mail Enabled

Having built-in e-mail enabling, allows a user to send queries and reports from within your query tool. A query tool should allow a user to bring up the e-mail interface from within, type comments, and send off a report to others who need it. There are several different protocols for e-mail, including MAPI, VIM, and MHS. MAPI is from Microsoft, VIM is from Lotus, and MHS is Novell's version.

17.3.8 Bells and Whistles

Every query tool vendor will tout a few features that are unique. They are the first you are likely to hear about from the vendor. Here are a few of the more interesting ones the author has noted:

- Scripting language
- Componentizing (C++ and OLE)
- Multidimensional data access

Scripting Language

Some tools providers offer scripting languages for embedding their query and reporting functionality for use with application and development. The real question with these languages is how robust they are and whether there is another alternative to them that may be easier. For example, if OLE objects are available to embed in an application, is a scripting language necessary?

Componentizing (OLE)

Many vendors are offering OLE components. For example, Microsoft Word is an OCX, which means it can be contained within what are known as OLE containers. OLE components are going to become plug-and-play enabled for application development as Windows 95 matures and Microsoft stabilizes the technology. Generic end-user query tools may well be replaced by customizable components.

Multidimensional Data Access

Many query tools are touting multidimensional features to claim their rightful place in the EIS and DSS marketplace.

17.3.9 Caveats: Things to Watch Out For

- Heterogeneous joins
- Performance issues
- Overcomplexity
- Ad hoc query

Heterogeneous Joins

The ability to join tables from different data sources, e.g., data between Oracle and Sybase database servers, is irresistible to some users; however, heterogeneous joins are problematic. Microsoft Access supports heterogeneous joins, but the manner in which they do it can become unmanageable for larger systems. In the case of Access, tables are joined by downloading the results of different tables to your PC. For client/server systems where tables routinely exceed 10,000 rows, the performance of such an operation can be paralyzingly slow.

If heterogeneous joins are a capability you wish to explore, understand how the process is being done; only a few vendors today offer a solution with reasonable performance for medium-to-large systems.

Performance Issues

A query tool should protect against an end user killing system performance. Some of the features mentioned to combat this were a query estimator, query limiter, and query stop features. With the query estimator, users determine the number of rows their query will retrieve before execution. A query limiter can limit the amount of rows a user can query for, and a query stop feature can halt a query that is slowing down a system.

Overcomplexity

The query process should be simple. Templates should exist for helping create new queries, reports, or graphs. With the state of the market today, if a solution is complex, a user may decide to look elsewhere.

Ad Hoc Query

No one wants to wait around for a download of hundreds of thousands of records. A user who requires additional data from tables other than the ones he or she downloaded (which may be quite often in an ad hoc query session) is out of luck. The best method to enhance performance is not to download all the data locally; it is better to enhance the retrieval mechanisms involved.

Even running "simple" queries can be damaging to the corporate network. Someone may create a query that accidentally fetches every single row in a 200,000 row table. A large query causes network bottlenecks and can possibly bring the database to a halt. An enterprise-conscious data access tool will provide the necessary features to prevent this situation from occurring.

17.4   EIS Systems

Query tools are used for decision support. Most query tools will position themselves for use in marketing, sales, and business analysis; however, several query products distinguish themselves as catering to more specialized analytical processing. They offer enhanced functionality and provide information or links to information that generic tools do not. These tools are commonly referred to as *Executive Information Systems*, or *EIS*. Another trait of EIS systems is that they will often be positioned as working not only with RDBMS but with specialized databases, either *multidimensional* databases (discussed below) or data warehouses (discussed in Chapter 18).

Many of the query tools already mentioned position their products as EIS systems. In fact, the distinguishing features between general tools and more specialized tools are starting to gray. The differentiating factor of the EIS vendors listed below is that their query tools are marketed specifically for the EIS market. Two examples of EIS companies are Comshare and IRI, which was acquired by Oracle. Comshare not only offers EIS query and reporting tools, but offers "agents," which they call Commander OLAP applications. These agents have connections to information from such companies as Dow Jones and Reuters (for analysis in the financial industry). IRI not only offers EIS query and reporting but, more specifically, is in the business of buying and selling information from retail business for use in business analysis.

Both IRI and Comshare use SQL and relational databases. Interestingly, they also both offer their own multidimensional databases for enhanced functionality.

Understanding the Multidimensional Model

While relational databases today are based on two-dimensional models, the SQL language is used with the multidimensional data model for the simple reason that larger amounts of data are stored in relational databases. While both relational and multidimensional data models support data analysis as well as the design and maintenance of analytical code, relational models have taken considerably greater effort to accomplish specific decision support solutions (DSS).

Figure 17-1 illustrates a representation of a multidimensional model, which can be represented by a cube.

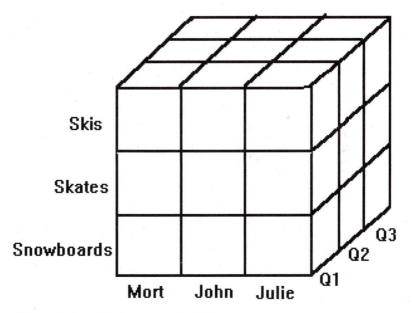

Figure 17-1   *Multidimensional Model*

The three accesses of this cube represent sales reps (Mort, John, and Julie), quarters (Q1, Q2, and Q3), and total sales for products (skis, skates, and snowboards).

Multidimensional databases associate a set of similar information as *dimensions.* For example, the sales reps Mort, John, and Julie can be thought of as a sales force dimension. The product totals of skis, skates, and snowboards can be thought of as a product sales dimension.

In Figure 17-1, the cube is easy to diagram. If we add another dimension, for example, a Sales Quotas dimension, which tracks expected sales as opposed to actual sales total, this model is harder to visualize. Multidimensional databases structure data with many dimensions so that the relationships between them can be easily viewed. *The biggest advantage to this data model is that join operations are easy to perform,* whereas in a straight relational model, the join operations get very complex as more dimensions are added.

Drill-down Capability

EIS systems frequently discuss the ability to *drill-down*, which can be defined as the ability to break down aggregate to more specific segmented data. For example, if a report shows the total sales of a company ($20 million), you may want to drill-down that data and find out what each sales region contributed to total sales (let us say, $6 million from the Southern Region, $4 million in the Eastern Region, $7 million in the Central Region, and $3 million in the Western Region). You may then want to drill-down and find out what each account in each region contributed to the total sales. You could drill-down even further in the data hierarchy.

EIS Players

All products are trademarks or registered trademarks of their respective companies.

Andyne Computing, Ltd (Pablo)

552 Princess St., 2nd
Fl. Kingston, ON, CD K7L 1C7
(800) 267-0665

PRODUCT: Pablo

PLATFORMS: Macintosh client

POSITION: Andyne's Pablo is a data access and reporting tool for multidimensional data. Andyne's architecture defines a HyperCube, which is a multidimensional structure that can be maintained in relational databases, providing drill-down and object-based information analysis. Included with Pablo is a Data Navigator, which can perform "information pivoting." Andyne supports most major RDBMS as back-end servers, including Informix, Oracle, Sybase, CA-Ingres, DB2, Tandem, and Teradata.

Business Objects, Inc. (BusinessObjects)
20183 Stevens Creek Blvd., Suite 100
Cupertino, CA 95014
(408) 973-9300

PRODUCT: BusinessObjects

PLATFORMS: Windows, Windows 95, Macintosh, and UNIX

POSITION: BusinessObjects straddles the fence between a general query tool and an EIS system. At the heart of this product is the ability to transfer knowledge of a relational database structure into objects or "Universes." Objects are defined by means of a GUI-based interface. These objects allow a user to create a central repository of "query objects," which can solve the same problems a multidimensional approach could. BusinessObjects has query, report, and graphing components as well as a BusinessAnalyzer for multidimensional analysis.

BusinessObjects supports access to Oracle, Sybase, DB2, Informix, Teradata, CA-Ingres, Red Brick, and DEC RDB, as well as ODBC access to AS/400, SQLBase, and others.

Cognos Corp. (PowerPlay)
67 S Bedford St., Ste 200W
Burlington, MA 01803
(617) 229-6600

PRODUCT: PowerPlay, PowerPlay Multidimensional Server

PLATFORMS: Windows for PowerPlay, DEC VAX, UNIX platforms including IBM AIX and HP-UX for PowerPlay Multidimensional Server

POSITION: While Cognos positions Impromptu as a generic query and reporting tool, PowerPlay is positioned as an EIS or DSS solution. PowerPlay includes sample solutions and data from applications centering around specific corporate analysis; for example, sales analysis, quality-control analysis, and marketing and demographic analysis. The components of this product include Explorer, Reporter, Portfolio, and Transformer.

Explorer and Reporter offer the query and reporting functionality. Portfolio is used for gathering and presenting collections of reports. Transformer handles the translation from two-dimensional data files to a multidimensional model, including data compression capability, special indexing for drill-down, and an easy GUI interface.

PowerPlay directly accesses Oracle and Sybase SQL Server and has a wide range of ODBC drivers. Access to dBASE, Paradox, FoxPro, Excel, and Lotus 1-2-3 is also provided.

Comshare, Inc. (Commander EIS)
3001 S State St., P.O. Box 1588
Ann Arbor, MI 48108
(800) 922-7979

PRODUCT: Commander EIS

PLATFORMS: Windows, Windows 95, OS/2, Macintosh, IBM MVS and VM systems, DEC VAX platforms

POSITION: Commander EIS provides query and reporting as well as a link to critical business information to aid decision support. Connections to SQL data sources, including DB2 and SQL/DS, are provided as is access to electronic news and competitive information. Comshare offers many packages to provide decision support in such areas as financial reporting, budgeting, profit management, and total quality analysis. Comshare also offers a multidimensional database called Commander Prism.

Information Advantage, Inc. (IA Decision Support Suite)
12900 Whitewater Drive, Suite 100
Minnetonka, MN 55343
(612) 938-7015

PRODUCT: IA Decision Support Suite includes IA Report, IA Analysis, IA Forecast, and IA Budget

PLATFORMS: Windows front-end; object library and decision support modules run on HP/UX, IBM AIX, Sun Solaris

POSITION: IA supports a high-end object library with DSS modules, which resides on an application server linked to a data warehouse. Data warehouses are supported by vendors like IBM, Informix, Oracle, and Red Brick Systems. IA has a modular approach to their software suite, with a Windows front end. IA Report is a reporting and monitoring package. IA Analysis is a query and data access module for historical data. IA Forecast is used for developing statistical analysis and forecasts on businesses. IA Budget is used for devising consistent budgets throughout a corporate business.

IRI Software, a Division of Oracle (Express EIS)
200 5th Ave
Waltham, MA 02154
(617) 890-1100

PRODUCT: Express EIS

PLATFORMS: Windows, Windows 95, DOS, Sun Solaris, IBM AIX, HP-UX

POSITION: Express EIS is the business intelligence system for drill-down data analysis and reporting. IRI sells a pcExpress multidimensional database to facilitate their decision support tools. They also offer add-on applications for financial planning and analysis, as well as marketing, sales, and business analysis for market-specific areas of consumer retail and financial services sectors.

Pilot Software, Inc., a Division of Dun and Bradstreet (Lightship)
1 Canal Park
Cambridge, MA 02141
(617) 374-9400

PRODUCT: Lightship, Command Center

PLATFORMS: Lightship runs on Windows; Command Center runs on IBM platforms, Sun Solaris, HP-UX, SCO UNIX, DEC VAX, DOS, and Macintosh

POSITION: Pilot Software was acquired by Dun and Bradstreet Corporation in 1994. Lightship is more than a EIS tool. It has a language, Lightship Basic language, with over 400 functions, for use in EIS systems or "business intelligence systems." Lightship is a query and reporting tool for business analysis: it includes such features as geographic mapping, object-oriented, drill-down approach to data analysis, and three-dimensional graphing. Through Lightship Link, Lightship allows links to SQL databases, including Oracle, Informix, Sybase, and SQLBase, among others.

Pilot's Commander software, with interfaces to Apple Macintosh and PCs, maintains EIS information for financial analysis, as well as business decision support solutions.

17.5   Exercises

Exercise 17.5.1: Creating a Query

1. Start Quest. Make sure that the database is connected to the GUPTA sample database. Click on **New** and then **Query.** Quest is displayed as shown below.

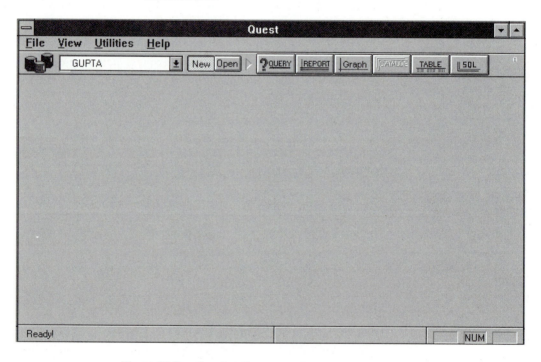

Figure 17-2   *Opening Quest*

2. The **Choose Tables/Views** window, as shown in Figure 17-3, is opened. Select the two tables: CUSTOMER_INVOICE and RETAIL_CUSTOMER. Click the **Summary** button on the form.

    The tables can be selected by the arrows in the middle of the dialog box.

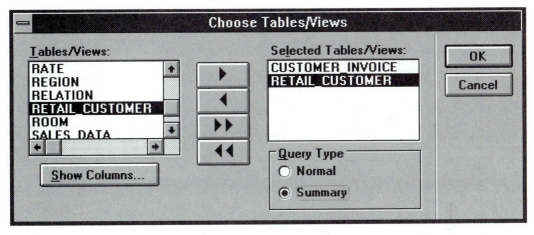

Figure 17-3 *Choose Tables/Views*

3. Click **OK**. The **Link Tables** dialog box shown below is displayed. No changes are necessary. Click **OK**.

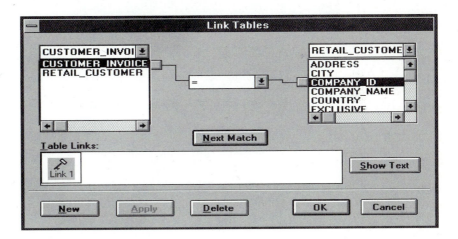

Figure 17-4 *Link Tables*

Build a Condition Statement

Quest can graphically build a condition statement. Figure 17-5 shows the condition, which, if built with SQL, would generate the clause,

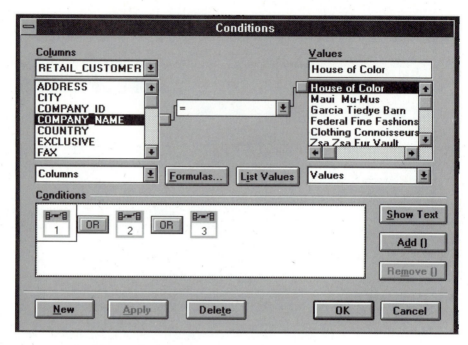

Figure 17-5   *Conditions*

where COMPANY_NAME="House of Color" OR
COMPANY_NAME="Federal Fine Fashions" OR
COMPANY_NAME="Gilligan Nautical"

To build the condition:

4. Choose the **Query** menu and select the **Conditions** option. You are prompted to select a table. Choose the RETAIL_CUSTOMER table. A set of three conditions will be built, based on the *Company_name* column.

5. For the first statement, select the column *Company_name*. Select = from the combo box. Select the value "House of Color." Click **Apply**.

6. Click on the **New** push button. A second condition is displayed. The two conditions are linked with an AND operator. Click on the AND operator; it will change to OR.

7. For the second statement, select the column *Company_name*. Select = from the combo box. Select the value "Federal Fine Fashions." Click **Apply**.

8. Click on the **New** push button. A third condition is displayed. The third condition is linked with an AND operator. Click on the AND operator; it will change to OR.

9. For the third statement, select the column *company_name*. Select = from the combo box. Select the value "Gilligan Nautical." Click **Apply.**

Figure 17-5 shows the conditions that have been built.

Choosing Columns

The query built so far shows all columns of a table. The following steps will limit the columns that will be returned.

10. Choose the **Query** menu again and select **Choose Columns**. From the RETAIL_CUSTOMER table (shown in upper left-hand pull-down list box), select the column COMPANY_NAME.

    From the CUSTOMER_INVOICE table (shown in the pull-down list box in Figure 17-6), choose the following columns: INVOICE_NO, INVOICE_DATE, INVOICE_TOTAL. Click **OK**.

    Figure 17-6 shows the results.

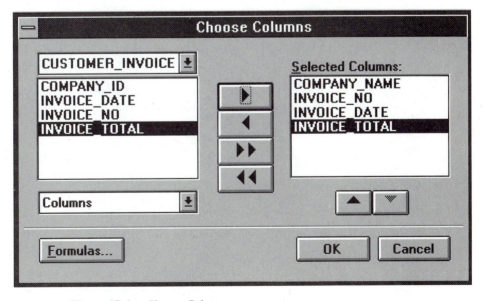

Figure 17-6 *Choose Columns*

Sorting the Result Set

11. Choose from the Query menu again and select the **Sort** option. Choose sort by the column *Company_name*. Click **OK**. Figure 17-7 shows the end results.

COMPANY_NAME	INVOICE_DATE	INVOICE_NO	INVOICE_TOTAL
Federal Fine Fashions	1/5/93	1	1,298.00
Federal Fine Fashions	2/22/93	4	845.25
Federal Fine Fashions	7/20/93	17	1,592.00
Federal Fine Fashions	8/2/93	19	3,820.70
Gilligan Nautical Duds	2/14/93	3	790.00
Gilligan Nautical Duds	6/22/93	16	1,511.25
Gilligan Nautical Duds	8/20/93	22	412.20
Gilligan Nautical Duds	12/7/93	32	694.75
House of Color	3/13/93	7	1,871.15
House of Color	5/3/93	11	645.25

Query - GUPTA:Query1

Figure 17-7 *Displaying the End Results*

12. Choose the Query menu again and select the **Show SQL** option. You should see the SQL statement that has been graphically built so far.

13. Save this file by pulling down the **File** menu and selecting **Save As.** Save the query as query1.qqt, as shown in Figure 17-8.

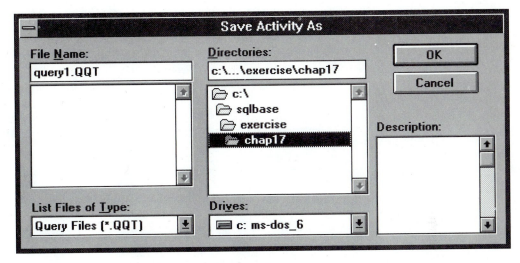

Figure 17-8 *Saving a Query File*

The query tools offer several features.

- The Query menu has an **Auto Execute OFF** option. Quest defaults to automatically run our queries once you select the tables. With the Auto Execute option switched on, Quest starts processing the query you are defining automatically. To manually execute a statement, choose the **Execute** option from the query menu.

- Since we chose the Summary option, as shown in Figure 17-2, we can define columns based on a formula editor. For example, we could create a column that is the sum of all invoices for each company.

- The **Auto Estimate** menu option shows the approximate size of a specific query.

Exercise 17.5.2: Creating a Graph

At this point, we simply want to demonstrate the graph activities.

1. If your query is not open, reopen it. Choose **OPEN** and then the **Query** button from the activity bar. Open the file query1.qqt, which we created in the first exercise. You can use the file, *query1.qqt*, if you have had any problems.

2. Click on the **NEW** button and then on the **Graph** button. You are asked if the graph is to link with query1.qqt. Click **OK**.

3. Pull down the Graph menu and select the **Label** option. From the Label Source, choose *Invoice_no*. From the Data Set, choose *Invoice_total*. Type in the title *Company/Invoice Percentage Chart.* (shown in Figure 17-9).

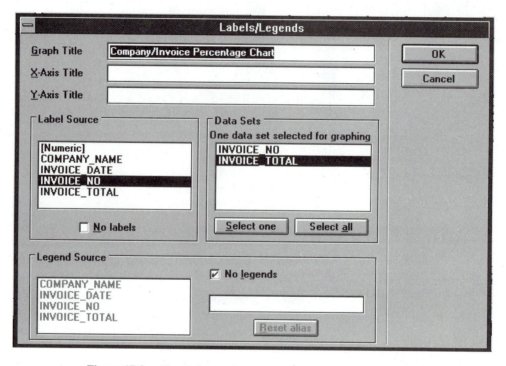

Figure 17-9 *Graph Setup*

4. Pull down the **Graph** menu and select the **Graph Type** option. Select the pie graph radio button. Figure 17-10 pictures a graph that shows what percent of total revenue each invoice has for the selected company.

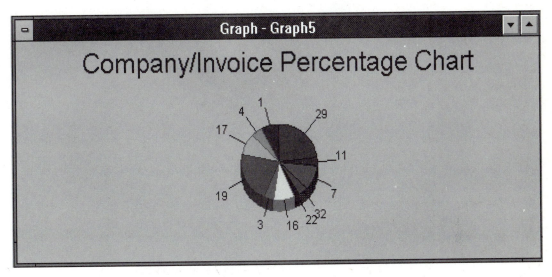

Figure 17-10 *Sample Graph*

5. From the activity bar, choose the **File** menu item and the **Close** option to close the graphing activity. To end the exercise and exit Quest, choose the **File** menu item and the **Exit** option.

17.6   Summary

This chapter showed the basic features of query tools, discussed some of the companies that provide these tools, and demonstrated very basic functionality with a hands-on exercise. The next chapter discusses reporting, which is a basic feature of most query tools, and is also sold by many companies in the form of a separate product. Chapter 18 complements Chapter 17.

18   Report Writers

Although query and report functionality of SQL databases is often integrated, as discussed Chapter 17, there are tools that specialize in report writing. This chapter discusses reporting in more detail than did Chapter 17. It also introduces popular report writers.

The chapter is organized as follows:

18.1   Report Writers

Most query tools marketed today offer report writing capabilities; however, buyers often find they can get extra power and functionality by buying best-of-breed components, similar to a buyer who mixes and matches stereo components. So, while report writers are bundled with query tools, other reporting options exist and sell well in the SQL market.

The report writers that specialize in report-only capabilities have done well in several specific areas, including the stand-alone PC report writing market, the report production server market, and component reporting for application development. Each of these three areas is discussed below.

18.1.1 Stand-alone PC Report Writers

Products, like ReportSmith™, Crystal Reports™, and R&R Report Writer™ are popular, easy-to-use report writers in the stand-alone PC market. Today, they have all added levels of SQL connectivity to their products. When connectivity to XBase products like Access, dBASE, Paradox, and also text files are necessary, these tools have a place in the SQL market. The main advantage these tools offer is ease of use for end users who want to develop quick reports from their own personal data.

18.1.2 Production Servers

Report writers like MITI's SQR Workbench™ and Information Builders' Focus Reporter™ offer another level of reporting by allowing cross-platform uniformity to report generation. Users may want to execute reports on a server where data is located rather than on a client machine. Sometimes this type of reporting capability is referred to as *batch* reporting. For complex reports that use large amounts of data, a server is more capable of executing and generating a report than is a PC. In examples like company payroll, a report generation process, which requires a production server, could take many hours to complete.

18.1.3 Component Reporting

With Microsoft's OLE 2.0 technology, vendors are now breaking their query and reporting functionality into *OLE controls*. With OLE and other object technology, it is possible to componentize report writers and run these objects on OLE servers. Report components are not only useful for application development, but they also allow reports to be pushed to back-end machines, such as a Windows NT server. For example, Microsoft's Access, Cognos's Impromptu, and Centura Software's Quest are all query tools that offer OLE componentry.

18.2   Report Generation Vendors

All products are trademarks or registered trademarks of their respective companies.

Borland International, Inc. (ReportSmith)
100 Borland Way
Scotts Valley, CA 95066-3249
(800) 233-2444; (408) 431-1000

PRODUCT: ReportSmith

PLATFORMS: Windows, Windows 95

POSITION: ReportSmith is a popular Windows reporting tool supporting such features as OLE 2.0 container support and compound reports, which can include charts, graphs, and integrated sound. ReportSmith offers four kinds of reports: columnar lists, cross-tabs, forms, and mailing labels. ReportSmith's WYSIWYG layout allows data to be dynamically updated as a report is changed. ReportSmith includes a macro language referred to as ReportBasic.

Connectivity includes native drivers to Oracle, MS SQL Server, Sybase SQL Server, SQLBase, CA-Ingres, DB2, and ODBC-compliant databases. PC database access includes dBASE, Access, FoxPro, Excel, and ASCII files.

Concentric Data Systems, Inc. (R&R Report Writer SQL Edition)
110 Turnpike Rd.
Westborough, MA 01581
(800) 325-9035; (508) 366-1122

PRODUCT: R&R Report Writer SQL Edition

PLATFORMS: Windows, Windows 95, DOS

POSITION: R & R Report Writer SQL Edition has five styles of reports: columnar, tabular, forms, letters, and mail tables. This report writer can join up to 100 tables or views in a report. One of its features includes over 90 functions to create calculated fields. For programmers, R & R works with Visual Basic and MS C++.

Connectivity includes 25 database formats with ODBC compliance. PC database access includes dBASE, Access, FoxPro, Excel, and ASCII files.

Crystal Computer Services, Inc. (subsidiary of Seagate Technology, Inc.) (Crystal Reports Professional)
1050 W. Pender St., Ste. 2200
Vancouver, BC, CD V6E 3S7
(800) 877-2340; (800) 663-1244

PRODUCT: Crystal Reports Professional

PLATFORMS: Windows, Windows 95

POSITION: Crystal Reports has been bundled with Visual Basic and dBASE, among other tools. Crystal Reports provides a development class library to help embed reports in development environments. Some of the features it offers include WYSIWYG interface, OLE 2.0 objects, and over 100 functions.

Connectivity includes 25 database formats with ODBC compliance. PC database access includes dBASE, Access, FoxPro, Excel, and ASCII files.

Information Builders, Inc. (Focus Reporter for Windows)
51250 Broadway
New York, NY 10001-3782
(212) 736-4433

PRODUCT: Focus Reporter for Windows

PLATFORMS: Windows, Windows 95; FOCUS Reporter applications are transportable to over 35 platforms, including DOS, OS/2, IBM mainframe, UNIX systems, DEC VMS

POSITION: Focus Reporter's cross-platform, uniform look for report generation is impressive. Information Builders makes use of its EDA/SQL middleware to offer over 35 databases with which to connect. Focus Reporter offers a WYSIWYG interface and over 50 charts and graphs to embed in their reports.

MITI (SQR Workbench)
2895 Temple Ave
Long Beach, CA 90806
(310) 424-4399

PRODUCT: SQR Workbench for Windows

PLATFORMS: DOS, Windows, Windows NT, OS/2, Sun Solaris, HP-UX, IBM AIX, most major UNIX systems, DEC VMS, IBM MVS

POSITION: SQR Workbench is more than an end-user query tool. SQR Workbench is made up of SQR, SQR Developers Kit, SQR Execute, and SQR Viewer. SQR is the report writer — a procedural 4GL for writing reports. SQR Developer's Kit is used for debugging. SQR Execute is used to deploy runtime versions for reporting. SQR Viewer is a report viewer. SQR Workbench has a 4GL- like interface that has SQL extensions. This allows production reports to be generated on server platforms. SQL works with most major development tools, including Visual Basic, SQL Windows, PowerBuilder, and Oracle Forms.

SQR Workbench is a multiplatform, production report writing system for corporate offices. Most major SQL database platforms are supported, including SQL Server, Oracle, Informix, DB2, RdB, CA-Ingres, and SQLBase. Reports can be done in a variety of styles including tabular, forms, letters, mailing labels, and master-detail reports. Reports can also include graphics, such as charts, graphs, signatures, and multimedia images.

18.3   Report Writer Checklist

Whether a report writer is part of the query tools mentioned in Chapter 17 or a stand-alone application, there are features that you should look for, such as:

- Ease of use and documentation
- Styles for reports
- Graphing and imaging capability
- Functionality
- Connectivity
- Bells and whistles

18.3.1 Ease of Use and Documentation

As with query tools, ease of installation, documentation, and support can easily outweigh increased functionality. Often the best, newest, greatest features are the same ones that are not documented and are the most confusing to use. The following is a list of criteria to evaluate ease of use and documentation. The list is similar to the checklist for a query tool.

- Ease of installation
- WYSIWYG
- Quick default reports
- Creation of reports for reuse
- Ability to link reports to different data sets
- Documentation

Ease of Installation

A report tool should be easy to set up. Initial installation is probably the easiest check-off item to gauge. The configurability of the query product, specifically for network solutions, is often the most complex item to evaluate. Networking most greatly affects performance of one product over another in client/server solutions and should be weighed heavily.

WYSIWYG

WYSIWYG (what you see is what you get) computing generally means that an application has graphical interfaces to allow easy formatting and configuration of reports, graphs, and forms. Most tools today have added such functionality, but there are exceptions.

Quick Default Reports

The Quick Reports feature transforms your query data into a presentation quality report — complete with titles and headings — with one touch of a button.

Creation of Reports for Reuse

Report writers don't have to build reports from scratch; end users should be able to inherit your report design and company headings. They can even use your report against other database tables, all the while maintaining your report formatting and styles.

Ability to Link Reports to Different Data Sets

Once a report template has been created, the ability to use and modify that template against different data sets and even different databases is valuable. In order to handle this correctly, a report generation tool must be able to easily handle the conversion of data types, which can vary among databases.

Documentation

Quality of the documentation directly relates to the quality of a software tool. Tools that have been in the market longer, and therefore the ones that are generally more stable, tend to be better documented.

18.3.2 Styles for Reports

Reports can be generated in many different styles. A good report generation tool should provide templates to illustrate many different styles of reports. Generally, there are five styles to evaluate as criteria:

- Matrix/cross-tab reports
- Tabular reports
- Form reports
- Form letters
- Master-detail reports

Tabular Reports

One of the most common ways of displaying data, as shown in the exercises at the end of the chapter, is through a tabular format. Data categories are separated by tabs and displayed horizontally across a page. Tabular reports should allow:

- Easy labeling of columns with background text
- Ability to highlight fields by color or underlining
- WYSIWYG features to alter how columns are formatted

Matrix/Cross-tab Reports

Crosstabs is a feature to allow a report to display a two-dimensional matrix of numeric data. The size of the matrix is based on the number of unique occurrences of the column and row categories you select when defining the crosstab.

A crosstab can be demonstrated by using the **Help** utility from within Quest and selecting *Simple Crosstab Tutorial*.

Master-Detail Reports

Reports can be generated based on queries that join several tables. A useful feature of a report tool is the ability to generate part of a report on a specific query, and then use a specific column of that query to define another query where the results are also part of the report. The relationship between the two result sets can be thought of as a *master-detail* relationship.

Mail Labels

Report writers should have the ability to generate mailing labels. Standard label formats should be available. Figure 18-1 shows an example of a report based on the generation of mailing labels for Avery-style labels.

Leonard Neuhoff
653 Rita Drive
Century City, CA 90067

Thomas Tester
456 Calico Street
Hacienda Heights, CA 93333

Clifford Stuart
617 East Lake Avenue
Apt. 233
Century City, CA 90067

Lionel Lakeland
902 Bluffside Road
Beverly Hills, CA 90067

Raymond Water
4932 Ocean View Road
Ventura, CA 93003

David McGough
550 Ash St.
Beverly Hills, CA 90067

Tony Butler
45 Macedonia Road
Inglewood, CA 90302

James Tate
2399 Western Avenue
Van Nuys, CA 91405

Peter McDermott
215 Howard St.
Apt F
Inglewood, CA 90302

John Roarke
878 Gallatin Road
Costa Mesa, CA 92627

Micheal Lear
254 Main Street
Thousand Oaks, CA 91360

Harry Greenstreet
12901 Norwalk Blvd.
Costa Mesa, CA 92627

Charles Randolph
894 Grigsby Road
El Cajon, CA 92020

Robert McClain
593 55th Street
Torrance, CA 90505

Robert Steveson
140 San Pablo Avenue
El Cajon, CA 92020

Athur Greystoke
897 Plaines Lane
Apt 124
Garden Grove, CA 92640

Larry Barell
392 Eastern Street
Los Angeles, CA 91214

Eric Baker
501 Kern Street
Garden Grove, CA 92640

Figure 18-1   *Mailing Labels*

Form Letters

Reports should also have a format to generate a form letter. For example, customer information — first name, last name, address, city, state, and zip code — can be represented as variables that will be replaced for each customer. This allows letters to be uniquely created for each and every customer. The form in Figure 18-2 demonstrates such a form letter.

The Haberdashery

Fine Men's Clothing Since 1895
1500 Fashion Ave
Laguna Hills, CA 92653

July 12, 1995

Chester Campbell
2716 Etoile Way
Hollywood, CA 90027

Dear Mr. Campbell:

Individualists are always sought after. We, at The Haberdashery, specialize in catering to your individual style.

Next month in our annual Sales Event at the Haberdashery. You'll find a full selection of stylish suites and sport coats that combine European flair and quality with American craftsmanship, many at unseasonably low prices. We guarantee one hour tailoring of any suit you want.

The Haberdashery is open every evening, except Sunday, until 10:00 PM. We welcome you to stop by our store and let us help you find a suit that matches your style. Our sales event lasts only till the end of the month, so please don't delay.

Sincerely,

Anthony Florentine

Figure 18-2 *Form Letter Generation*

18.3.3 Graphing and Imaging Capability

Report generation tools should be able to embed graphics based on the data used in the reports. Here are some criteria to evaluate graphing and imaging capabilities in reports.

- Inclusion of graphs in reports
- Inclusion of images in reports
- Creation of pie, bar, line, area, and log-line graphics
- Support of image formats

Inclusion of Graphs in Reports

The first check-off item for reporting tools and graphing is to determine if graphs are allowed in report tools.

Inclusion of Images in Reports

Bitmap images should be easy to import into a report.

Creation of Pie, Bar, Line, Area, and Log-line Graphics

A graphing tool should be able to present your data as bar, line, or pie charts, in 2-D and 3-D. Graphs that can represent multidimensional data are valuable for EIS solutions.

Support for Image Formats

Images can be stored in a number of formats, including BMP, TIFF, and GIF file formats. There are conversion utilities to convert one format to another. A reporting tool should support at least BMP and TIFF images.

18.3.4 Advanced Functionality

Some of the report writers are designed for personal computing. Others are specifically SQL-oriented, and client/server oriented. Feature functionality between report writers can vary greatly. Here are a few features to look for:

- Ability to create two-pass reports
- Drill-down ability
- Formula editor capabilities

Ability to Create Two-pass Reports

Use powerful two-pass reporting to compute data in a report that is reused in other parts of that same report. Quest Reporter computes the totals for each group of data in the first pass, then tallies the grand total in the second pass, using the data from the first pass. Calculate intricate "total of totals" information with the two-pass feature.

Drill-down Ability

If a report generates a figure for the total revenue for a company, can you drill-down to find the breakdown of total revenue by region? For more sophisticated reporting tools, another click of the mouse should give you the revenue in each sales region by sales rep.

Formula Editor Capabilities

A formula editor is an editor that allows you to perform summations and other useful analytical functions against your result data. The same formula editor used with querying should be integrated with reporting, providing mathematical, statistical, and financial functions. Use these functions in the formula editor to manipulate your data or build your own custom functions. Use the formula editor to present standard deviation information and loan amortization and to present value calculations in your reports.

With many reporting tools, users who are familiar with their Oracle or Sybase functions must relearn the equivalents for the report generation they are using, which is a time-consuming process. A formula editor should incorporate all native functions of the server database to maximize the data manipulation capabilities that are available.

18.3.5 Connectivity

Connectivity criteria for query tools were covered in Chapter 17. Connectivity criteria for query and reporting are nearly identical, so the discussion is not repeated here. Here are the connectivity criteria discussed in the last chapter:

- Native connectivity support to relational databases
- Level of ODBC support
- ODBC vendors supported
- Access to Xbase databases and spreadsheets
- Extras to connect to your desired platform
- OLE support
- E-mail enabled

18.3.6 Bells and Whistles

Here is a list of criteria for report tools not covered in the previous sections:

- Macro language
- Componentizing
- Back-end reporting

Macro language

Some tools providers offer scripting languages for embedding their reporting functionality for use with application and development. The real question with these languages is how robust they are and whether there is another alternative to them that may be easier. For example, if OLE objects are available to embed in an application, is a scripting language necessary?

Componentizing

With OLE, software vendors now provide reporting OLE controls and servers that can be embedded within applications. A generic end-user query tool may well be replaced by a customizable component.

Back-End Reporting

Reports generated on servers, rather than on client machines have several advantages.

- They produce the reports on the same machine where the database may reside, thus eliminating network traffic.
- Reports can be off-loaded from the client machines onto more powerful machines.
- Reports can be regulated. For instance, you can generate a whole batch of reports every Saturday night at 2 A.M.

18.4 Exercises with Report Writers

Exercise 18.4.1: Creating a Custom Report

This procedure explains how to create and save a custom report template, using the default report template available in the Report activity.

1. From the activity bar, click **New** and then **Query**. Open the file, sales.qqt, as shown in Figure 18-3.

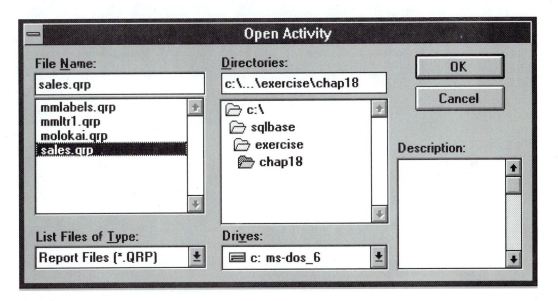

Figure 18-3 *Opening a Report File*

Click **OK**. The predefined query, with a results table, is displayed.

2. From the activity bar, click **New** and then **Report**. Quest asks whether you wish to link the query and the report, as shown below. Click **Yes**.

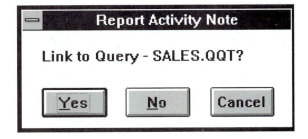

Figure 18-4 *Creating a Link to a Query*

3. You will now see a quick report, as shown in Figure 18-5.

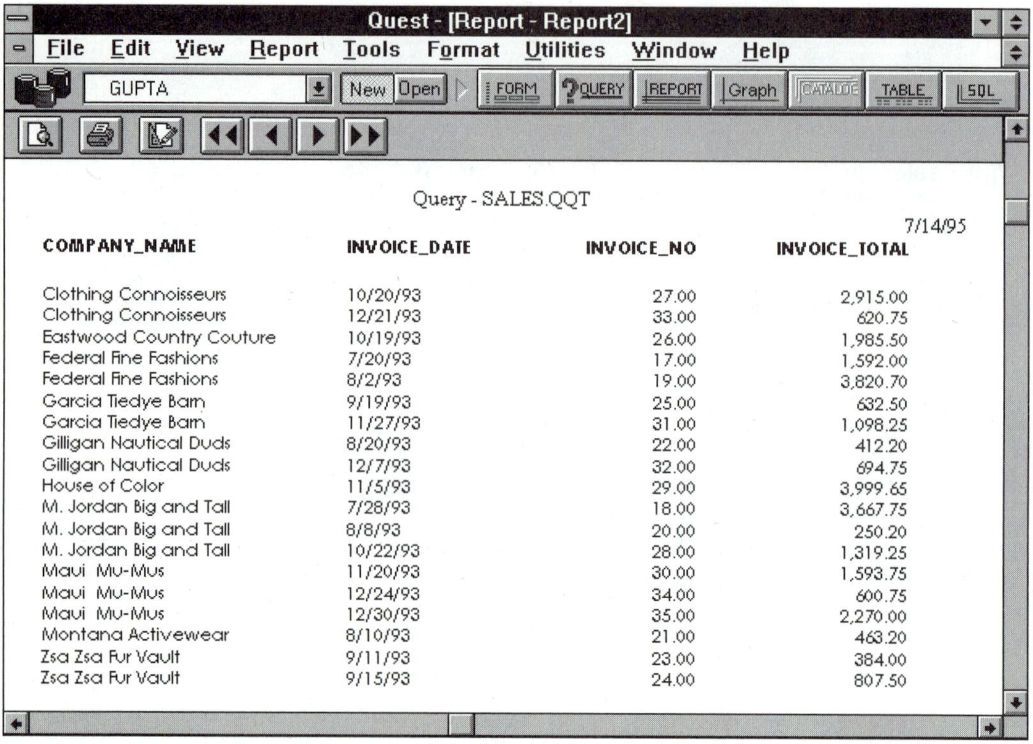

COMPANY_NAME	INVOICE_DATE	INVOICE_NO	INVOICE_TOTAL
Clothing Connoisseurs	10/20/93	27.00	2,915.00
Clothing Connoisseurs	12/21/93	33.00	620.75
Eastwood Country Couture	10/19/93	26.00	1,985.50
Federal Fine Fashions	7/20/93	17.00	1,592.00
Federal Fine Fashions	8/2/93	19.00	3,820.70
Garcia Tiedye Barn	9/19/93	25.00	632.50
Garcia Tiedye Barn	11/27/93	31.00	1,098.25
Gilligan Nautical Duds	8/20/93	22.00	412.20
Gilligan Nautical Duds	12/7/93	32.00	694.75
House of Color	11/5/93	29.00	3,999.65
M. Jordan Big and Tall	7/28/93	18.00	3,667.75
M. Jordan Big and Tall	8/8/93	20.00	250.20
M. Jordan Big and Tall	10/22/93	28.00	1,319.25
Maui Mu-Mus	11/20/93	30.00	1,593.75
Maui Mu-Mus	12/24/93	34.00	600.75
Maui Mu-Mus	12/30/93	35.00	2,270.00
Montana Activewear	8/10/93	21.00	463.20
Zsa Zsa Fur Vault	9/11/93	23.00	384.00
Zsa Zsa Fur Vault	9/15/93	24.00	807.50

Figure 18-5 *A Quick Report*

4. Close the report. From the activity bar, click **File** and then **Close**.

Exercise 18.4.2: Modifying a Report

Once a report is created, as in Exercise 18.4.1, it can easily be modified and reformatted to look more presentable. This exercise opens a modified version of the previous report to show how a report can be modified. Two simple modifications of this report are discussed: changing the title of the report and creating an input field based on a formula.

1. If sales.qqt is not open, reopen the file.

2. From the activity bar, click **Open** and then **Report**. Open the file, sales.qrp, as shown in Figure 18-6.

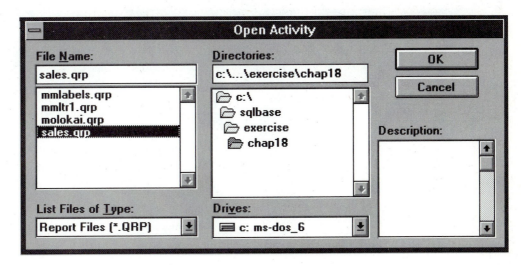

Figure 18-6   *Opening a Report File*

Sales.qrp is a report file template. Salest.qqt is the query file we created. These file name extensions are conventions of the Quest product.

Click **OK**.

3. A modified report based on the query, sales.qqt, is displayed.

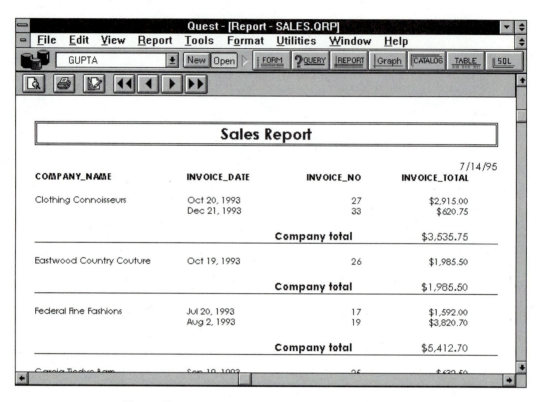

Figure 18-7 *Report SALES.QRP*

Use the **Preview** command from the **Report** menu at any time in this procedure to see how each step affects the structure and format of your report.

4. The report is now in **Preview** mode. Modification of this report will be done in **Design** mode. Choose **Design** from the **Report** menu (**Alt**, **R**, **D**) or **Ctrl+D** to return to your template. Figure 18-8 shows the report in design mode.

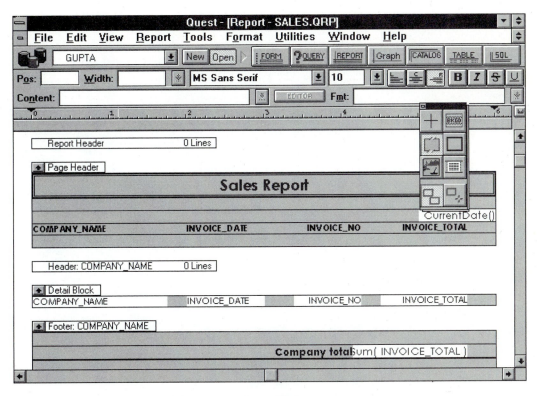

Figure 18-8   *Report Design Mode*

Notice the report line marked **Detail Block**. The detail block contains fields with input items that will be linked to the query result set. The detail block has a Header titled COMPANY_NAME. This means that detail blocks will be created in this report arranged by company names.

Changing the Title of a Report

5. The title now reads: Sales Report. To change title, select the text, Sales Report (as shown in Figure 18-9), using the right mouse button; double-click to open the **Format Background Text** dialog box.

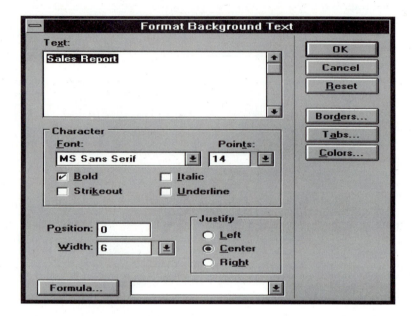

Figure 18-9   *Format Background Text*

The font has been set to MS Sans Serif 14, but you can change it now if you wish. Click on the **Colors** button to change the color of the title from blue to red.

Using the Formula Editor

6. Choose the input field shown below by clicking the right mouse button on the field.

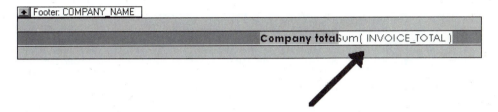

Figure 18-10 *Choosing an Input Field*

7. Press the Editor push button as shown below.

Figure 18-11 *The EDITOR Button*

8. A Formula Editor (Figure 18-12) is displayed. The formula editor defines a formula that calculates the sum of all invoice_totals. Notice that the formula editor has a list of functions, formulas, and fields of the database tables to which the report is linked.

As mentioned in step 4, the headers for detail blocks in this report are company names. This means that this formula calculates the sum of all invoice_totals per company. The "per company" is not explicitly stated in the formula, but it is effectively done this way because of the way the report is organized.

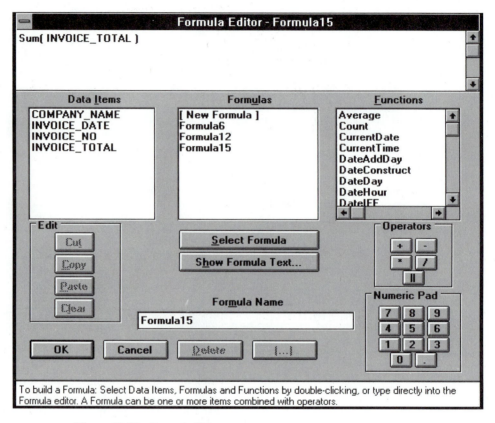

Figure 18-12 *Formula Editor*

9.   Click on **OK** to exit the Formula Editor.

10. Select **File** from the activity menu and pull down the **Save** option to save this file as modified.

Exercise 18.4.3: Creating a Form Letter

This exercise demonstrates use of a report tool to create a template form letter that can be used to generate letters to any number of individuals.

1. From the activity bar, click **New** and then **Query**. Open the file, molokai.qqt.

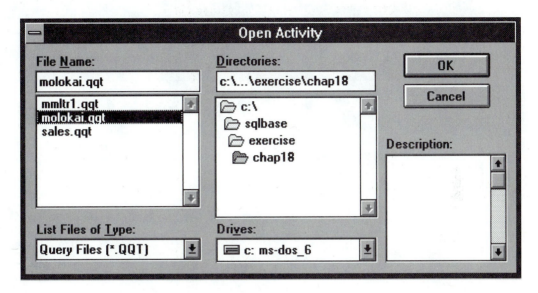

Figure 18-13 *Opening a Query File*

Click **OK**. The predefined query, with a results table, is displayed.

2. From the activity bar, click **Open** and then **Report**. Choose the file, molokai.qrp. Click **OK**.

3. Quest asks whether you wish to link the query and the report. Click **Yes**.

4. You should now see one of many form letters that have been created.

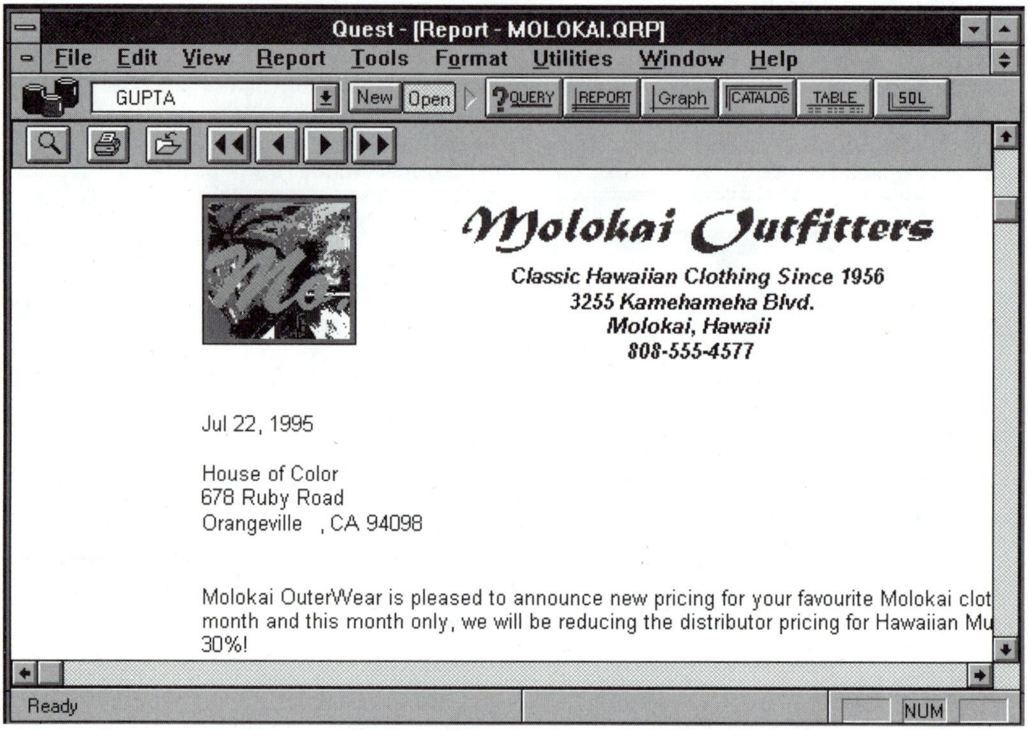

Figure 18-14 *Report, MOLOKAI.QRP*

5. Choose **File** from the Activity menu and then choose **Exit.**

Exercise 18.4.4: Creating Mailing Labels

This exercise demonstrates using a report tool to create mailing labels that can be printed on standard format mailing label; in this case, standard Avery mail label format is used.

1. From the activity bar, click **New** and then **Query**. Open the file, mmltr1.qqt.

2. From the activity bar, click **Open** and then **Report**. Choose the file mmltr1.qrp. Click **OK**.

3. Quest asks whether you wish to link the query and the report. Click **Yes**.

The mailing labels are displayed.

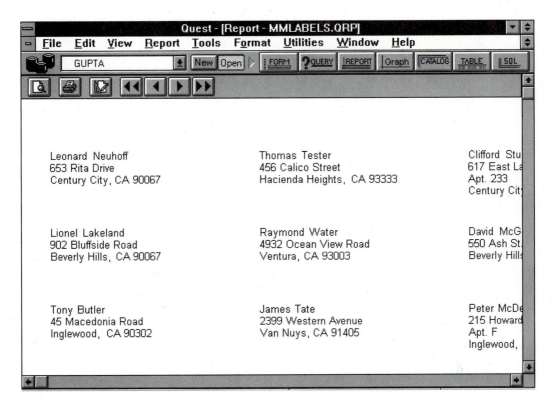

Figure 18-15 *Label Report, MMLABELS.QRP*

4.   Choose **File** from the Activity menu and then choose **Exit**.

18.5   Summary

This chapter covered general functionality of report writers and introduced several report writer vendors who sell stand-alone report writers. Most query tool vendors introduced in Chapter 17 also include report writing as a component of their tool. The exercises in this chapter provided an understanding of what report writers can do and showed the general styles of reports.

19   Database Directions

Although the future direction of relational database technology is hard to predict, the topics making the headlines are ideas that are not new: data warehousing, parallel databases, object-oriented databases, replication strategies, databases on the Internet, as well as lightning-fast performance on 64-bit operating systems.

The chapter is organized as follows:

Section 19.1 Data Warehousing
Section 19.2 Parallel Databases
Section 19.3 Object-Oriented Databases (OODBMS)
Section 19.4 Replication Strategies
Section 19.5 Performance and the 64-bit OS
Section 19.6 Relational Technology and the Internet
Section 19.7 Summary

19.1   Data Warehousing

Data warehousing is not a new concept, but it is one that is rapidly gaining in popularity and becoming more useful with the advancements in software, hardware, and client/server technology. The idea is to transform operational data, usually from many production databases, into a specialized database where end users, like executives and analysts, can access information relevant to decision support. Specifically, companies are interested in using operational data to understand business trends, to make forecasts, and to draw conclusions about customer patterns.

19.1.1 Data Warehousing Servers

One concept data warehouses make heavy use of is *meta data.* Meta data is data about data. For example, when using information for decision support, it is important to store information over long periods of time, defining multiple versions of data over a time period. In operational databases, there is typically just one view of data. Meta data provides a method of describing multiple versions of the structure and content of data over time. This is also described as making data *multidimensional.*

Analysts are extending the data warehousing paradigm, and are now referring to smaller decision support data systems as *data marts* or *data kiosks.*

Data warehousing differs greatly from most production, transaction-based systems. Transaction-based databases have many users connected to them and are designed to optimize inserts and updates of data. Data warehouses typically have few users and are optimized to extract information by querying the database with complex SELECT statements. Decision support requires the transformation and integration of data, which poses challenges to traditional on-line transaction processing (OLTP) systems. For example, extracting information might require joining ten or twenty tables. A transaction-based system will usually have poor performance under these conditions.

19.1.2 Data Warehousing and Data Access

Query and report tools were discussed in Chapters 17 and 18. With the creation of specialized databases for data warehousing has come the appearance of specialized data access tools. These tools are specifically designed for decision support. These tools are often referred to as EIS, or executive information systems. Vendors in the data analysis and EIS fields worry about different issues than do most data access vendors, including multidimensional views of data. Vendors with this class of access tools include Information Advantage, Business Objects, IRI Software, Comshare, Cognos, and Pilot Software. Their tools were discussed in Chapter 17.

19.1.3 Data Warehousing Vendors

All products are trademarks or registered trademarks of their respective companies.

AT&T Global Information Services (Teradata)
1700 S. Patterson Blvd.
Dayton, OH 45479
(513) 445-5000

PRODUCT: Teradata

PLATFORMS: AT&T (NCR)

POSITION: This information is repeated for parallel technology. Teradata is a parallel database architecture that is suited for data warehousing (probably before data warehousing and parallel databases became popular terms). Teradata is one of the oldest parallel databases on the market. AT&T has both massively parallel and symmetric multiprocessing versions of the Teradata database. Teradata boasts databases containing terabytes of data. One of the highlights of this product is the rich feature set and full parallelization of SQL that has come with maturity.

Carleton Corp. (Passport)
8 New England Executive Park
Burlington, MA 01803
(617) 272-4310

PRODUCT: Passport

PLATFORMS: OS/2, Windows, and UNIX

POSITION: Carleton Passport is a database-independent data warehouse solution like Prism. Passport generates COBOL programs in order to extract data as sources and produce meta data. Users import the data to a relational database and access SQL. Passport has a strong graphical front end to its solution.

Some data sources include IBM DB2, IMS, IDMS, Adabas, Cincom Supra, VSAM, sequential files, and others. Carlton has specialized loading utilities to import data into Oracle, Sybase, and DB2, but it supports all relational databases.

Evolutionary Technologies, Inc. (Extract Tool Suite)
4301 Westbank Drive
Austin, TX 78746
(512) 327-6994

PRODUCT: Extract Tool Suite

PLATFORMS: IBM AIX, Sun Solaris, HP-UX, and other UNIX solutions

POSITION: Extract Tool Suite is a database-independent solution to data warehousing. Evolutionary Technology's Extract Tool Suite provides a GUI for generating data extraction routines, including COBOL and C.

This tool can act as a bidirectional gateway among data sources that can transform data, although it does not create meta data. Most databases are supported by ETI, including Oracle, Sybase, Informix, IBM DB2, and IMS.

IBM Corp. (IBM DB2 Parallel Edition)
Old Orchard Rd
Armonk, NY 10504
(800) 426-3333

PRODUCT: IBM DB2 Parallel Edition

PLATFORMS: IBM SP2 and RS/6000 clustered nodes

POSITION: Like Informix and Oracle, IBM is using its entry into the parallel market to push data warehousing. With near-linear performance improvements on queries as processors are added, this is possible today.

Informix Software, Inc. (INFORMIX-OnLine Dynamic Server)
4100 Bohannon Drive
Menlo Park, CA 94025
(415) 926-6300

PRODUCT: INFORMIX-OnLine Dynamic Server

PLATFORMS: HP-UX, Sun, IBM, Sequent Dynex, most UNIX systems that support symmetric multiprocessing

POSITION: Informix is positioning its scalable, parallel query architecture for use in the data warehousing market. The enterprise-level database vendors are all positioning their parallel databases as serving the same market as more specialized vendors. Informix also purchased Stanford Technology, a leader in data warehousing technology to strengthen their position in this market.

Oracle Corp. (Parallel Query Option)
500 Oracle Parkway
Redwood Shores, CA 94086
(800) 633-0583

PRODUCT: Oracle with Parallel Query Option

PLATFORMS: DEC OSF/1, HP-UX, Pyramid, Sequent Dynex, Sun Solaris

POSITION: Oracle is positioning its Parallel Query Option as a data warehousing solution. Oracle has announced many future plans and is definitely positioning for a strong play in this market with the purchase of EIS vendor and information provider, IRI Software.

Prism Solutions, Inc. (Prism Warehouse Manager)
1000 Hamlin Court
Sunnyvale, CA 94089
(408) 752-1888

PRODUCT: Prism Warehouse Manager

PLATFORMS: Windows, DOS, and OS/2. Server dependent on back-end database it works with.

POSITION: Prism Warehouse Manager provides a data-independent approach to data warehousing. The PC-based software performs data extraction and transformation among a wide variety of databases. This product creates automated COBOL programs to facilitate the complexities of data extraction for use in decision support. Data can be extracted from relational and nonrelational data, including Oracle, Informix, Digital Rdb and RMS, Sybase SQL Server, VSAM, IMS, IDMS, sequential files on a variety of platforms, and others.

Prism Warehouse Manager creates meta data that can then be supported by a number of host databases, including Oracle, Informix OnLine, Sybase SQL Server, IBM DB2, Tandem NonStop SQL, Red Brick Warehouse, and Teradata.

Red Brick Systems, Inc. (Red Brick Warehouse)
485 Alberto Way
Los Gatos, CA 95032
(408) 353-7214

PRODUCT: Red Brick Warehouse

PLATFORMS: HP-UX, Sun Solaris, Sequent Dynex, DEC OSF/1

POSITION: Red Brick Systems is a specialized database for database warehousing. While it is not as prevalent as more generic RDBMs, it offers much faster query, loading, and indexing performance (as much as ten times faster in many circumstances). They have a join accelerator, called STAR-join, that creates a special index for multiple table joins.

Red Brick offers SQL extensions to expand on the types of queries users can perform, specifically for decision support on historical data. Red Brick provides an attractive price/performance solution for decision support systems, offering symmetric multiprocessing systems.

19.2   Parallel Databases

Want to join together tables with hundreds of millions of rows of data, perform a query with a result set over several millions of rows, and retrieve that data in 30 minutes or less? Parallel database technology is rapidly making this affordable to do. As an example, Tandem recorded a 1994 benchmark of over 20,918 tpmC using their parallel database, NonStop SQL, a screamingly fast benchmark by today's standards. With corporate databases rapidly approaching terabytes of data, mainstream database vendors are pushing aggressively ahead to "parallelize" their database.

19.2.1 Not All Parallel Is Equal

Vendors often gloss over the differences in their parallel designs. Underlying parallel processing are the advancements in hardware platforms, where multiple CPUs are supported by one or a cluster of internetworked machines. There are two primary approaches to supporting parallel computing:

- **Symmetric multiprocessing (SMP)**

  In this scenario, you commonly find one machine with shared memory and disks that support one to many processors. Two of the more popular such systems include Sun's System 2000 and Hewlett

Packard's T500, which support eight and sixteen CPUs without a huge performance hit. Hardware vendors are now offering symmetric multiprocessing with Windows NT platforms, further driving down costs. These machines can also be termed *tightly coupled*. While this class of platforms is increasingly powerful, they ultimately run into scalability issues because of locks caused by memory and disk contention.

- **Massively parallel processing (MPP)**

In this scenario, each CPU, or node, has its own memory, operating system, disks, and database software. The system may pass certain data to one CPU or another, depending on how the database is divided. This approach offers almost unlimited scalability but proves to be more difficult to write software for. This technology has also been referred to as "loosely coupled" or "shared nothing" architecture. Vendors like AT&T GIS, with Teradata, and Tandem, with NonStop SQL, have traditionally been strong in the MPP arena, but today all vendors are moving into this area.

Software vendors are starting to support clusters of SMP-based machines, which could be thought of as a hybrid to the two appoaches. As this technology advances, the database performance we will see will dwarf today's standards.

19.2.2 Parallel Database Vendors

There are no new players in the market to introduce. The major database vendors are all working on parallel database servers. Here is a brief description of what they are doing in this arena. All products are trademarks or registered trademarks of their respective companies.

AT&T Global Information Services (Teradata)
1700 S Patterson Blvd
Dayton, OH 45479
(513) 445-5000

PRODUCT: Teradata

PLATFORMS: AT&T (NCR)

POSITION: Teradata is one of the oldest parallel databases on the market. AT&T has both MPP and SMP versions of the Teradata database. Teradata boasts databases containing terabytes of data. One of the highlights of this product is the rich feature set and full parallization of SQL that has come with maturity.

IBM Corp. (DB2/6000 Parallel Edition)
Old Orchard Rd
Armonk, NY 10504
(800) 426-3333

PRODUCT: IBM DB2/6000 Parallel Edition

PLATFORMS: IBM SP2 and RS/6000 nodes.

POSITION: The Parallel Edition is geared to a loosely coupled environment for massively parallel machines, although a tightly coupled environment is also supported by clustering interconnected SMP RS/6000 nodes.

Informix Software, Inc. (OnLine XPS and OnLine Dynamic Server)
4100 Bohannon Drive
Menlo Park, CA 94025
(415) 926-6300

PRODUCT: OnLine XPS and OnLine Dynamic Server

PLATFORMS: Sequent Dynex, Sun Solaris, HP-UX, IBM AIX, DEC OSF/1, and other UNIX platforms

POSITION: Informix's dynamic scalable architecture (DSA) works with both tightly coupled SMP environments and loosely coupled MPP environments. Informix has been viewed by many to be an early leader of the UNIX database vendors in providing a scalable solution working both in SMP and MPP systems. Applications developed on SMP platforms can be easily ported to MPP systems. Informix supports very large database configurations (VLDBs) by backing up databases at the fragment level. If a table partition becomes corrupted, that partition can be restored while the rest of the table remains on-line.

Microsoft Corp. (SQL Server 95)
One Microsoft Way
Redmond, WA 98052
(206) 882-8080

PRODUCT: SQL Server 95

PLATFORMS: Windows NT

POSITION: Microsoft is supporting a tightly coupled SMP design, where queries are parallelized across a single database instance. Microsoft makes use of Windows NT's threaded design and support for multiple processors. While Microsoft scales for the workgroup market with this offering, they clearly have the intention of expanding their foothold in this area.

Oracle Corp. (Parallel Query Option)
500 Oracle Parkway
Redwood Shores, CA 94086
(800) 633-0583

PRODUCT: Oracle with Parallel Query Option (PQO)

PLATFORMS: The Parallel Query Option is a module that is added to Oracle database sites, especially to UNIX systems with more than one processor.

POSITION: The Parallel Query Option with an Oracle server is designed for tightly coupled systems and symmetric multiprocessing (SMP). Simply put, the parallel query breaks down SQL statements into subtasks and performs the subtasks concurrently on multiple processors in order to increase speed. Oracle has separate products for tightly coupled and loosely coupled designs. Loosely coupled systems use Oracle's Parallel Server discussed below. To make use of PQO, systems should have more than one processor.

Oracle Corp. (Parallel Server)
500 Oracle Parkway
Redwood Shores, CA 94086
(800) 633-0583

PRODUCT: Oracle Parallel Server

PLATFORMS: Supports clustered and massively parallel systems, including DEC VAXcluster, IBM, Pyramid, Sequent, nCUBE, Encore Computer, and NCR

POSITION: Oracle Parallel Server makes use of MPP and clustered systems with a loosely coupled design. Multiple computers (nodes) can share a common set of disks connected together. As a business grows, the system is expanded by adding more nodes without modification to the actual database. For high availability, multiple nodes can concurrently run on Oracle DBMS.

Sybase, Inc. (Navigation Server)
6475 Christie Ave
Emeryville, CA 94608
(800) 426-4785

PRODUCT: Sybase Navigation Server

PLATFORMS: Runs on UNIX-based massively parallel systems, from vendors like AT&T, NCR, IBM, Sequent, and Pyramid

POSITION: The Sybase Navigation Server is designed specifically for loosely coupled environments, including massively parallel processors (MPP). Nothing is shared in Sybase's parallel design; they have control servers, with instances of an SQL Server DBMS, that manage parallel operations.

Tandem Computers, Inc. (NonStop SQL)
19191 Vallco Parkway
Cupertino, CA 95014
(408) 285-6000

PRODUCT: NonStop SQL

PLATFORMS: Tandem Himalaya

POSITION: Tandem supports a loosely coupled MPP system. Tandem has gained a reputation for providing a high-end system with the ability to keep running. Built-in redundancy provides a robust environment.

19.3 Object-Oriented Databases (OODBMS)

Object-oriented databases are a relatively new technology compared with relational DBMS. At the heart of this technology is the notion of treating data as objects. Objects are defined by a *type* and a *class*, and their structure and functionality can be *inherited* by another class. Classes *encapsulate* the data structure of the information and define procedures or *methods*. The OODBMS offers the benefit of reuse of development efforts for future products but, until now, has added to the complexity of the initial creation of a database. For simplistic data relationships, it is unlikely that OODBMS will replace relational technology, but for complex data types and relationships, OODBMS have many benefits to offer.

19.3.1 SQL and Object-Oriented Technology

Many OODBMS vendors have interleaved relational and object-oriented technology in an attempt to form a hybrid technology more palatable to mainstream users. These vendors include HP, UniSQL, Omniscience, Objectivity, Ontos, Poet, and Cincom.

19.3.2 Object-Oriented Vendors with SQL Extensions

All products are trademarks or registered trademarks of their respective companies.

Hewlett Packard Co. (OpenODB)
3000 Hanover St.
Palo Alto, CA 94304
(800) 752-0900

PRODUCT: OpenODB

PLATFORMS: HP-UX, HP MPE-IX

POSITION: OpenODB is designed to build very large, multiuser applications, where data access to existing data in relational and nonrelational systems is still possible. Because of external function hooks, the database can link to data and code anywhere on the system. It can work with multimedia as well as integrate with existing applications. HP has an API for this management system in C, C++, COBOL, Fortran, and Pascal. HP supports an object-oriented SQL and has a component referred to as the Relational Storage Manager.

Objectivity, Inc. (Objectivity/DB)
301 B E. Evelyn Ave.
Mountain View, CA 94041
(415)254-7100

PRODUCT: Objectivity/DB

PLATFORMS: Windows, Window 95, Windows NT, DEC VMS and OSF/1, DG, HP-UX, IBM AIX, Sun Solaris, Silicon Graphics IRIS, NEC

POSITION: Objectivity's object-oriented engine has ANSI-standard SQL and ODBC support, as well as interfaces to C++ and Smalltalk. They have a multithreaded architecture that is scalable over a wide range of platforms.

Omniscience Object Technology, Inc. (ORDBMS)
3080 Olcott St., Suite 100C
Santa Clara, CA 95054
(408)562-0799

PRODUCT: Omniscience ORDBMS

PLATFORMS: Windows, Windows NT, Sun Solaris, and Macintosh

POSITION: Omniscience offers an application interface for both object-oriented and relational methods. Available with ODBC 2.0 support and with support of the ANSI SQL-92 standard.

Ontos, Inc. (Ontos DB)
Three Burlington Woods
Burlington, MA 01803
(617) 272-7110

PRODUCT: Ontos DB 3.0

PLATFORMS: HP-UX, Sun Solaris, IBM AIX, DEC OSF/1, and other UNIX platforms

POSITION: Ontos DB is the central component of Ontos's Virtual Information Architecture, which is an object-oriented methodology for data distribution. Ontos DB supports an SQL interface and also an Object Center development environment for C++ and Objectworks/C++.

Poet Software Corp. (Poet)
4633 Old Ironsides Dr, Ste 110
Santa Clara, CA 95054
(408) 748-3403

PRODUCT: Poet

PLATFORMS: Windows, Windows NT, Macintosh, Novell, OS/2, NextStep, Sun Solaris, HP-UX, IBM AIX, and SCO UNIX

POSITION: Poet has a C++ interface for adding database functionality while keeping the language's object-oriented features. Poet refers to the technology as Persistent Objects and Extended Database Technology. Poet has support for ODBC and their own OQL (object query language).

UniSQL, Inc. (UniSQL/X DBMS)
8911 N Capital of Texas Hwy, Ste 2300
Austin, TX 78759
(512) 343-7297

PRODUCT: UniSQL/X DBMS

PLATFORMS: Windows NT, Sun Solaris, SGI IRIS, HP-UX, IBM AIX, DEC OSF/1

POSITION: UniSQL has both object-oriented and relational capabilities. UniSQL supports ODBC and ANSI SQL, as well as interfaces to access most major relational databases. Users can also use an object SQL query language and interface the DBMS with C, Smalltalk, or C++ (among a number of other development environments). Users can create complex objects that can be accessed and queried interactively by SQL/X nonprocedural queries.

19.4   Replication Strategies

Data replication, like data warehousing and parallel servers, is a concept that has existed for a while. Replication is also being taken in different directions. Historically, vendors like Tandem, Oracle, Sybase, Informix, and CA-Ingres have provided data replication. A major purpose of their replication has been to allow *high availability*, in other words, data is replicated from one system to another system to avoid system failures when components malfunction. In many mission-critical systems for large corporations, such as hospital and manufacturing control systems, a malfunction of a computer database is a major crisis.

Data replication has until recently been largely *homogeneous* (meaning that your Oracle server will be replicated to another Oracle server, and your Informix Online server will be replicated to another Informix OnLine server.) Today, vendors are rapidly working on solutions that will provide low-cost data replication that will allow distributed and *heterogenous* data transfer.

This section discusses a direction that database replication is moving toward: the concept of *decentralized data replication*. Decentralized data replication will be heterogeneous in nature. It will allow data to travel both horizontally and vertically within corporate organizations. The SQL language is a *structured* query language. The word structured is italicized because decentralized, SQL-based data replication will add structure to how data is transferred on the corporate perimeter. Today, most data at the corporate perimeter is held in unstructured media, like spreadsheets and personal, flat-file data structures.

19.4.1 Decentralized Data Replication

Many organizations are confronted with the same problem. They are very good at accumulating data but not good at disseminating it to the people who need it. This problem is most severe on the front lines of an organization, where branch offices and field employees have only remote access to corporate data. It's the classic "fat pipe in, thin pipe out" problem.

Over the next decade, competitive advantage will be gained by those organizations that address the "fat pipe in, thin pipe out" problem and better leverage their information assets. This change will be most visible on the corporate perimeter, where a new generation of front-line applications will redefine how organizations interact with their customers, business partners, and suppliers.

Many organizations are addressing this issue by decentralizing subsets of corporate data to branch offices, workgroups, and individual PCs and mobile laptops. By decentralizing data, organizations can better leverage their informational assets — delivering data to the people who need it. Indeed, decentralizing data is an integral part of what client/server is all about.

One key challenge to creating a decentralized environment is to ensure that data does not become isolated on "islands" throughout an organization. Decentralized subsets of data must be synchronized to support corporate entities that share access to the same corporate data. This facilitates decentralized data processing, reducing system contention for the same data and providing flexibility for application development. Replication is one of the key, emerging technologies that address this issue.

Replication is an automated process in which changes to a local database are captured, then propagated to targeted, disparate databases. The principal advantage of data replication is that two or more disparate data sets can be kept in sync with relatively little overhead.

Replication solutions have been available since 1993. These solutions can be classified in two categories, basic "data pumps" and more sophisticated "store-and-forward" solutions. Data pumps simply move data from a target to a source. Typically, this involves running a SELECT statement against a table in the source database and propagating the result set to the target database. Store-and-forward solutions are more sophisticated in that they attempt to synchronize the target database with its source, rather than just copy data. They ensure greater data integrity by maintaining and applying changes on a transaction-by-transaction basis. They also provide tools for reintegrating data after it is initially replicated, using conflict avoidance and resolution mechanisms.

Decentralized versus Distributed Replication

Unfortunately, the replication solutions offered by most database vendors fall short when addressing the distinct demands of decentralized data. This is not surprising given that these solutions were designed with a different problem in mind—facilitating distributed database implementations.

Distributed replication is used to provide end users with a consistent, singular view of the data that is spread across multiple servers. Historically, consistency was maintained by use of a "two-phase commit" protocol. Two-phase commit, however, requires tremendous overhead, since it requires all servers sharing the distributed data to participate in all update, insert, or delete operations. Replication provides an alternative, low-overhead way to maintain consistency.

A decentralized paradigm places distinct demands on a replication solution. The requirements for a successful decentralized replication solution are in Table 19-1.

Table 19-1 *Replication Requirements*

Replication for Decentralized Data	Replication for Distributed Data
Vertically structured	Horizontally structured
Heterogeneous parent/child	Homogeneous peers
Extract sliced subsets data	Maintain a consistent, singular view of data
Occasionally connected	Connected across a WAN or LAN
Large number of participants	Small number of participants
Client-centric	Server-centric

Decentralized Replication Is Vertically Organized

The biggest fundamental difference between decentralized and distributed replication is the direction in which data flows. Decentralized replication is vertically organized, pumping data up and down the organization. This typically involves replicating subsets of data between corporate operational systems and informational systems located on the front lines. These informational systems may be servers located in branch offices or workgroups, or desktop databases deployed on mobile laptops.

For example, every evening an insurance company downloads data from its corporate mainframe to servers located in each of its branch offices. Branch offices use this data to process claims and review policy information. When agents from the office go into the field, they also take relevant claim and policy information with them on their laptops so they can work with it when they are with a customer. Changes to this data, as well as new policy information, are then placed back on the branch server, which in turn propagates back up to the mainframe. Decentralized replication manages the flow of data from the corporate mainframe, to the branch office server, to agents' laptops, and then back again.

Distributed replication is more horizontal in nature. It focuses on maintaining a consistent view of data spread across multiple operational systems. This typically involves synchronizing several peer servers or a single master with several slave servers.

For example, a transportation company once centrally processed all invoices with a single, large database. As this database grew in size, response time continued to get slower. This problem was solved by offloading parts of this database to several minicomputers located throughout the organization in New York, Chicago, and L.A. Distributed replication is used to keep all of these servers synchronized. As far as applications are concerned, they are still running against a single, logical database.

Decentralized Replication Is Heterogeneous

Decentralized replication, because it is vertically organized, must move data between corporate-wide systems and decentralized systems. This requires a heterogeneous interface, since systems at different tiers in an organization are typically implemented with different DBMS products. Corporate-wide data is often stored on mainframes and minicomputers in products such as DB2 or Oracle. Decentralized data, stored on LAN servers as well as on desktops and laptops, is typically stored in products such as SQLBase.

Distributed replication tends to be homogenous in nature. First, the tight synchronization needed to support a distributed model can best be found in solutions implemented with DBMS products from the same vendor. This is not going to change in the near future, because database vendors are likely to continue to optimize their distributed capabilities within their own product line.

Decentralized Replication Manages a Large Number of Occasionally Connected Participants

The relationship among participants in each of the two replication processes is also quite different. Decentralized replication is loosely coupled among many servers, whereas distributed replication is tightly coupled among a few servers.

Decentralized replication pushes data out toward the corporate perimeter. This typically involves replicating data from a few corporate-wide servers to twenty or thirty branch offices or workgroups or to hundreds of mobile employees with laptops.

Data is replicated according to an occasionally connected model that assumes communication can only occur at discrete instants in time. This may be at a specific moment explicitly defined by an end user, e.g., salespeople may replicate their local data when they dial in from the road. Replication may also occur at a regular interval, e.g., every evening in a branch office.

Distributed data assumes a networked connection among a few servers. The replication process may be data-driven, where changes to data will automatically initiate a synchronization process, or time-driven at frequent intervals.

Decentralized Replication Moves "Slices" of Information

The data that is replicated also varies between decentralized and distributed solutions. You decentralize to help end users get to the data that they need. This typically involves more than just mirroring data that exists at the corporate level. Indeed, decentralized data is usually sliced and formatted to the needs of a specific workgroup or individual. This may involve horizontally selecting rows or vertically selecting columns to take part in the replication process.

For example, your sales people need certain information when they are with a customer. They don't need all the information that's out there, just what pertains to that day's sales calls. Decentralized replication extracts the relevant information for each salesperson (name and phone number of clients assigned to their district) to their laptop database. This lets the salesperson locally access and manipulate the data when visiting customers.

Distributed replication is primarily concerned with maintaining a single, consistent view of data, keeping it as synchronized and up-to-date as possible. There is relatively little need to manipulate data as it is copied, other than merging or dividing well-defined fragments of data.

19.4.2 Decentralized Replication Vendors

All products are trademarks or registered trademarks of their respective companies.

Centura Software Corp. (SQLBase Ranger)
1060 Marsh Road
Menlo Park, CA 95054
(415) 321-9500

PRODUCT: SQLBase Ranger

PLATFORMS: Windows, Windows 95, Windows NT, OS/2, NetWare

POSITION: Centura Software's SQLBase Ranger provides a store-and-forward replication solution specifically designed to support decentralized data. SQLBase replication supports heterogeneous databases and ensures data integrity and consistency, even when transactions are performed against the same data on two or more different databases. It is ideally suited to support mobile or occasionally connected applications that perform transactions against a compact local database, then synchronize a central database with the updates from those transactions, either through a LAN connection (when possible) or through a messaging service. A complete solution, SQLBase replication provides point-and-click management and monitoring tools for easy implementation and administration.

Microsoft Corp. (SQL Server 6.0)
One Microsoft Way
Redmond, WA 98052
(206) 882-8080

PRODUCT: SQL Server 6.0

PLATFORMS: Window NT

POSITION: Microsoft has implemented a distributed publish-and-subscribe data replication capability. Currently, SQL Server's replication is homogeneous with the intent of providing a heterogeneous replication strategy. Microsoft has also defined a Distributed Management Framework, SQL-DMF, for providing management of distributed systems.

Praxis International, Inc. (OmniReplicator)
Four Cambridge Center
Cambridge, MA 02142
(617) 661-9790

PRODUCT: OmniReplicator

PLATFORMS: Software runs on an IBM PC with Windows. Support of replication on HP-UX, Sun Solaris, IBM AIX, Sequent Dynex, DEC OSF/1, Teradata systems. Bidirectional support for replication for Oracle, DB2, Sybase, and unidirectional support for Informix, DB2/6000, CA-Ingres, Rdb, and Teradata

POSITION: Support for heterogeneous, bidirectional data replication. The product makes use of SequeLink middleware from TechGnosis, Inc. The software allows for replication via a store-and-forward paradigm. Two or more locations can share a common table and update a common set of data.

Sybase, Inc. (Sybase SQL Anywhere)
6475 Christie Ave
Emeryville, CA 94608
(800) 426-4785

PRODUCT: Sybase SQL Anywhere

PLATFORMS: Windows, Windows 95, Windows NT, OS/2, NetWare

POSITION: Sybase SQL Anywhere provides quick, asynchronous replication of data from SQL Anywhere to Sybase SQL Server. If Sybase SQL Server is a replication server, it is also possible to replicate data from other database vendors.

Trinsic Corp. — a Subsidiary of Platinum Technology (InfoPump)
101 University Ave
Palo Alto, CA 94301
(415) 328-9595

PRODUCT: InfoPump

PLATFORMS: Windows NT, OS/2, and IBM AIX

POSITION: This is a server-based replication software package. You can move and synchronize data from multiple data sources, including Oracle,

Sybase SQL Server, Microsoft SQL Server, CA-Ingres, Informix, DB2/2, DB2/6000, as well as nonrelational data sources like Lotus Notes and dBASE.

19.5 Performance and the 64-bit OS

Digital Equipment Corporation was the first to offer a mainstream 64-bit operating system. When an RDBMS makes use of a 64-bit operating system, there are immediate benefits: Specifically, it is much easier to map large amounts of data to physical addresses in memory. This means that if you buy enough RAM, you can load an entire database into RAM. How much faster is this than when you access a database from a disk? Consider this: Seek times on disks are in the millisecond range. Seek times for memory are in the nanosecond range. Given that disk access is a sizable chunk of database access time, the speed gains will be impressive.

This technology is still young and very expensive, but given time, this will help drive database performance through the roof. Large financial institutions and traders on Wall Street can almost immediately justify the large cost of buying machines to support this architecture today.

Oracle Corporation, Sybase, Computer Associates, and Informix are all porting their software to 64-bit platforms. With 32-bit systems, the largest amount of data that can be stored in memory is 2 gigabytes. That limit will be considerably larger with 64 bits. Oracle plans initial support for 14 gigabytes in memory.

19.6 Relational Technology and the Internet

The speed at which the Internet, or World Wide Web (WWW), has become pervasive is astonishing. At very little cost, almost anyone will be able to access incredible amounts of information. Does this present an opportunity to relational database vendors? You bet!

Companies like Sybase, Oracle, Informix, IBM, and hordes of startups are looking at the infinite ways to connect SQL technology and the web. SQL vendors realize the opportunity in having web servers connect to relational engines. All the major RDBMS vendors are jumping at this opportunity. With the increased speeds that cable hookups can offer into the home, relational data types may expand to handle all sorts of multimedia data. Similarly, front-end relational engines that work with web browsers will have a place on the Internet. Very few software companies will be unaffected by the web!

HTML, Java, and CGI

The contents that web browsers, like those from Netscape, hook to, are pages written in what is called *Hypertext Markup Language*, or *HTML*. HTML allows form-based applications on the web. These HTML forms are managed by web servers, which immediately implies that there is an opportunity to integrate large RDBMS to these HTML pages and web servers.

The way that databases hook in with HTML pages and web browsers is through what is known as the *Common Gateway Interface*, or *CGI*. CGI actually is an interface that can call any type of application, but relational vendors find it specifically useful for integration with web browsers and servers.

Java, developed by Sun Microsystems, is the object-oriented language that has been accepted by most vendors involved with the Internet as the development language for the web. Again, relational vendors are exploring ways to integrate with this language.

SQL Vendors on the Internet

The explosion in the number of companies developing products for the web seems to coincide with the explosion of end users connecting to the web. The following is a sampling of software companies active is this arena or integrating relational technology with the web. All products are trademarks or registered trademarks of their respective companies.

- Spider Technologies Inc. (Spider) in Palo Alto, CA

- Netscape Communications (LiveWire) in Mountain View, CA

- Nomad Development Corp (WebDBC) in Seattle, WA

- Edify Corp (Electronic Workforce) in Santa Clara, CA

- The Information Atrium Inc. (LivePage) in Waterloo, Ontario, Canada

These companies and many more are active in the development of software for relational databases and the web. With the changes occurring in this market today, it is not likely that an accurate listing of all the players in the market would last more than a few weeks.

Following is a short list of leading RDBMS vendors who are tackling integration of RDBMS technology and the Internet, specifically IBM, Informix, Microsoft, Oracle, and Sybase.

IBM Corp. (DB2 World Wide Web Connection)

Old Orchard Rd
Armonk, NY 10504
(800) 426-3333

PRODUCT: IBM World Wide Web Connection

POSITION: IBM has provided CGI gateways to DB2. Multimedia integration with DB2 and the web is a subject of much interest at IBM. At the time of this writing, the announcements are forthcoming.

Informix Software, Inc. (INFORMIX-4GL CGI Interface Kit, Web DataBlade)

4100 Bohannon Drive
Menlo Park, CA 94025
(415) 926-6300

PRODUCT: Web DataBlade, INFORMIX-4GL CGI Interface Kit

POSITION: Informix has CGI gateways interfaces to integrate the Informix engine with web servers, like the INFORMIX-4GL CGI Interface Kit. More interesting is Informix's purchase of Illustra Information Technologies, Inc., and the Web DataBlade product offering. Illustra integrates object-relational database with web servers.

Microsoft Corp. (Internet Database Connector)

One Microsoft Way
Redmond, WA 98052
(206)882-8080

PRODUCT: Internet Database Connector

POSITION: Microsoft will likely release a variety of web products. They have an Internet Database Connector that integrates ODBC data sources to web servers. Microsoft SQL Server uses ODBC as the native API. An SQL Server/web server bundle is likely not too far off.

Oracle Corp. (Oracle Web System, Oracle World Wide Web Interface Kit)
500 Oracle Parkway
Redwood Shores, CA 94086
(800) 633-0583

PRODUCT: Oracle Web System, Oracle World Wide Web Interface Kit

POSITION: Oracle has aggressively worked toward allowing developers to create CGI gateways, using PL/SQL for Oracle databases. They provide a series of applications through a kit to facilitate this. The Oracle Web System will provide programs for Oracle-based web servers and client software.

Sybase, Inc. (Sybase WebSQL, Sybperl)
6475 Christie Ave
Emeryville, CA 94608
(800) 426-4785

PRODUCT: Sybase WebSQL

POSITION: Sybase is developing WebSQL, which will connect to web server software. Sybase will use their Open Client Interface (OCI) to interface. Sybase uses a UNIX-based application language, *Perl*, which has also been popular for web CGI application development. Sybase calls their version of the Perl language, Sybperl. More products are likely to follow.

19.7   Summary

SQL has certainly matured since its introduction back in 1973, when the technology was documented. As evidenced by the number of vendors mentioned in this book, a wide breadth of solutions has been created surrounding the language and relational databases.

This last chapter addressed future areas where considerable advancement will occur in the SQL market. Data warehousing, parallel databases, SQL and object-oriented databases, decentralized replication, integrated database/web servers, and databases on 64-bit architectures are all technologies that are moving rapidly ahead.

****

You finished the book!

We hope you have a better understanding of how SQL is used and of the many vendors involved in the relational database market. Given all the dynamic and creative work that has occurred over the last five years alone, the process of learning this technology will be an ongoing battle. It is not inconceivable that within several years every home will have a computer/phone/fax/multimedia station that contains a SQL-based relational system. Given SQL's pervasiveness in the market, it is reasonable to say that this language will continue to evolve and provide new ways to use information.

A   SQL Vendors

Appendix A provides addresses of SQL vendors in the following order:

- Section A.1   Relational Database Players
- Section A.2   Logical Modeling Vendors
- Section A.3   Data Translation Tool Vendors
- Section A.4   4GL Vendors
- Section A.5   Connectivity: Direct Access Solution Vendors
- Section A.6   Connectivity: Vendors with ODBC Drivers
- Section A.7   Connectivity: Vendors with Multidatabase APIs
- Section A.8   Connectivity: Gateways
- Section A.9   Connectivity: Vendors with Middleware Products
- Section A.10   End-User Query Vendors
- Section A.11   EIS Players
- Section A.12   Report Generation Vendors
- Section A.13   Data Warehousing Vendors
- Section A.14   Parallel Database Vendors
- Section A.15   Object-Oriented Databases with SQL Extensions
- Section A.16   Decentralized Replication Vendors
- Section A.17   Database Internet Vendors

A.1   Relational Database Players

Borland International, Inc. (Interbase)
100 Borland Way
Scotts Valley, CA 95066
(408) 431-1000

Centura Software Corp. (SQLBase)
1060 Marsh Rd.
Menlo Park, CA 94025
(415) 321-9500

Cincom Systems, Inc. (Supra)
2300 Montana Ave.
Cincinatti, OH 45211
(800) 543-3010

Computer Associates International, Inc. (CA-Ingres)
One Computer Associates Plaza
Islandia, NY 11788
(516) 543-3010

IBM Corp. (DB2, DB2/2, DB2/6000)
Old Orchard Road
Armonk, NY 10504
(914) 765-1900

Informix Software, Inc. (INFORMIX-Online, INFORMIX-SE)
4100 Bohannon Dr.
Menlo Park, CA 94025
(415) 926-6300

Microsoft Corp. (SQL Server)
One Microsoft Way
Redmond, WA 98052
(206) 882-8080

Oracle Corp. (Oracle)
500 Oracle Parkway
Redwood Shores, CA 94065
(415) 506-7000

Oracle Corp. (Rdb/VMS)
500 Oracle Parkway
Redwood Shores, CA 94065
(415) 506-7000

Progess Software Corp. (Progress)
14 Oak Park
Bedford, MA 01730
(617) 280-4000

Quadbase Systems, Inc. (Quadbase-SQL)
2855 Kifer Rd., Ste. 203
Santa Clara, CA 95051
(408) 982-0835

Sybase, Inc. (SQL Server)
6475 Christie Avenue
Emeryville, CA 94608
(510) 596-3500

Sybase, Inc. (SQL Anywhere)
Watcom, a subsidiary of Sybase.
Waterloo, Ontario
(519) 886-3700

Tandem Computers, Inc. (NonStop SQL)
19333 Vallco Parkway
Cupertino, CA 95014
(408) 285-6000

XDB Systems, Inc. (XDB)
14700 Sweitzer Lane
Laurel, MD 20707
(301) 317-6800

4th Dimension Software, Inc. (4D First and 4D Server)
One Park Plaza, 11th Fl.
Irvine, CA 92714
(714) 757-4300

A.2   Logical Modeling Vendors

Asymetrix Corp. (InfoModeler)
110 110th Ave. N.E., Suite 700
Bellevue, WA 98004
(206) 462-0501

Logic Works, Inc. (ERwin)
1060 Route 206
Princeton, NJ 08540
(609) 252-1177

Sybase, Inc. (S-Designer)
6475 Christie Avenue
Emeryville, CA 94608
(510) 596-3500

A.3   Data Translation Tool Vendors

Tools and Techniques, Inc. (Data Junction)
2201 Northland Dr.
Austin, TX 78756
(512) 459-1308

A.4   4GL Vendors

Blythe Software, Inc. (Omnis 7)
989 E. Hillsdale Blvd. #400
Foster City, CA 94404
(415) 571-0222

Borland International, Inc. (Delphi)
100 Borland Way
Scotts Valley, CA 95066-3249
(800) 233-2444; (408) 431-1000

Centura Software Corp. (Centura, SQLWindows)
1060 Marsh Rd.
Menlo Park, CA 94025
(415) 321-9500

IBM Corp. (VisualAge)
Old Orchard Road
Armonk, NY 10504
(914) 765-1900

Informix Software, Inc. (INFORMIX-NewEra)
4100 Bohannon Dr.
Menlo Park, CA 94025
(415) 926-6300

Microsoft Corp. (Visual Basic)
One Microsoft Way
Redmond, WA 98052
(206) 882-8080

Oracle Corp. (Power Objects)
500 Oracle Parkway
Redwood Shores, CA 94065
(415) 506-7000

Powersoft Corp — a Subsidiary of Sybase (PowerBuilder)
561 Virginia Rd.
Concord, MA 01742
(508) 287-1500

Progress Software Corp. (Progress)
14 Oak Park
Bedford, MA 01730
(617) 280-4000

A.5 Connectivity: Direct Access Solution Vendors

Informix Software, Inc. (INFORMIX-Net)
4100 Bohannon Dr.
Menlo Park, CA 94025
(415) 926-6300

Oracle Corp. (SQL*Net)
500 Oracle Parkway
Redwood Shores, CA 94065
(415) 506-7000

Sybase, Inc. (Open Client/ C Developers Kit)
6475 Christie Ave.
Emeryville, CA 94608
(510) 596-3500

A.6   Connectivity: Vendors with ODBC Drivers

Intergraph Corp. (ODBC Drivers)
One Madison Industrial Park
Huntsville, AL 35894
(205) 730-2000

Intersolv, Inc. (Q+E ODBC Pack)
3200 Tower Oaks Blvd.
Rockville, MD 20852
(301) 230-3200

Microsoft Corp. (ODBC SDK)
One Microsoft Way
Redmond, WA 98052
(206) 882-8080

Openlink Software, Ltd. (ODBC Drivers)
15 Cherry Orchard Rd.
Croydon CR9 6BB, United Kingdom
44-81-681-7701

Simba Technologies, Inc. (ODBC Pack)
2125 Western Ave. Ste. 301
Seattle, WA 98121
(206) 441-0340

Syware, Inc. (Dr DeeBee)
P.O. Box 91, Kendall Station
Cambridge, MA 02142
(617) 497-1376

Visigenic Software, Inc. (ODBC SDK)
951 Mariner's Blvd. Ste. 460
San Mateo, CA 94404
(415) 286-1900

A.7 Connectivity: Vendors with Multidatabase APIs

Apple Computer, Inc. (DAL)
One Infinite Loop
Cupertino, CA 95014
(408) 966-1010

Borland International, Inc. (IDAPI)
100 Borland Way
Scotts Valley, CA 95066
(408) 431-1000

Centura Corp. (SQLNetwork API)
1060 Marsh Rd.
Menlo Park, CA 94025
(415) 321-9500

Information Builders, Inc. (EDA/SQL)
1250 Broadway
New York, NY 10001
(212) 736-4433

TechGnosis, Inc. (SequeLink)
5 Burlington Woods Dr., Suite 202
Burlington, MA 01803
(617) 229-6100

A.8 Connectivity: Gateways

Centura Software Corp. (SQLHost)
1060 Marsh Rd.
Menlo Park, CA 94025
(415) 321-9500

Computer Associates, Inc. (CA-Ingres Gateways)
One Computer Associates Plaza
Islandia, NY 11788
(516) 543-3010

IBM Corp. (DDCS)
Old Orchard Rd.
Armonk, NY 10504
(914) 765-1900

Information Builders, Inc. (Database Gateways)
1250 Broadway
New York, NY 10001
(212) 736-4433

MDI — a Sybase Company (OmniSQL)
3035 Center Green Dr.
Boulder, CO 80301
(303) 443-2706

Oracle Corp. (Transparent Gateway for DRDA, Open Gateway Technology)
500 Oracle Parkway
Redwood Shores, CA 94065
(415) 506-7000

A.9   Connectivity: Vendors with Middleware Products

Attachmate Corp. (SELECT! Professional 5.0)
3617 131st Ave., SE
Bellevue, WA 98006
(206) 644-4010

Cincom Systems, Inc. (ObjectHub)
2300 Montana Ave.
Cincinnati, OH 45211
(800) 543-3010

Informix Software, Inc. (INFORMIX-Star)
4100 Bohannon Dr.
Menlo Park, CA 94025
(415) 926-6300

MDI — a Sybase Company (InfoPump)
3035 Center Green Dr.
Boulder, CO 80301
(303) 443-2706

Platinum Technology, Inc. (Integrator)
1815 S Meyers Rd.
Oakbrook Terrace, IL 60181
(708) 620-5000

Techsmith Corp. (Remote NetLib)
3001 Coolidge Rd., Ste. 400
East Lansing, MI 48823
(517) 333-2100

Wall Data, Inc. (Rumba)
11332 NE 122nd Way
Kirkland, WA 98034
(206) 814-9255

VMARK Software, Inc. (HyperSTAR)
50 Washington St.
Westboro, MA 01581
(508) 366-3888

A.10   End-User Query Vendors

Andyne Computing, Ltd. (GQL)
552 Princess St., 2nd
Fl. Kingston, ON, CD K7L 1C7
(800) 267-0665

Blythe Software, Inc. (True Access)
989 East Hillsdale Blvd.
Foster City, CA 94404
(415) 571-0222

Brio Technology, Inc. (BrioQuery)
444 Castro St., Ste. 700
Mountain View, CA 94041
(800) 486-2746

Business Objects, Inc. (BusinessObjects)
20813 Stevens Creek Blvd., Ste. 100
Cupertino, CA 95014
(408) 973-9300

Centura Software Corp. (Quest)
1060 Marsh Rd.
Menlo Park, CA 94025
(800) 584-8782; (415) 321-9500

Cognos Corp. (Impromptu)
67 S. Bedford St., Ste. 200 W.
Burlington, MA 01803-5164
(800) 4-COGNOS; (800) 267-2777

Computer Associates International, Inc. (CA-Visual Express)
One Computer Associates Plaza
Islandia, NY 11788-7000
(800) CALL-CAI; (516) 342-5224

Information Builders, Inc. (Business Intelligence Suite)
1250 Broadway, 30th Fl.
New York, NY 10001-3782
(800) 969-INFO; (212) 736-4433

IntelligenceWare, Inc. (Iconic Query)
55933 W. Century Blvd., Ste. 900
Los Angeles, CA 90045
(800) 888-2996; (310) 216-6177

Intersolv, Inc. (Q+E)
53200 Tower Oaks Blvd.
Rockville, MD 20852
(800) 547-4000; (301) 230-3200

IQ Software Corp. (IQ, IQ Access)
3295 River Exchange Dr., Ste. 550
Norcross, GA 30092-9909
(800) 458-0386; (404) 446-8880

Microsoft Corp. (Access & MSQuery)
One Microsoft Way
Redmond, WA 98052
(206) 882-8080

Oracle Corp. (Oracle Data Query, Oracle Forms, and Oracle Reports)
500 Oracle Parkway
Redwood Shores, CA 94065
(415) 506-7000

Powersoft Corp — a Subsidiary of Sybase
(PowerViewer, PowerMaker)
561 Virginia Rd.
Concord, MA 01742
(508) 287-1500

Software AG of North America, Inc. (Esperant)
11190 Sunrise Valley Dr.
Reston, VA 22091
(703) 860-5050

Trinzic Corp. — a Subsidiary of Platinum Technology
(Forest & Trees)
101 University Ave.
Palo Alto, CA 94301
(800) 952-8779

A.11   EIS Players

Andyne Computing, Ltd. (Pablo)
552 Princess St., 2nd
Fl. Kingston, ON, CD K7L 1C7
(800) 267-0665

Business Objects, Inc. (BusinessObjects)
20183 Stevens Creek Blvd., Suite 100
Cupertino, CA 95014
(408) 973-9300

Cognos Corp. (PowerPlay)
67 S Bedford St., Ste. 200W
Burlington, MA 01803
(617) 229-6600

Comshare, Inc. (Commander EIS)
3001 S State St., P.O. Box 1588
Ann Arbor, MI 48108
(800) 922-7979

Information Advantage, Inc. (IA Decision Support Suite)
12900 Whitewater Drive, Suite 100
Minnetonka, MN 55343
(612) 938-7015

IRI Software, a Subsidiary of Oracle (Express EIS)
200 5th Ave.
Waltham, MA 02154
(617) 890-1100

Pilot Software, Inc., a Division of Dun and Bradstreet (Lightship)
1 Canal Park
Cambridge, MA 02141
(617) 374-9400

A.12   Report Generation Vendors

Borland International, Inc. (ReportSmith)
100 Borland Way
Scotts Valley, CA 95066-3249
(800) 233-2444; (408) 431-1000

Concentric Data Systems, Inc. (R&R Report Writer SQL Edition)
110 Turnpike Rd.
Westborough, MA 01581
(800) 325-9035; (508) 366-1122

Crystal Computer Services, Inc., a Subsidiary of Seagate Technology, Inc. (Crystal Reports Professional)
1050 W. Pender St., Ste. 2200
Vancouver, BC, CD V6E 3S7
(800) 877-2340; (800) 663-1244

Information Builders, Inc. (Focus Reporter for Windows)
51250 Broadway
New York, NY 10001-3782
(212) 736-4433

MITI (SQR Workbench)
2895 Temple Ave.
Long Beach, CA 90806
(310) 424-4399

A.13 Data Warehousing Vendors

AT&T Global Information Services (Teradata)
1700 S Patterson Blvd.
Dayton, OH 45479
(513) 445-5000

Carleton Corp. (Passport)
8 New England Executive Park
Burlington, MA 01803
(617) 272-4310

Evolutionary Technologies, Inc. (Extract Tool Suite)
4301 Westbank Drive
Austin, TX 78746
(512) 327-6994

IBM Corp. (IBM DB2 Parallel Edition)
Old Orchard Rd.
Armonk, NY 10504
(800) 426-3333

Informix Software, Inc. (INFORMIX-OnLine Dynamic Server)
4100 Bohannon Drive
Menlo Park, CA 94025
(415) 926-6300

Oracle Corp. (Parallel Query Option)
500 Oracle Parkway
Redwood Shores, CA 94086
(800) 633-0583

Prism Solutions, Inc. (Prism Warehouse Manager)
1000 Hamlin Court
Sunnyvale, CA 94089
(408) 752-1888

Red Brick Systems, Inc. (Red Brick Warehouse)
485 Alberto Way
Los Gatos, CA 95032
(408) 353-7214

A.14   Parallel Database Vendors

AT&T Global Information Services (Teradata)
1700 S Patterson Blvd.
Dayton, OH 45479
(513) 445-5000

IBM Corp. (DB2/6000 Parallel Edition)
Old Orchard Rd.
Armonk, NY 10504
(800) 426-3333

Informix Software, Inc. (Online XPS & OnLine Dynamic Server)
4100 Bohannon Drive
Menlo Park, CA 94025
(415) 926-6300

Microsoft Corp. (SQL Server 95)
One Microsoft Way
Redmond, WA 98052
(206) 882-8080

Oracle Corp. (Parallel Query Option)
500 Oracle Parkway
Redwood Shores, CA 94086
(800) 633-0583

Oracle Corp. (Parallel Server)
500 Oracle Parkway
Redwood Shores, CA 94086
(800) 633-0583

Sybase, Inc. (Navigation Server)
6475 Christie Ave.
Emeryville, CA 94608
(800) 426-4785

Tandem Computers, Inc. (NonStop SQL)
19191 Vallco Parkway
Cupertino, CA 95014
(408) 285-6000

A.15 Object-Oriented Databases with SQL Extensions

Hewlett Packard Co. (OpenODB)
3000 Hanover St.
Palo Alto, CA 94304
(800) 752-0900

Objectivity, Inc. (Objectivity/DB)
301 B E. Evelyn Ave.
Mountain View, CA 94041
(415) 254-7100

Omniscience Object Technology, Inc. (ORDBMS)
3080 Olcott St., Suite 100C
Santa Clara, CA 95054
(408) 562-0799

Ontos, Inc. (Ontos DB)
Three Burlington Woods
Burlington, MA 01803
(617) 272-7110

Poet Software Corp. (Poet)
4633 Old Ironsides Dr., Ste. 110
Santa Clara, CA 95054
(408) 748-3403

UniSQL, Inc. (UniSQL/X DBMS)
8911 N. Capital of Texas Hwy., Suite 2300
Austin, TX 78759
(512) 343-7297

A.16   Decentralized Replication Vendors

Centura Software Corp. (Centura Ranger)
1060 Marsh Road
Menlo Park, CA 95054
(415) 321-9500

Microsoft Corp. (SQL Server 6.0)
One Microsoft Way
Redmond, WA 98052
(206) 882-8080

Praxis International, Inc. (OmniReplicator)
Four Cambridge Center
Cambridge, MA 02142
(617) 661-9790

Sybase, Inc. (SQL Anywhere)
Watcom, a Subsidiary of Sybase
Waterloo, Ontario
(519) 886-3700

Trinsic Corp. — a Subsidiary of Platinum Technology (InfoPump)
101 University Ave.
Palo Alto, CA 94301
(415) 328-9595

A.17 Database Internet Vendors

IBM Corp. (DB2 World Wide Web Connection)
Old Orchard Rd.
Armonk, NY 10504
(800) 426-3333

Informix Software, Inc. (INFORMIX-4GL CGI Interface Kit, Web DataBlade)
4100 Bohannon Drive
Menlo Park, CA 94025
(415) 926-6300

Microsoft Corp. (Internet Database Connector)
One Microsoft Way
Redmond, WA 98052
(206) 882-8080

Oracle Corp. (Oracle Web System, Oracle World Wide Web Interface Kit)
500 Oracle Parkway
Redwood Shores, CA 94086
(800) 633-0583

Sybase, Inc. (Sybase WebSQL, Sybperl)
6475 Christie Ave.
Emeryville, CA 94608
(800) 426-4785

B   Installing SQL Solo

This appendix steps through the installation of the exercises and SQL Solo software used in this book.

Section B.1 is for:

- Windows 3.1
- Windows for Workgroups 3.1.1
- 16-bit applications on Windows NT 3.5
- OS/2 Warp Win/OS/2

Section B.2 is for:

- Windows 95

B.1   Installing CD-ROM Software

On-line Help

You can get help at any point in this install process by referring to the Install section of on-line help.

B.1.1 Step 1 Installing SQL Solo

We are now ready to install SQL Solo, using the included CD-ROM. To do this, follow these steps:

1. Start Microsoft Windows on your PC.

2. Put the CD in your CD-ROM drive. Normally, this is Drive D, but may be different for you.

3. Choose **Run** from the **File** menu in the Windows Program Manager.

4. Enter D:SETUP in the Run dialog box and click **OK.**

5. Click on the Quick Installation button; a dialog box asks the name of the directories where you want to install the components. The default directory names appear in the dialog box as c:\gupta and c:\sqlbase. Choose **OK**.

The CD-ROM will build the Gupta Program Group for you when the install program finishes. The program group looks like this:

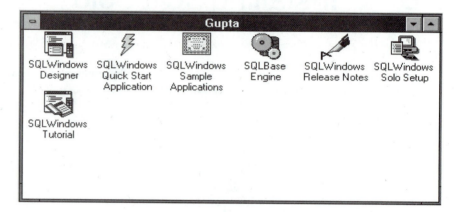

B.1.2 *Step 2* Adding Quest Program Item

Quest is a query tool that is available upon installing SQL Solo in Windows 3.1 and Windows 3.1.1; however, there is no icon for this program. The following steps create the icon for Quest.

1. Click your mouse in the Gupta Program Group window so that you have highlighted the window shown in **Step 1**.

2. Choose **New** from the **File** menu in the Windows Program Manager.

Choose **Program Item** from the New window.

3.   Fill in Program Item Properties as shown below. Click **OK**.

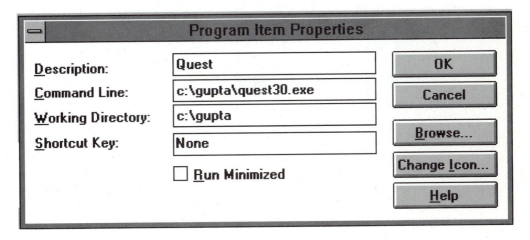

4.   Your program should now look like this:

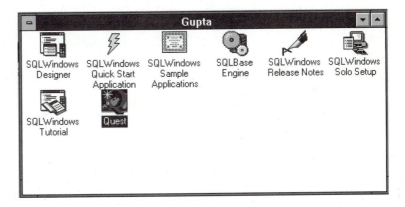

B.1.3 **Step 3** Copying Exercises to your Local Disk Drive

The following steps copy the book's exercises into your local database directory. By default, this directory is in the c:\sqlbase directory, the default database directory when installing SQL Solo.

1. Pull down the **File** menu from the Program Manager and choose **Run**:

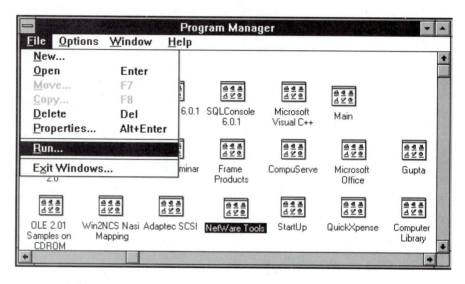

2. Make sure your CD-ROM is in the drive. Open another window and drill-down to the d:\labs directory on your CD-ROM.

3. Type in d:\labs\labs.bat:

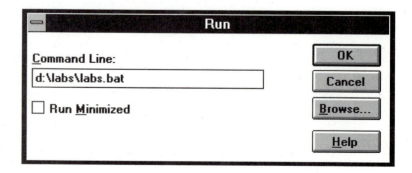

4.   The labs.bat file will create a directory, c:\sqlbase\exercise, and place all the exercises for the book in this directory. If you changed the default directory, c:\sqlbase, when installing SQL Solo, then you will have to alter the labs.bat file to successfully install.

B.2   *Installing SQL Solo on Windows 95*

SQL Solo is known to run on Windows 95. The following is included in the Centura SQL Solo read-me file concerning Windows 95 Support:

"This version of SQLWindows 5.0.2 has been certified by Gupta's Quality Assurance department to run on Microsoft Windows 95, Final Build. When the final release of Windows 95 is available from Microsoft, we will test and certify SQLWindows on that release, and post notice of the certification on Gupta's CompuServe forum."

On-line Help

You can get help at any point in this install process by referring to the Install section of on-line help. You can also consult the Centura Forum on Compuserve or Centura's web site for the latest information on SQL Solo.

B.2.1 **Step 1** *Installing SQL Solo*

We are now ready to install SQL Solo, using the included CD-ROM. To do this, follow these steps:

1.   Start Microsoft Windows 95 on your PC.

2.   Put the CD in your CD-ROM drive. Normally, this is Drive D, but may be different for you.

3.   Choose **Run** under the Start push button located on the lower left side of your screen.

4.   Enter D:SETUP in the Run dialog box and click **OK.**

5.   Click on the Quick Installation button; a dialog box asks the name of the directories where you want to install the components. The default directory names appear in the dialog box as c:\gupta and c:\sqlbase. Choose **OK**.

The CD-ROM will build the pull-down menus for you (under the Gupta menu Item) when the install program finishes.

B.2.2 **Step 2** Adding Quest Program Item

Quest is a query tool that is available upon installing SQL Solo in Windows 95. If for any reason you should not see it from your pull down menu for running applications on Windows 95, you will find the executable as c:\gupta\quest30.exe.

B.2.3 **Step 3** Copying Exercises to your Local Disk Drive

The following steps copy the book's exercises into your local database directory. By default, this directory is in the c:\sqlbase directory, the default database directory when installing SQL Solo.

1. Use the Windows Explorer to find the file D:\labs\labs.bat (assuming D: is the CD-ROM drive).

2. Select **labs.bat** from the Windows Explorer and double-click to execute it.

3. The labs.bat file will create a directory, c:\sqlbase\exercise, and place all the exercises for the book in this directory. If you changed the default directory, c:\sqlbase, when installing SQL Solo, then you will have to alter the labs.bat file to successfully install.

Note: The exercises in this course use bitmaps with the Windows 3.1 look and feel. The windows you will see with Windows 95 will vary.

C   The LEAD Toolkit: A Demonstration

The demonstration in this appendix shows the LEAD Toolkit from Client Server Designs. The LEAD toolkit generates a physical database as well as a working application from a logical model.

Client Server Designs, via a point-and-click interface, quickly generates a database schema and a working template application. This process is based on the existence of a logical model diagram. While this process will not provide a production-ready application, once the working application template has been designed, it can be modified and expanded upon. Clearly, for a new application developer, this can save much time!

The following demonstration steps through the process of generating a database and application, using the LEAD toolkit.

There are four main components to the LEAD toolkit:

- **Open Case Tool**
  Provides links to existing logical model tools (like ERwin or S-Designer) in order to open for viewing the logical diagram used for the generation of the database and application template.

- **Data Generator**
  Connects to a database server and creates a database if one has not already been created. The steps to this process are Connect, Load, and Begin.

- **App Generator**
  Builds a SQLWindows application based on the logical model diagram. Client Server Designs has object components they use to build a working application that can access the created database. They are also working to allow application creation for other development tools, like Visual Basic.

- **Launch App**
  Once the application is created, the application can be launched. An application can easily be modified and expanded upon. (This demo does not include the underlying source code that the product uses. Source code is part of the commercially available product.)

1. Open the File Manager. Go to the directory c:\sqlbase\exercise\lead. Pull down the **File** menu option and choose the **RUN** option.

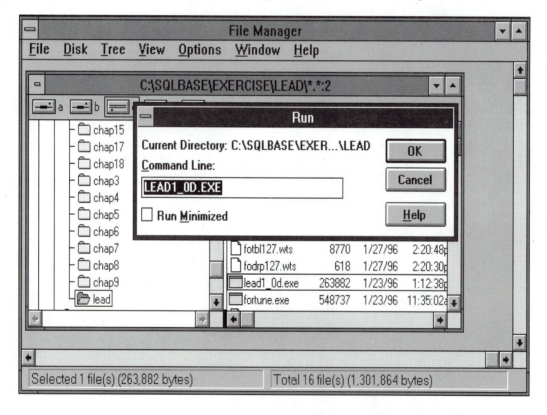

Type in the file, LEAD1-OD.EXE and click **OK**.

The application will open.

2.   The first screen to appear is shown below.

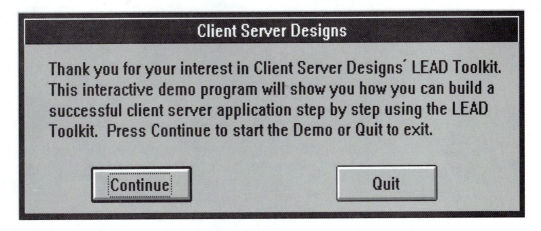

Press **Continue**.

3.   You are first prompted to press the **Open Case Tool** button.

Notice that there are arrows under the text that goes along with this demo. If you want to step through the demo without performing the actions, use the arrows to go back and forth. In this case, press the **Open Case Tool** button.

4.   A logical model diagram for our sample database, designed in ERwin, is displayed. Press **Continue**.

5. Press the **Data Generator** button.

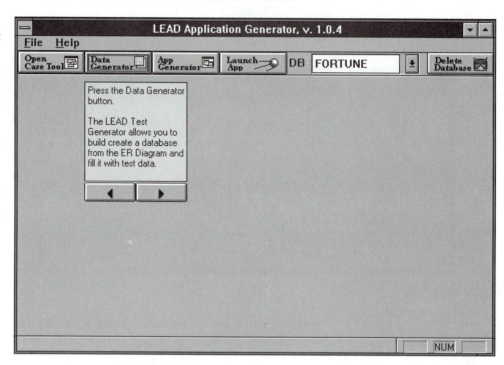

Three new buttons are displayed: **Connect**, **Load**, and **Begin**. The screen displayed after you press the **Data Generator** button prompts you to press the **Connect** button.

6. Press the **Connect** button. There will be no Fortune database to connect to, so you will be prompted to create this database. Press **Yes**.

This demo is configured to create the Fortune database. The commercial product will allow you to choose the database you will either connect to or create.

7. Press the **Load** button. Use the arrows at the bottom of the text to navigate the next several steps.

8. The demo asks you to load a *.erx file. This is an exported file from the logical model diagram tool, which will be used to create our application.

Press **Cancel** to continue. Normally, you would select a file. In this demonstration, the file is hard-coded.

9. Press **Begin**.

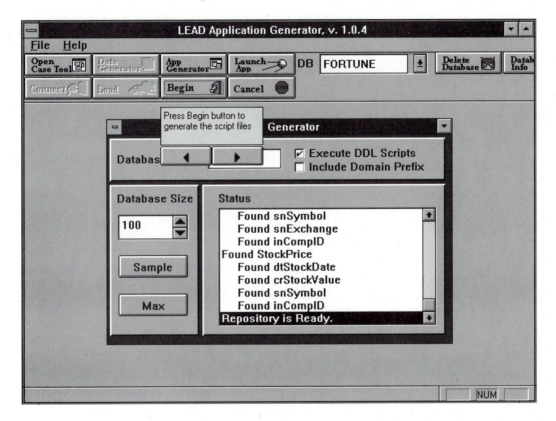

10. The process of generating the database takes a few minutes. Sit back and watch the SQL scripts run. When it is finished, the demo selects the **App Generator** button.

11. Press the **App Generator** button.

    The **App Generator** button triggers a form. Use the arrows to step through this form. The form indicates information about the application you will generate. You will then press a new button, **Generate App**. The application name you will generate for this demo is again hard-coded.

    Your application code is being generated for you!

12. Press **Launch App**. You will see the window shown below.

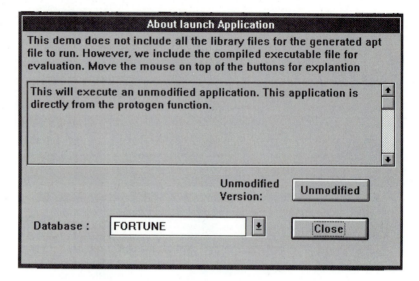

Press the **Unmodified** button, which will launch the newly generated application.

13. The login window is shown below. You need not enter a user or password; simply press **OK**.

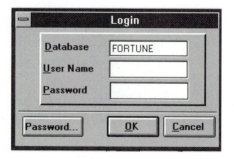

14. The application is displayed as shown below. Pull down the **Open** menu option from the File menu and choose **Company**.

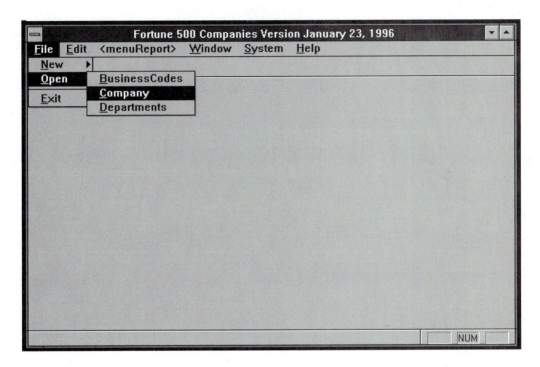

15. You will see a new set of buttons appear; press **Search**.

16. The application asks if you want to retrieve all the companies. Press **OK**.

You should now see the application shown below. You can do any number of things at this point.

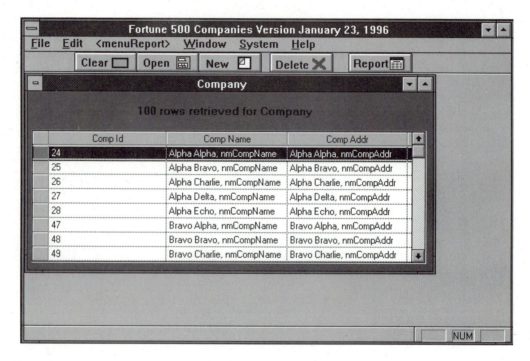

17. To see company information, double-click on row 24; the window shown below appears. If you scroll down the window that opens, you will see that all tables in the database are visible with information specific to the company identification number you chose.

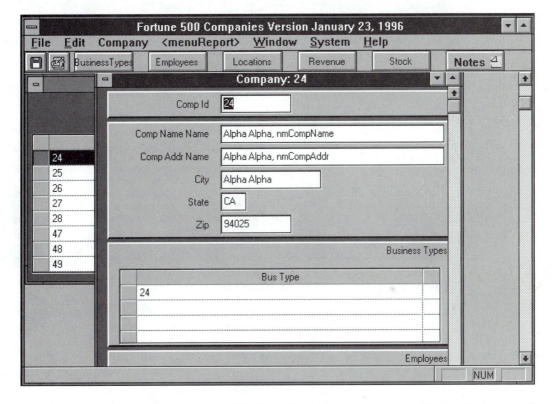

Notice that the LEAD toolkit added a Notes capability to display stored text about companies.

18. Pull down the left-hand icon and choose the **Close** option from the window Company: 24.

19. Press the **Report** button shown at step 16.

    You will see this report generated.

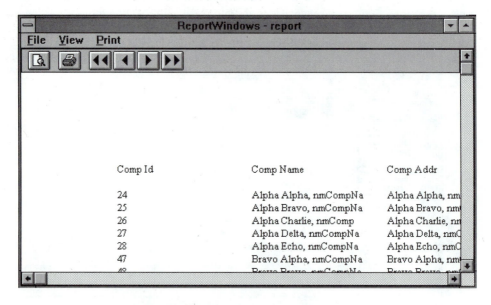

20. Pull down **Close Report** from the **File** menu.

    You can play with this application and see many more features, all of which were generated automatically. With the LEAD toolkit, source code is generated, so once this application is generated, you can modify it and add more features.

21. To close this application, pull down the **File** menu and choose the **Close** menu option.

Index

LICENSE AGREEMENT AND LIMITED WARRANTY

READ THE FOLLOWING TERMS AND CONDITIONS CAREFULLY BEFORE OPENING THIS SOFTWARE MEDIA PACKAGE. THIS LEGAL DOCUMENT IS AN AGREEMENT BETWEEN YOU AND PRENTICE-HALL, INC. (THE "COMPANY"). BY OPENING THIS SEALED SOFTWARE MEDIA PACKAGE, YOU ARE AGREEING TO BE BOUND BY THESE TERMS AND CONDITIONS. IF YOU DO NOT AGREE WITH THESE TERMS AND CONDITIONS, DO NOT OPEN THE SOFTWARE MEDIA PACKAGE. PROMPTLY RETURN THE UNOPENED PACKAGE AND ALL ACCOMPANYING ITEMS TO THE PLACE YOU OBTAINED THEM FOR A FULL REFUND OF ANY SUMS YOU HAVE PAID.

1.   **GRANT OF LICENSE:** In consideration of your payment of the license fee, which is part of the price you paid for this product, and your agreement to abide by the terms and conditions of this Agreement, the Company grants to you a nonexclusive right to use and display the copy of the enclosed software program (hereinafter the "SOFTWARE") on a single computer (i.e., with a single CPU) at a single location so long as you comply with the terms of this Agreement. The Company reserves all rights not expressly granted to you under this Agreement.

2.   **OWNERSHIP OF SOFTWARE:** You own only the magnetic or physical media (the enclosed CD-ROM) on which the SOFTWARE is recorded or fixed, but the Company retains all the rights, title, and ownership to the SOFTWARE recorded on the original CD-ROM copy(ies) and all subsequent copies of the SOFTWARE, regardless of the form or media on which the original or other copies may exist. This license is not a sale of the original SOFTWARE or any copy to you.

3.   **COPY RESTRICTIONS:** This SOFTWARE and the accompanying printed materials and user manual (the "Documentation") are the subject of copyright. You may not copy the Documentation or the SOFTWARE, except that you may make a single copy of the SOFTWARE for backup or archival purposes only. You may be held legally responsible for any copying or copyright infringement which is caused or encouraged by your failure to abide by the terms of this restriction.

4.   **USE RESTRICTIONS:** You may not network the SOFTWARE or otherwise use it on more than one computer or computer terminal at the same time. You may physically transfer the SOFTWARE from one computer to another provided that the SOFTWARE is used on only one computer at a time. You may not distribute copies of the SOFTWARE or Documentation to others. You may not reverse engineer, disassemble, decompile, modify, adapt, translate, or create derivative works based on the SOFTWARE or the Documentation without the prior written consent of the Company.

5.   **TRANSFER RESTRICTIONS:** The enclosed SOFTWARE is licensed only to you and may not be transferred to any one else without the prior written consent of the Company. Any unauthorized transfer of the SOFTWARE shall result in the immediate termination of this Agreement.

6.   **TERMINATION:** This license is effective until terminated. This license will terminate automatically without notice from the Company and become null and void if you fail to comply with any provisions or limitations of this license. Upon termination, you shall destroy the Documentation and all copies of the SOFTWARE. All provisions of this Agreement as to warranties, limitation of liability, remedies or damages, and our ownership rights shall survive termination.

7.   **MISCELLANEOUS:** This Agreement shall be construed in accordance with the laws of the United States of America and the State of New York and shall benefit the Company, its affiliates, and assignees.

8.   **LIMITED WARRANTY AND DISCLAIMER OF WARRANTY:** The Company warrants that the SOFTWARE, when properly used in accordance with the Documentation, will operate in substantial conformity with the description of the SOFTWARE set forth in the Documentation. The Company does not warrant that the SOFTWARE will meet your requirements or that the operation of the SOFTWARE will be uninterrupted or error-free. The Company warrants that the

media on which the SOFTWARE is delivered shall be free from defects in materials and workmanship under normal use for a period of thirty (30) days from the date of your purchase. Your only remedy and the Company's only obligation under these limited warranties is, at the Company's option, return of the warranted item for a refund of any amounts paid by you or replacement of the item. Any replacement of SOFTWARE or media under the warranties shall not extend the original warranty period. The limited warranty set forth above shall not apply to any SOFTWARE which the Company determines in good faith has been subject to misuse, neglect, improper installation, repair, alteration, or damage by you. EXCEPT FOR THE EXPRESSED WARRANTIES SET FORTH ABOVE, THE COMPANY DISCLAIMS ALL WARRANTIES, EXPRESS OR IMPLIED, INCLUDING WITHOUT LIMITATION, THE IMPLIED WARRANTIES OF MERCHANTABILITY AND FITNESS FOR A PARTICULAR PURPOSE. EXCEPT FOR THE EXPRESS WARRANTY SET FORTH ABOVE, THE COMPANY DOES NOT WARRANT, GUARANTEE, OR MAKE ANY REPRESENTATION REGARDING THE USE OR THE RESULTS OF THE USE OF THE SOFTWARE IN TERMS OF ITS CORRECTNESS, ACCURACY, RELIABILITY, CURRENTNESS, OR OTHERWISE.

IN NO EVENT, SHALL THE COMPANY OR ITS EMPLOYEES, AGENTS, SUPPLIERS, OR CONTRACTORS BE LIABLE FOR ANY INCIDENTAL, INDIRECT, SPECIAL, OR CONSEQUENTIAL DAMAGES ARISING OUT OF OR IN CONNECTION WITH THE LICENSE GRANTED UNDER THIS AGREEMENT, OR FOR LOSS OF USE, LOSS OF DATA, LOSS OF INCOME OR PROFIT, OR OTHER LOSSES, SUSTAINED AS A RESULT OF INJURY TO ANY PERSON, OR LOSS OF OR DAMAGE TO PROPERTY, OR CLAIMS OF THIRD PARTIES, EVEN IF THE COMPANY OR AN AUTHORIZED REPRESENTATIVE OF THE COMPANY HAS BEEN ADVISED OF THE POSSIBILITY OF SUCH DAMAGES. IN NO EVENT SHALL LIABILITY OF THE COMPANY FOR DAMAGES WITH RESPECT TO THE SOFTWARE EXCEED THE AMOUNTS ACTUALLY PAID BY YOU, IF ANY, FOR THE SOFTWARE. SOME JURISDICTIONS DO NOT ALLOW THE LIMITATION OF IMPLIED WARRANTIES OR LIABILITY FOR INCIDENTAL, INDIRECT, SPECIAL, OR CONSEQUENTIAL DAMAGES, SO THE ABOVE LIMITATIONS MAY NOT ALWAYS APPLY. THE WARRANTIES IN THIS AGREEMENT GIVE YOU SPECIFIC LEGAL RIGHTS AND YOU MAY ALSO HAVE OTHER RIGHTS WHICH VARY IN ACCORDANCE WITH LOCAL LAW.

ACKNOWLEDGMENT

YOU ACKNOWLEDGE THAT YOU HAVE READ THIS AGREEMENT, UNDERSTAND IT, AND AGREE TO BE BOUND BY ITS TERMS AND CONDITIONS. YOU ALSO AGREE THAT THIS AGREEMENT IS THE COMPLETE AND EXCLUSIVE STATEMENT OF THE AGREEMENT BETWEEN YOU AND THE COMPANY AND SUPERSEDES ALL PROPOSALS OR PRIOR AGREEMENTS, ORAL, OR WRITTEN, AND ANY OTHER COMMUNICATIONS BETWEEN YOU AND THE COMPANY OR ANY REPRESENTATIVE OF THE COMPANY RELATING TO THE SUBJECT MATTER OF THIS AGREEMENT.

Should you have any questions concerning this Agreement or if you wish to contact the Company for any reason, please contact in writing at the address below.

Robin Short
Prentice Hall PTR
One Lake Street
Upper Saddle River, New Jersey 07458